Autodesk® Inventor® 2019 Advanced Part Modeling

Learning Guide
Mixed Units - 1st Edition

ASCENT - Center for Technical Knowledge®
Autodesk® Inventor® 2019
Advanced Part Modeling

Mixed Units - 1st Edition

Prepared and produced by:

ASCENT Center for Technical Knowledge
630 Peter Jefferson Parkway, Suite 175
Charlottesville, VA 22911

866-527-2368
www.ASCENTed.com

Lead Contributor: Jennifer MacMillan

ASCENT - Center for Technical Knowledge is a division of Rand Worldwide, Inc., providing custom developed knowledge products and services for leading engineering software applications. ASCENT is focused on specializing in the creation of education programs that incorporate the best of classroom learning and technology-based training offerings.

We welcome any comments you may have regarding this guide, or any of our products. To contact us please email: feedback@ASCENTed.com.

© ASCENT - Center for Technical Knowledge, 2018

All rights reserved. No part of this guide may be reproduced in any form by any photographic, electronic, mechanical or other means or used in any information storage and retrieval system without the written permission of ASCENT, a division of Rand Worldwide, Inc.

The following are registered trademarks or trademarks of Autodesk, Inc., and/or its subsidiaries and/or affiliates in the USA and other countries: 123D, 3ds Max, Alias, ATC, AutoCAD LT, AutoCAD, Autodesk, the Autodesk logo, Autodesk 123D, Autodesk Homestyler, Autodesk Inventor, Autodesk MapGuide, Autodesk Streamline, AutoLISP, AutoSketch, AutoSnap, AutoTrack, Backburner, Backdraft, Beast, BIM 360, Burn, Buzzsaw, CADmep, CAiCE, CAMduct, Civil 3D, Combustion, Communication Specification, Configurator 360, Constructware, Content Explorer, Creative Bridge, Dancing Baby (image), DesignCenter, DesignKids, DesignStudio, Discreet, DWF, DWG, DWG (design/logo), DWG Extreme, DWG TrueConvert, DWG TrueView, DWGX, DXF, Ecotect, Ember, ESTmep, FABmep, Face Robot, FBX, Fempro, Fire, Flame, Flare, Flint, ForceEffect, FormIt 360, Freewheel, Fusion 360, Glue, Green Building Studio, Heidi, Homestyler, HumanIK, i-drop, ImageModeler, Incinerator, Inferno, InfraWorks, Instructables, Instructables (stylized robot design/logo), Inventor, Inventor HSM, Inventor LT, Lustre, Maya, Maya LT, MIMI, Mockup 360, Moldflow Plastics Advisers, Moldflow Plastics Insight, Moldflow, Moondust, MotionBuilder, Movimento, MPA (design/logo), MPA, MPI (design/logo), MPX (design/logo), MPX, Mudbox, Navisworks, ObjectARX, ObjectDBX, Opticore, P9, Pier 9, Pixlr, Pixlr-o-matic, Productstream, Publisher 360, RasterDWG, RealDWG, ReCap, ReCap 360, Remote, Revit LT, Revit, RiverCAD, Robot, Scaleform, Showcase, Showcase 360, SketchBook, Smoke, Socialcam, Softimage, Spark & Design, Spark Logo, Sparks, SteeringWheels, Stitcher, Stone, StormNET, TinkerBox, Tinkercad, Tinkerplay, ToolClip, Topobase, Toxik, TrustedDWG, T-Splines, ViewCube, Visual LISP, Visual, VRED, Wire, Wiretap, WiretapCentral, XSI.

NASTRAN is a registered trademark of the National Aeronautics Space Administration.

All other brand names, product names, or trademarks belong to their respective holders.

General Disclaimer:

Notwithstanding any language to the contrary, nothing contained herein constitutes nor is intended to constitute an offer, inducement, promise, or contract of any kind. The data contained herein is for informational purposes only and is not represented to be error free. ASCENT, its agents and employees, expressly disclaim any liability for any damages, losses or other expenses arising in connection with the use of its materials or in connection with any failure of performance, error, omission even if ASCENT, or its representatives, are advised of the possibility of such damages, losses or other expenses. No consequential damages can be sought against ASCENT or Rand Worldwide, Inc. for the use of these materials by any third parties or for any direct or indirect result of that use.

The information contained herein is intended to be of general interest to you and is provided "as is", and it does not address the circumstances of any particular individual or entity. Nothing herein constitutes professional advice, nor does it constitute a comprehensive or complete statement of the issues discussed thereto. ASCENT does not warrant that the document or information will be error free or will meet any particular criteria of performance or quality. In particular (but without limitation) information may be rendered inaccurate by changes made to the subject of the materials (i.e. applicable software). Rand Worldwide, Inc. specifically disclaims any warranty, either expressed or implied, including the warranty of fitness for a particular purpose.

AS-INV1901-APM1MU-SG   //   IS-INV1901-APM1MU-SG

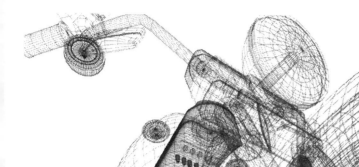

Contents

Preface ix

In this Guide xiii

Practice Files xvii

Chapter 1: Tips & Tools 1-1

    1.1 **Design Philosophies** 1-2
        Origin Features 1-2
        Base Feature 1-2
        Sketching Plane 1-2
        Sketch Options 1-2
        Feature Relationships 1-3
        Dimensions 1-3
        Depth Options 1-3
        Feature Order 1-3
        Equations 1-3

    1.2 **Sketching Tips** 1-4
        Simple Sketches 1-4
        Sketch Degrees of Freedom 1-4
        Constraints 1-4
        Reference in 3D 1-5
        Fillets and Chamfers 1-6
        Construction Entities 1-6
        Sketched Sections 1-6
        Dynamic Input & Dimensioning for Sketching 1-7
        Precise Input 1-7

    1.3 **Display Options** 1-10
        Visual Style 1-10
        Ray Tracing 1-11
        Ground Plane 1-13
        Shadows 1-14
        Reflections 1-14
        Lighting Styles 1-15
        Perspective & Orthographic Views 1-18

1.4 Appearances	1-19
Create a New Appearance	1-23
Assign an Appearance	1-26
Adding Appearances to the Document	1-26
Practice 1a Create a Sketch using Precise Coordinates	**1-27**
Practice 1b Create a Lighting Style	**1-36**
Practice 1c Working with Appearances	**1-39**
Chapter Review Questions	**1-47**
Command Summary	**1-50**
Chapter 2: Sketching Tools	**2-1**
2.1 Splines	2-2
Editing a Spline	2-4
2.2 3D Sketches	2-8
3D Sketch Tools	2-9
Modifying 3D Sketch Entities	2-17
Dimensioning & Constraining	2-18
Practice 2a Create a Swept Cut using a 3D Sketch	**2-20**
Practice 2b Imported Point Data	**2-25**
Chapter Review Questions	**2-33**
Command Summary	**2-35**
Chapter 3: Multi-Body Part Modeling	**3-1**
3.1 Multi-Body Part Modeling	3-2
Creating the First Solid Body	3-3
Creating Additional Solid Bodies	3-4
Assigning Features to Solid Bodies	3-4
Manipulating Solid Bodies	3-4
Solid Body Display	3-8
Solid Body Properties	3-9
Practice 3a Complex Part Design	**3-10**
Practice 3b Multi-Body Part Design	**3-19**
Chapter Review Questions	**3-29**
Command Summary	**3-31**
Chapter 4: Advanced Work Features	**4-1**
4.1 Grounded Work Points	4-2
Convert an Existing Work Point to a Grounded Work Point	4-2
Create a Grounded Work Point	4-2

4.2 User Coordinate Systems 4-4
Locating the UCS Relative to the Model Origin............................... 4-5
Locating the UCS Relative to Existing Geometry............................ 4-6
Redefining UCS Placement 4-6
UCS Visibility and Naming 4-7

Practice 4a Creating Geometry using a UCS 4-8

Chapter Review Questions 4-16

Command Summary 4-18

Chapter 5: Advanced Lofts, Sweeps, and Coils 5-1

5.1 Area Lofts 5-2

5.2 Advanced Sweeps... 5-5
Path & Guide Rail Sweep.. 5-5
Path & Guide Surface Sweep 5-7

5.3 Coils 5-8

Practice 5a Area Loft... 5-12

Practice 5b Sweeps 5-16

Practice 5c Creating a Coil 5-22

Chapter Review Questions 5-24

Command Summary 5-26

Chapter 6: Analyzing a Model 6-1

6.1 Analysis Types 6-2
Zebra Analysis 6-2
Draft Analysis 6-2
Curvature Analysis 6-3
Surface Analysis 6-4
Cross Section Analysis 6-5

6.2 Analysis Procedures... 6-7

Practice 6a Analyzing Continuity.. 6-13

Practice 6b Draft Analysis 6-21

Practice 6c Section Analysis... 6-24

Chapter Review Questions 6-30

Command Summary 6-32

Chapter 7: Generative Shape Design 7-1

7.1 Shape Generator 7-2
Preparing a Model for Shape Generator 7-3
Opening Shape Generator 7-3

      Material Assignment.. 7-4
      Applying Constraints... 7-5
      Applying Loads.. 7-6
      Shape Generator Settings... 7-8
      Preserving Regions.. 7-9
      Assigning Symmetry.. 7-10
      Run the Shape Generator... 7-11
      Promote the 3D Mesh Model... 7-12

  Practice 7a Generating a Design using Shape Generator................. 7-14

  Chapter Review Questions.. 7-25

  Command Summary 7-27

Chapter 8: Introduction to Surfacing 8-1

  8.1 Introduction to Surfaces... 8-2

  8.2 Basic Surfaces 8-3

  8.3 Patch Surfaces 8-4

  8.4 Ruled Surfaces 8-5

  8.5 Stitch Surfaces 8-7

  8.6 Sculpting with Surfaces 8-9

  8.7 Thickening & Offsetting a Surface 8-11

  8.8 Surfaces in Drawing Views 8-14
        Surfaces in Child Views 8-16
        Annotating Surfaces in a Drawing... 8-16

  Practice 8a Creating a Surface I.. 8-17

  Practice 8b Creating a Surface II 8-20

  Practice 8c Sculpting a Surface... 8-23

  Practice 8d Ruled Surface Creation 8-26

  Chapter Review Questions.. 8-32

  Command Summary 8-34

Chapter 9: Additional Surfacing Options 9-1

  9.1 Extend and Trim Surfaces... 9-2
        Trim Surface.. 9-2
        Extend Surface.. 9-3

  9.2 Replace Face with a Surface 9-5

  9.3 Delete Faces 9-6

  9.4 Copy Surfaces 9-7

  Practice 9a Extending Surfaces... 9-9

Contents

    Practice 9b Copying Surfaces 9-11

    Practice 9c Deleting a Surface 9-15

    Practice 9d Creating a Solid from Surfaces 9-20

    Practice 9e Deleting a Face 9-25

    Chapter Review Questions 9-28

    Command Summary 9-30

Chapter 10: Copying Between Parts (iFeatures) 10-1

    10.1 Creating iFeatures 10-2

    10.2 Inserting iFeatures 10-6

    10.3 iFeatures vs. Copy Feature 10-10

    10.4 Table-Driven iFeatures 10-11

    10.5 Editing iFeatures 10-15
        Edit Inserted iFeature 10-15
        Edit iFeature file 10-15
        Editing the iFeature Image 10-16
        Placement Help 10-16

    Practice 10a Create and Insert an iFeature 10-18

    Practice 10b Table-Driven iFeature 10-27

    Practice 10c (Optional) Slotted Hole iFeature 10-35

    Chapter Review Questions 10-40

    Command Summary 10-42

Chapter 11: iParts 11-1

    11.1 iPart Creation 11-2

    11.2 iPart Placement 11-12
        Placing a Standard iPart 11-13
        Placing a custom iPart 11-14
        Replacing an iPart 11-14

    11.3 Editing an iPart Factory 11-15
        Edit Table 11-15
        Adding Features to an iPart 11-15

    11.4 Creating iFeatures from a Table-Driven iPart 11-16

    11.5 Tables for Factory Members 11-17

    Practice 11a Bolt iPart Factory 11-19

    Practice 11b Create an iPart Factory 11-26

    Practice 11c iParts in Assemblies 11-36

    Practice 11d iPart Member Tables 11-38

    Chapter Review Questions 11-42

    Command Summary 11-44

Chapter 12: Importing & Editing CAD Data 12-1

    12.1 Importing CAD Data (AnyCAD) 12-2

    12.2 Exporting Geometry 12-7

    12.3 Editing the Base Solid 12-9

    12.4 Direct Edit 12-13
        Move 12-14
        Size 12-16
        Scale 12-17
        Rotate 12-19
        Delete 12-21

    12.5 Attaching Point Cloud Data 12-23

    Practice 12a Opening a CATIA Assembly 12-28

    Practice 12b Opening STEP Files 12-32

    Practice 12c Direct Edit 12-37

    Chapter Review Questions 12-48

    Command Summary 12-52

Chapter 13: Working with Imported Surfaces 13-1

    13.1 Importing Surfaces 13-2

    13.2 Repairing Imported Surfaces 13-4

    Practice 13a Repairing Imported Data 13-13

    Practice 13b Manipulating Imported Surfaces 13-26

    Chapter Review Questions 13-30

    Command Summary 13-32

Chapter 14: Working with AutoCAD Data 14-1

    14.1 Opening AutoCAD Files 14-2
        Opening DWG Files 14-2
        Importing DWG Files 14-3

    14.2 DWG File Underlays 14-9
        Importing a DWG File as an Underlay 14-9
        Controlling Layer Visibility 14-10
        Moving an Underlay 14-11
        Cropping an Underlay 14-11
        Using an Underlay to Create Geometry 14-12

Contents

Practice 14a Import an AutoCAD DWG File into Autodesk Inventor 14-15

Practice 14b Open AutoCAD DWG Data to Create a Solid 14-20

Practice 14c Import Associative DWG Data into a Part File 14-26

Practice 14d Associative DWG Layout 14-38

Chapter Review Questions 14-48

Command Summary 14-50

Chapter 15: Introduction to Freeform Modeling 15-1

15.1 Creating Freeform Geometry 15-2
Creating Standard Freeform Shapes 15-2
Creating a Face Freeform 15-6
Converting Geometry to a Freeform 15-7
Deactivating and Activating Freeform Mode 15-9

15.2 Editing Freeform Geometry 15-10
Edit Form 15-10
Working with Edges 15-15
Working with Faces 15-21
Working with Points 15-23
Thickening Freeform Geometry 15-25
Controlling Symmetry 15-27
Mirroring Freeform Geometry 15-28
Deleting Entities 15-29

Practice 15a Box Freeform Modeling 15-31

Practice 15b Cylinder Freeform Modeling 15-43

Practice 15c Working with Existing Geometry 15-53

Practice 15d (Optional) Bridging Freeform Geometry 15-61

Chapter Review Questions 15-64

Command Summary 15-67

Appendix A: Creating Emboss and Decal Features A-1

A.1 Emboss Features A-2
Creating the Emboss Profile A-2
Creating the Emboss Feature A-3

A.2 Decal Features A-5
Creating a Decal A-6

Practice A1 Emboss and Decals A-7

Chapter Review Questions A-12

Command Summary A-13

Appendix B: Custom Sketched Symbols B-1

- **B.1 Create Sketched Symbols** B-2
  - Editing Sketched Symbols B-5
- **B.2 Place Sketched Symbols** B-6
- **B.3 AutoCAD Blocks** B-9
- Practice B1 Custom Sketched Symbols I B-11
- Practice B2 Custom Sketched Symbols II B-17
- Chapter Review Questions B-22
- Command Summary B-24

Appendix C: CAD Management C-1

- **C.1 Title Block and Border Customization** C-2
  - Use Existing Title Blocks and Borders C-2
  - Create a New Title Block and Border C-3
- **C.2 Style Library Manager** C-5
  - Style C-5
  - Style Library C-5
  - Style Library Manager C-6
  - Copy Styles Between Style Libraries C-8
  - Rename or Delete Styles C-8
  - Create a New Style Library C-8
- Practice C1 Customizing the Title Block C-9
- Practice C2 Managing Styles C-14
- Chapter Review Questions C-20
- Command Summary C-22

Appendix D: Engineer's Notebook D-1

- **D.1 Engineer's Notebook** D-2
- **D.2 Notes** D-3
- Practice D1 Engineer's Notebook D-8
- Chapter Review Questions D-15
- Command Summary D-16

Appendix E: Autodesk Inventor Certification Exam Objectives E-1

Index Index-1

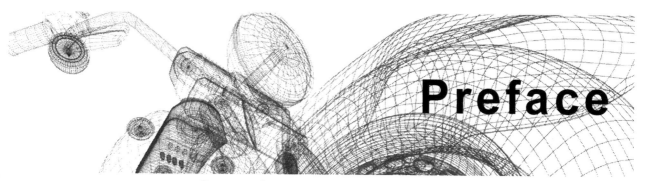

Preface

Autodesk® Inventor® 2019: Advanced Part Modeling is the second in a series of learning guides on the Autodesk® Inventor® software that is published by ASCENT. The goal of this guide is to build on the skills acquired in the *Autodesk Inventor Introduction to Solid Modeling* learning guide by taking students to a higher level of productivity when designing part models using the Autodesk Inventor software.

In this learning guide, the student considers various approaches to part design. Specific advanced part modeling techniques covered include multi-body design, advanced lofts, advanced sweeps, coils, generative shape design, surface modeling, and Freeform modeling. Material aimed at increasing efficiency includes: iFeatures for frequently used design elements, iParts for similar designs, and how to work with imported data. The guide also covers some miscellaneous drawing tools such as custom sketches symbols, working with title blocks and borders, and documenting iParts.

Topics Covered

- Advanced model appearance options
- 2D and 3D sketching techniques
- Multi-body part modeling
- Advanced geometry creation tools (work features, area lofts, sweeps, and coils)
- Analysis tools
- Generative shape design using Shape Generator
- Creating and editing basic surfaces, importing surfaces, and surface repair tools
- iFeatures and iParts
- Importing data from other CAD systems and making edits
- Working with AutoCAD DWG files
- Freeform modeling
- Emboss and Decal features
- Advanced Drawing tools (iPart tables, surfaces in drawing views, and custom sketched symbols)
- Adding notes with the Engineer's Notebook

Prerequisites

- Access to the 2019 version of the software. The practices and files included with this guide might not be compatible with prior versions.

- The material assumes a mastery of Autodesk Inventor basics as taught in *Autodesk Inventor Introduction to Solid Modeling*. Students should know how to create and edit parts, use work features, create and annotate drawing views, etc. The use of Microsoft Excel is required for this training course.

Note on Software Setup

This guide assumes a standard installation of the software using the default preferences during installation. Lectures and practices use the standard software templates and default options for the Content Libraries.

Students and Educators can Access Free Autodesk Software and Resources

Autodesk challenges you to get started with free educational licenses for professional software and creativity apps used by millions of architects, engineers, designers, and hobbyists today. Bring Autodesk software into your classroom, studio, or workshop to learn, teach, and explore real-world design challenges the way professionals do.

Get started today - register at the Autodesk Education Community and download one of the many Autodesk software applications available.

Visit www.autodesk.com/education/home/

Note: Free products are subject to the terms and conditions of the end-user license and services agreement that accompanies the software. The software is for personal use for education purposes and is not intended for classroom or lab use.

Lead Contributor: Jennifer MacMillan

With a dedication for engineering and education, Jennifer has spent over 20 years at ASCENT managing courseware development for various CAD products. Trained in Instructional Design, Jennifer uses her skills to develop instructor-led and web-based training products as well as knowledge profiling tools.

Jennifer has achieved the Autodesk Certified Professional certification for Inventor and is also recognized as an Autodesk Certified Instructor (ACI). She enjoys teaching the training courses that she authors and is also very skilled in providing technical support to end-users.

Jennifer holds a Bachelor of Engineering Degree as well as a Bachelor of Science in Mathematics from Dalhousie University, Nova Scotia, Canada.

Jennifer MacMillan has been the Lead Contributor for *Autodesk Inventor Advanced Part Modeling* since its initial release in 2007.

In this Guide

The following images highlight some of the features that can be found in this guide.

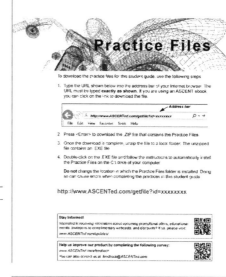

Practice Files

The Practice Files page tells you how to download and install the practice files that are provided with this guide.

Link to the practice files

Chapters

Each chapter begins with a brief introduction and a list of the chapter's Learning Objectives.

Learning Objectives for the chapter

Autodesk Inventor 2019: Advanced Part Modeling

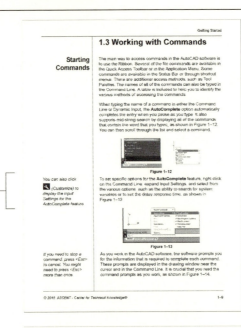

Side notes

Side notes are hints or additional information for the current topic.

Instructional Content

Each chapter is split into a series of sections of instructional content on specific topics. These lectures include the descriptions, step-by-step procedures, figures, hints, and information you need to achieve the chapter's Learning Objectives.

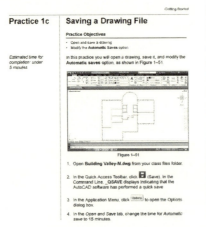

Practice Objectives

Practices

Practices enable you to use the software to perform a hands-on review of a topic.

Some practices require you to use prepared practice files, which can be downloaded from the link found on the Practice Files page.

Chapter Review Questions

Chapter review questions, located at the end of each chapter, enable you to review the key concepts and learning objectives of the chapter.

Command Summary

The Command Summary is located at the end of each chapter. It contains a list of the software commands that are used throughout the chapter, and provides information on where the command is found in the software.

Autodesk Certification Exam Appendix

This appendix includes a list of the topics and objectives for the Autodesk Certification exams, and the chapter and section in which the relevant content can be found.

Practice Files

To download the practice files for this guide, use the following steps:

1. Type the URL shown below into the address bar of your Internet browser. The URL must be typed **exactly as shown**. If you are using an ASCENT ebook, you can click on the link to download the file.

2. Press <Enter> to download the .ZIP file that contains the Practice Files.

3. Once the download is complete, unzip the file to a local folder. The unzipped file contains an .EXE file.

4. Double-click on the .EXE file and follow the instructions to automatically install the Practice Files on the C:\ drive of your computer.

   Do not change the location in which the Practice Files folder is installed. Doing so can cause errors when completing the practices.

http://www.ASCENTed.com/getfile?id=porcellus

Stay Informed!

Interested in receiving information about upcoming promotional offers, educational events, invitations to complimentary webcasts, and discounts? If so, please visit:

www.ASCENTed.com/updates/

Help us improve our product by completing the following survey:

www.ASCENTed.com/feedback

You can also contact us at: *feedback@ASCENTed.com*

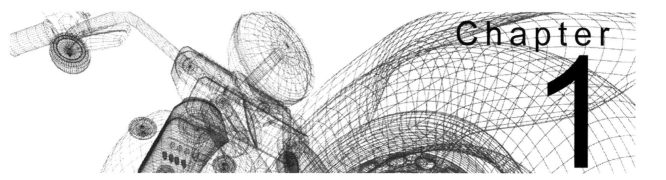

Chapter 1

Tips & Tools

There are a number of tips and tools that can help you improve your efficiency when working in the Autodesk® Inventor® software. These include such things as an understanding of general design philosophies, tips and tricks to be used when sketching the model, and modifying the display options or assigning visual appearances to help enhance the model's display for editing or presenting.

Learning Objectives in this Chapter

- Understand how the creation options and modeling sequence helps to create robust models.
- Understand how sketching, dimensioning, referencing, and constraining techniques enable you to create an accurate and modifiable sketch.
- Enhance the appearance of the surfaces and edges of a model by assigning visual styles, ray tracing, reflections, shadows, and a ground plane to the model.
- Customize and assign lighting styles to control the number, color, and intensity of light sources in a model.
- Manipulate the visual appearance of a material using the in-canvas appearance and texture tools.
- Create, assign, and edit existing appearances in the model using the Appearance Browser.

1.1 Design Philosophies

Before creating any part, consider the design intent of the part to maximize the flexibility of the design. Considering "what if" scenarios helps to create a robust model that is easy to modify.

When starting a new model, consider the following:

- Origin Features
- Base Feature
- Sketching Plane
- Sketch Options
- Feature Relationships
- Dimensions
- Depth Options
- Feature Order
- Equations

Origin Features

Origin Planes are an excellent selection as parents for subsequent features because they reduce the number of unwanted feature relationships.

Base Feature

The base feature is the first geometry feature added to the part. Create the sketch and select the base feature's form that best captures the fundamental shape of the model.

The Primitive tools are not displayed on the ribbon by default.

- Consider using one of the Primitive shapes to quickly create the base feature without explicitly accessing the Sketch environment or Feature creation dialog box.

Sketching Plane

Sketch planes must be carefully considered as they establish feature relationships. Whenever possible, use an origin plane to minimize the number of unwanted feature relationships. The selection of sketching plane for the base feature also affects the default orientation of the Home view for the model.

Sketch Options

Sketching efficiently is important. There are a number of options in the *Sketch* tab of the Application Options that helps you manipulate sketched entities. Becoming familiar with these options is beneficial. Sketches do not have to be complex. In some situations, creating multiple sketches or sharing a sketch and using multiple features can lead to the same results.

Feature Relationships	Feature relationships are established when selecting sketching planes and sketch references, as well as all other references made to existing geometry throughout feature definition. Carefully consider the references that are established to ensure they capture the required design intent. Sketch references can be removed and added in each sketch as required.
Dimensions	Carefully consider which dimensions are required to drive the design. The dimensions should be placed so that they enable modifications and represent the values that will be used in drawing views.
Depth Options	The choice of depth options affects the feature. Remember that some depth options result in feature relationships (i.e., **To Next, To, Between, Distance from Face**).
Feature Order	Carefully consider what feature order would best capture the design intent. The feature order of a model is important and can affect the resulting geometry. The Model browser enables you to easily review feature order. Feature order can be changed by selecting and dragging features. Keep in mind that parent features must exist prior to any features that reference them.
Equations	Equations are user-defined mathematical relations used to capture and control design intent in a model. Use equations in features, parts, and assemblies to capture design intent.

1.2 Sketching Tips

The Sketch environment provides a variety of ways to incorporate design intent.

Simple Sketches

Keep sketches as simple as possible. If it becomes very complex, consider whether the feature being sketched should be created as two or more simpler features. If a complex section cannot be avoided, sketch, dimension, and constrain a small number of entities at a time.

Sketch Degrees of Freedom

Determine the degrees of freedom remaining in a sketch by clicking (Show All Degrees of Freedom) in the Status Bar. Reviewing the remaining degrees of freedom can help determine where additional constraints and dimensions are required.

Constraints

Constraints control how sketched entities behave. For example, if two lines are constrained to be equal lengths they remain equal lengths even when the geometry changes.

- To show or hide all constraints, toggle (Hide All Constraints) in the Status Bar or use <F8> and <F9>.

- To view constraints applied to individual entities, in the Constrain panel, click (Show Constraints) and select the entity. Alternatively, you can select an entity to display its constraints. Constraints display similar to those in Figure 1–1.

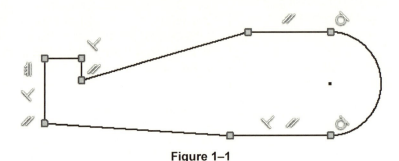

Figure 1–1

Tips & Tools

Controlling Constraint Inference

As you sketch geometry, constraints are automatically applied as you drag the cursor within a certain tolerance of other sketched entities. Symbols display on the entity that is being sketched, indicating which constraint is applied. Consider enabling/disabling constraint inference or modifying the inference scope to help capture design intent when sketching.

Although constraint inference may be disabled for a specific constraint, you can still manually apply a constraint if required.

- To toggle inference on and off, in the Constrain panel, click (Constraint Settings) and select the *Inference* tab. Enable or disable the **Infer constraints** option and select the constraints that should be inferred in the *Selection for Constraint Inference* area.

- To control the inference scope, in the expanded Constrain panel, click (Constraint Inference Scope). The Constraint Inference Scope dialog box opens and enables you to specify one of the following:
  - **Geometry in Current Command:** Constraints are inferred to the geometry created in the current command.
  - **All Geometry:** Constraints are inferred to in all of the active sketch geometry.
  - **Select:** Constraints should be inferred to only selected geometry.

Constraint Persistence

As an alternative, you can press and hold <Ctrl> to disable Constraint Inference and Constraint Persistence during the sketching process.

With the **Infer constraints** option enabled in the Constraint Settings dialog box, you have an additional option called **Persist constraints**. This option controls whether or not the inferred constraint is permanently assigned once the sketch entity is placed. By default, **Persist constraints** is enabled in a new sketch. To disable it, clear this option in the Constraint Settings dialog box. If **Infer constraints** is disabled, **Persist constraints** is also automatically disabled.

Reference in 3D

When assigning references, orient the part into a three-dimensional view. You can then be certain of the references that you are selecting. Always remember that referencing entities results in feature relationships. Avoid dimensioning or constraining to edges created from fillets, drafts, and chamfers.

Fillets and Chamfers

Create fillets and chamfers as separate features instead of sketching them in a feature. This helps simplify sketches and makes the model more robust.

Construction Entities

Use construction entities to help you sketch geometry. Construction entities are used as a reference and do not create solid geometry. It is common to use construction lines in sketching to indicate that arcs or circles lie along the same line or to indicate the midpoint of a line. An example of a use for construction circles is shown in Figure 1–2.

To sketch a construction entity, in the Format panel, click

 (Construction) *and sketch an entity (e.g., line, arc, etc.). To toggle an already sketched entity from solid to construction (or vice versa), select the entity and click the icon again.*

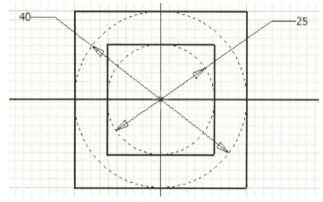

Figure 1–2

Sketched Sections

The sketch associated with a feature is separate from the remaining elements. The feature group can be expanded in the Model browser to display the section, as shown in Figure 1–3. This enables you to edit the sketch or its references independently of the entire feature.

You can reuse a consumed sketch by selecting **Share Sketch** *in the shortcut menu. Alternatively, select and drag a sketch to the top-level to share it or toggle on its visibility to reuse it. The sketch is copied above its parent. All edits to a shared sketch update all features that use it.*

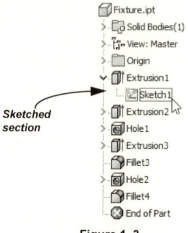

Figure 1–3

Tips & Tools

Dynamic Input & Dimensioning for Sketching

When creating a Line, Rectangle, Circle, Arc, Slot, or Point entity, a dynamic input line displays as soon as you drag the cursor onto the graphics window. This line provides input fields to define the start location of an entity (relative to 0,0,0), values to extend the entity, and angular values to position the entity, as shown in Figure 1–4. The field highlighted in blue is the active value. To toggle to alternate fields, press <Tab>.

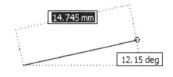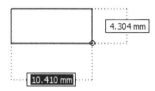

Figure 1–4

*To change the coordinate type, right-click and expand **Coordinate Type**.*

As soon as you enter a value into a dynamic input field and press <Enter>, the entity is placed and a dimension is automatically created. If multiple values must be entered in various fields, enter a value, press <Tab> to toggle to the next field, and enter its value. Only press <Enter> once all values are defined.

- When creating a Primitive as the base feature, you must use the Dynamic Input method to create dimensions that are associated with the feature.

- To disable dynamic input, in the Application Options dialog box (*Tools* tab>Options panel> (Application Options)), in the *Sketch* tab, clear the **Enable Heads-Up Display (HUD)** option.

- To disable the automatic creation of dimensions when entities are created using dynamic input, in the Constraint Settings dialog box, in the *General* tab, clear the **Create dimensions from input values** option.

Precise Input

Similar to dynamically entering coordinate and entity values upon entity placement, precise input also enables more precise sketching using coordinates rather than simply selecting points on the screen.

- Unlike dynamic input, precise input is available for Spline, Ellipse, and Polygon entities, and is the only option for precise location in a 3D sketch.

Dynamic input locates the first point with an absolute Cartesian coordinate and all additional points are defined relative to it.

*Precise Input is also available for many of the sketch editing tools (e.g., **Move**, **Copy**, **Rotate**, etc.).*

- Using precise input, you can enter coordinates either by typing their absolute Cartesian coordinates or by typing the distances from the last point you selected.

- When precise input is used, dimensions are not automatically placed. You must explicitly add dimensions.

How To: Enter Precise Values when Creating Geometry

1. Select the type of entity to sketch in the Create panel.
2. Expand the Create panel by clicking ▼ and then click
   (Precise Input), as shown in Figure 1–5.

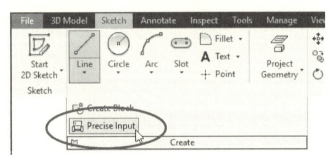

Figure 1–5

3. Select a precise input type from the drop-down list, as shown in Figure 1–6 for a 2D sketch. These options enable you to define how you enter the precise values to locate your geometry. The options vary depending on if you are working with a 2D or 3D sketch. For example, if you use precise input for a 3D sketch you only have one option which is to enter an X, Y, and Z value.

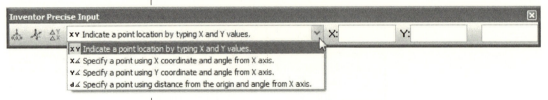

Figure 1–6

4. By default, all values are measured from the model origin.

Tips & Tools

- To change the location of the model origin, click
  (Precise Redefine). The origin displays on the model as a triad symbol. Select the blue sphere at the center of the origin and select a new location. A red dot displays under the cursor when you hover over a possible location for the origin. This location must be fully located in the model (e.g., a vertex, point, etc.).
- The newly defined origin for precise input remains until it is explicitly changed. To reset the origin back to the model origin, in the Inventor Precise Input toolbar, click
  (Reset to Origin).

5. Enter dimensional values in the toolbar, measured relative to the origin triad.

   - Once you have entered one value it constrains movement of the cursor based on what you have entered.
   - For example, if you click the x∠ input type, set the X value to 1 and leave the angle field blank, you can move the cursor along the X=1 line (parallel to the x-axis). However, if you leave the X field blank and set the angle field to 15, you can move the cursor along the 15 degree angle line, as shown in Figure 1–7.

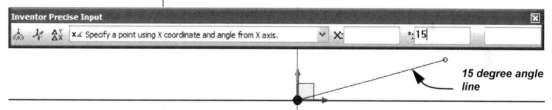

Figure 1–7

- Once you enter the required values to define the first point, press <Enter> to locate it. Continue to enter points as required to fully define the entity that has been selected. For example, if you are creating a two point rectangle you must enter two points to define the extent of the rectangle.

- The ΔY/ΔX icon enables you to enter relative to the last point rather than from the origin (0,0,0). This is not available for the first point.

1.3 Display Options

In the *View* tab>Appearance panel there are a number of options that can be used to improve the appearance of a model, as shown in Figure 1–8.

Figure 1–8

Visual Style

The *Visual Style* drop-down list contains options that can be assigned to provide model surfaces and edges with an enhanced appearance. The choice of visual style can be dependent on whether you are working on the model's design or presenting the design once it is completed. The available visual styles are shown in Figure 1–9.

Figure 1–9

Figure 1–10 shows a few of the available visual styles.

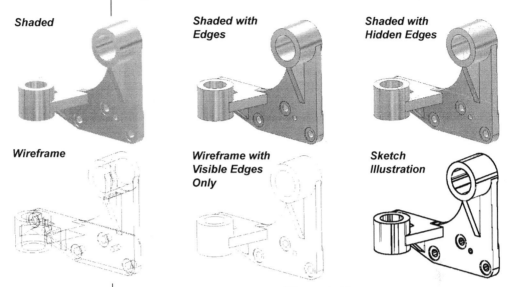

Figure 1–10

Incorporating any of the visual styles with the remaining options on the Appearance panel (e.g., Shadows, Reflections, etc.) can substantially improve the visual appearance of your models.

Ray Tracing

The **Ray Tracing** option enables you to enhance a model's visualization results when using either the **Realistic** or **Monochrome** visual styles. Ray tracing generates images by tracing the path of light through pixels in an image to simulate the effect. This technique produces an image that is highly realistic, without having to render the model in another environment.

To enable Ray tracing, in the *View* tab>Appearance panel, click (Ray Tracing). The Ray Tracing Quality window, (shown in Figure 1–11) opens when Ray Tracing is enabled.

The render sample rates are:
Low: *4 samples/pixel*
Draft: *16 samples/pixel*
High: *64 samples/pixel*

Figure 1–11

- The Progress bar indicates the rendering percentage and time display.

- Hover the cursor over the title bar of the window to expand it to set the quality (Low, Draft, or High) of the image generation.

- Click **Save**, **Pause**, or **Disable** at the bottom of the window, as required. You can also disable the render by selecting **Ray Tracing** on the ribbon.

- While **Ray Tracing** is enabled, the Ray Tracing Quality window remains open. To optimize visual space in the graphics window, it might fade from the display. Hover the cursor over the lower right-hand corner of the graphics window to display it again.

In the examples shown in Figure 1–12, a model has been assigned the **Metal-AL-6061 (Polished)** color, and the visual styles settings have been manipulated to vary the displayed image.

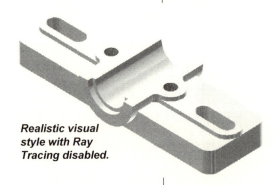
Realistic visual style with Ray Tracing disabled.

Realistic visual style with Ray Tracing enabled.

Figure 1–12

Ground Plane

In the Appearance panel, the (Ground Plane) option enables you to toggle the display of a plane that represents the ground. The ground plane can be included to help represent the up direction of the model. It is also used in conjunction with shadows and reflection to set realistic visual display settings. Consider the following about the ground plane:

- The ground plane is parallel with the Origin's XZ plane.

- The ground plane is tied to the model. If you rotate the model, the ground plane rotates with it.

- When viewing the ground plane from the top, a plane with a grid is displayed. When viewing the model from beneath the plane, only the exterior outline of the plane is displayed.

- To customize the ground plane, in the *View* tab>Appearance panel, in the Ground Plane drop-down list, select **Settings**. This option enables you to relocate the X, Y, and Z locations, its appearance, grid display, and reflection settings.

- All settings for the ground plane are stored with the document only, and do not affect other models in the current session.

An example of a model with its ground plane displayed is shown in Figure 1–13.

The ground plane does not need to be displayed in order for ground shadows and reflections to be used.

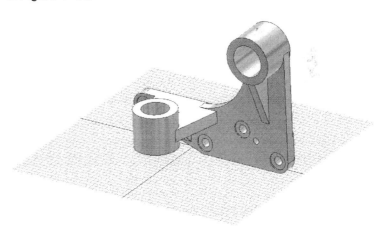

Figure 1–13

Shadows

The *Shadows* drop-down list ( ) enables you to control the shadows that are assigned in a model for enhanced model visualization. Shadows can be enabled so they display on the ground, on the object, or so that ambient shadows are used. Shadows can be enabled individually or in any combination of the three shadow types. Figure 1–14 displays a model with the various shadowing effects.

Figure 1–14

To customize shadow settings, in the Shadows ( ) drop-down list, select **Settings** to access the active Lighting Style. Customize the shadow values in the *Shadows* tab for the active Lighting Style.

Reflections

Reflections can be cast on the ground plane by enabling (Reflections) in the Appearance panel on the *View* tab. Shadows reflect the visual style that is set in the model. By changing the Z location of the ground plane, the resulting reflection is varied. The **Settings** option in the Reflection drop-down list enables you to customize the Ground Plane which affects reflections.

Note that the ground plane does not need to be displayed in order for ground reflections to be assigned in the model.

Tips & Tools

Lighting Styles

The appearance of parts can be changed by adjusting the lighting style. In a lighting style, you can control the number, color, and intensity of light sources for a file, as well as assign image-based lighting and shadows. Use the Lighting Style drop-down list to quickly assign a lighting style as an alternative to accessing the Style and Standard Editor. The default list of lighting styles are shown in Figure 1–15.

Lighting styles can be set in a part, assembly, or presentation.

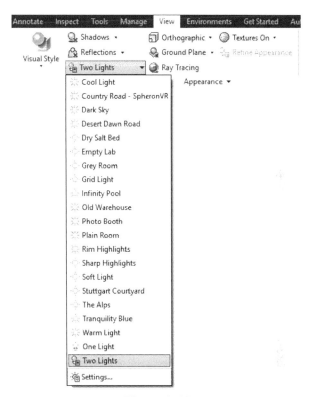

Figure 1–15

Many styles assign an image, as shown in the **Old Warehouse** and **Empty Lab** styles shown in Figure 1–16. Models can be positioned relative to the image to enhance model realism.

For image-based lighting styles, use the Perspective orientation to improve realism.

Figure 1–16

© 2018, ASCENT - Center for Technical Knowledge® 1–15

If a new lighting style is required, you can use either of the following techniques to access the Style and Standard Editor:

- In the *View* tab>Appearance panel, in the Lighting drop-down list, select **Settings**.

- In the *Manage* tab>Styles and Standards panel, click 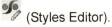 (Styles Editor).

The Style and Standard Editor opens as shown in Figure 1–17.

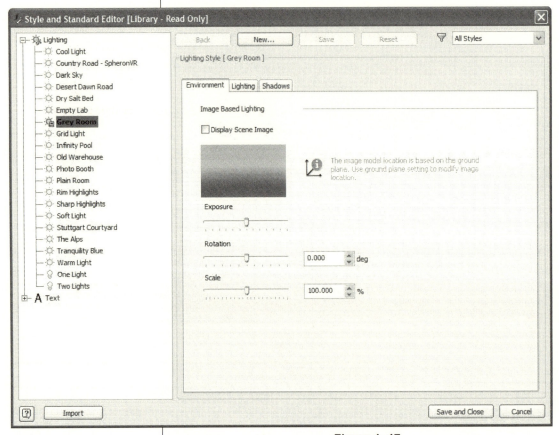

Figure 1–17

Select a lighting style to edit or create a new style. To create a new style, right-click on an existing style and select **New Style**. The selected style is copied and can be used as a starting point for the creation of the new style.

The table below describes the lighting style settings.

Tabs		Description
Environment tab		
	Image Based Lighting	Set the image-based lighting effects for the active light style. This tab is only available if an image has been assigned to the lighting style. To display the image in the actual scene, select **Display Scene Image**. Without this option enabled, the image is not displayed; however, by toggling this option on and off, you can control the image-based lighting effect without losing all of the specified settings. You can also adjust its exposure, rotation, and scale.
Lighting tab		
	Light# tabs	Select a light number tab to activate it for editing. Click ![icon] on each tab to toggle the specific light source on or off.
	Standard Light Settings	Control the horizontal/vertical position of the active light source using the sliders that surround the image of the light. You can also select the color and control the brightness of the light source. Using the two Relative movement options, you can specify that the light is fixed to the view's camera (![icon]) or that the light maintains a fixed direction relative to the Viewcube (![icon]).
	All Lights	Control the brightness and ambience of the light sources for all standard lights. Use the *Brightness* slider to control the light intensity and use the *Ambience* slider to set the contrast between lit and unlit areas in the scene.
Shadows tab		
	Shadow Settings	Set the lighting style's shadow setting by selecting from a predefined list of shadow directions. You can also specify the shadow's density, softness, and ambient shadow intensity.

Edits you make in the dialog box are dynamically displayed on the part. You must save the edits to preserve them. Edits are saved to the active lighting style in the file.

Perspective & Orthographic Views

Traditional mechanical drawings show parts in orthographic (parallel) views, where parallel edges on the part display parallel in the drawing. Perspective views display the way that the eye sees, where parallel edges seem to converge at a vanishing point, as shown in Figure 1–18. To change to a perspective view, select the *View* tab. In the Appearance panel, expand (Orthographic) and click (Perspective).

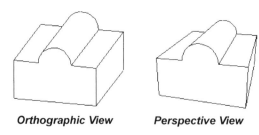

Orthographic View   **Perspective View**

Figure 1–18

While in a perspective view, you can zoom, pan, and rotate, but the results may differ slightly than that in an Orthographic view. Refer to the "About Perspective Views" Help topic for more information on view manipulation for Perspective views.

Tips & Tools

1.4 Appearances

Colors and textures can be added to a model to further enhance its visualization. Color and texture are combined within the appearance definition of a material. When a material is assigned, the visual appearance specified for that material is assigned to the model. The Materials and Appearance Override drop-down lists in the Quick Access Toolbar display the current material and its appearance, as shown in Figure 1–19.

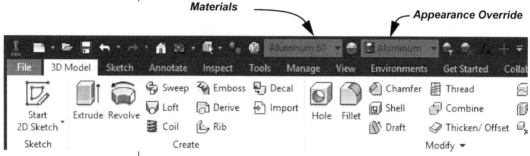

Figure 1–19

To assign a different appearance to the model while maintaining the material setting and therefore its iProperty data, select an alternate material in the Appearance Override drop-down list, as shown in Figure 1–20.

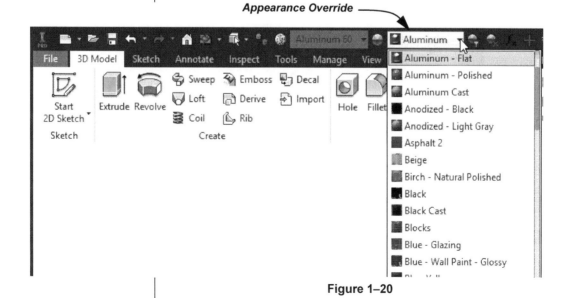

Figure 1–20

The predefined list of appearances provided in the Appearance Override drop-down list are pulled from provided libraries. By default, the Inventor Material Library is set as the active library. To switch between libraries in the drop-down list, select an alternate library name, as shown in Figure 1–21.

The default library can be set in the Project File.

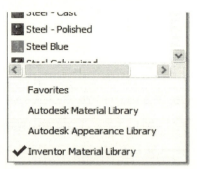

Figure 1–21

To quickly manipulate the assigned appearance, you can use the in-canvas tools.

In-Canvas Appearance and Texture Tools

The in-canvas appearance and texture tools provide you with a convenient way to change the color of an appearance or the texture mapping on the model. The tools are provided in a mini-toolbar and the icons can be used directly on the model.

How To: Edit the Existing Appearance using the In-canvas Tools

1. In the *Tools* tab>Material and Appearance panel, click (Adjust). The Appearance mini-toolbar opens as shown in Figure 1–22.

Figure 1–22

2. Using the model, select the appearance that is to be edited. You can select directly on the model when the cursor displays as the eyedropper ( ), or you can select the appearance from the Appearances drop-down list in the mini-toolbar.

Tips & Tools

- When using the cursor, if you want to edit the color of the entire model, ensure that you select the entire model.
- To change only selected faces, surfaces, bodies, or features, select them individually. Use the Select Other drop-down list to select the required option.
- Selecting the appearance in the Appearances drop-down list enables you to first edit the Appearance and then apply it to the model.

3. Select the method for defining the color.
   - Defining the color as a red, green, and blue value (**RGB Values**) is the default option.
   - Select the RGB Values drop-down list and select **HSL Values** to define the color with a hue, saturation, and lightness value.

4. For either the **RGB** or **HSL Values** options, use the color wheel to define its values.
   - Drag the line around its perimeter to change the value.
   - To refine the color, activate and drag the square node on the internal diamond shape at the center of the color wheel.
   - If the appearance was selected directly from the model, it will update as you are changing the color.

5. If you selected the appearance from the drop-down list, you are required to assign it to the model. Using the cursor, now displayed as a paint can ( ), select the model or individual faces, surfaces, bodies, or features, to assign the edited appearance.

6. If the Appearance has a texture assigned to it, you can scale and rotate the texture using the   and   icons that display once the model or individual faces, surfaces, bodies, or features are selected.
   - Hover the cursor over the icons until they are active (yellow) and then press and hold the mouse button to scale and rotate.

7. If the Appearance has a texture assigned to it, you can vary how it is mapped to the surface of the model. Expand the   drop-down list and select a mapping option.
   - By default, **Automatic** is used and generally provides a good representation of the texture on the model.
   - Hovering the cursor over the other mapping options displays them in the model.

8. Click   to complete the edit and close the mini-toolbar.

The scale and rotate icons are displayed for non-textured appearances. Manipulating these icons will not affect the overall appearance.

Once an appearance is adjusted using the in-canvas tools, a new appearance is created that has (1) appended to the end of the name. For example, if you were adjusting the Red appearance, the adjusted appearance would be called Red(1).

Appearance Browser

The Appearance Browser (shown in Figure 1–23), is used as an alternative to the Appearance Override drop-down list to assign appearances. It provides thumbnail previews to identify appearances, and can be used to create new appearances.

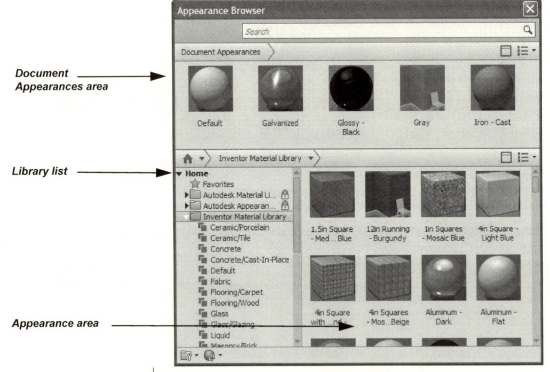

Figure 1–23

The Appearance Browser is divided into the following three areas:

- *Document Appearances* area - This area includes all appearances that have been assigned to the model.

- Library list - The library list enables you to select the libraries where you want to look for different appearances. The Favorites node enables you to quickly access any of the appearances from the three libraries that you have marked as Favorites.

Tips & Tools

Create a New Appearance

- *Appearance* area - Once a library is expanded and a group type selected, its appearances are displayed in the *Appearance* area. Using this area, appearances can be added to the *Document Appearances* area for use.

How To: Use the Appearance Browser to Create a New Appearance

1. In the *Tools* tab>Material and Appearance panel, click (Appearance). The Appearance Browser opens as shown in Figure 1–24. The current file only has one appearance that was assigned to it (Default) as shown in the *Document Appearances* area and the **Inventor Material Library** is selected. If an appearance override was assigned, it would also be displayed here.

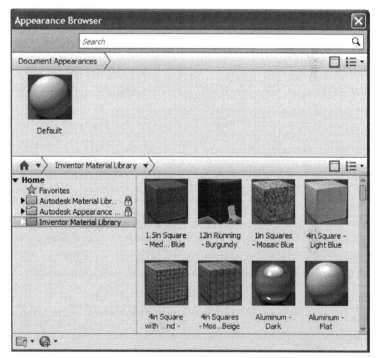

Figure 1–24

2. Right-click on an existing appearance in the *Document Appearances* area and select **Duplicate** to create its copy. The selected appearance should be one that closely resembles the settings that you want as a new appearance.

   Alternatively, click at the bottom of the Appearance Browser and select from the list of types to start the creation of a new appearance.

3. Select the default name, *right-click on it, and select* **Rename**. Enter a new name for the appearance.

4. Right-click on the new appearance and select **Edit**. The Appearance Editor opens, as shown in Figure 1–25.

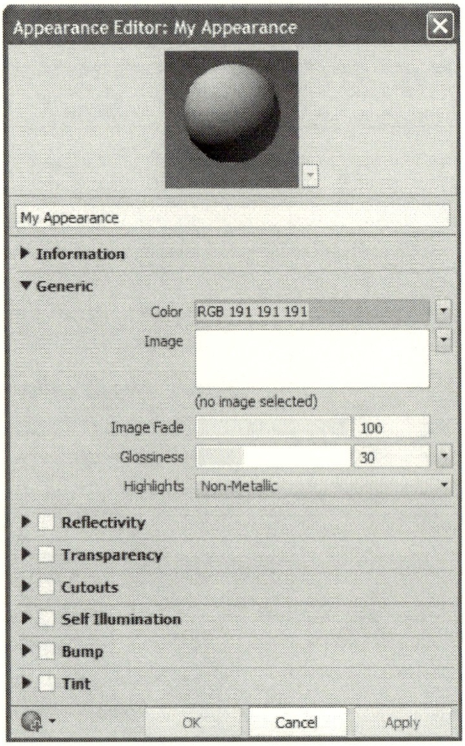

Figure 1–25

5. Define the appearance, as required.
   - Select in the *Color* field to access the Color dialog box to select or customize a new color.
   - Select in the *Image* field to import a texture for the appearance.
   - Change the settings of the *Image Fade*, *Glossiness*, and *Highlights* to customize the appearance of the texture.
   - Use other options in the Appearance Editor to further customize the new appearance by adding reflectivity, transparency, bump maps, self illumination, etc.
6. Click **OK** to complete the creation of the new appearance. The thumbnail image in the *Document Appearances* area updates to reflect the changes that were made in the Appearance Editor.

To edit an existing appearance, right-click on the appearance name in the *Document Appearances* area of the Appearance Browser and select **Edit**. Edit the options, as required, to reflect the required change.

Hint: Textures

Textures are files that can be added to any appearance. Bump maps enable you to further control the display of an image by assigning a bumpiness value. Texture images are assigned in the Generic node while that for Bump Maps are assigned in the Bump node. Similarly, maps can be assigned to other nodes.

To assign an image, select in the *Image* field for the node and use the Material Editor Open File dialog box to browse to and select an image.

To modify the placement of the image, right-click on the *Image* field and select **Edit Image**. The Texture Editor opens as shown in Figure 1–26. You can refine the image's position, rotation, scale, repeat, and (in the case of a bump map) vary the amount of bumpiness.

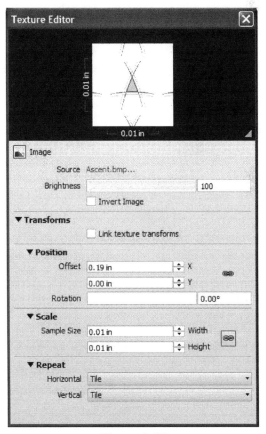

Figure 1–26

Assign an Appearance

Alternatively, you can assign the new appearance using the Material Override drop-down list in the Quick Access Toolbar. Once assigned, the appearance is automatically added to the Document Appearances area.

How To: Use the Appearance Browser to Assign an Appearance to the Model

1. In the *Tools* tab>Material and Appearance panel, click (Appearance).
2. To assign a new appearance, select the entire model or individual surfaces on the model, right-click on the appearance thumbnail in the *Document Appearances* area and select **Assign to Selection**.
   - To help identify what is being selected in the model, before selecting, hover the cursor over the model so that the preview displays the entire model (dashed lines) or individual surfaces (solid lines).
3. Click to close the Appearance Browser.

Adding Appearances to the Document

How To: Use the Appearance Browser to Add a Material from a Library to the Document Appearances area

1. In the *Tools* tab>Material and Appearance panel, click (Appearance).
2. Expand the appropriate library in the Library list.
3. Select an appearance type. The list of appearances associated with the selected type display in the *Appearance* area on the right side of the Appearance Browser.
4. Right-click an appearance and select **Add To>Document Materials** to add it to the *Document Appearances* area for use in the model.

To display the model so that any of the image's texturing settings are consistently displayed, set the *Visual Style* to **Realistic**. If not, only the color of the appearance might display on the model.

Practice 1a

Create a Sketch using Precise Coordinates

Practice Objectives

- Create sketched entities by entering their starting locations and dimension sizes.
- Reposition the origin triad in a sketch so that dimensions can be entered relative to a defined location rather than the origin of the model.
- Create sketched entities by entering their extents using the Precise Input dialog box versus sketching and dimensioning them independently.

In this practice you will create a part. For some sketch features, you will use either dynamic input or precise input to create the entities in the model. The completed part is shown in Figure 1–27.

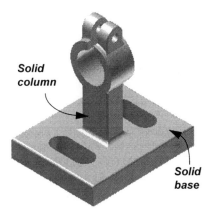

Figure 1–27

Task 1 - Create a new part file.

1. In the *Get Started* tab>Launch panel, click (Projects) to open the Projects dialog box. Project files identify folders that contain the required models.

This project file is used for the entire learning guide.

2. Click **Browse**. In the practice files folder, select **Advanced Part.ipj**. Click **Open**. The Projects dialog box updates and a checkmark displays next to the new project name, indicating that it is the active project. The project file tells Autodesk Inventor where your files are stored. Click **Done**.

3. Create a new part using the standard Metric template.

Task 2 - Create the solid base.

The sketch for the solid base is a 300 X 240mm rectangle.

1. In the *3D Model* tab>Sketch panel, click (Start 2D Sketch). The Origin planes are temporarily displayed in the graphics window enabling you to select the sketch plane.

   *Alternatively, you can right-click on the plane name in the Model browser or in the graphics window and select **New Sketch**.*

2. Select the XZ Plane in the graphics window to start a new sketch. You are placed in the Sketch environment, the XZ Plane is the current sketch plane, and the *Sketch* tab is active.

3. Project the YZ and XY planes onto the sketch plane to locate and dimension the sketch.

4. In the Create panel, click (Rectangle).

5. Press <Tab> to activate the *X* field in the dynamic input display. Enter **120** in the *X* field, press <Tab> to toggle to the *Y* field, and enter **150** in the *Y* field. The point is measured from the absolute origin (0,0). Press <Enter> after you have entered the values.

6. Enter **240** in the *X* field, press <Tab>, and enter **300** in the *Y* field. Press <Enter> after you have entered the values. The point is measured from the previous point (120,150). The rectangle displays as shown in Figure 1–28 with the defined dimensions.

You might have to zoom out to be able to see the rectangle.

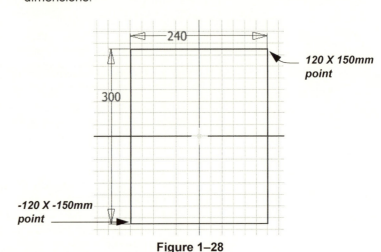

Figure 1–28

7. Press <Esc> to cancel the command.

8. Constrain the sketch to ensure symmetry with respect to the projected work planes. The sketch displays as shown in Figure 1–29.

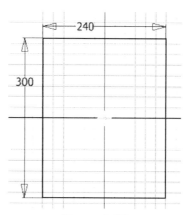

Figure 1–29

9. Finish the sketch. Extrude the sketch by **40mm** in the positive z-direction. The extrusion displays as shown in Figure 1–30. The model is displayed in the isometric Home view.

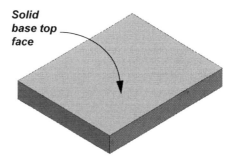

Figure 1–30

Task 3 - Create the solid column.

The sketch for the solid column is a 240 X 80mm rectangle. The coordinates for a solid column sketch are given from the center of the solid base top face.

1. Create a work point to provide a reference for the Precise Input. The reference point should be at the center of the solid base top face. Create the work point using **Center Point of Loop of Edges** or **Intersection of Three Planes** (at the intersection of the solid base top face, and the XY and YZ planes).

2. In the Model browser, right-click on the XY plane and select **New Sketch**, or use any of the other options to create a new sketch.

3. Project the YZ plane onto the sketch plane to locate and dimension the sketch.

4. Project the work point that was previously created.

5. In the Create panel, click ▢ (Rectangle).

6. Expand the Create panel and click 🖮 (Precise Input).

7. In the Inventor Precise Input toolbar, click ✶ (Precise Redefine) and select the black sphere at the center of the origin triad.

8. Select the projected work point. The origin triad displays as shown in Figure 1–31. Your sketch might be displayed from the other side of the XY plane. The new location you define remains the active origin until you select a new point or you reset it back to the model origin using the ⚛ (Reset to Origin) icon.

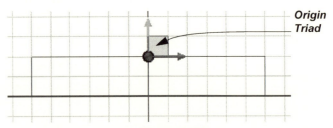

Figure 1–31

9. Enter **40** in the X field and **240** in the Y field. The point is measured from the relative origin. Press <Enter> after you have entered the values.

10. Enter **-40** in the X field and **0.00** in the Y field. Press <Enter> after you have entered the values.

11. Dimension and constrain the sketch, as shown in Figure 1–32. You will need to assign the symmetric and coincident constraints.

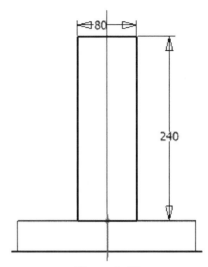

Figure 1–32

- In this case, Precise Input enabled you to change the origin point from which the dimensions were entered. Although it would have been easier to adjust the coordinate entries for values that were relative to the origin, Precise Input can be valuable if the provided values are more complex. In addition, consider that you had to manually assign the dimensions, while with dynamic input, they were assigned for you.

12. Finish the sketch and close the Precise Input dialog box. Extrude the sketch by **25mm** on either side of the XY plane. The extrusion displays as shown in Figure 1–33. The model is displayed in the isometric Home view and is shaded.

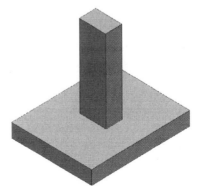

Figure 1–33

Task 4 - Create the slots in the solid base.

1. Right-click on the solid base top face and select **New Sketch**, or use any of the other options to create a new sketch.

2. Project the YZ and XY planes onto the sketch plane to locate and dimension the sketch.

3. Sketch the slot shown in Figure 1–34. Use dynamic input to enter the dimensions. Add the additional 70 dimension to locate the slot and assign a symmetry constraint to fully locate the slot.

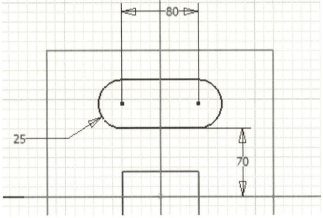

Figure 1–34

4. Finish the sketch and extrude the sketch as a cut through the entire model.

5. Mirror the slot using the XY plane as the mirroring plane. The model displays as shown in Figure 1–35.

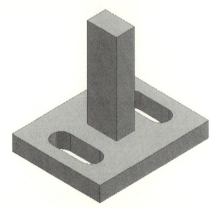

Figure 1–35

Task 5 - Create the extrusion.

1. Create the extrusion shown in Figure 1–36. Select the XY plane as the sketching plane. Locate the center of the circular sketch using either dynamic input or precise input. Locate the center of the circular sketch at **0, 180** with a diameter of **120mm**. Extrude the sketch by **35mm** on either side of the XY plane. Ensure that the sketch is fully constrained.

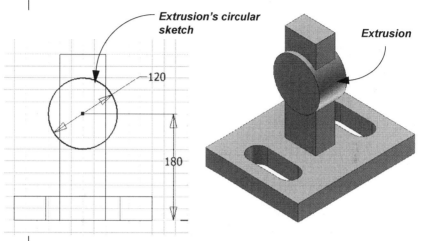

Figure 1–36

Task 6 - Create a Through All hole.

1. Create the concentric, through all hole shown in Figure 1–37. The hole diameter is **80mm**.

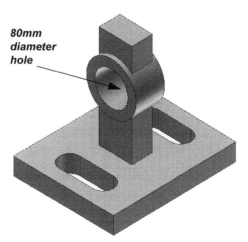

Figure 1–37

Task 7 - Create an extruded cut.

1. Select the XY plane as the sketching plane and sketch the section shown in Figure 1–38. The cut should always cut through to the concentric hole. By referencing existing geometry and using constraints you can create the section using only one dimension.

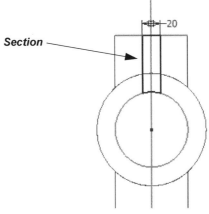

Figure 1–38

2. Finish the sketch.

3. Create an extruded cut through both sides of the XY plane. The model displays as shown in Figure 1–39.

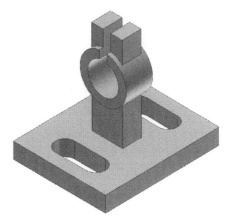

Figure 1–39

Task 8 - Create fillets and a hole.

1. Create the full round fillets and the hole shown on the left side of Figure 1–40. The diameter for the hole is **20mm**.

2. Create the **2mm** fillets shown on the right side of Figure 1–40.

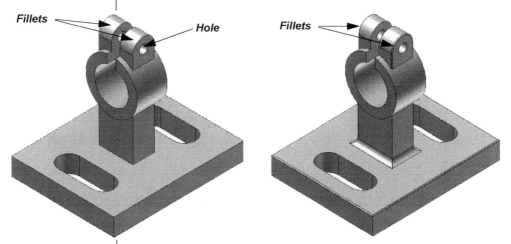

Figure 1–40

3. Save the part as **Precise_Input.ipt** and close the model.

Practice 1b

Create a Lighting Style

Practice Objectives

- Create a new lighting style based on an existing style.
- Edit a lighting style to change its ambience setting and include multiple colored lights.
- Change the lighting style that is applied to the model using the Styles and Standards Editor and the options in the Appearance panel.

In this practice, you will create a new lighting style and assign it for use with a part file. The part is shown in Figure 1–41.

Figure 1–41

Task 1 - Open a part file and create a new lighting style.

1. Open **handle.ipt**.

2. In the *Manage* tab>Styles and Standards panel, click (Styles Editor). The Style and Standard Editor dialog box opens.

3. Expand the **Lighting** branch and select **Two Lights**.

4. Click **New**. The New Local Style dialog box opens.

5. Enter **handle** in the *Name* field and click **OK**. The handle style is now listed in the Lighting branch.

6. Double-click on **handle** in the list to activate it. The active style is bold in the list and is applied to the model.

7. Move the *Ambience* slider to increase the amount of ambient light on the screen for all lights. Note how the model updates as you move the slider.

8. Return the *Ambience* slider to approximately the middle of the scale.

9. In the *Standard Lights* area of the *Lighting* tab, ensure that the *Light 1* tab is selected and that the 💡 (yellow light bulb) icon is active. This represents the first direct light.

10. Move the vertical slider on the right side of the image to the top and the slider on the bottom to the left side to place the light.

11. Click the **Color** icon located above the *Brightness* slider. Select one of the blue colors from the color palette. Click **OK**. Note the effect on the part.

12. Select the *Light 2* tab to activate it. Ensure that the 💡 icon is enabled (yellow). Select it, if not. The blue light you created in the last step will now have less influence on the part. Change the color of the second light to red, and move the sliders to the bottom and right positions to place this light.

13. Click **Save and Close**. Note the effect on the part.

14. Rotate the part. You will see different shades and colors on the part, depending on where you placed the lights.

Task 2 - Manipulate the appearance of the model.

1. Select the *View* tab.

2. In the Appearance panel, note that the handle light style is currently active. In the Lighting Style drop-down list, select **Two Lights**. Note how the model updates to reflect the settings in this style.

3. Select some of the various options in the Visual Style drop-down list to manipulate the model's appearance. Leave the style set to **Shaded with Edges.**

4. In the Lighting Style drop-down list, select **Empty Lab**.

5. The default scale of the model relative to the image is incorrect. In the Lighting Style drop-down list, select **Settings**. In the *Image Based Lighting* area in the *Environment* tab, reduce the *Scale* to approximately **15%**. Click **Save and Close**.

6. In the Orthographic drop-down list, select **Perspective** to obtain a more realistic image.

7. Zoom in and orient the model. The **Shaded with Edges** visual style is not very realistic for product presentation. Change the visual style to **Realistic**.

8. Select a darker color in the Appearance Override drop-down list in the Quick Access toolbar, shown in Figure 1–42.

Appearance Override

Figure 1–42

9. The model should display similar to that shown in Figure 1–43.

Figure 1–43

10. Save the part and close the window.

Practice 1c Working with Appearances

Practice Objectives

- Override the visual appearance of a material.
- Create, edit, and assign appearances to a model using the Appearance Browser and the Appearance Override drop-down list.

In this practice, you will assign a material to a model and then override its visual appearance. You will apply appearances to the entire model as well as individual surfaces. The final model is shown in Figure 1–44.

Figure 1–44

Task 1 - Open a model and assign a material.

1. Open **bearing_journal.ipt**. The part is currently assigned the Generic material and visual appearance, as shown in the Material and Appearance Override drop-down lists in the Quick Access Toolbar in Figure 1–45.

Figure 1–45

2. In the Quick Access Toolbar, in the Material drop-down list, set the material to **Stainless Steel**. The visual appearance is set as Semi-Polished which is the default setting for the Stainless Steel material. The model displays as shown in Figure 1–46.

The model's color is now Semi-Polished.

Figure 1–46

Task 2 - Assign and new visual appearance and edit it.

1. In the Quick Access Toolbar, in the Appearance Override drop-down list, set the color to **Yellow**. The visual appearance of the model changes to yellow, as shown in Figure 1–47, but the material remains Stainless Steel.

The model's color is now Yellow.

Figure 1–47

2. In the *Tools* tab>Material and Appearance panel, click (Adjust) to open the appearance mini-toolbar.

3. Hold <Ctrl> and select the two surfaces shown in Figure 1–48.

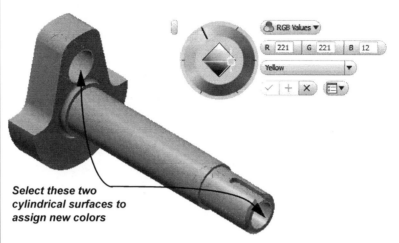

Select these two cylindrical surfaces to assign new colors

Figure 1–48

4. Maintain the RGB Values setting and use the color wheel to define the values. Drag the line around its perimeter to change the value to red. Because the surfaces were preselected, the surfaces update as you change the RGB value.

5. Click ✓ to complete the change and close the mini-toolbar. The model should display similar to that shown in Figure 1–49.

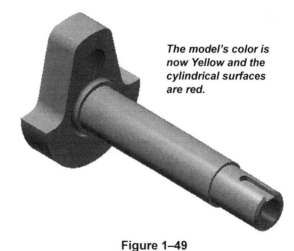

The model's color is now Yellow and the cylindrical surfaces are red.

Figure 1–49

6. In the Appearance Override drop-down list, select **Rust**. The model should display similar to that shown in Figure 1–50. Note that the surface overrides on the internal surfaces that were changed to red are maintained and the Rust appearance is applied to the rest of the model. The Rust appearance was created using a texture image.

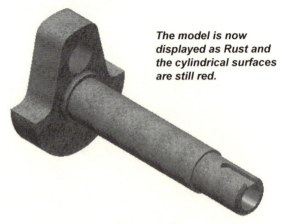

The model is now displayed as Rust and the cylindrical surfaces are still red.

Figure 1–50

7. In the *Tools* tab>Material and Appearance panel, click (Adjust) to open the appearance mini-toolbar.

8. Hover the cursor over the model so that its entire boundary is highlighted in dashed red lines and click to select the model. If required, use the Select Other drop-down list to select the solid in order to highlight all the geometry. This enables you to edit the Rust appearance on the entire model.

9. Try and change the color of the appearance. Note how it does not change because this appearance is using a texture image.

10. Click to open the drop-down list and roll the cursor over each of the mapping options. By default, **Automatic** is used and it provides a good representation of the rust texture on the model. Depending on the surface and model shapes being assigned a textured appearance the other options might provide better representations.

11. Hover the mouse over the icon until the cursor changes to the icon. This indicates that you can now scale the texture. Drag the cursor to scale the texture.

Tips & Tools

12. Hover the cursor over the ○ icon until the cursor changes to the ↻ icon indicating that you can now rotate the texture. Drag the cursor to rotate the texture.

13. Click ✕ to cancel the edit and close the mini-toolbar. The original texture scale and rotation is maintained.

Task 3 - Create a new appearance and assign it to the model.

1. In the *Tools* tab>Material and Appearance panel, click 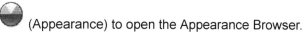 (Appearance) to open the Appearance Browser.

   Alternatively, you can also click ◐ in the Quick Access Toolbar. The Appearance Browser displays as shown in Figure 1–51.

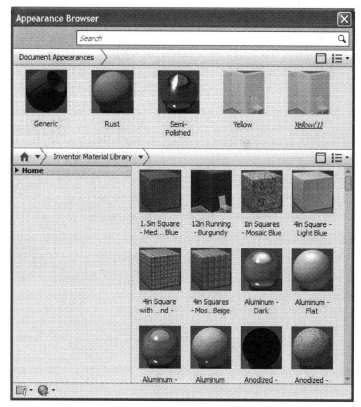

Figure 1–51

Note that there are currently five appearances listed in the *Document Appearances* area. These correspond to all of the appearances that you have assigned to the model. **Generic** was the appearance that was set when the file was opened, **Semi-Polished** was used when the material was set to Stainless Steel, **Yellow** was used to override the visual appearance of the Stainless Steel Material, and **Yellow(1)** represents the edits that were made using the mini-toolbar to create the red color. Finally, **Rust** was the final override material that was used. Only appearances that have been used in the model are shown here.

2. Right-click on **Yellow(1)** and select **Rename**. Enter **MyRed** as the new name.

3. Right-click on **Generic** and select **Duplicate**. This creates a copy of the Generic appearance that you can use it as the base for a new appearance.

4. Right-click on **Generic(1)** and select **Rename**. Enter **MyColor** as the new name for the duplicated appearance.

5. Double-click on **MyColor** to open the Appearance Editor.

6. Select in the *Color* field and assign a new color to the appearance using the Color dialog box. Increase the *Glossiness* value and change the *Highlights* to **Metallic**. Additional settings can be made using other nodes in the Appearance Editor to further customize the appearance.

7. Click **OK** to complete the edit and close the Appearance Editor.

8. Hover the cursor over the model so that its entire boundary is highlighted in dashed lines and click to select the model.

9. In the Appearance Browser, right-click on **MyColor** and select **Assign to Selection** to assign the new appearance to the model. Note that the red surface overrides are still maintained.

10. Click ☒ to close the Appearance Browser.

Tips & Tools

Task 4 - Clear appearance overrides.

1. In the *Tools* tab>Material and Appearance panel, click (Clear) to open the mini-toolbar.

2. Press and hold <Ctrl> and select the two surfaces that were assigned the **MyRed** appearance.

3. Click to clear the appearance override on these surfaces. Note that the entire model now has the **MyColor** appearance assigned.

4. In the *Tools* tab>Material and Appearance panel, click (Clear) to open the mini-toolbar again.

5. Click **Select All** in mini-toolbar and click to clear all overrides in the model. This returns the visual appearance back to Semi-Polished, which was assigned with the Stainless Steel material.

Task 5 - Add an appearance from the Inventor Material Library to the model.

1. In the *Tools* tab>Material and Appearance panel, click (Appearance) to open the Appearance Browser.

2. In the (Home) drop-down list, select **Inventor Material Library** to display of materials in this library. You can also expand the **Home** node and select **Inventor Material Library**.

3. Expand the **Inventor Material Library** drop-down list. Select **Metal/Steel** to display the list of appearances in the Metal/Steel category.

4. Right-click the **Machined 02** appearance and select **Add To>Document Materials**.

5. Select the model and assign the **Machined 02** appearance to the selection.

6. Close the Appearance Browser. The model updates as shown in Figure 1–52.

The model is now displayed with the Machined 02 material.

Figure 1–52

The appearance could also have been assigned by selecting it and using the Appearance Override drop-down list to select the Machined 02 appearance. In this case, once selected it would have been assigned and added to the *Document Appearances* area. This is an alternative method to adding materials using the Appearance Browser. The benefit of the Appearance Browser is that you can review the thumbnail images and copy existing materials to use as a base for new appearances.

7. Save the part and close the window.

The additional material libraries can also be expanded and used to access other appearances. By default, their appearances are not listed in the appearance override drop-down list so they must be added through the Appearance Browser.

Chapter Review Questions

1. In the Inventor Precise Input dialog box, which tool enables you to change the origin point so that it is used as the reference point from which values are measured?

    a. [icon]

    b. [icon]

    c. [icon]

2. The custom placement of the origin used with the Precise Input tool, is only set as long as the entity that was being sketched at the time is active.

    a. True
    b. False

3. Which of the following statements are true regarding dynamic input and dimensioning when creating sketched entities. (Select all that apply.)

    a. Dynamic input is available for all sketched entity types.
    b. When dynamically entering the first dimension value (the locating dimension value) for an entity, the coordinate entry is always measured from (0,0,0).
    c. By default, values entered in a dynamic input field automatically display as dimensions in the sketch.
    d. Dynamic input cannot be disabled when sketching entities.

4. Which of the following Appearance tools are available when the Visual Style for the model is set as **Shaded**? (Select all that apply.)

    a. Shadows
    b. Reflections
    c. Lights
    d. Ground Plane
    e. Ray Tracing

5. The ground plane must be enabled (displayed) for the shadows and ground reflections to be visible in the model.

    a. True

    b. False

6. Which of the following statements are true regarding lighting styles. (Select all that apply.)

    a. An Image-based lighting style enables you to use a predefined background image in the style.

    b. Multiple standard lights can be combined in a single lighting style.

    c. Multiple lighting styles can be applied at one time.

    d. Shadow settings are controlled in a lighting style.

7. The following icons display when working with the in-canvas appearance and texture tool. Which icon enables you to scale a texture in a material?

    a.

    b.

    c.

    d.

8. Which of the following statements is true regarding the Appearance Browser dialog box shown in Figure 1–53. (Select all that apply.)

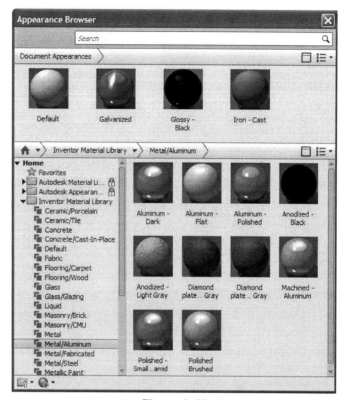

Figure 1–53

a. Four appearances have been applied to the model.

b. The Favorites list is currently being displayed in the *Appearance* area.

c. The Metal/Aluminum category in the Inventor Material Library is currently active.

d. The Aluminum - Dark material is the currently assigned material to the model.

Command Summary

Button	Command	Location
	Adjust (color)	• **Ribbon:** *Tools* tab>Appearance panel
	Appearance (Browser)	• **Ribbon:** *Tools* tab>Appearance panel
N/A	Appearance Override	• **Quick Access Toolbar** • **Appearance Browser**
	Clear (color)	• **Ribbon:** *Tools* tab>Appearance panel
	Constraint Inference Scope	• **Ribbon:** *Sketch* tab>expanded Constrain panel
	Constraint Settings	• **Ribbon:** *Sketch* tab>expanded Constrain panel
	Construction	• **Ribbon:** *Sketch* tab>Format panel
	Ground Plane	• **Ribbon:** *View* tab>Appearance panel
	Hide All Constraints	• **Sketch Status Bar** • **Keyboard:** Toggle with <F8> and <F9>
N/A	Lighting Styles	• **Ribbon:** *View* tab>Appearance panel
	Orthographic	• **Ribbon:** *View* tab>Appearance panel
	Perspective	• **Ribbon:** *View* tab>Appearance panel
	Precise Input	• **Ribbon:** *Sketch* tab>expanded Create panel
	Ray Tracing	• **Ribbon:** *View* tab>Appearance panel
	Reflections	• **Ribbon:** *View* tab>Appearance panel
	Shadows	• **Ribbon:** *View* tab>Appearance panel
N/A	Share Sketch	• **Context Menu:** in Model browser with sketch name selected
	Show All Degrees of Freedom	• **Sketch Status Bar**
	Show Constraints	• **Ribbon:** *Sketch* tab>Constrain panel
	Styles Editor (lighting)	• **Ribbon:** *Manage* tab>Styles and Standards panel
	Visual Style	• **Ribbon:** *View* tab>Appearance panel

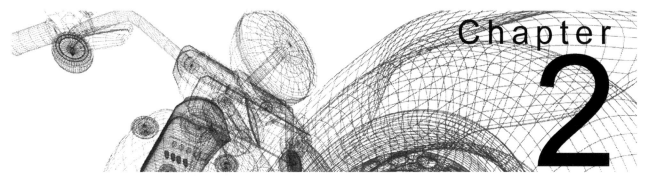

Chapter 2

Sketching Tools

The fundamental level sketch entities that can be created in a 2D sketch include lines, arcs, rectangles, etc. The Spline options provide additional flexibility to create smooth curved entities for creating geometry. Splines and entities such as lines and arcs can also be created in a 3D sketch. 3D sketches enable you to create entities that exist in 3D space without a sketch plane. Along with splines, lines, and arcs, there are a number of additional 3D sketch tools that can be used to create a sketch to generate complex geometry.

Learning Objectives in this Chapter

- Create a spline entity by placing vertices to define its control frame.
- Create a spline entity by placing points that define the exact spline shape.
- Create a 3D sketch that consists of linear, helical, arc, and bend entities.
- Create a 3D sketch by entering an equation that defines the x, y, and z coordinates over a specified range.
- Create 3D curves that are based on intersections of planes or the projection of geometry onto non-planar surfaces.
- Create a 3D curve that is sketched on a curved face.

2.1 Splines

You can draw curves using Arc and Ellipse entities, but those curves can be too rigid. To create a free-form curve consider using a Spline. There are two types of splines that can be sketched: **Control Vertex** and **Interpolation**.

- For a Control Vertex Spline, the points that are placed to create the spline define the vertices of the control frame. The control frame defines the shape of the spline, as shown in Figure 2–1.

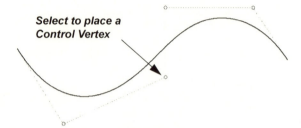

Figure 2–1

- For an Interpolation Spline, the spline is fit through the selected points, as shown in Figure 2–2.

Figure 2–2

You can use splines in models for many purposes, such as a base for creating surfaces, parting lines for splitting molds and drafts, or a sweep path, as shown in Figure 2–3.

Figure 2–3

Multiple splines can be sketched and constrained to one another using the (Smooth (G2)) constraint to produce a smooth transition between entities. This constraint can also be used to constrain a spline to other sketched entities.

Sketching Tools

How To: Create a Spline

1. Select the type of spline that is required.

   - In the *Sketch* tab>Create panel, click (Spline Interpolation).
   - In the *Sketch* tab>Create panel, click (Spline Control Vertex).
   - If creating a spline in 3D sketch, the commands are located in the *3D Sketch* tab>Draw panel, in their own drop-down list.

2. Sketch the free-form spline by placing points or by selecting existing work points, end points, or midpoints.
   - An Interpolation spline is sketched by selecting points that will lie on the exact path of the spline.
   - A Control Vertex spline is sketched by selecting points that define the control frame.

The Spline options for a 2D Sketch are located with the line entities on the Create panel.

You cannot add fillets or chamfers to a spline and you cannot select the midpoint of a spline.

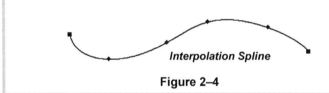

Hint: Identifying Spline Points

To help identify splines, the end points of a Interpolation Spline display as a square shape, while the fit points along the curve display as a diamond, as shown in Figure 2–4.

Interpolation Spline

Figure 2–4

3. Add dimensions and constraints to the spline's points and control vertices, similar to that shown in Figure 2–5. Interpolation Splines can be dimensioned in a similar way between points.

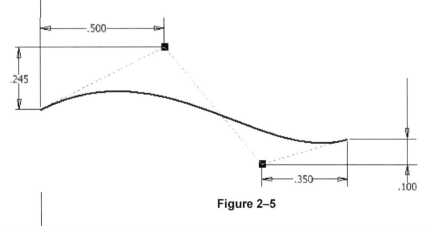

Figure 2–5

Editing a Spline

4. Right-click and select **Create** or click ![check] in the mini-toolbar. You can also select **Cancel [Esc]** to cancel sketching and deactivate the command, or select **Restart** to restart the spline.

Once the spline is complete, you can select the spline to edit it as follows:

- Select and drag the shape points (control vertices or interpolation points) to new locations. For Interpolation Splines, if you press and hold <Alt> while dragging, other unconstrained points also move.

- For Interpolation Splines, select and drag the tangent handles displayed at all shape points, as shown in Figure 2–6, to manipulate the shape of the spline. The handle must be activated to modify. To activate a handle, select the shape point, right-click and select **Activate Handle**.

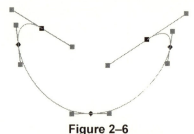

Figure 2–6

You can also edit the spline attributes using options in the shortcut menu. The spline editing options include the following:

- Select **Insert Point** or **Insert Vertex** in the shortcut menu to add additional internal shape points for interpolation or control vertex splines, respectively.

- Click **Display Curvature** in the marking menu to display a curvature comb that indicates the curvature along the spline, as shown in Figure 2–7. The length of each comb line is inversely proportional to the radius of the curve at that point. If the curvature comb does not display, right-click and select **Setup Curvature Display** to modify the comb's density and scale.

The options available in the shortcut menu depend on whether the spline was created as a control vertex or an interpolation spline. Additionally, where you right-click on the spline can affect which options are displayed.

Sketching Tools

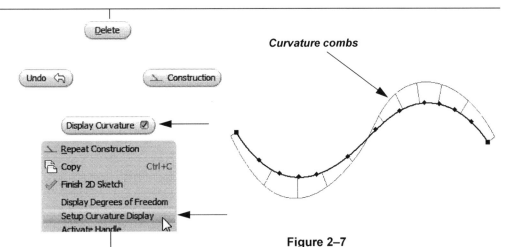

Figure 2–7

The options in the shortcut menu vary depending on whether the spline, point, or handles are selected.

- Select **Activate Handle**, **Curvature**, or **Flat** in the shortcut menu to control the shape of the spline at the shape points. The shape point nearest to where you right-clicked is affected. The spline shown in Figure 2–8 has **Activate Handle** applied to it. This option displays a line tangent to the spline (called a handlebar) on the shape point; adjust the direction of the handlebar by dragging either end. The handlebar rotates about the shape point.

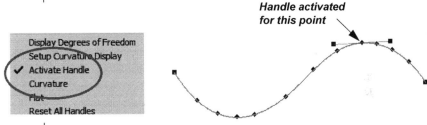

Figure 2–8

- The **Curvature** option provides an arc (called a curvature bar) on the shape point in addition to the tangent line, as shown in Figure 2–9. Drag either end of the curvature bar to change the curvature. The **Flat** option removes the curvature at the selected point.

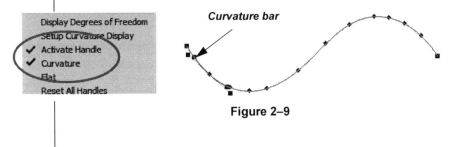

Figure 2–9

- Select **Spline Tension** in the shortcut menu to adjust how straight the spline is between shape points for an interpolation spline. Higher tensions force the spline to become straighter (and the curvature at the shape points becomes tighter). Figure 2–10 shows a spline with zero tension on the left side and maximum (100%) tension on the right side. A start point, end point, and one shape point were used to create the spline.

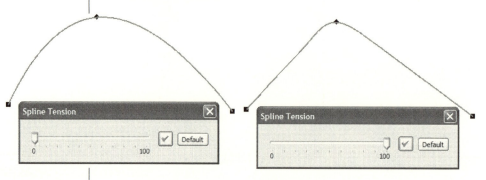

Figure 2–10

*If the spline tension is modified, the spline is automatically converted to the **Minimum Energy** Fit Method.*

- Select **Fit Method** in the shortcut menu to edit the spline transition between shape points in an interpolation spline. The three methods available enable you to create a spline that transitions smoothly between shape points (**Standard**), a spline that uses the AutoCAD fit method (**AutoCAD**), and a spline with smoother continuity and better curvature distribution (**Minimum Energy**). The Minimum Energy method increases the file size and requires longer calculation times.

- Select **Close Spline** in the shortcut menu for an interpolation spline to join the start and end points, as shown in Figure 2–11.

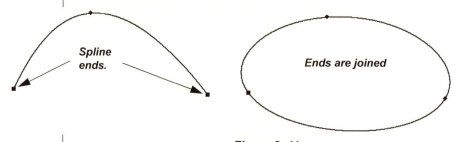

Figure 2–11

Sketching Tools

- Once spline handles have been reset for an interpolation spline, you can restore all or individual handles to their natural solve state using **Reset All Handles** or **Reset Handle**. The **Reset All Handles** option, as shown in Figure 2–12, is available on the shortcut menu when the spline is selected. The **Reset Handle** option is available on the shortcut menu when a handle is selected.

Resetting a single handle restores it to a natural solve state based on the position of the other handles, not necessarily to its original solve state.

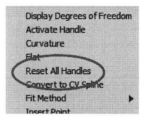

Figure 2–12

- The **Convert to CV Spline** option and **Convert to Interpolation** options enable you to switch a control vertex spline to a spline that was created using interpolation points, and vice versa. The spline shown in Figure 2–13 was originally an interpolation spline that was converted to a Control Vertex spline using **Concert to CV Spline**.

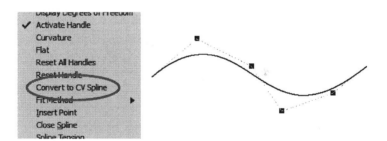

Figure 2–13

2.2 3D Sketches

3D sketches can be used as profiles, rails in a loft, a path to define a 3D sweep, complex surfaces, etc.

While 2D sketching is performed in a plane, 3D sketching takes place in 3D space without a sketch plane. 3D sketches must be drawn from existing points (e.g., work points) or points on existing objects. The 3D sketch is automatically constrained to the selected vertices as it is sketched, as shown in Figure 2–14.

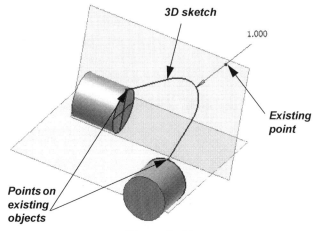

Figure 2–14

How To: Create a 3D sketch

1. In the *3D Model* tab>Sketch panel, click ![icon] (Start 3D Sketch). The command can be found on the expanded **Start 2D Sketch** command, as shown in Figure 2–15.

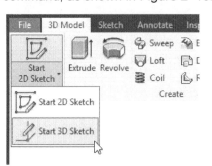

Figure 2–15

Sketching Tools

2. Use the tools on the *3D Sketch* tab (shown in Figure 2–16) to create 3D entities.

Figure 2–16

3. Modify the entities, as required, using tools on the Modify panel.
4. Using the Constrain panel, add dimensions and constraints to locate the 3D sketched entities, as required.
5. Once you finish sketching, in the Exit panel, click ✓ (Finish Sketch) or select **Finish 3D Sketch** in the context menu.
6. To edit a 3D sketch, right-click on its name in the Model browser and select **Edit 3D Sketch** or double-click on the 3D Sketch in the Model browser.

3D Sketch Tools

The following options in the Draw panel enable you to create entities in a 3D sketch.

Line

To sketch lines, click ／ (Line) in the Draw panel or right-click and select **Create 3D Line**. Select points to define the line. You can also reference existing work points, sketch points, vertices, and end points. Since 3D sketches are often used to define sweeps for tubing and cabling, the sketch may need to be curved. Auto-Bend places a radius at all corners, as shown in Figure 2–17. To toggle Auto-Bend on or off, right-click and select **Auto-Bend** when creating the Line.

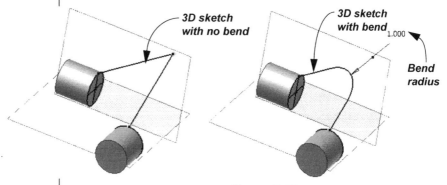

Figure 2–17

- To change the default setting for the Auto-Bend radius for the current file, click ▢ (Document Settings) (*Tools* tab> Options panel), select the *Sketch* tab and change the value in the *Auto-Bend Radius* field. If the radius value is too large for the sketch, the bend is not applied.

> **Hint: Improving Sketch Accuracy**
>
> Consider using the ▢ (Ortho Mode) and ▢ (Snap Object) options in the Status bar at the bottom of the graphics window to better control how the entities are sketched. With **Ortho Mode** enabled, you can restrict sketching to the X, Y, and Z planes. With **Snap Object** enabled, you can snap to existing entities when sketching new entities.

Helical Curve

Click ▢ (Helical Curve) in the Draw panel or right-click and select **Helical Curve** to create a helical/spiral curve. The types can include a Constant Helical Curve (▢) or Variable Helical Curve (▢). For each type, you can define how the curve is created using the options in the *Definition* area. The creation types include the following:

- **Pitch and Revolution**
- **Revolution and Height**
- **Pitch and Height**
- **Spiral** (only available for Constant Helical Curves)

The values that are available to define a constant helical curves depend on the creation type that was selected. Once the sizes are entered, select the required point(s) directly on the model to define the curve. You can also set the revolution direction by clicking the ▢ and ▢ (Rotation) icons in the dialog box.

Figure 2–18 shows a Constant Helical Curve and the options used to create it.

Sketching Tools

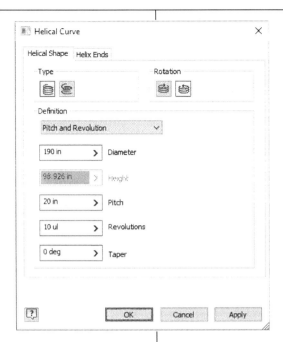
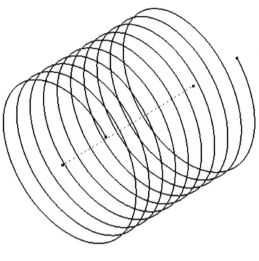

Figure 2–18

In the Helical Curve dialog box, the dimensions for variable helical curves are entered in a table format to define the varying sizes curves across its entire length, as shown in Figure 2–19.

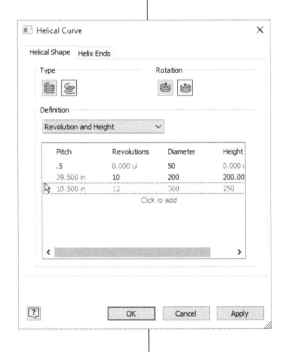
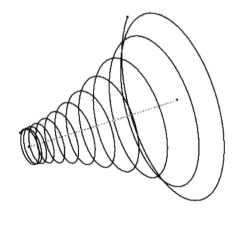

Figure 2–19

Arc

Click ◯ (Arc Three Point) or ◯ (Arc Center Point) to create an arc as you would in a 2D sketch. The Three Point arc can also be started by right-clicking and then selecting **Three Point Arc**.

Spline

Click ◯ (Spline Interpolation) or ◯ (Spline Control Vertex) to create a spline as you would in a 2D sketch.

> **Hint: Entering Precise Values**
>
> Consider using **Precise Input** in the expanded Draw panel to precisely define the X, Y, and Z location of the entities that are placed in the 3D sketch. This can be used for lines, helical curves, arcs, splines, and points. The Precise Input mini-toolbar enables you to enter values. To close the mini-toolbar once active, expand ▤▾ and click **Close**. The interface used for Precise Input varies slightly from that used for 2D sketch creation. In 3D, the interface uses a mini-toolbar.

> **Hint: Aligning and Reorienting the Sketch Triad**
>
> As you are sketching you can right-click and access commands that enable you to align and reorient the model to accurately sketch the entities. The shortcut menu options enable you to do the following:
>
> - **Align to Plane:** Aligns the sketch triad to a plane.
>
> - **Orient Z** and **Orient to World:** Reorients the sketching triad to a custom Z direction or to the world coordinate system. To define a custom Z direction, you can select an edge, line, axis, plane, vertex or point.
>
> - **Snap Intersection:** Snaps an entity to the intersection of entities. This is only available when **Ortho Mode** is enabled.

Sketching Tools

Equation Curve

An Equation curve enables you to create complex entities by entering an equation that defines the entities path in the X, Y, and Z axes. To create an equation curve, in the Draw panel, click (Equation Curve). A mini-toolbar opens, as shown in Figure 2–20, providing you with the fields that you can use to define the curve and the range of values to evaluate.

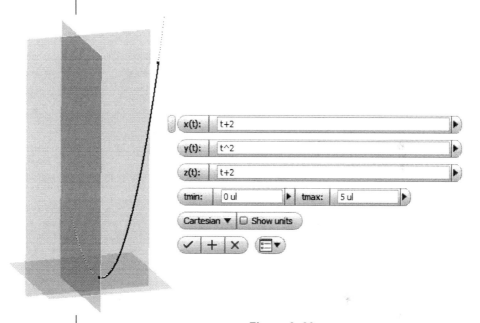

Figure 2–20

Point

Click (Point) to create sketch points or center points for use in creating your 3D sketch.

Bend

If you place lines without bends and later decide to add them, click (Bend) in the Draw panel or right-click and select **Bend**. Enter a radius in the Bend dialog box and select the two lines for the bend to join. The lines to which the bend is applied must meet at a corner.

Intersection Curve

You can create a 3D sketch curve from the intersection of two surfaces, splines, lines, work planes, or parts. The sketch automatically updates if you change either of the two objects.

Click (Intersection Curve), select the two objects to define the 3D sketch, and click **OK** to create the 3D sketch. If you are using one work plane and another object, select the work plane first. A 3D sketch created by intersecting an extruded surface and the XY Plane is shown in Figure 2–21.

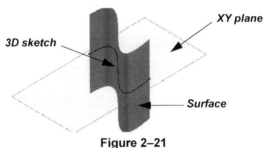

Figure 2–21

Project Curve to Surface

Click (Project to Surface) to create a sketch that is projected onto a face (2D or 3D) from a selected curve(s), as shown in Figure 2–22. The projection output can be along a selected vector, to a closest point, or wrapped to a surface that is flat, cylindrical, or conical.

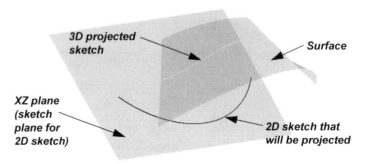

Figure 2–22

Sketching Tools

Silhouette Curve

A silhouette curve represents the contour of the model relative to a specific pull direction. The curve can include both the inner and outer design model boundaries, as shown in Figure 2–23. The curve can be best explained by imagining a light shining on the model. The curve is placed wherever there is a silhouette.

Silhouette curves are commonly used for generating parting lines for plastic part design, or for use in multi-body part design.

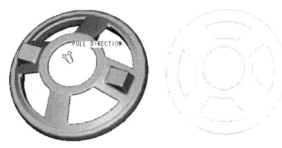

Figure 2–23

Click (Silhouette Curve) and select the *Body* to use as the geometry to create the silhouette curve. In the *Exclusion* area, select whether faces, straight faces, or internal faces are to be excluded from the curve. The curve will be placed on the selected body. Define the *Direction* from which to derive the silhouette curve. The direction can be defined by a plane, face, edge, or axis.

The models shown in Figure 2–24 show two examples of silhouette curves created on similar models. In the left model, the silhouette curve feature creates two curves because the straight faces were excluded, and in the right model, it creates a single curve around the entire model because nothing was excluded.

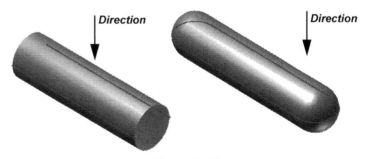

Figure 2–24

Curve on Face

A curve can be sketched directly on a face using the **Curve on Face** command. This enables you to easily locate the sketch directly on a non-planar face without having to project entities. To sketch a curve on a face, click (Curve on Face) in the Draw panel. You can select vertices, edges, or miscellaneous points to define the curve. The curve is placed on the face that is highlighted in red and is generated as a 3D interpolation spline, similar to that shown in Figure 2–25. Once sketched, you have access to the shortcut menu to close the sketch or add additional points. You can also use constraints and dimensions to fully define the curve.

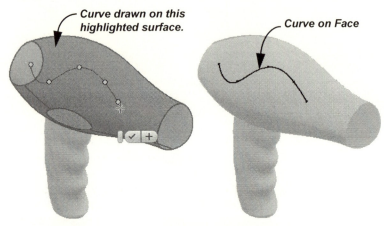

Figure 2–25

Include Geometry

To include edges from 3D objects and 2D sketches in the 3D sketch, click (Include Geometry) and select the geometry to include. Alternatively, you can select **Include Geometry** in the shortcut menu to initiate the command. If you change an object that was used with the option, the sketch also updates to reflect this change.

Sketching Tools

Mirror

Use the ▯▮ (Mirror) option in the Pattern panel to mirror 3D sketch entities. Like mirroring in a 2D sketch, the mirror plane can be a planar face, an origin plane, or a work plane.

Points

Use the 🗒 (Points) option in the Insert panel to insert points from a selected Microsoft Excel file. The requirements for the spreadsheet are:

- Coordinates are on the first sheet.
- Cell A1 lists the unit of measure (a blank cell assumes the default units).
- Row 2 shows column headers (e.g., X, Y, Z).
- Row 3 and thereafter show the coordinates.
- Points reference the sketch origin.

> **Hint: Work Features**
>
> Use the work feature options to create work planes, axis, and points in the 3D Sketch. The Work Feature panel is not displayed by default, you must add it to the panel to use it.

Modifying 3D Sketch Entities

To activate a 3D sketch for editing, double-click on its name in the Model browser, or select it and click ⬇ (Edit 3D Sketch).

You can edit using any of the following:

- Select and drag vertices, center points, or any section on a 3D entity to reposition it without entering exact coordinates.
- Double-click on the dimensions to change their value.
- Right-click and select **Construction** to convert a sketched entity into a construction entity.
- Select **Delete** in the shortcut menu to delete an object in the 3D sketch. If you delete an object that was added with the **Include Geometry** option, the source object is not affected.
- Use **Extend**, **Trim**, and **Split** in the Modify panel to refine the sketch's shape. These options are also available when sketching.

- Use **3D Transform** in the Modify panel to reposition geometry in a 3D sketch. Once activated, you are provided with the transform triad and mini-toolbar. Select a manipulator handle on the triad to reposition the selected entity linearly, rotationally, or on a plane. The mini-toolbar updates as required and enables you to enter values to define the move. The mini-toolbar can also be used to control the orientation of the triad to the world, view, or local coordinate systems. In Figure 2–26, a spline entity is being moved along the X axis of the world coordinate system.

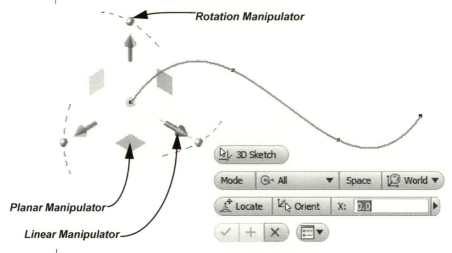

Figure 2–26

Use standard copy and paste functionality to create copies of existing sketched entities in the same sketch or in different sketches. This enables you to efficiently duplicate entities in a 3D sketch. Use the 3D Transform tool to move the pasted entities, as required. If pasted in the same sketch the new entities are pasted over the source entities and must be moved.

Dimensioning & Constraining

The dimensions must reference geometry and work points.

Using the Constrain panel, add dimensions and constraints to locate the sketched entities. The available constraint options are shown in Figure 2–27.

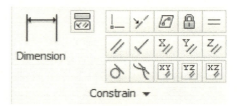

Figure 2–27

Sketching Tools

*Assigned constraints can be deleted by right-clicking on the constraint symbol in the graphics window and selecting **Delete**.*

- The **Coincident**, **Parallel**, **Tangent**, **Collinear**, **Perpendicular**, **Smooth (G2)**, **Fixed**, and **Equal** constraints can be used in the same way as in a 2D sketch.

- The ⬚ (On Face) constraint enables you to constrain points, lines, arc, or spline to a planar face. Optionally, you can constrain individual points to a curved face.

- The ⬚, ⬚, and ⬚ constraint types can be used to constrain a line, curve, or spline handle to lie parallel with the X, Y, or Z axis, respectively.

- The ⬚, ⬚, and ⬚ constraint types can be used to constrain a line, curve, or spline to lie parallel with the XY, YZ, or XZ planes, respectively.

When dimensioning and constraining, you can also consider setting the **Dynamic Dimension** and **Infer Constraints** options in the Status Bar to aid in the sketching process.

- ⬚ (Dynamic Dimension): Enables you to toggle whether the dynamic dimension field appears as you are sketching. This field enables you to enter exact values. When disabled, you can only select points to place the entities.

- ⬚ (Infer Constraints): Enables you to control whether constraints are inferred by the Autodesk Inventor software as you are sketching or not.

- ⬚ (Show/Hide Constraints): Enables you to toggle the display of constraint symbols on and off in the sketch.

> **Hint: 3D Sketch Properties**
>
> The Geometry Properties dialog box, shown in Figure 2–28, controls 3D sketch properties. To open the dialog box, select the entity, right-click and select **Properties**. 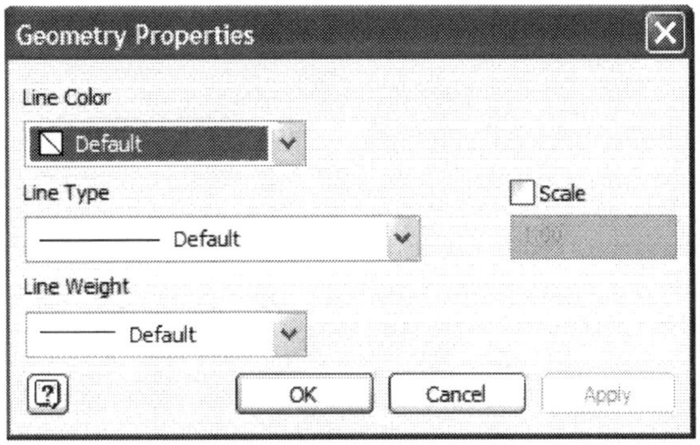
>
> **Figure 2–28**

Practice 2a

Create a Swept Cut using a 3D Sketch

Practice Objectives

- Create a 3D sketch by placing points in the model and using those points to define the location of a 3D spline.
- Create a swept cut that references a sketched profile and a 3D sketched path.

In this practice, you create a swept cut through the model shown on the left of Figure 2–29. You use 3D sketch options to create the path for the sweep. You are provided with work planes and the order in which to create work points that are used to define the 3D sketch. Many of the menu selections are left out so that you can practice feature creation. The final model is shown on the right of Figure 2–29. The model guides a follower while rotating about the X Axis.

X Axis

Figure 2–29

Task 1 - Create work points.

In this task, you create four work points as the basis for the swept cut's 3D path.

1. Open **barrel_cam.ipt**. The work planes that have been provided will be used as references for the work points that you will create.

2. Create four work points. The planes that will be referenced to create the work points are shown in Figure 2–30.

    - Intersection of the planes 2, 6, and the XY plane.
    - Intersection of the planes 1, 3, and the XZ plane.
    - Intersection of the planes 2, 5, and the XY plane.
    - Intersection of the planes 1, 4, and the XZ plane.

*Sometimes changing the selection priority to **Feature Priority** and zooming into the model can help to select planes in a model.*

It is recommended that you select each plane directly in the Model browser to ensure that you are selecting the correct planes. If a work point does not get created after selecting three planes, then one of the planes selected might be incorrect. Most commonly it is due to selecting a plane that does not intersect with the other two.

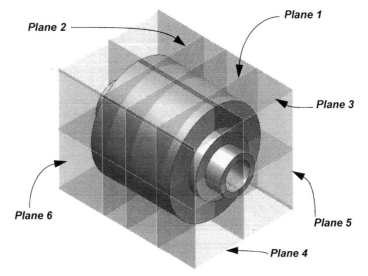

Figure 2–30

3. In the *View* tab>Visibility panel, expand **Object Visibility** and clear the **User Work Planes** and **Origin Planes** options to toggle off the visibility of all work planes and Origin planes.

4. Display the model in Wireframe (*View* tab>Appearance panel>**Visual Style**) and orient the model to the Right view. The model and work points display as shown in Figure 2–31. The model is displayed parallel to the YZ plane.

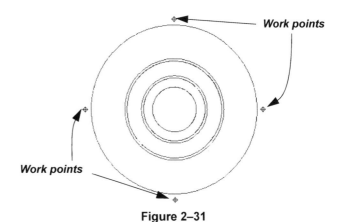

Figure 2–31

Task 2 - Create a 3D sketch.

In this task, you use the 3D sketch options to create the path for the swept cut.

1. Display the model in isometric Home view.

2. Start a 3D sketch by right-clicking and selecting **New 3D Sketch**, or on the ribbon, on the *3D Model* tab, select **Start 3D Sketch**.

3. In the Draw panel, click (Spline Interpolation) and select the existing work points in the order they were created. The model displays as shown in Figure 2–32. You must select the start point a second time to close the spline.

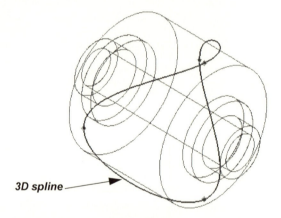

Figure 2–32

4. In the Exit panel, click (Finish Sketch).

Task 3 - Create a swept cut profile.

1. Set the three default origin planes as visible.

2. Select the XZ plane in the Model browser, right-click and select **New Sketch** to activate the 2D sketch environment.

3. Project the YZ and XY work planes onto the sketch plane. You use these projected planes to locate and dimension the profile.

4. Project the work point at the intersection of 1, 3, and the XZ plane (Work Point2) onto the sketch plane. The work point location is shown in Figure 2–33. You project the work point because the sweep path must intersect the sketch plane of the profile.

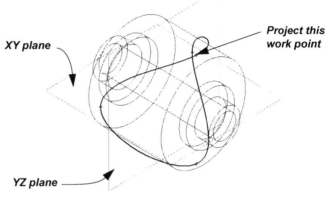

Figure 2–33

5. Sketch and dimension the profile, as shown in Figure 2–34. Constrain the sketch to the projected work point.

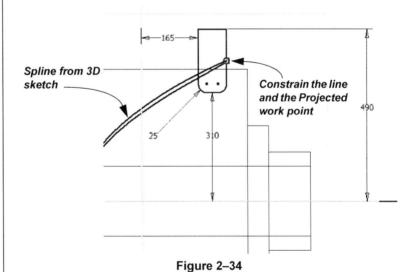

Figure 2–34

6. In the Exit panel, click ✓ (Finish Sketch).

Task 4 - Create a swept cut.

1. Create a swept cut using the path and profile that have just been created. Return the model to the Shaded view display. The model displays as shown in Figure 2–35.

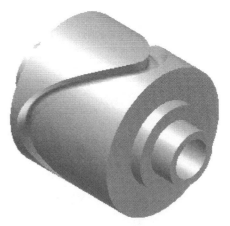

Figure 2–35

2. Add fillets of **10 mm** on the outside edges of the swept cut to remove sharp edges. Return the model to its shaded display. The model displays as shown in Figure 2–36.

Figure 2–36

3. Save and close the model.

Practice 2b

Imported Point Data

Practice Objectives

- Create a 2D and 3D sketch that reads points from a Microsoft Excel spreadsheet file.
- Set the options for imported points in a 3D sketch to import points only, import the points with connecting lines, or import points with a connecting spline.
- Create a swept extrusion that references a sketched profile and a 3D sketched path.

In this practice, you will import point data to create both 3D and 2D sketches. Using this data, you will then create the swept geometry shown in Figure 2–37.

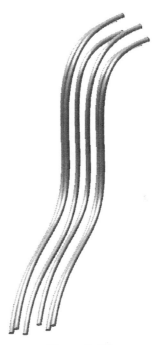

Figure 2–37

Task 1 - Create a 3D sketch.

The 3D sketch can be sketched using the tools in the Draw panel, or you can import point data. In this task, you will import point data using a few different methods.

1. Create a new part file with the standard English template, **Standard (in).ipt**.

2. In the *3D Model* tab>Sketch panel, click (Start 3D Sketch). The *3D Sketch* tab is now the active tab.

3. In the Insert Panel, click (Points).

4. Select **chute_path.xls** and click **Open**. The spreadsheet was created for this practice and contains the X, Y, and Z coordinates for six points, as shown in Figure 2–38. Figure 2–38 shows the points in the default Home view.

Figure 2–38

5. In the Model browser, expand **Origin** and place the cursor over the Center Point work feature. Note that the Center Point and one of the imported points are coincident. Imported points reference the sketch origin (Center Point).

6. In the Draw panel, click (Line).

7. Right-click in the graphics window and verify that **Auto Blend** is disabled in the shortcut menu.

8. Reorient the model so that it is in the Home view, if not already. Starting from the top most point (sketch origin), select each point to draw lines between each of them, as shown in Figure 2–39. Right-click and select **OK**.

Figure 2–39

The line joining the points is not smooth. To smooth out the line, you can delete linear entities, add arcs, and assign tangency; however, doing so will change the point locations. Depending on your design intent, this might be acceptable, but for this design the points must remain as originally assigned.

9. Select all points and entities, and then delete them from the sketch.

10. In the *Tools* tab>Options panel, click (Application Options). In the Application Options dialog box, select the *Sketch* tab and enable **Auto-bend with 3D line creation** at the bottom of the window. Close the dialog box.

11. Select the *3D Sketch* tab.

12. In the Insert Panel, click ▦ (Points).

13. Select **chute_path.xls** and click **Options**.

14. Select **Create lines** and click **OK** in the File Open Options dialog box. This dialog box enables you to control how the points are brought into the sketch. The default option only brings in the points from the file.

15. Click **Open** to bring the points into the sketch. Note that the points have been added and lines have been drawn for you. In addition, because **Auto Blend** was enabled, the curve is smoother. The data displays as shown in Figure 2–40.

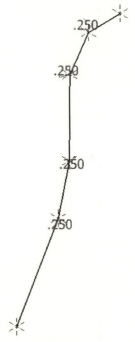

Figure 2–40

16. Select all points and entities, and then delete them from the sketch.

17. In the Insert Panel, click ▦ (Points).

18. Select **chute_path.xls** and click **Options**.

Sketching Tools

19. Select **Create spline** and click **OK** in the File Open Options dialog box.

20. Click **Open** to bring the points into the sketch as a spline. The data displays as shown in Figure 2–41.

Figure 2–41

21. In the Exit panel, click (Finish Sketch).

Depending on the design intent of your model, you can consider using any one of the three methods for importing point data and using it in the 3D sketch. For the remainder of this practice, you will use the data that was brought into the 3D sketch as a spline.

Task 2 - Create a 2D sketch.

1. In the *3D Model* tab>Sketch panel, click (Start 2D Sketch). Select the XY plane as the sketch plane. The *Sketch* tab is now the active tab.

2. In the Insert Panel, click (Points).

3. Select **chute_profile.xls**. Before importing the data, verify in the File Open Options dialog box that it will be brought in as points. Open the file.

4. Click **Yes** in the dialog box that opens, as shown in Figure 2–42. This message notes that although X, Y, and Z coordinates are in the file, only the X and Y coordinates will be used to import the data.

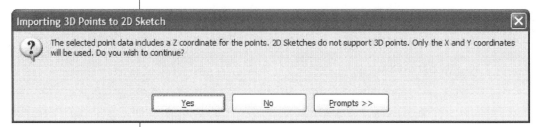

Figure 2–42

5. Reorient the model to the Front view and zoom in, as shown in Figure 2–43. Six new points have been imported.

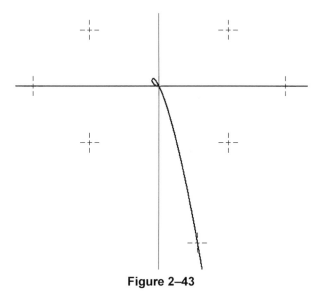

Figure 2–43

6. Sketch circular entities on all six points. Create a **.375** diameter dimension on one of the entities. Use the equal and fix constraints to locate the points where they have been imported. This ensures that all circular entities have the same diameter. The final sketch is shown in Figure 2–44.

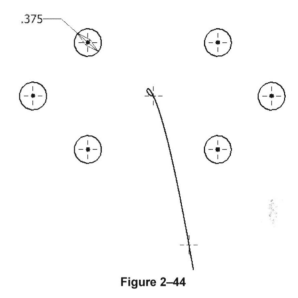

Figure 2–44

7. In the Exit panel, click (Finish Sketch).

Task 3 - Create swept geometry using the 2D and 3D sketches.

1. In the *3D Model* tab>Create panel, click (Sweep).

2. Select the interior of one of the circular entities as a Profile for the sweep.

3. Disable the **Optimize for Single Selection** option, if enabled. This enables you to select multiple references. Select the remaining circular entities (six total). If the **Optimize for Single Selection** option is enabled, you must manually enable the *Profile* reference selector to select each of the six profiles.

4. Once all six circular entities are selected as profiles, activate the (Path) reference selector.

5. Select the 3D spline curve (imported in an earlier task) as the Path reference.

6. Complete the feature. The model displays as shown in Figure 2–45.

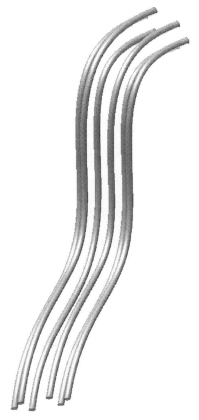

Figure 2–45

7. Save the model and close the window.

Chapter Review Questions

1. Which of the following correctly describes the difference between a 3D sketch and a 2D sketch? (Select all that apply.)
   a. In a 3D sketch there is no sketch plane.
   b. In a 3D sketch you use the **Fillet** command to add a bend between two linear entities.
   c. In a 3D sketch you have access to all of the same sketching constraints as those available in a 2D sketch.
   d. In a 3D sketch you can import points as can be done in a 2D sketch.

2. Which of the following describes how the **Include Geometry** option can be used in a 3D sketch?
   a. It enables you to copy sketched entities in a 3D sketch.
   b. It provides access to geometry creation options for creating 3D geometry using the 3D sketched entities.
   c. It enables you to reference existing entities in a model in a 3D sketch.
   d. It enables you to constrain entities in a 3D sketch.

3. Which 3D sketch tool can be used to create a curved entity that is defined by entering a formula for the x, y, and z axes?
   a. **Interpolation Spline**
   b. **Control Vertex Spline**
   c. **Equation Curve**
   d. **Bend**

4. You can create a 3D sketch curve from the intersection of two surfaces, work planes, or parts.
   a. True
   b. False

5. What are the three ways that imported point data can be brought into a 3D sketch?
   a. Points only
   b. Points with arcs connecting the points
   c. Points with lines connecting the points
   d. Points with a spline connecting the points

6. Which 3D sketch tool was used to create the entity shown in Figure 2–46?

Figure 2–46

   a. **Equation Curve**
   b. **Helical Curve**
   c. **Arc**
   d. **Control Vertex Spline**
   e. **Interpolation Spline**

7. Only the endpoints of a spline can be dimensioned in a sketch.

   a. True
   b. False

8. If a handlebar displays on a spline point, which type of spline was created?

   a. **Control Vertex Spline**
   b. **Interpolation Spline**

Command Summary

Button	Command	Location
N/A	3D Move/Rotate (3D Sketch)	• **Context menu:** In the graphics window
	Arc Center Point (3D Sketch)	• **Ribbon:** *3D Sketch* tab>Draw panel
	Arc Three Point (3D Sketch)	• **Ribbon:** *3D Sketch* tab>Draw panel • **Context menu:** In the graphics window
	Bend (3D Sketch)	• **Ribbon:** *3D Sketch* tab>Draw panel • **Context menu:** In the graphics window
	Create 3D Sketch	• **Ribbon:** *3D Model* tab>Sketch panel
N/A	Delete (3D Sketch entity)	• **Context menu:** In the graphics window
N/A	Edit 3D Sketch (3D Sketch)	• **Context menu:** In Model browser • **Context menu:** In the graphics window
	Equation Curve (3D Sketch)	• **Ribbon:** *3D Sketch* tab>Draw panel
	Helical Curve (3D Sketch)	• **Ribbon:** *3D Sketch* tab>Draw panel • **Context menu:** In the graphics window
	Include Geometry (3D Sketch)	• **Ribbon:** *3D Sketch* tab>Draw panel • **Context menu:** In the graphics window
	Intersection Curve (3D Sketch)	• **Ribbon:** *3D Sketch* tab>Draw panel
	Line (3D Sketch)	• **Ribbon:** *3D Sketch* tab>Draw panel • **Context menu:** In the graphics window
	Mirror (3D Sketch)	• **Ribbon:** *3D Sketch* tab>Pattern panel
	Point (3D Sketch)	• **Ribbon:** *3D Sketch* tab>Draw panel
	Points (3D Sketch)	• **Ribbon:** *3D Sketch* tab>Insert panel
	Project to Surface (3D Sketch)	• **Ribbon:** *3D Sketch* tab>Draw panel
N/A	Properties (3D Sketch)	• **Ribbon:** *3D Sketch* tab>Format panel • **Context menu:** In the graphics window

	Silhouette Curve (3D Sketch)	• **Ribbon:** *3D Sketch* tab>Draw panel
	Spline Control Vertex	• **Ribbon:** *Sketch* tab>Create panel • **Ribbon:** *3D Sketch* tab>Draw panel
	Spline Interpolation	• **Ribbon:** *Sketch* tab>Create panel • **Ribbon:** *3D Sketch* tab>Draw panel

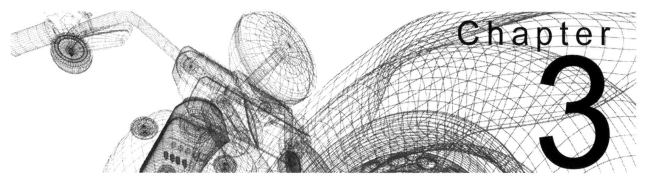

Chapter 3

Multi-Body Part Modeling

Top-down design is an engineering CAD methodology used in the Autodesk® Inventor® software where you create single part files in the context of an assembly model. Using the multi-body part modeling technique, the top-down design approach has been made even easier. Multi-body modeling is also used for the creation of complex plastic or cast parts that require very intricate geometry.

Learning Objectives in this Chapter

- Create multiple solid bodies in a single part model to ease feature creation.
- Add features to existing solid bodies instead of creating a new solid body for each feature.
- Manipulate existing solid bodies to add or remove features, move the position of bodies, split bodies, or combine multiple bodies into one body.
- Control the visibility, display settings, and properties of individual solid bodies in a model.

3.1 Multi-Body Part Modeling

Multi-body part files enable you to create your entire assembly design in the Part environment using part modeling feature commands. This technique is commonly used when creating complex plastic or cast parts that require very intricate geometry. The design is arranged into separate bodies in the single part file. Figure 3–1 shows a model that has two solid bodies (listed in the **Solid Bodies** node). **Solid2** is selected and highlighted on the model. These separate bodies can then be extracted into individual parts for a new assembly.

Multi-body assembly modeling is introduced in this learning guide to explain the modeling procedure; however, the specifics on using this technique for top-down design is taught in the Autodesk Inventor Advanced Assembly Modeling course.

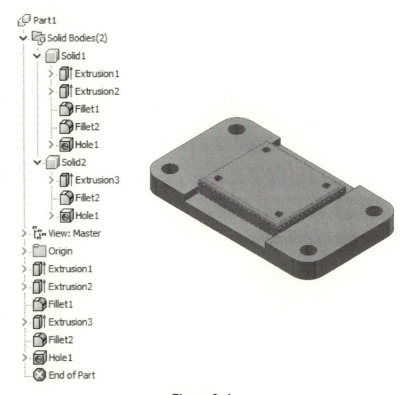

Figure 3–1

The advantages of building a part file using multi-bodies include the following:

- Top-down design is streamlined. You do not set up an initial complex file and directory structure to design in the context of a top-level assembly. The entire design resides in a single file, helping you design faster and accurately capture the model's design intent. Bodies are extracted to create parts.

*For models that have surfaces, a **Surface Bodies** node is also added as a separate entry.*

- A complex part file can be better organized using separate bodies with respect to their function or position in the model.

- Relationships between bodies can be easily set up and broken.

- You can control the visibility of bodies as a group rather than at the individual feature level.

- This method is useful for plastic part design, where interior components for a predefined shape can be designed in context and then extracted.

Creating the First Solid Body

With the creation of the first feature in any part file, the first solid body is automatically created. This is because the (New Solid) icon in the feature creation dialog box and the mini-toolbar is selected automatically and cannot be cleared, as shown in Figure 3–2. Once the base feature is created, the *Solid Bodies* folder displays in the Model browser and the first solid body is added to the folder.

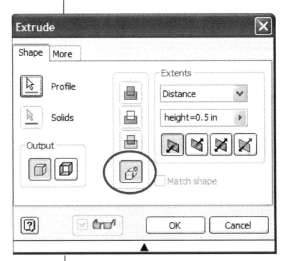
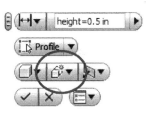

Figure 3–2

Each additional feature is automatically applied to the existing solid body, as long as the (New Solid) icon is not selected when additional features are created.

Creating Additional Solid Bodies

Once the first solid body is added to the model, each additional feature is automatically applied to it, unless a new feature is explicitly set to be created as a new solid body. To create the new solid body, create its feature as you normally would; however, click ▢ (New Solid) in the feature creation dialog box. Once selected, a second body is added to the model.

Assigning Features to Solid Bodies

Once two or more solid bodies are in a model, the selection of the placement/sketch planes are important to correctly locate the new feature in the required solid body. Consider the following:

- When creating a sketched feature, it is by default added to the same solid body as that of the sketching plane. For features to be added to a different solid body, click ▢ (Solids) in the feature dialog box and then select the required solid body.

- When creating a pick-and-place feature, it is by default added to the same solid body as the placement references. In the case of a fillet, for example, it is added to the same solid body as the parent feature of the placement edge. If multiple edges are selected that belong to multiple solid bodies, the feature is added to each solid body.

- When creating a sketch-based or pick-and-place feature, it is only extended through its parent solid body, even if the **Through All** depth option is selected. For features to interact with another solid body, click ▢ (Solids) in the feature dialog box and then select additional solid bodies to be included.

Manipulating Solid Bodies

The Autodesk Inventor Advanced Assembly Modeling course discusses further manipulation options that enable you to insert additional bodies from other models, or use them to create separate parts and assemblies.

Once multiple solid bodies exist in the model, you can further manipulate them. You can redefine them as part of another solid body, move them, split them, and combine them.

Redefining/Removing Features in Solid Bodies

Once a feature is created and assigned to a solid body, you can re-assign it to another solid body or remove a solid body from interacting with the feature. To do so, redefine the original feature and click ▢ (Solids) to activate it. You can select the new solid to apply it to or, if you want to remove a solid body from the initial selection set, hold <Ctrl> and select the solid body to remove.

Multi-Body Part Modeling

Moving Bodies

You might need to move the various bodies in a multi-body part.

How To: Move a Solid Body

*The **Move** command is only available when working with solid bodies.*

1. In the *3D Model* tab>expanded Modify panel, click (Move Bodies). The Move Bodies dialog box opens.
2. Select the solid bodies to move. If you need to select multiple bodies, you must click (Bodies) again after selecting the first body in order to select additional bodies.
3. Select a move operation using the drop-down list in the Move Bodies dialog box, as shown in Figure 3–3.

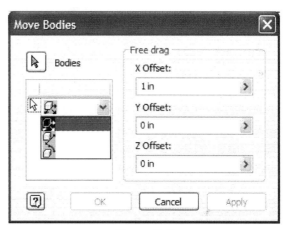

Figure 3–3

Each icon in the list enables you to move the body, as follows:

- (Free drag): Enables you to enter a precise X, Y, or Z offset value, or drag the preview in any direction.

- (Move along ray): Enables you to enter a precise offset value, or drag the preview offset from a selected reference.

- (Rotate about line): Enables you to enter a precise rotational angle value, or drag the preview around a selected axis.

4. Depending on the move operation selected, enter values and select references using the right side of the dialog box to define the movement.

5. To define a second move operation, if required, select **Click to add** and select a new move operation, as shown in Figure 3–4.

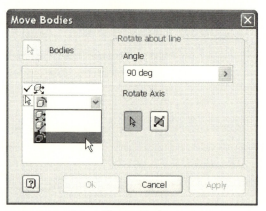

Figure 3–4

6. Continue to add move operations as required for the selected body.
7. Click **OK** to complete the feature. A Move Body feature is added to the bottom of the Model browser, as well as in each Solid Body that was moved.

*To edit the Move Body feature, right-click on it and select **Edit feature**.*

Splitting Bodies

You can split a single body so that you can manipulate the resulting bodies independently.

How To: Split a Solid Body

1. In the *3D Model* tab>Modify panel, click (Split).
2. Click (Split Solid) as the split method. The Split dialog box updates as shown in Figure 3–5.

*The **Split** command is available when working with solid bodies or Autodesk Inventor features.*

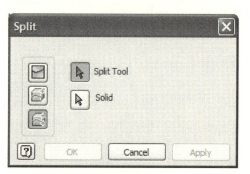

Figure 3–5

Multi-Body Part Modeling

3. Select a work plane or a sketch as the *Split Tool*. The split tool defines where the split occurs.
4. Select the *Solid* body to split. If a sketch was selected as the split tool, the solid body to which the sketch plane belongs is automatically selected as the solid to be split. You can reselect this reference, if required.
5. Click **OK** to complete the split.

Combining Bodies

If you created two solid bodies separately during an initial design, you may decide later that they should be combined. Using the **Combine** command, you can add or remove material based on selected bodies.

How To: Combine Features

*The **Combine** command is only available when working with solid bodies.*

1. In the *3D Model* tab>Modify panel, click (Combine). The Combine dialog box opens as shown in Figure 3–6.

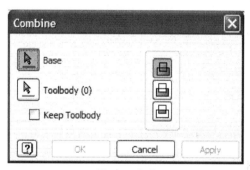

Figure 3–6

2. Select the solid body to use as the *Base* reference. The base body is the solid body on which the operation will be performed.

You can only select one base body, but you can select multiple toolbodies, if required.

3. Select the solid body to use as the *Toolbody* reference. The toolbody is the solid body or bodies that will perform the operation.
4. (Optional) To maintain the toolbody as a solid body after the operation, select **Keep Toolbody**. If you select this option, toolbody becomes invisible. This option is only available during the initial combine operation, not during the editing process.

5. Select an operation to perform on the base. The available operations include joining ▢, cutting ▢, and intersecting ▢ the toolbody from the base.
6. Click **OK** to complete the feature. The Combine feature is listed at the bottom of the Model browser and in the solid body used as the base reference.

Solid Body Display

Once multiple solid bodies exist in a model, you may want to individually control the visibility of various solid bodies. To control the visibility of a solid body, right-click on the solid body and enable or disable the **Visibility** option.

A representation of the model can be saved using a Design View. This enables you to capture the visibility settings of the Solid Bodies for reuse at a later time without having to enable and disable visibility.

How To: Save a Solid Body Display Configuration

1. Right-click on the *View* folder and select **New**. By default, the model exists as a Master view. When a new view is created it is automatically set to be active.
2. Configure the view display.
3. Select the new view, click again (do not double-click) and enter a descriptive name for the view.
4. To lock the design view, right-click on the view name in the Model browser and select **Lock**. Locking restricts you or others from making changes to the design view representation.

To display an alternate Design view, right-click on its name in the Model browser and select **Activate**. Alternatively, you can double-click on its name.

A Design view can also store other display options such as section view settings and colors.

Design views can be used when creating drawing views.

Solid Body Properties

To access the properties for a solid body, right-click on the solid body name and select **Properties**. The Body Properties dialog box opens as shown in Figure 3–7.

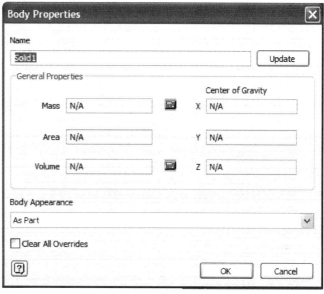

Figure 3–7

Using the Body Properties dialog box, you can do the following:

- Rename the solid body. You can also rename a solid body directly in the Model browser.

- Update and provide the general properties for the solid body.

- Set a color style for the solid body.

*The **Clear All Overrides** option removes color overrides from individual faces contained in the solid body.*

Practice 3a

Complex Part Design

Practice Objectives

- Create multiple solid bodies in a single part model to facilitate feature creation.
- Add features to existing solid bodies instead of creating a new solid body for each feature.
- Combine multiple solid toolbodies into the selected base body.

In this practice, you learn how using multi-body modeling to create a part can help you achieve complex results, without dealing with complex work arounds or lengthy Work Feature creation. The completed model is shown in Figure 3–8.

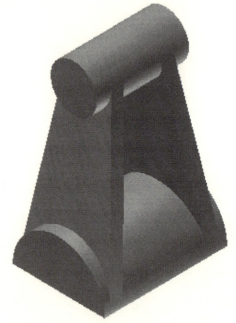

Figure 3–8

Task 1 - Create an extrusion.

1. Start a new part model using the **Standard (in).ipt** template.

2. Create the sketch shown in Figure 3–9 on the XY plane. Constrain the half circle to the origin of the part file.

Multi-Body Part Modeling

Consider renaming parameters throughout this practice to create a more dynamic and stable model that will be able to accommodate any required design changes.

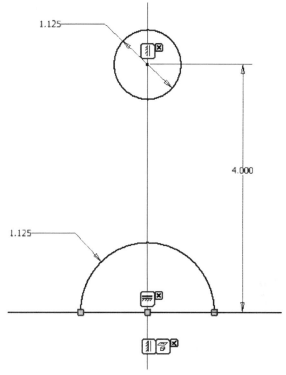

Figure 3–9

3. Extrude the half circle portion of **Sketch1** as the profile and extrude it **3 in** symmetrically, as shown in Figure 3–10. Note that (New Solid) is selected automatically as it is the first feature in the model and the first solid body must be created at the same time as the first feature.

 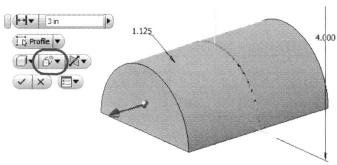

Figure 3–10

4. Review the Model browser. **Extrusion1** displays below the Origin, as it is a feature of the part. Expand the **Solid Bodies** node and note that currently, only one Solid Body is in the model, called **Solid1**. Expand **Solid1** and note that **Extrusion1** displays there as well, as shown in Figure 3–11.

Figure 3–11

Task 2 - Create a second solid body.

1. In the Model browser, right-click on **Sketch1** and select **Share Sketch**. Sketch1 is used to create the second solid body so it must be shared.

2. Extrude the circular portion of **Sketch1** as the profile and extrude the profile **2.25 in** symmetrically. Note that (New Solid) is not selected in either the dialog box or the mini-toolbar, because this is the second feature in the model and it defaults as being added as a feature in the first solid body.

3. In the Extrude dialog box or in the mini-toolbar, click (New Solid), as shown in Figure 3–12, to create the extrude feature as a separate solid body.

*As an alternative to using the **Share Sketch** command you can also turn on the visibility of a sketch to reuse it.*

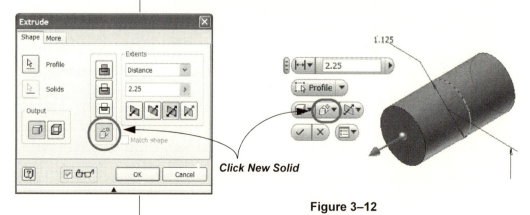

Figure 3–12

4. Complete the extrude.

5. For clarity, in the Model browser, right-click on **Sketch1** and clear the **Visibility** option.

6. Review the Model browser. **Extrusion2** has been added after **Extrusion1**. Expand the **Solid Bodies** node and note that two Solid Bodies are now in the model. **Extrusion1** is a feature of **Solid1**, and **Extrusion2** is in **Solid2**, as shown in Figure 3–13.

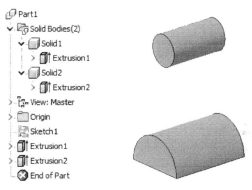

Figure 3–13

Task 3 - Create a third solid body.

1. Create a new sketch using the YZ origin plane as the sketching plane.

2. Project the XY origin plane, and the edges of **Solid1** and **Solid2**, as shown in Figure 3–14. Create and constrain the entities and complete the sketch.

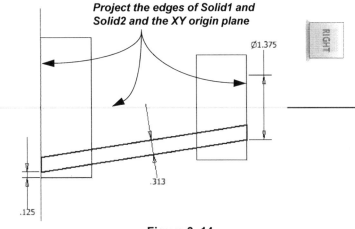

Figure 3–14

The exact depth of the extrusion is not important as long as it extends past the limits of the other solids.

3. Extrude the new sketch profile, **2.75in** symmetrically, as shown in Figure 3–15.

4. In the Extrude dialog box or in the mini-toolbar, click (New Solid), as shown in Figure 3–15, to create the extrude feature as a separate solid body.

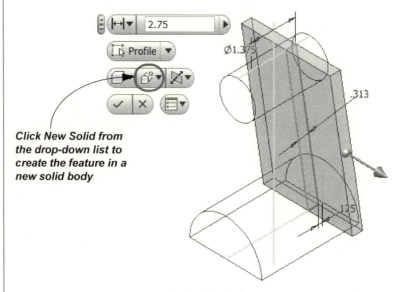

Figure 3–15

5. Complete the extrude.

Task 4 - Add a new feature to an existing solid body.

1. Create a new sketch using the XY origin plane as the sketching plane.

2. Project the edge of the circle and the half circle geometry.

3. Create the sketch as shown in Figure 3–16. Use tangent constraints between the four end points of the lines and the projected curves to fully constrain the entities without dimensions.

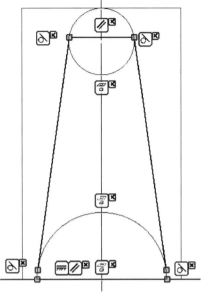

Figure 3–16

4. Extrude the new sketch profile.

5. In the mini-toolbar, in the drop-down list, select **Select Solid**. In the Model browser, select **Solid3** to include this extrusion as part of this solid body.

6. In the mini-toolbar, in the Extents drop-down list, select **Through All**.

7. In the mini-toolbar, in the drop-down list, select **Intersect**, as shown in Figure 3–17.

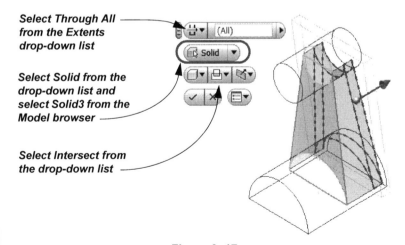

Figure 3–17

8. Complete the extrude. The model displays as shown in Figure 3–18.

Figure 3–18

Task 5 - Mirror a solid body.

1. In the Pattern panel, click ▶◀ (Mirror).

2. In the Mirror dialog box, click 🗐 (Mirror solids).

3. In the Model browser, select **Solid3** as the solid.

4. Click ▷ (Mirror Plane) and select the **XY Plane**.

5. Complete the mirror. The model displays as shown in Figure 3–19.

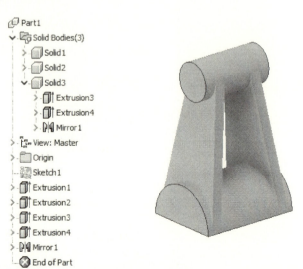

Figure 3–19

Task 6 - Combine the solid bodies.

The solid selected as the base will be the solid that remains.

1. In the Modify panel, click (Combine).

2. In the Model browser, select **Solid1** as the base.

3. In the Model browser, select **Solid2** and **Solid3** to add to the Toolbody. The Combine dialog box displays as shown in Figure 3–20.

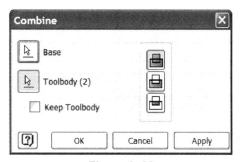

Figure 3–20

4. Click **OK** to complete the combine. The model displays as shown in Figure 3–21.

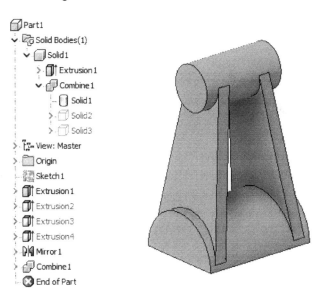

Figure 3–21

The combine tool has created a complex shape that will be easier to fillet and construct from origin planes than the alternative methods of complex plane creation and additional modeling references.

Task 7 - (Optional) Complete the model.

1. Complete the model by adding the additional features shown in Figure 3–22. No additional new solids need to be created.

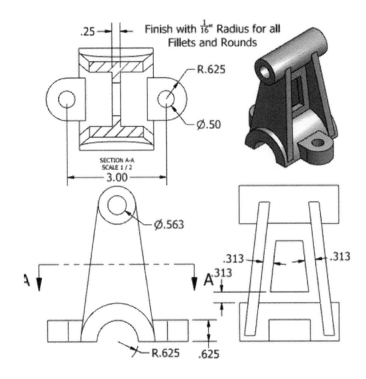

Figure 3–22

2. Save the file as **complex_part.ipt** and close the window.

Practice 3b

Multi-Body Part Design

Practice Objectives

- Create features as multiple solid bodies in a single part model to ease feature creation.
- Add features to existing solid bodies instead of creating a new solid body for each feature.

In this practice, you will create a single part file containing two solid bodies. In creating these solid bodies, you will use the commands that are available for multi-body design. You will learn to create multiple bodies in a model, add features to the bodies, and make changes to the bodies. The completed model is shown in Figure 3–23.

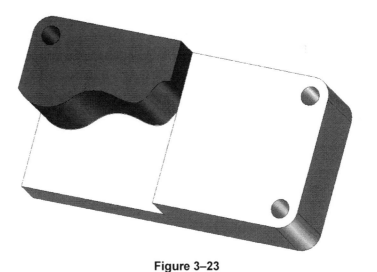

Figure 3–23

Task 1 - Create a new model.

1. Start a new part model using the **Standard (in).ipt** template.
2. Create a new sketch on the XY plane.
3. Project the YZ and XZ planes.

4. Sketch a rectangular entity centered on the projected origin planes, as shown in Figure 3–24.

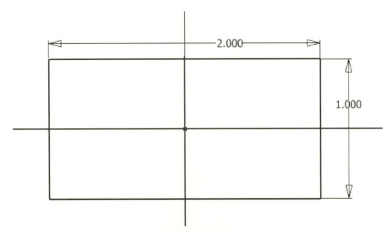

Figure 3–24

Assigning a parameter name to a dimension directly in the Edit Dimension dialog box prevents having to do so in the Parameters dialog box.

5. With the sketch still active, double-click on the 2.000 dimension and enter **width=2in**, as shown in Figure 3–25.

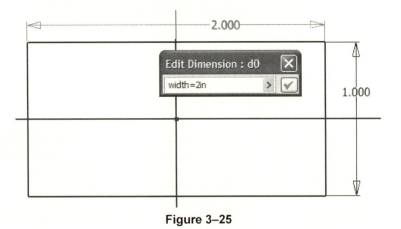

Figure 3–25

6. Double-click on the 1.000 dimension and enter **depth=1in**.

7. Finish the sketch.

Multi-Body Part Modeling

8. Extrude the rectangular sketch a distance of 0.5 inches by entering **height=0.5 in** as the extent value in either the Extrude dialog box or on the mini-toolbar. Note that ![icon] (New Solid) is selected automatically, because it is the first feature in the model and the first solid body must be created at the same time as the first feature. The Extrude dialog box and mini-toolbar should display as shown in Figure 3–26.

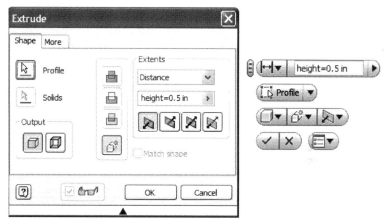

Figure 3–26

9. Complete the extrude.

10. Review the Model browser. **Extrusion1** displays below the Origin, as it is a feature of the part. Expand the **Solid Bodies** node and note that currently, only one Solid Body is in the model, called **Solid1**. Expand **Solid1** and **Extrusion1** displays there as well, as shown in Figure 3–27.

Figure 3–27

Task 2 - Create additional features in the model.

1. Create a new sketch on the surface shown in Figure 3–28.

2. Project the YZ plane.

3. Sketch the linear entity shown in Figure 3–28. Align it to the YZ work plane through the center of the model. Project any additional edges to create an enclosed section on the left-hand side of the sketch plane.

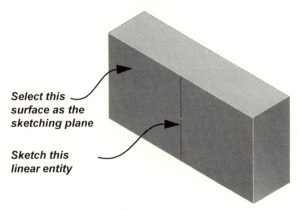

Figure 3–28

4. Finish the sketch.

5. Create an Extrude. In the Extrude dialog box or in the mini-toolbar, click ⬜ (Cut) and select the left section to remove.

6. Set the depth value to **cutdepth=height/2**. Note that ⬜ (New Solid) is not selected in either the dialog box or the mini-toolbar, because this is the second feature in the model and it defaults to being a feature in the first solid body.

7. Complete the extrude.

8. Add two **.125 in** fillets to the geometry shown in Figure 3–29.

9. Review the Model browser. **Extrusion2** and **Fillet1** have been added after **Extrusion1**. Expand the **Solid Bodies** node. Note that only one Solid Body, **Solid1**, is in the model, and that **Extrusion2** and **Fillet1** have been added there as well. **Extrusion1**, **Extrusion2**, and **Fillet1** are all features in **Solid1**. The model and the Model browser are shown in Figure 3–29.

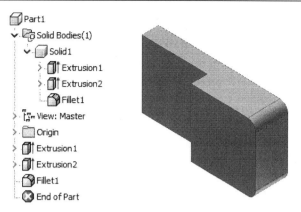

Figure 3–29

Task 3 - Review the modified parameter names.

1. In the *Manage* tab>Parameters panel, click f_x (Parameters). The Parameters dialog box opens as shown in Figure 3–30. The parameter names and equations that were entered during model creation are assigned in the dialog box.

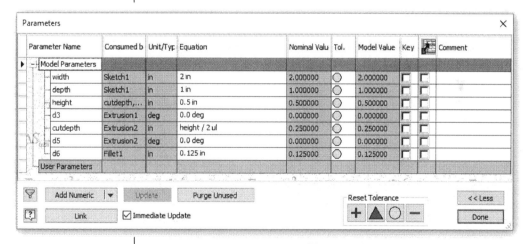

Figure 3–30

2. Close the Parameters dialog box.

Task 4 - Create a second solid body in the model.

1. Create a 2D sketch on the lower surface of the model that was just cut away.

2. Sketch a spline similar to that shown in Figure 3–31. Project the required edges to create a closed sketch above the spline. Ensure that the spline and projected edges are constrained as Coincident.

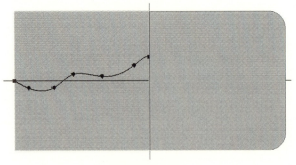

Figure 3–31

3. Once compete, click ✓. Once the spline is complete, points display on each spline point to enable you to edit the spline in the sketch.

4. Select the points and manipulate the shape of the spline. Do not worry about dimensioning the sketch.

5. Finish the sketch.

6. Create an Extrude. Select the upper section of the sketch as the section to extrude.

7. In the Extrude dialog box or in the mini-toolbar, click ☐ (New Solid) to create the extrude feature as a separate solid body.

8. Set the depth value to **height**. This creates a relationship between the two features.

9. Complete the feature.

Multi-Body Part Modeling

10. Review the Model browser. **Extrusion3** has been added after **Fillet1**. Expand the **Solid Bodies** node and note that two Solid Bodies are now in the model. **Extrusion1**, **Extrusion2**, and **Fillet1** are all features in **Solid1**, and **Extrusion3** is in **Solid2**. A re-oriented version of the model and the Model browser display as shown in Figure 3–32.

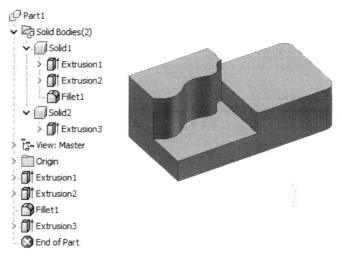

Figure 3–32

Task 5 - Modify the properties of a solid body.

1. In the Model browser, right-click on **Solid2** (under the **Solid Bodies** node) and select **Properties**.

2. In the *Body Appearance* drop-down list, select **Blue - Wall Paint - Glossy** to change the color of **Body2**.

3. Click **Update** to update the Mass, Area, and Volume of this single body.

4. Click **OK** to close the Body Properties dialog box.

You can assign a new name to the solid body in the Body Properties dialog box.

Task 6 - Add features to the solid bodies.

1. Create a Fillet on the two edges as shown in Figure 3–33. The two edges are from different solid bodies. Keep the default **.125 in** value as the radius for the fillets.

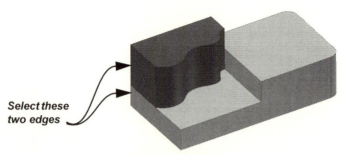

Figure 3–33

2. Complete the feature.

3. Review the Model browser. **Fillet2** has been added after **Extrusion3**, as well as to both of the solid bodies. A re-oriented version of the model and the Model browser are shown in Figure 3–34. The benefit of having them created together is that if the value changes, both update. If you want them separated, you must create them as separate features.

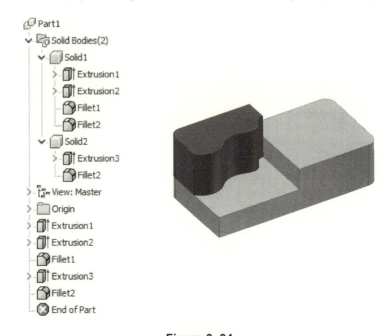

Figure 3–34

4. Re-orient the model to display the bottom of the model, as shown in Figure 3–35.

5. Create a sketch on the bottom surface and create three points at the centers of the fillets, as shown in Figure 3–35.

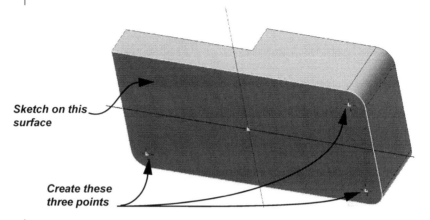

Figure 3–35

6. Complete the sketch.

7. Create holes at all three points. Set the *Termination* to **Through All** and the diameter to **.125in**.

8. Complete the feature.

9. Rotate the model, as shown in Figure 3–36, and note that the holes extrude through all of **Solid1** but not through **Solid2**. Hole1 is listed as a feature in the Model browser and a feature under the **Solid1,Solid Bodies** node. A feature is automatically added to the body from which the sketch plane is selected.

Figure 3–36

10. Double-click on **Hole1** in either location in the Model browser to edit the hole.

11. In the Hole dialog box, select in the *Solids(s)* field to activate it and select **Solid2** to include the holes as part of this solid body. All sketched features enable you to assign the feature to multiple bodies.

12. Complete the feature. The holes now extrude through both solid bodies, as shown in Figure 3–37.

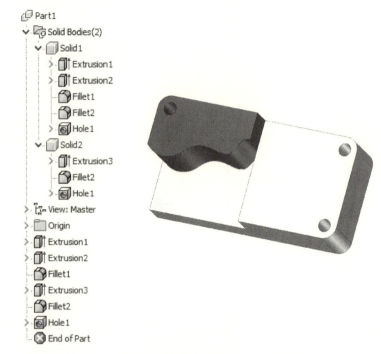

Figure 3–37

13. In the Parameters dialog box (*Manage* tab), modify the *height* parameter to **1**. You can also set it by editing the dimensions associated with **Extrusion1**.

14. In the Quick Access Toolbar, click (Local Update) to update the model, if required. Changes to both **Solid1** and **Solid2** are due to the relationships that you set while entering the original values for the features.

15. Save the model as **solid body practice.ipt**.

Chapter Review Questions

1. Which of the following best describes how the solid body that is created second is added to the model?
   a. The second feature is automatically applied to the first solid body, unless set otherwise.
   b. The second feature is created as its own solid body.

2. Which of the following statements are true regarding how to assign features to solid bodies? (Select all that apply.)
   a. When creating a sketched feature, it is by default added to the same solid body as that of the sketching plane.
   b. Sketched entities created as part of a feature in one solid body can reference features in a second solid body.
   c. When creating a pick-and-place feature, it is by default added to the same solid body as the placement references. If multiple references are selected that belong to multiple solid bodies, the feature fails to be created.
   d. When using a **Through All** depth option for a feature, the feature automatically extends through all solid bodies it comes in contact with.

3. Which option enables you to create a single solid body from two solid bodies?
   a. **Split**
   b. **Combine**
   c. **Move Bodies**
   d. **Patch**

4. By reviewing the list of features in the Model browser, you can determine how many solid bodies exist in the model.
   a. True
   b. False

5. Match the description of the type of Move Body operation in the left column to its icon in the right column.

Operation	Icon	Answer
a. Free Drag	![icon]	_____
b. Move along ray	![icon]	_____
c. Rotate about line	![icon]	_____

Command Summary

Button	Command	Location
	Combine	• **Ribbon:** *3D Model* tab>Modify panel
	Move Bodies	• **Ribbon:** *3D Model* tab>Modify panel
N/A	**Properties** (solid bodies)	• **Context menu:** In Model browser with Solid Body node selected
	Split	• **Ribbon:** *3D Model* tab>Modify panel

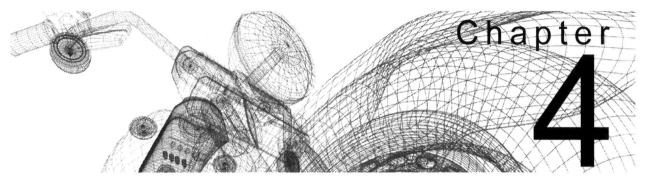

Chapter 4

Advanced Work Features

In the *Autodesk® Inventor® Introduction to Solid Modeling* learning guide, you learned how to use the Origin features that are provided in a new model and create basic work planes, axis, and points to help design a model. Grounded work points and user coordinate systems are additional work features that can be used to create model geometry.

Learning Objectives in this Chapter

- Convert an existing work point to a grounded work point.
- Create a new grounded work point relative to existing geometry.
- Create a user coordinate system that is accurately placed and oriented relative to the origin of the model.
- Create a user coordinate system that is accurately placed and oriented, in a required x- and y-direction, relative to existing geometry of the model.
- Edit the translational and rotational positions and visibility of a user coordinate system.

4.1 Grounded Work Points

A grounded work point maintains its position in space, even if the reference objects in the file change. Grounded work points can be created in part or assembly files. A grounded work point can be created on its own or you can convert an existing work point.

Convert an Existing Work Point to a Grounded Work Point

To ground an existing work point, right-click on it in the Model browser and select **Ground**. To restore its parametric association with the part, select **Ground** again in the shortcut menu to clear its checkmark. You cannot restore associativity with the references if the grounded work point has been edited with the 3D Move/Rotate mini-toolbar.

Create a Grounded Work Point

How To: Create a Grounded Work Point

1. In the *3D Model* tab>Work Features panel, click (Grounded Point), as shown in Figure 4–1.

Figure 4–1

2. Select a point on the model to locate the grounded work point.
   - A triad displays on the screen at the selected location. The triad shows the positive X, Y, and Z axes and the XY, YZ, and XZ planes.
3. Using the 3D Move / Rotate mini-toolbar (shown in Figure 4–2), precisely locate the grounded work point by entering values in the entry fields.

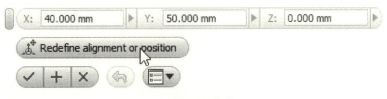

Figure 4–2

Alternatively, you can also move a grounded work point using the triad. The movement options depend on where you select the triad. The available selection areas on a triad are shown in Figure 4–3.

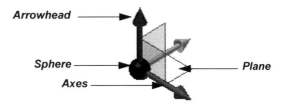

Figure 4–3

- Select the arrowhead to change its location by dragging it or by entering a value.
- Select an axis to rotate the triad by dragging it or by entering an angle. Rotating does not affect its position, but enables you to move in a particular direction.
- Select a plane to move the triad in that plane by dragging it or by entering a distance.
- Select the sphere to drag the triad freely.

4. Click ✓ or + in the 3D Move / Rotate mini-toolbar to complete the creation. Clicking + enables you to continue adding grounded work points.

- The symbol for a grounded work point in the Model browser is a ✣ (pushpin), as opposed to the ✣ symbol for a work point.

4.2 User Coordinate Systems

A User Coordinate System (UCS) is similar to the Origin that exists as one of the initial nodes in any part or assembly file. Like the Origin, a UCS consists of three planes, three axes, and a center point. The only difference is that you can have multiple UCSs in a single model that can all be oriented differently. Once created, a UCS is listed in the Model browser at the point it was created. It is identified by a special triad icon, as well as by a sequential number associated with its feature name, as shown in Figure 4–4.

Figure 4–4

The following are practical uses for a UCS in a model:

- A UCS enables you to design models relative to any of its work features. When selecting a UCS as a 2D sketch reference, the sketch is automatically placed on the XY plane of the UCS. Alternatively, you can select an alternate plane in a UCS as the sketch plane by manually selecting it in the Model browser. Additionally, sketch geometry can be aligned to any of the axes in the UCS. Changes made to plane or axis placement will reflect in any features that are children.

- A UCS can be used to provide a sketch plane for a feature that would be difficult to create using work planes alone.

- A UCS can be used for measuring.

- A UCS triad can be used as a View Face reference for orienting.

When a UCS or a UCS plane is used as a 2D sketch plane, the Center Point for the UCS is automatically projected into the sketch.

Advanced Work Features

- A UCS can be used as a reference in constraining components.
- Work features in a UCS can be displayed in a drawing.

A UCS can be located in a model so that it is either located relative to the model's origin or relative to existing geometry.

Locating the UCS Relative to the Model Origin

How To: Create a UCS Relative to the Model's Origin

1. In the *3D Model* tab>Work Features panel, click ╚ (UCS).
2. Locate the UCS in the main window by dragging the cursor to the required location. The UCS displays with an attached status bar. This indicates the absolute location of the UCS relative to the model origin, as shown in Figure 4–5. Click to place the UCS or enter specific values in the entry fields.

Figure 4–5

3. To refine the location of the UCS in the model, select and drag the various triad segments, as shown below:

The colors that display on each axis of the UCS triad correspond to the same colors for the model's triad. Red represents the X axis, green is the Y axis, and blue is the Z axis.

The cursor displays when the cursor is not placed on any of the triad segments. It prompts you to select a triad segment to define the type of transform.

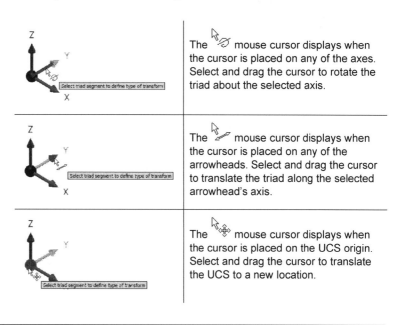

© 2018, ASCENT - Center for Technical Knowledge®

4–5

- Alternatively, you can select a triad segment, enter an exact value and press <Enter> once any of the triad segments are active. To toggle through multiple fields in the Heads Up Display, press <Tab>.

4. To complete the UCS placement, right-click and select **Finish**.
   - The additional options in the shortcut menu enable you to restart UCS placement (**Restart**), and cancel UCS placement (**Done [Esc]**).

Locating the UCS Relative to Existing Geometry

How To: Create a UCS Relative to Existing Geometry in a Part Model

1. In the *3D Model* tab>Work Features panel, click ⊾ (UCS).
2. As you move the cursor over existing geometry, the triad snaps to geometry (e.g., center points, vertex, midpoints, points). Locate the UCS relative to existing geometry by selecting references. (Note that you cannot create a UCS relative to existing geometry when working in an assembly model.)
3. The UCS status bar prompts you to specify the direction of the X axis. Select a point on the model to define the X direction reference. The UCS reorients once selected.
4. The UCS status bar prompts you to specify the direction of the Y axis. Select a point on the model to define the Y direction reference. The UCS reorients once selected and the UCS placement is automatically completed.
5. Once the Y axis direction is defined, the UCS is automatically created.
   - The additional options in the shortcut menu enable you to restart UCS placement (**Restart**), cancel UCS placement (**Done [Esc]**), and undo the most recent reference selection (**Back**).

The colors that display on each axis of the UCS triad correspond to the same colors for the model's triad. Red represents the X axis, green is the Y axis, and blue is the Z axis.

Each UCS adds six parameters to the model: three positional and three angular. Each parameter is initially listed in the Parameters dialog box using its default naming convention. If these parameter values are to be used in equations, it is recommended to rename them with more descriptive names.

Redefining UCS Placement

Whether a UCS is placed relative to the model origin or relative to existing geometry, the feature's placement can be redefined.

Advanced Work Features

- To redefine a UCS, right-click on the feature in the Model browser and select **Redefine Feature** or right-click on the feature in the model and select **Redefine Feature**. Select and drag the various triad segments (axis, arrowhead, or origin) to redefine its placement.

Alternatively, you can double-click on a UCS name in the Model browser to redefine it.

- For UCS features that were created by referencing existing geometry, you can right-click and select **Show Inputs** to show the references that were selected as the X and Y axis references. This will help you identify the entities that were used to create the feature.

- Alternatively, you can modify the location of a UCS by editing its values in the Parameters dialog box (*Manage* tab> Parameters panel>click f_x (Parameters)). Review the **Consumed By** column to identify what feature the parameter is consumed by.

UCS Visibility and Naming

You can control the default visibility of work features in a UCS and specify an alternate prefix for UCS names using the UCS Settings dialog box. To access these options, in the *Tools* tab> Options panel, click (Document Settings). In the Document Settings dialog box, select the *Modeling* tab and click **Settings** in the *User Coordinate System* area to open the UCS Settings dialog box, as shown in Figure 4–6.

The naming convention used for the work features in a UCS cannot be altered. Their names are dependent on the UCS name.

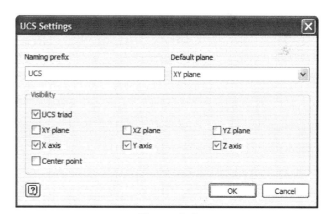

Figure 4–6

In addition to changing the naming prefix and visibility, you can specify the default plane for a UCS. The default plane is the plane that is used if the UCS is selected as a 2D sketching reference. The settings specified in the UCS Settings dialog box pertain to all UCSs in the model. Settings cannot be specified for a UCS on an individual basis.

Practice 4a Creating Geometry using a UCS

Practice Objectives

- Create a user coordinate system that is accurately placed and oriented in a required X and Y direction.
- Edit the translational and rotational X, Y, and Z positions of existing user coordinate systems.

In this practice, you will create the lofted geometry shown in Figure 4–7. The geometry is created by sketching sections on user coordinate systems (UCS) and then creating a loft between the sections. To complete the practice, you redefine the positions and sketches on the UCS to manipulate the shape of the geometry.

Figure 4–7

Task 1 - Create a user coordinate system.

1. Open **Intake.ipt**.

2. In the Work Features panel, click ⌐ (UCS).

3. Move the cursor around the model. Note how the triad snaps to geometry.

4. Position the cursor over the circular edge shown in Figure 4–8. The triad snaps to the center of the circular edge. The status line indicates the UCS is offset 40 mm in the X direction, 0mm in the Y direction, and -30mm in the Z direction from the Model Origin.

The colors that display on each axis of the UCS triad correspond to the same colors for the model's triad. Red represents the X axis, green is the Y axis, and blue is the Z axis.

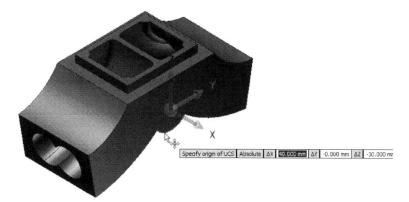

Figure 4–8

5. Select the edge.

6. The UCS Status Bar prompts you to specify the direction of the X axis. Hover the cursor over the midpoint vertex shown in Figure 4–9 and select this point. The UCS reorients once selected.

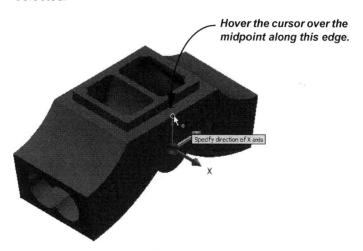

Figure 4–9

7. The UCS status bar prompts you to specify the direction of the Y axis. Select the point shown in Figure 4–10 to define the Y direction reference. The UCS reorients as shown in Figure 4–11.

Figure 4–10   Figure 4–11

Any work features that are created in a UCS can be used for feature creation.

8. In the Work Features panel, click ∠ (UCS).
9. Create a second UCS using the same references.
10. Create a third UCS using the same references. The three UCS features are located directly on top of one another. The model and Model browser display as shown in Figure 4–12.

Figure 4–12

Task 2 - Modify the location of the UCS.

1. In the Model browser, double-click on **UCS2** to activate the UCS for modification.

2. Click and hold the arrowhead for the Z axis, as shown in Figure 4–13.

Figure 4–13

3. Drag the cursor away from the model until the status bar reads that it is offset by approximately 50mm. Release the mouse button to locate the UCS. To obtain an exact value, click and release the arrowhead for the Z axis and enter **50** while the Z field is active (highlighted in blue) and press <Enter>.

4. Click and hold the axis of the Y axis, as shown in Figure 4–14.

Figure 4–14

5. Drag the cursor until the status bar reads that it is approximately 5 deg (rotated towards top of model). Release the mouse button to locate the UCS. To obtain an exact value, click and release the mouse button on the axis for the Yaxis and enter **5** while the field is active (highlighted in blue) and press <Enter>. You might need to enter **-5 deg**.

6. Right-click and select **Finish** to complete the modification of UCS2.

7. Double-click on **UCS3** in the Model browser.

8. Press and hold the left mouse button on the arrowhead for the Z axis and drag it away from the model. Drag the cursor until the status bar reads that it is offset by approximately 125mm, or enter the exact value. Release the left mouse button to locate the UCS.

9. Click and hold the axis of the Y axis. Drag the mouse until the status bar reads that it is approximately 15 deg (rotated towards top of model) or enter the exact value. Release the mouse button to locate the UCS. You might need to enter **-15 deg**.

10. Click and hold the arrowhead for the X axis and drag it until the status bar reads that it is offset by approximately **12mm**, or enter the exact value. Release the mouse button to locate the UCS.

11. Right-click and select **Finish** to complete the modification of UCS3. The updated model displays as shown in Figure 4–15.

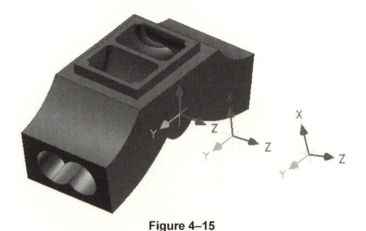

Figure 4–15

Task 3 - Sketch sections on each UCS that is used to create a loft.

1. In the Sketch panel, click ▱ (Start 2D Sketch).

Advanced Work Features

2. In the Model browser, select **UCS1** as the reference for the sketch. By default, if a UCS is selected as the sketch reference, the XY plane is used as the sketch plane. The Sketch tab is activated.

3. In the Create panel, click (Project Geometry) and select the circular edge that was used to place all the UCS features.

4. In the Create panel, click (Circle). Sketch the circular entity so that it is aligned with the center of the UCS and the projected edge. The sketch should be fully constrained based on these selections.

5. In the Exit panel, click (Finish Sketch).

6. In the Sketch panel, click (Start 2D Sketch) and in the Model browser, select **UCS2**.

7. In the Create panel, click (Circle). Sketch a circular entity so that it is centered on the UCS, as shown in Figure 4–16.

8. Create the 40 mm diameter dimension as shown in Figure 4–16.

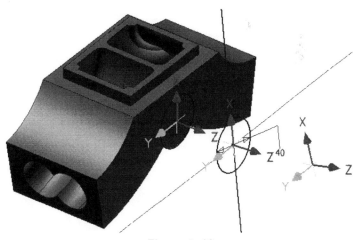

Figure 4–16

9. In the Exit panel, click .

10. Create a third circular sketch that references UCS3, as shown in Figure 4–17.

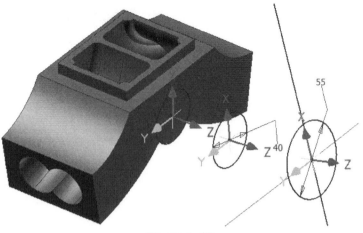

Figure 4–17

Task 4 - Create a loft feature.

1. In the *3D Model* tab>Create panel, click (Loft).

2. To define the sections for the loft, first select the sketch that was created referencing UCS1 (**Sketch1**), then select the sketch that was created referencing UCS2 (**Sketch2**). To complete the loft, select the final section that was sketched referencing UCS3.

3. Click **OK** to complete the loft. The model displays similar to that shown in Figure 4–18.

Figure 4–18

Task 5 - Modify the loft's shape by modifying the UCS features.

1. In the Model browser, double-click on **UCS3** to modify it.

2. Click and hold the arrowhead for the Y axis and drag it to a new location. Release the mouse button.

3. Click and hold the axis of the Y axis. Drag the cursor to change its angular location. Release the mouse button.

4. Right-click and select **Finish** to complete the change. The model updates to reflect the change.

   As an alternative, you can modify the location of a UCS by editing its values in the Parameters dialog box (*Manage* tab> Parameters panel>click f_x (Parameters)). Review the **Consumed By** column to identify which dimensions are associated with which UCS. To show the references from which the UCS was created and the dimensions were measured, in the Model browser, right-click on the UCS and select **Show Inputs**.

5. Continue to modify the geometry, UCS features, and sketches to refine the shape of the loft, similar to that shown in Figure 4–19.

Figure 4–19

6. Save the model and close the window.

Chapter Review Questions

1. The location of grounded work points is parametric. If there is a change made to the objects on which the points are dependent, the point location also changes.

    a. True

    b. False

2. In the Model browser, which of the following icons represents a grounded work point?

    a. ◈

    b. ◆

    c. ✸

3. If the mini-toolbar is being displayed as shown in Figure 4–20, which of the following features is currently being created?

    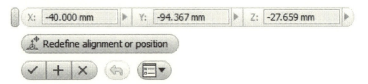

    Figure 4–20

    a. Work Point

    b. Grounded Work Point

    c. Center Point

    d. UCS

4. Which of the following planes associated with a UCS, is the default sketching plane if the UCS is selected as a reference for sketching?

    a. YZ Plane

    b. XZ Plane

    c. XY Plane

5. Which area in a grounded work point's triad, as shown in Figure 4–21, enables you to freely locate the point in the model?

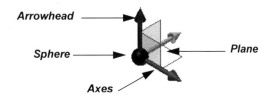

Figure 4–21

a. Arrowhead
b. Sphere
c. Axes
d. Plane

6. Which of the triad areas, as shown in Figure 4–22, is not available for use when creating a UCS?

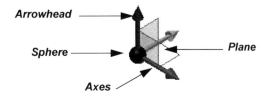

Figure 4–22

a. Arrowhead
b. Sphere
c. Axes
d. Plane

Command Summary

Button	Command	Location
	Grounded Work Point	• **Ribbon:** *3D model* tab>Work Features panel
	UCS	• **Ribbon:** *3D model* tab>Work Features panel

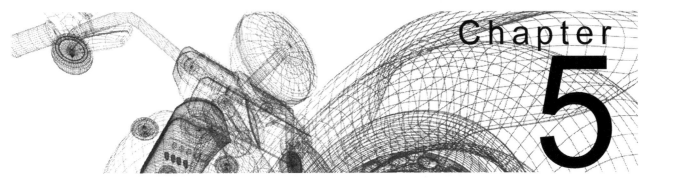

Chapter 5

Advanced Lofts, Sweeps, and Coils

Creating the required geometry in a model can be accomplished using many different techniques. There is no right or wrong way to create geometry. Instead, what is important is that the resulting geometry should capture your design intent and be designed in such a way that any required changes can be made easily. Understanding how to use the advanced modeling features and the advanced options for standard features will provide you with additional flexibility when you are creating geometry.

Learning Objectives in this Chapter

- Create an Area Loft that blends geometry between multiple profiles and intermediate points along a centerline.
- Define accurate position and area dimensions for the intermediate points that are selected along the Area Loft Centerline.
- Create a Path & Guide Rail Sweep to control the scale and twist of a sweep by selecting an additional curve to use as a guiding reference for the profile.
- Create a Path & Guide Surface Sweep which uses a surface normal to control the twist of the profile along the path.
- Create coil shaped geometry that adds or removes material from the model.

5.1 Area Lofts

An Area Loft feature is similar to a Rail and Center Line Loft in that it enables you to create geometry by blending between multiple profiles. Area Lofts expand on the Center Line Lofts by enabling you to define the area of sections at specified points along the path as well as define new sections along the centerline and define their areas. The shape in Figure 5–1 has been blended between three selected sections. Each shows its position on the centerline and its area.

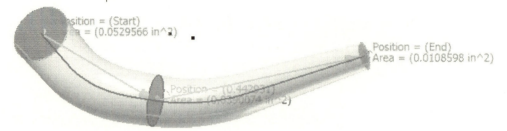

Figure 5–1

How To: Create an Area Loft

1. In the *3D Model* tab>Create panel, click (Loft).
2. Click (Area Loft). The Loft dialog box refreshes as shown in Figure 5–2.

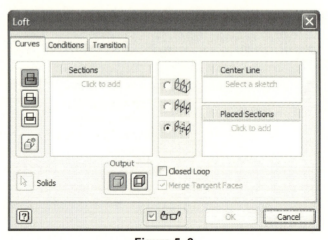

Figure 5–2

Select **Closed Loop** to create the loft so that the first and last section are joined.

3. Select how the geometry will be added to the model. The options include adding material using a join (▣), removing material with a cut (▣), or adding material that is the result of an intersection (▣).
4. Define whether the new geometry is added as a new solid body or is combined with an existing body.
   - If the loft is the first solid feature in the model, the feature is automatically added as the first solid body.
   - If the loft is added as a secondary solid feature, you can click ▣ to add the feature as a new solid body.
   - If there are more than two solids in the model, you can select which solid to apply the loft to by clicking ▣ and selecting the body to which to apply it.
5. Select the output option as Solid (▣) or Surface (▣).
6. Select the sections to be blended, similar to that shown in Figure 5–3.

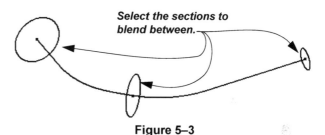

Select the sections to blend between.

Figure 5–3

- You can either select a sketched profile or an existing planar face as a profile. Existing planar faces are selected directly from the model, and can only be used as the start and end sections.

7. Activate the *Center Line* area of the dialog box and select the Center Line geometry to define the path that the loft will follow. The resulting geometry is previewed on the screen, similar to that shown in Figure 5–4.

Figure 5–4

When editing the Start and End or any other selected sketched section, you cannot change the Section Position values. Only internally placed section positions can be changed.

Click (Driven Section) option to disable all Section Size controls and only control the section position.

8. Activate the *Placed Section* area of the dialog box and select other points on the Center Line to control additional areas for the Loft.
   • Note how the Position and Area dimensions are provided for each selected section or placed section.
9. In the Section Dimensions dialog box (shown in Figure 5–5), click (Driving Section) to enable you to control the area of the internal sections. For placed sections you can also control their position. Edit the values, as required.

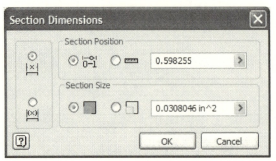

Figure 5–5

10. Click **OK** to close the Section Dimensions dialog box.
11. Click **OK** to complete the feature or right-click in the graphics window and select **OK [Enter]**. Figure 5–6 displays the completed model used in this example.

*The **Area Loft** option provides support for the design of hydraulic and pneumatic components.*

Figure 5–6

5.2 Advanced Sweeps

Path sweeps create geometry by sweeping a profile along a path. Path & Guide Rail Sweeps and Path & Guide Surface Sweeps are two advanced types of path sweeps.

Path & Guide Rail Sweep

The Path & Guide Rail Sweep enables you to select an additional curve (Guide Rail).

How To: Create a Path & Guide Rail Sweep

1. In the *3D Model* tab>Create panel, click (Sweep).
2. Select the Profile and Path references (similar to a Path sweep).
3. Select **Path & Guide Rail** from the *Type* drop-down list.
4. Select a Guide Rail reference.
5. Select how the geometry will be added to the model. The options include adding material using a join ( ), removing material with a cut ( ), or adding material that is the result of an intersection ( ).
6. Define whether the new geometry is added as a new solid body or is combined with an existing body.
    - If the loft is the first solid feature in the model, the feature is automatically added as the first solid body.
    - If the loft is added as a secondary solid feature, you can click to add the feature as a new solid body.
    - If there are more than two solids in the model, you can select which solid to apply the loft to by clicking and selecting the solid.
7. Select the output option as Solid ( ) or Surface ( ).

8. Define the required *Profile Scaling* option, as shown in Figure 5–7. They enable you to control the direction(s) in which the Guide Rail should affect the profile scale along the sweep. Figure 5–8 shows an example of how the scaling affects the resulting geometry.

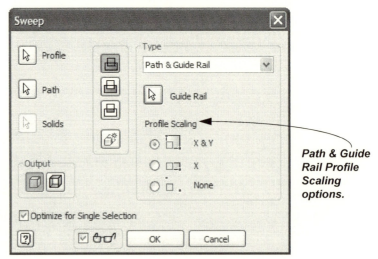

Figure 5–7

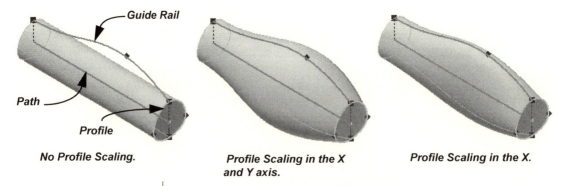

Figure 5–8

9. Once the sweep feature is defined, click **OK**. Alternatively, right-click in the graphics window and select **OK [Enter]** or press <Enter>.

Path & Guide Surface Sweep

The Path & Guide Surface Sweep enables you to select both a surface whose normal controls the twist of the sweep and a path, as shown in Figure 5–9.

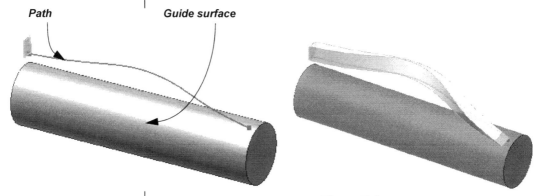

Figure 5–9

The procedure for creating this type of sweep is the same as that for a traditional Path sweep, except that the **Path & Guide Surface** option is selected and a guide surface is assigned. Figure 5–10 shows the Path & Guide options.

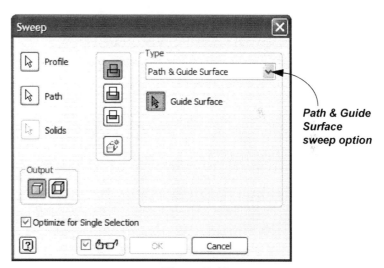

Figure 5–10

5.3 Coils

A helical shape is used to create springs, threads, and augers. You can create these shapes using a Coil. A coil profile is swept along a helical path or a spiral path, as shown in Figure 5–11.

Similar to extrusions and revolutions, you can use a coil to add or remove material.

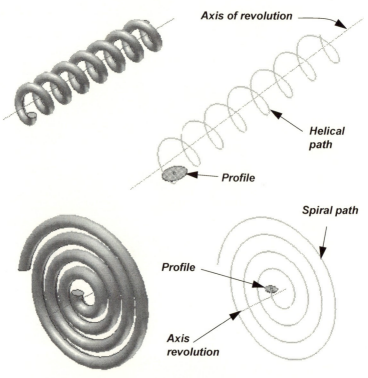

Figure 5–11

A profile and axis of revolution must exist in the model prior to creating a Coil feature.

- The profile for a coil can be defined from sketches or existing planar faces.

- The axis of revolution can be a line in a sketch or a work axis. The axis of revolution must be sketched in the same sketch as the profile, unless you are selecting a work axis or a part edge. The axis can be in any orientation, but cannot intersect the profile.

How To: Create a Coil

1. In the *3D Model* tab>Create panel, click ⬚ (Coil) once the profile and axis of the revolution are defined. The Coil dialog box opens as shown in Figure 5–12.

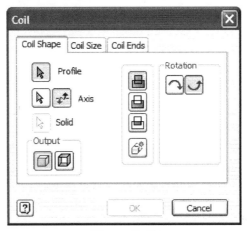

Figure 5–12

2. Select the Profile, Axis, and the Axis direction in the Shape section of the *Coil Shape* tab.
3. Define the direction of rotation using the ⬚⬚ icons.
4. Select how the geometry will be added to the model. The options include adding material using a join (⬚), removing material with a cut (⬚), or adding material that is the result of an intersection (⬚).
5. Define whether the new geometry is added as a new solid body or is combined with an existing body.
   - If the loft is the first solid feature in the model, the feature is automatically added as the first solid body.
   - If the loft is added as a secondary solid feature, you can click ⬚ to add the feature as a new solid body.
   - If there are more than two solids in the model, you can select which solid to apply the loft to by clicking ⬚ and selecting the solid.
6. Select the output option as Solid (⬚) or Surface (⬚).

7. Select the *Coil Size* tab to define the coil size and select a type from the Type drop-down list, as shown in Figure 5–13. Depending on the type that is selected you can enter values for **Pitch**, **Height**, **Revolution**, and **Taper**.

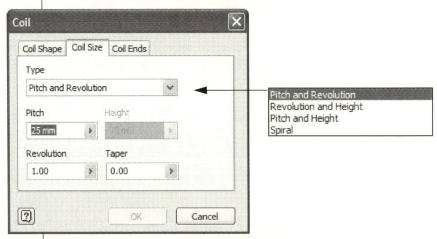

Figure 5–13

- Pitch sets the length per turn. For example, if the pitch is set to 0.5, there will be 0.5 units between adjacent coils.

- Height sets the height of the coil centerline. This option is not available for a Spiral type.

- Revolution sets the total number of revolutions of the coil.

- Taper enables you to determine how the radius of each turn changes over the length of the coil, so the coil is cone-shaped. A positive number increases the radius; a negative number decreases the radius. This option is not available for a Spiral type.

8. Select the *Coil Ends* tab to define the start and end shape of the coil.
    - The end of a spring might be formed so that the spring can stand upright on a flat surface. Part of the coil can be flat or at a different angle than the rest of the spring. When **Natural** is selected, the spring is uniform along its length; when **Flat** is selected, the coil is deformed at the end to enable the spring to sit flat, as shown in Figure 5–14.

Advanced Lofts, Sweeps, and Coils

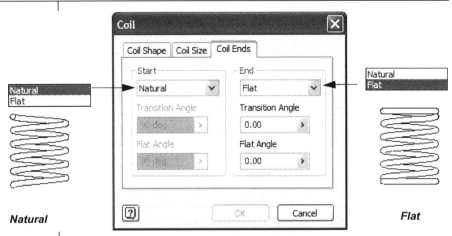

Natural **Flat**

Figure 5–14

- When **Flat** is selected a transition angle specifies how many degrees over which the transition between the body of the spring and the flat end of the spring is achieved. For example, if set to 180 degrees, the change from the body of the spring to flat happens over one half of a rotation. When **Flat** is selected, the flat angle specifies how much of the last coil should be flat (no pitch). A flat angle of 360 degrees makes a complete turn at the end of the coil.

9. Once the coil feature is defined, click **OK**. Alternatively, right-click in the graphics window and select **OK [Enter]**.

Alternatively, you can create coil type geometry using a 3D Helical Curve and sweeping a circular section along it. When using a Coil feature you have more control over the ends of the coil.

Practice 5a Area Loft

Practice Objectives

- Create an Area Loft that blends geometry between multiple profiles and intermediate points along a centerline.
- Define accurate position and area dimensions for the intermediate points that are selected along the Area Loft centerline.

In this practice, you will use an Area loft feature to create the bottle shown in Figure 5–15. By defining the position and area of multiple sections along the entire length of the bottle you will shape of the bottle.

Figure 5–15

Task 1 - Open a part file.

1. Open **bottle.ipt**. The part displays as shown in Figure 5–16.

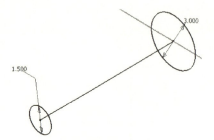

Figure 5–16

Task 2 - Create a centerline loft.

1. In the *3D Model* tab>Create panel, click (Loft).

2. In the Loft dialog box, click (Area Loft).

3. Select the two circular entities as the sections. Select the larger diameter circle for the first section (start) and the small circle for the second section (end).

4. Activate the *Center Line* area and select **Sketch 4** as the Center Line. The preview displays as shown in Figure 5–17.

You might need to select Sketch4 directly on the model and not in the Model browser to obtain an immediate preview of the loft feature; otherwise, the preview should display when you assign additional sections.

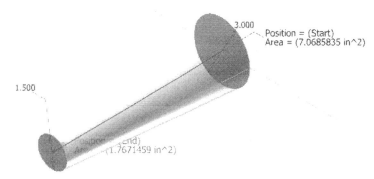

Figure 5–17

5. Orient the model similar to that shown in Figure 5–18. This is being done so you can see the dimensions of the sections and easily compare them to the graphics provided in the practice.

6. In the *Placed Sections* area, click **Click to add** and select the location, as shown in Figure 5–18, to add a section. This placement is approximate and will be modified.

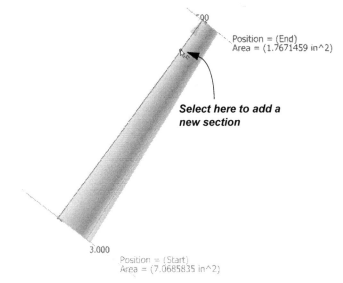

Figure 5–18

7. Ensure that is enabled to enable the section area to be driven by user-defined values. Enable the *Section Size* and *Section Position* options, if required. Change the *Section Size* to **1.75 in^2** and the *Section Position* to **0.9**. Figure 5–19 shows the Section Dimensions dialog box and the model.

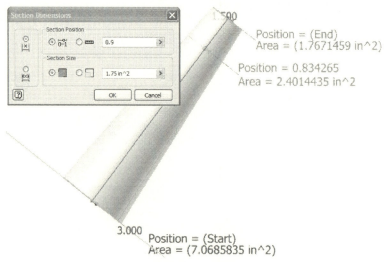

Figure 5–19

8. Click **OK** to accept the new dimensions.

9. In the *Placed Sections* area, click **Click to add**, select and dimension a second internal section, as shown in Figure 5–20.

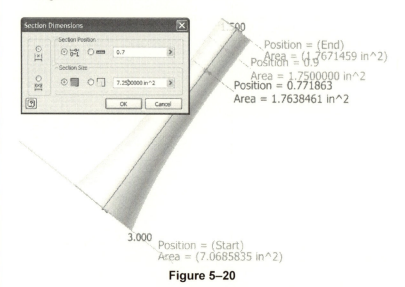

Figure 5–20

10. Continue to add sections to the loft using the Position and Area values shown in Figure 5–21.

For this practice you are not going to change the Position and Area for the Start and End sections; however, this type of modification is possible.

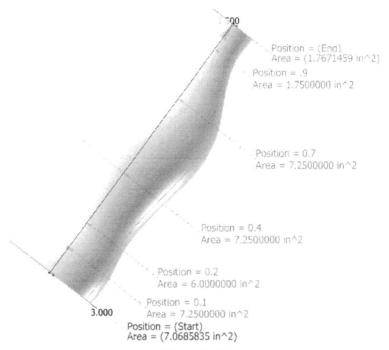

Figure 5–21

11. Click **OK** to create the loft.

12. Add a **0.5 in** fillet to the bottom of the bottle and a **0.1 in** shell. The model displays as shown in Figure 5–22.

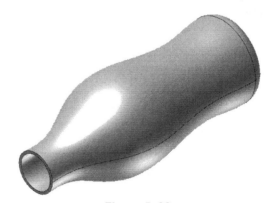

Figure 5–22

13. Save and close the model.

Practice 5b | Sweeps

Practice Objectives

- Create a Path & Guide Rail sweep that incorporates the use of a profile, path, and guide rail curve to define shape of the model.
- Create a cut using the Path & Guide Surface sweep that keeps the profile normal to a surface along the path.

In this practice, you will create the geometry shown in Figure 5–23. All of the geometry is created using the **Path & Guide Rail** and **Path & Guide Surface** sweep options. Different options in each type are used to create the geometry.

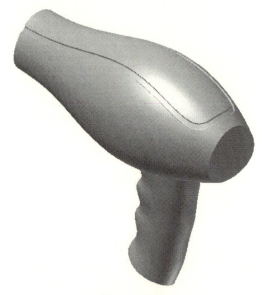

Figure 5–23

Task 1 - Create a sweep to represent the body of the hairdryer.

In this task, you create a Path & Guide Rail Sweep to create the body of the hairdryer model. You will also manipulate the profile scaling option to see how it affects the geometry's shape.

1. Open **Hairdryer.ipt**. A number of different curves and profiles have been created for you.

2. In the *3D Model* tab>Create panel, click (Sweep). The sweep type is set to **Path** by default. Select the **BodyProfile** sketch as the profile for the sweep. Select the **BodyPath** sketch as the path for the sweep. Both references, and the previewed geometry, are shown in Figure 5–24.

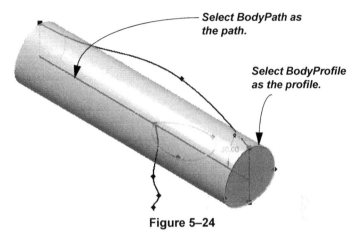

Figure 5–24

3. To enhance the shape of the body of the hairdryer, an additional curve will be included to drive the shape. In the *Type* drop-down list, select **Path & Guide Rail**.

4. Select the **BodyGuideRail** sketch as the Guide Rail reference, as shown in Figure 5–25. The preview updates to show the enhanced shape once the additional guide curve is added.

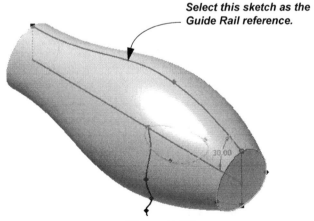

Figure 5–25

5. In the *Profiling Scaling* area of the Sweep dialog box, select **None**. The preview changes to eliminate the influence of the guide curve.

6. Select **X** in the *Profile Scaling* area. The X direction is the only direction that is influenced by the Guide Curve, as shown in Figure 5–26.

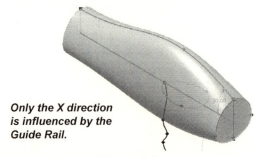

Only the X direction is influenced by the Guide Rail.

Figure 5–26

7. Change the *Profile Scaling* option back to **X & Y** to have the guide rail influence the sweep's shape in both the x and y directions.

8. Complete the feature.

Task 2 - Create a sweep to represent the handle of the hairdryer.

In this task, you create another Path & Guide Rail Sweep to create the handle of the hairdryer model.

1. Start the creation of another Sweep feature.

2. Select **HandleProfile** as the profile for the feature and **3D Sketch** as the path for the sweep. Both references and the previewed geometry are shown in Figure 5–27.

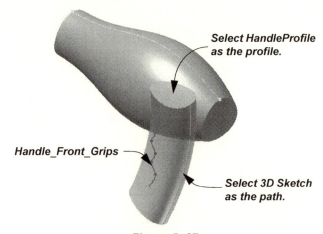

Select HandleProfile as the profile.

Handle_Front_Grips

Select 3D Sketch as the path.

Figure 5–27

3. In the *Type* drop-down list, change the sweep to **Path & Guide Rail**.

4. Select **Handle_Front_Grips** as the guide rail reference

5. Under *Profile Scaling*, select **X**.

6. Complete the feature. The model updates as shown in Figure 5–28.

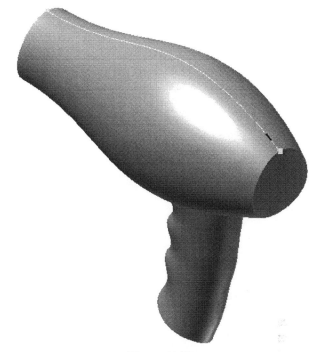

Figure 5–28

Task 3 - Create a sweep that cuts away material from the top of the hairdryer.

In this task, you create a Path & Guide Surface Sweep to cut away material on the top of the hairdryer model.

1. Right-click **IntersectionSurface** in the Model browser and select **Visibility**.

2. Start the creation of a new 3D sketch.

3. Using the **Intersection Curve** option, create a new curve at the intersection of **IntersectionSurface** and the surface of the body of the hairdryer. Finish the sketch. The curve should appear as shown in Figure 5–29.

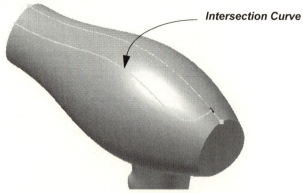

Figure 5–29

4. Start the creation of another **Sweep** feature.

5. The **Groove** sketch is preselected as the profile for the sweep because it is the only remaining section that is closed.

6. Select the curve that was just created using **Intersection Curve** as the path.

7. Set the sweep to remove material from the model and complete the feature.

8. Reorient the model to see the nozzle of the hairdryer, as shown in Figure 5–30. The cut does not remain normal to the surface of the hairdryer as it sweeps along the path.

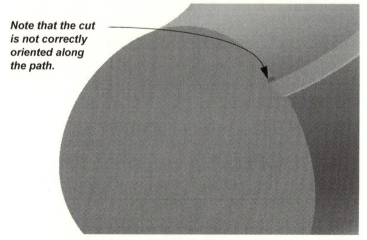

Figure 5–30

9. Edit the last Sweep feature.
10. Select **Path & Guide Surface** as the sweep type.
11. Maintain the **Profile** and **Path** options that were originally defined. Select the surface of the body of the hairdryer as the *Guide Surface* reference.
12. Complete the feature. The model updates to show that the swept cut now remains normal to the surface along the entire path, as shown in Figure 5–31.

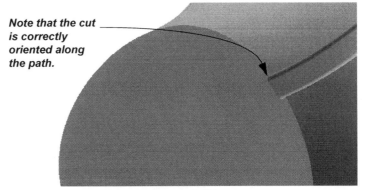

Note that the cut is correctly oriented along the path.

Figure 5–31

13. Mirror the cut as shown in Figure 5–32.

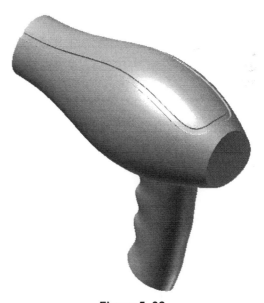

Figure 5–32

14. Save and close the model.

Practice 5c   Creating a Coil

Practice Objectives

- Create appropriate profile and axis features that can be used to create the required Coil feature.
- Create coil shaped geometry that removes material from the model.

In this practice, you create a coil on an existing part to create a drill bit. The completed drill bit is shown in Figure 5–33.

Figure 5–33

Task 1 - Sketch the coil profiles.

1. Open **drillbit.ipt**. Review the features in the Model browser. User-defined work features will be used to place and dimension the coil profile.

2. Create a sketch on Work Plane1. Project Work Axis1 onto the sketch plane to locate and dimension the coil profiles.

3. Sketch and dimension the two circular profiles so that they are symmetric about the projected Work Axis1, as shown in Figure 5–34.

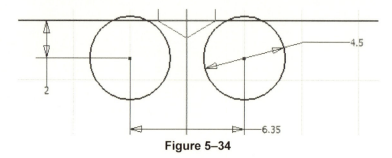

Figure 5–34

4. Finish the sketch.

Advanced Lofts, Sweeps, and Coils

Task 2 - Create the coil.

1. In the *3D Model* tab>Create panel, click (Coil). The Coil dialog box opens.

2. Select one of the sketched circles as the profile.

3. Click (Axis) and select the **Work Axis1**. Flip the coil direction, if required, so the path extends along the part.

4. Click to set the operation to cut away material.

5. Select the *Coil Size* tab and in the *Type* drop-down list, select **Pitch and Height**. Set the *Pitch* to **25 mm** and the *Height* to **75 mm**.

6. Select the *Coil Ends* tab and verify that **Natural** is selected as the **Start** and **End** options.

7. Click **OK**. The model displays as shown in Figure 5–35.

Figure 5–35

8. In the Model browser, expand the Coil feature, right-click the Sketch and select **Share Sketch**. Alternatively, select and drag the sketch out to the top-level to share it.

9. In the *3D Model* tab>Create panel, click (Coil) again and select the other circular profile to create another coil with the same settings as above.

10. Clear the visibility of the shared sketch. The model displays as shown in Figure 5–36.

Figure 5–36

11. Save and close the model.

Chapter Review Questions

1. Which of the following best describes an Area Loft? (Select all that apply.)

   a. It enables you to only create geometry between only two sketched sections.

   b. It enables you to control the shape of the geometry using Rail references.

   c. It enables you to control the area of a section.

   d. It enables you to control intermediate points along a center line.

2. An area value can be assigned to either the start section or the end section of an Area Loft?

   a. True

   b. False

3. When the Driven ( ) option is selected in the Section Dimensions dialog box, which section type(s) is not available (i.e., driven by the model geometry)?

   a. Section Position

   b. Section Size

   c. Both Section Position and Section Size

4. What does the Path & Guide Rail sweep enable you to control? (Select all that apply.)

   a. Control the orientation of the profile along the path of the sweep.

   b. Control the shape of the profile by referencing two curves.

   c. Control the scale and twist of the sweep.

   d. Control the shape of the sweep using the normal from a reference surface.

5. What sweep option enables you to control the twist of the sweep using a surface?

   a. Path

   b. Path & Guide Rail

   c. Path & Guide Surface

6. Which Coil End option was used to create the coil geometry shown in Figure 5–37?

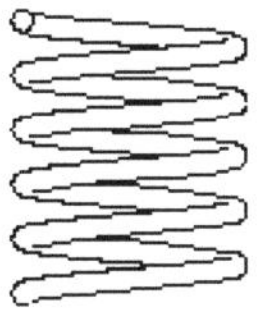

Figure 5–37

   a. Natural
   b. Flat

7. If a sketched line is being used as the axis of revolution for a Coil feature, it must exist as an independent feature and must be created prior to initiating the creation of the coil.

   a. True
   b. False

Command Summary

Button	Command	Location
	Coil	• **Ribbon:** *3D model* tab>Create panel
	Loft	• **Ribbon:** *3D model* tab>Create panel
	Sweep	• **Ribbon:** *3D model* tab>Create panel

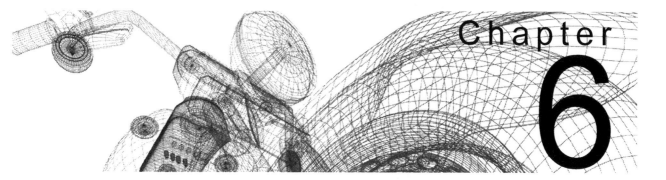

Chapter 6

Analyzing a Model

The ability to analyze models prior to manufacturing is a valuable tool in digital prototyping. The Autodesk® Inventor® software offers a variety of basic tools that can be used to verify such things as continuity, draft, curvature, and cross-sections in model geometry. Understanding how to use these tools during the design process helps to ensure that there are fewer issues prior to finalizing a model or sending it to a more complex analysis software tool.

Learning Objectives in this Chapter

- Conduct a Zebra analysis that evaluates continuity between surfaces.
- Conduct a Draft analysis that enables you to visually evaluate whether the applied draft values in a model are within a specified range.
- Conduct a Curvature analysis that evaluates whether continuity exists between surfaces based on the results of flow lines.
- Conduct a Gaussian, Mean Curvature, or Maximum Curvature analysis for points on a surface.
- Conduct a Cross Section analysis that displays the model sectioned through a single plane.
- Conduct a Cross Section analysis that displays the model sectioned through a series of planes and also identifies areas of the model that conflict with specified maximum and minimum wall thickness values.

6.1 Analysis Types

There are five analysis types that are available to analyze model geometry. These types are Zebra, Draft, Curvature, Surface, and Section.

Zebra Analysis

A Zebra Analysis projects parallel lines onto a model to determine if continuity between surfaces exists.

- If the stripes are parallel, the surface/face is flat.
- If the stripe edges do not line up, then the two surfaces are not tangent.
- If the stripe edges line up, but display a sharp angle, then the boundary is tangent but not curvature continuous.
- If the stripe edges are continuous (no sharp angles) across the boundary of two surfaces, then the transition is curvature continuous.

Figure 6–1 shows the three continuity options.

Stripe edges do not line up between surfaces (i.e., not tangent)

Stripe edges line up between surfaces; however there is a sharp angle (not continuous)

Stripe edges line up between surfaces and there is no sharp angle

Figure 6–1

Draft Analysis

A Draft Analysis determines if the drafts that have been added to the model are satisfactory for manufacturing. Based on a draft's maximum and minimum permissible values, a color gradient is displayed so that you can compare it to the model.

- If the draft falls within the permissible range (i.e., faces with adequate draft angles), the color of the selected faces/surfaces can be distinguished in the color gradient.
- If the colors on the model are outside the gradient, the draft angle is outside the range and further analysis of the surface should be done.

Figure 6–2 shows an example of a model whose draft angle is within the permissible range.

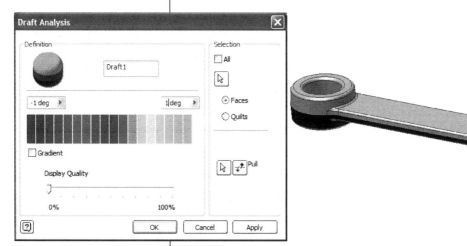

Figure 6–2

Curvature Analysis

An edge is generated where two surfaces meet, and a vertex is generated where two curves meet. The term continuity refers to how the faces/surfaces or end points meet. A Curvature analysis enables you to visually analyze the results of continuity calculations for flow lines (curvature comb) on selected faces or quilts or between them. The connections between curves and surfaces are described as follows:

G-1	Curves or surfaces <u>do not</u> share a common end point. There is no continuity.
G0	Curves or surfaces <u>do</u> share a common end point. They are not tangent to one another.

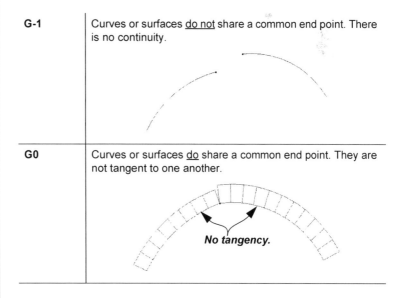

G1	Curves or surfaces are tangent to each other and share a common boundary, but have differing curvature magnitudes at their intersection. 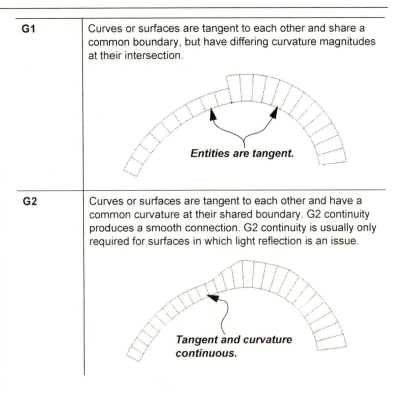
G2	Curves or surfaces are tangent to each other and have a common curvature at their shared boundary. G2 continuity produces a smooth connection. G2 continuity is usually only required for surfaces in which light reflection is an issue.

Surface Analysis

Surface analysis tools provide three analysis types: Gaussian, Mean Curvature, and Maximum Curvature, as shown in Figure 6–3.

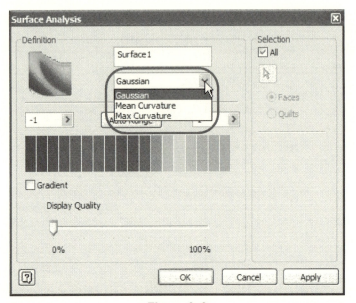

Figure 6–3

The three surface analysis types are described as follows:

- A **Gaussian** analysis is the product of the minimum curvature and maximum curvature for a given point on a surface. It is used to locate areas of high and low surface curvature and values can be either positive or negative. Minimum curvature values display in blue and maximum values display in green. All other values are assigned a color between blue and green. The Gaussian curvature for planar and cylindrical surfaces are zero because the curvature is always zero in at least one direction. Figure 6–4 shows a Gaussian Curvature analysis performed on two different parts.

Figure 6–4

- The **Mean Curvature** surface analysis provides information on the curvature of the u and v surfaces. Similar to a Gaussian analysis, it displays the results using a color gradient.

- The **Maximum Curvature** surface analysis shows the largest normal curvature at every point on the surface. Similar to a Gaussian analysis, it displays the results using a color gradient.

Cross Section Analysis

A Cross Section (Section) analysis obtains information about a cross-section through a part. You can perform two types of analyses: Simple and Advanced.

- A simple section analysis displays the model as a cutaway view of the part based on the selected plane and enables visual inspection. This view is similar to the slice graphics option, as shown in Figure 6–5.

Simple Analysis

Figure 6–5

- An advanced section analysis enables you to define multiple section planes by either selecting or creating them. It can also verify the maximum and minimum wall thickness and area. For an advanced section analysis, areas in a section that are thicker than the maximum highlight in red on the model and are listed in the *Results* area. Areas thinner than the minimum part thickness highlight in blue on the model and are listed in the *Results* area. A sample Advanced Section analysis is shown in Figure 6–6, where the part contains one cross-section that is too thick, one that is within the thickness range, and one that is too thin.

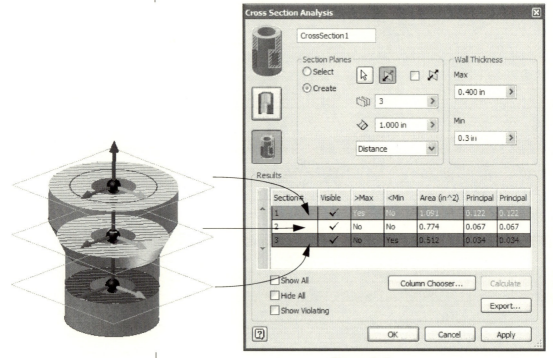

Figure 6–6

6.2 Analysis Procedures

Regardless of which analysis tool you use, the procedure for analyzing a model is similar.

General Steps

Use the following general steps to perform an analyses on a model:

1. Start the analysis.
2. Select the references.
3. Define the options.
4. Complete and review the analysis.
5. Display or edit an existing analysis.

Step 1 - Start the analysis.

In the *Inspect* tab>Analysis panel, select the required analysis type, as shown in Figure 6–7.

Figure 6–7

The corresponding dialog box opens. For all analyses, specify a name for the analysis or use the default.

- For a Surface Analysis, you must also select the type of surface analysis: **Gaussian**, **Mean Curvature**, or **Max Curvature**.

- For a Section Analysis you must also select the type of section analysis as **Simple** or **Advanced**.

Step 2 - Select the references.

Reference selection is required to define which geometry on the model is to be analyzed.

- For the Zebra, Draft, Curvature, and Surface analyses you must select surfaces to analyze. The default is to analyze all surfaces; however, you can clear the **All** option and select either **Faces** or **Quilts**, as shown in Figure 6–8. If either **Faces** or **Quilts** are to be used you must select the entities to analyze. For a Draft analysis, you must also select a reference for the pull direction.

Figure 6–8

- For a Section analyses, select a plane that cuts through the part at the required angle.

  - For a Simple Section analysis, an offset can be added from the plane by entering an offset value or by clicking and dragging it in the graphics window. The options for a simple section analysis are shown in Figure 6–9.

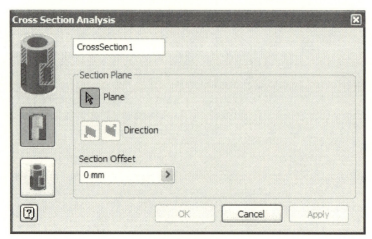

Figure 6–9

  - For an Advanced Section analysis, specify the number of sections and the section spacing (i.e., the distance between sections), as shown in Figure 6–10.

Analyzing a Model

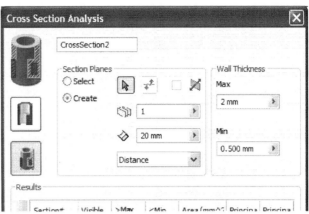

Figure 6–10

Step 3 - Define the options.

Once you have selected references for the analysis, you can define the options.

Zebra Analysis

For a Zebra analysis, select one of the three direction icons as shown in Figure 6–11. Select the direction that most clearly shows the transition between surfaces. You can leave it with the default direction first, define the other options, apply the analysis, and then edit the analysis to change the direction, as required. Adjust the Thickness, Density, Opacity, and Display Quality values to modify the proportion of white to black, number of stripes, transparency, and resolution for the zebra pattern, respectively.

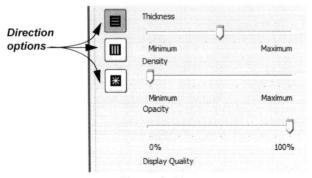

Figure 6–11

Draft Analysis

Enter minimum and maximum angles, as shown in Figure 6–12. Selected faces or quilts that fall between the specified angles will display in a color corresponding to the measured angle, based on the pull direction. Activate the **Gradient** option to display the color band as a continuous gradient, rather than discrete color bands. Adjust the display quality to control the quality of the color shown on the selected faces and quilts.

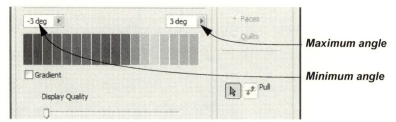

Figure 6–12

Curvature Analysis

To control the visual display of a curvature analysis you must manipulate the Comb Density, Comb Scale, and Surface Density. The (Comb Density) option controls the spacing between the spines. The (Comb Scale) option controls the scale or length of the spines. The (Surface Density) controls the density of the sample curves for interior faces. In the Direction section, specify having the curvature comb display in Direction1, Direction2, or both. The options are shown in Figure 6–13.

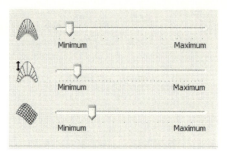

Figure 6–13

Surface Analysis

Enter minimum and maximum curvature ratio values, as shown in Figure 6–14. Selected faces or quilts that fall between the specified curvature ratios display in a color corresponding to the measured curvature ratio. Click **Auto Range** to set the minimum curvature ratio to the smallest value found on the selected faces and the maximum curvature ratio to the largest value found on the selected faces. Activate the **Gradient** option to display the color band as a continuous gradient, rather than discrete color bands. Adjust the display quality to control the quality of the color shown on the selected faces and quilts.

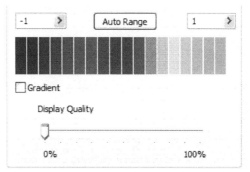

Figure 6–14

Cross Section Analysis

With a Simple Section analysis, you can only change the section offset value and the direction. For Advanced, additional options enable you to specify minimum and maximum thicknesses, as shown in Figure 6–15.

Figure 6–15

Step 4 - Complete and review the analysis.

Click **Apply** to run the analysis. The analysis is added to the Model browser. Review the results to ensure that they display as required.

- Rotate the model, as required, to better view the results. Rotating the model for a Zebra analysis is particularly helpful in determining how well the stripe edges line up.

You might want to clarify or adjust the results by changing the direction(s) selected for a Zebra or Curvature analysis, or you might want to adjust the minimum and maximum values for a Draft, Gaussian, or Section analysis. Make adjustments, as required, and click **Apply**. Continue adjusting, as required, and click **Cancel**.

Step 5 - Display or edit an existing analysis.

To display an analysis you already created, double-click on it in the *Analysis* folder in the Model browser. The analysis result displays on the model. To toggle off the visibility of all analyses, right-click on the *Analysis* folder and select **Analysis Visibility**, as shown in Figure 6–16.

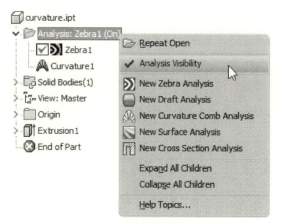

Figure 6–16

To edit an analysis you already created, right-click on it in the Model browser and select **Edit**.

Practice 6a

Analyzing Continuity

Practice Objectives

- Conduct a Zebra analysis that evaluates whether continuity exists between adjacent surfaces based on the results of stripes applied to the surfaces.
- Conduct a Curvature analysis that evaluates whether continuity exists between adjacent surfaces based on the results of flow lines that extend normal to the surfaces.

In this practice, you analyze a model using the Zebra and Curvature analysis tools. The Zebra analysis enables you to investigate the continuity between adjacent faces or quilts, while the Curvature analysis investigates the curvature of a face or quilt, as well as between boundaries.

Task 1 - Perform a Zebra analysis.

Perform a Zebra analysis to determine if continuity exists between surfaces.

1. Open **zebra.ipt**. Rotate the part to appear similar to that shown in Figure 6–17.

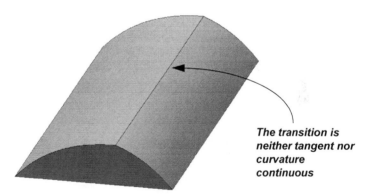

The transition is neither tangent nor curvature continuous

Figure 6–17

2. In the *Inspect* tab>Analysis panel, click ⟫ (Zebra). The Zebra Analysis dialog box opens.

3. Keep the default name of **Zebra1**. In the Selection area, clear the **All** option. Select the two curved surfaces in the model.

4. Set the *Thickness* slider halfway between Minimum and Maximum, the *Density* slider at approximately 75%, the *Opacity* at 100%, and the *Display Quality* at 100%, as shown in Figure 6–18.

Figure 6–18

5. Click **Apply** to run the analysis while leaving the dialog box open. The model displays similar to that shown in Figure 6–19. Note how the stripes on any one face do not line up with the stripes on the adjacent face The orientation of the model affects the display of the results. Try and spin the model so that you obtain something similar to that shown.

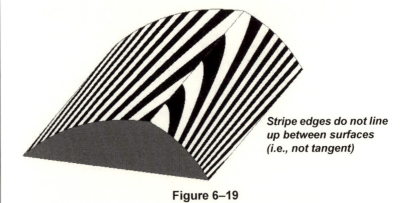

Stripe edges do not line up between surfaces (i.e., not tangent)

Figure 6–19

6. Close the Zebra Analysis dialog box. The analysis is listed in the Model browser, as shown in Figure 6–20.

Figure 6–20

7. In the Model browser, right-click on **Analysis:Zebra1 (On)** and select **Analysis Visibility**. This toggles off the display of the stripes on the model; however, the analysis remains in the model.

Task 2 - Change the tangency between the two curved surfaces.

1. Edit the sketch associated with **Extrusion1**.

2. In the *Sketch* tab>Constrain panel, click . Select the two sketch entities shown on the left side of Figure 6–21 to make them tangent. Select the left edge first and the right second. The sketch updates as shown on the right side.

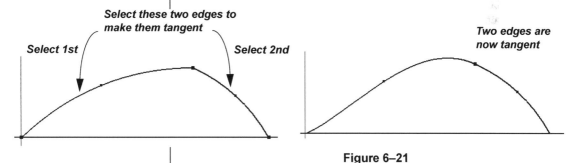

Figure 6–21

3. Finish the sketch.

4. In the Model browser, right-click on **Analysis:Zebra1 (Off)** and select **Analysis Visibility**. This toggles on the display of the stripes on the model, as shown in Figure 6–22. The stripes have updated to reflect the change in tangency between the two surfaces. They now line up with each other; however, they do not smoothly transition to the stripes on the adjacent face. There is an angle between the two.

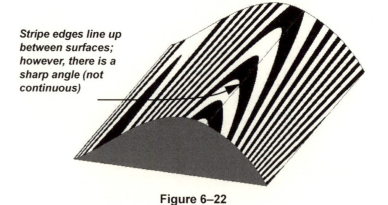

Stripe edges line up between surfaces; however, there is a sharp angle (not continuous)

Figure 6–22

Task 3 - Change the continuity between the two curved surfaces.

1. Edit the sketch associated with **Extrusion1**.

2. In the *Sketch* tab>Constrain panel, click [icon]. Select the two sketch entities shown on the left side of Figure 6–23 to make them G2 Continuous. Select the right edge first and the left second. The sketch updates as shown on the right side.

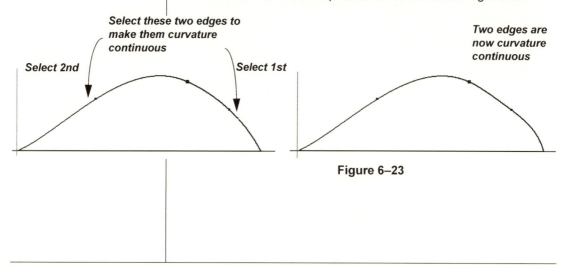

Select these two edges to make them curvature continuous

Select 2nd   *Select 1st*

Two edges are now curvature continuous

Figure 6–23

Analyzing a Model

3. Finish the sketch. The stripes have updated to reflect the change in curvature continuity between the two surfaces, as shown in Figure 6–24. The stripes now line up with one another; and smoothly transition to the stripes on the adjacent face. There is no angle between the two.

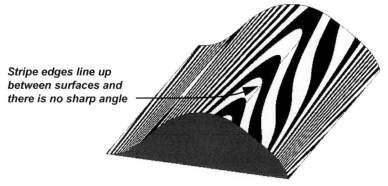

Stripe edges line up between surfaces and there is no sharp angle

Figure 6–24

4. Save the model and close the window.

Task 4 - Perform a Curvature analysis.

Perform a Curvature analysis to obtain a visual representation (in the form of a curvature comb) of the curvature on selected faces. In the next series of tasks, you will use the same model and similar steps to review non-continuous, tangent, and curvature continuity on surfaces.

1. Open **curvature.ipt**. The Zebra analysis has also been included in this model and is automatically toggled off when a model is initially opened.

2. In the *Inspect* tab>Analysis panel, click (Curvature). The Curvature Analysis dialog box opens.

3. Keep the analysis name as **Curvature1**. Select the two curved surfaces on the model, maintain the default settings, and click **OK**. The curvature spines are too small to easily see the curvature change between the two surfaces.

4. In the *Analysis* folder, right-click on **Curvature1** and select **Edit**.

5. Adjust the sliders for each option, as shown in Figure 6–25.

   - (Comb Density): Controls the spacing between the spines.
   - (Comb Scale): Controls the scale or length of the spines.
   - (Surface Density): Controls the density of the sample curves for interior faces.

6. Click **OK**. The model displays as shown on the right side of Figure 6–25.

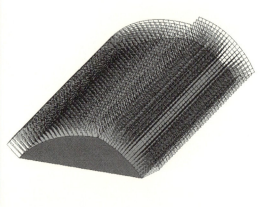

Figure 6–25

7. Orient the model to the Front view using the ViewCube. The model should display similar to that shown in Figure 6–26. Note that the curvature comb separates at the boundary between the two surfaces. This means that the two surfaces are discontinuous.

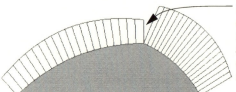

Separation of the curvature comb along the boundary indicates the adjacent faces are discontinuous (i.e., not tangent)

Figure 6–26

8. Using the sketching techniques previously discussed, apply tangency between the two surfaces. The Curvature analysis display updates, as shown in Figure 6–27. It might vary slightly based on the slider values that you set.

Continuation of the curvature comb with different lengths indicates that the adjacent faces are tangent (but not curvature continuous)

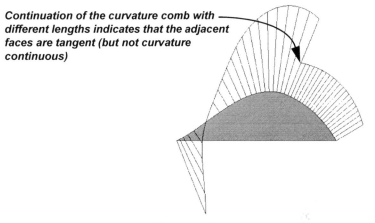

Figure 6–27

9. Using the sketching techniques previously discussed, apply curvature continuity between the two surfaces. Be sure to select the curves in the same order as was described earlier. The Curvature analysis display updates, as shown in Figure 6–28. It might vary slightly based on the slider values that you set.

Continuation of the curvature comb at the same length indicates that the adjacent faces are curvature continuous

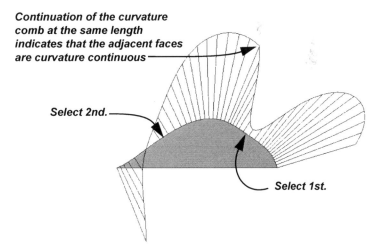

Figure 6–28

Task 5 - Activate and edit an existing analysis.

1. Currently, the **Curvature1** analysis is active. In the Model browser, double-click on the **Zebra1** analysis to activate it. The Zebra analysis displays on the model.

2. In the Model browser, right-click on **Zebra1** and select **Edit**. The Zebra Analysis dialog box opens with the current settings.

3. Increase the Density slider to the maximum value. Click **OK** to apply the changes and close the dialog box. The Zebra analysis updates with more stripes.

4. Right-click on the *Analysis* folder and select **Analysis Visibility** to toggle off the display of all analyses. The model displays without any visible analysis results.

5. Save the model and close the window.

Practice 6b

Draft Analysis

Learning Objective

- Conduct a Draft analysis that enables you to visually evaluate whether the applied draft values in a model are within a specified range.

In this practice, you analyze the draft on a model. The results of the Draft analysis are shown in Figure 6–29, where two distinct draft angles are detected.

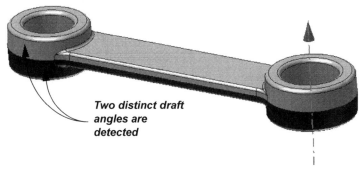

Figure 6–29

Task 1 - Perform a Draft analysis.

1. Open **analyze_connecting_rod.ipt**. Orient the model as shown in Figure 6–30.

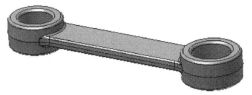

Figure 6–30

2. In the *Inspect* tab>Analysis panel, click (Draft). The Draft Analysis dialog box opens.

3. In the *Selection* area, clear the **All** option and verify that **Faces** is selected.

4. Select all 16 surfaces, including the opposite side's, as shown in Figure 6–31.

5. In the dialog box, in the *Pull* area, click 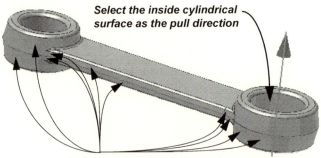 and select the inside cylindrical surface of one of the holes, as shown in Figure 6–31.

Figure 6–31

6. Specify the start and end draft angles as **-1** and **1** degrees respectively, as shown in Figure 6–32.

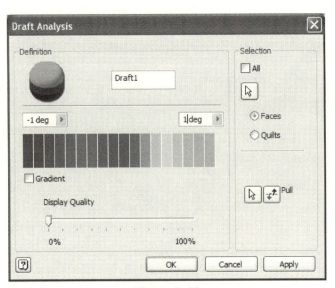

Figure 6–32

7. Click **Apply**.

8. The sides of the part turn two different colors, indicating that the draft angle is different on the top than the bottom. It might be difficult to identify from that shown in Figure 6–33. Compare the color on the model to that in the dialog box; you should be able to tell that the current draft angle on the model is outside of the +/-1 range.

Figure 6–33

9. Click **Cancel**. In the next step you are required to change the range. You cannot reset the range without closing the analysis and editing it.

10. In the Model browser, expand the *Analysis* folder and double-click on **Draft1** to edit it.

11. Change the range to **+/-5** degrees and **Apply** the change. The colors on the model change and now indicate that the draft is within this range. If this is not accurate enough for you can continue to reduce the range or use other tools to measure or show the dimension on these surfaces.

12. Click **Cancel**.

13. Save the model and close the window.

Practice 6c Section Analysis

Learning Objectives

- Conduct a Cross Section analysis that displays the model sectioned through a single plane.
- Conduct a Cross Section analysis that displays the model sectioned through a series of planes and also identifies areas of the model that conflict with specified maximum and minimum wall thickness values.

In this practice, you analyze the sections through a model using a simple section analysis and an advanced section analysis. The results of the analyses are shown in Figure 6–34.

Figure 6–34

Task 1 - Perform a simple cross-section analysis.

A simple cross-section analysis enables you to display the model sectioned through a plane on the part.

1. Open **section_analysis.ipt**. The model displays as shown in Figure 6–35.

Figure 6–35

Analyzing a Model

2. In the *Inspect* tab>Analysis panel, click (Section). The Cross Section Analysis dialog box opens.

3. Keep the default name of **CrossSection1**.

4. On the left side of the dialog box, verify that (Simple) is selected. This enables you to conduct a simple cross-section analysis.

5. The XZ origin plane is already displayed. Select this plane.

6. Flip the direction of the cross-section. The arrow points in the direction where the material is to be removed.

7. Maintain the *Section Offset* value as **0 mm**.

8. Click **OK**. A cutaway view of the part based on the selected plane is displayed, as shown in Figure 6–36.

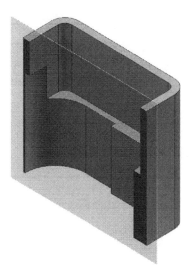

Figure 6–36

9. Clear the visibility of the XZ plane in the model.

10. In the Model browser, right-click on **Analysis:CrossSection1 (On)** and select **Analysis Visibility**. This toggles off the display of the active sectioned view of the model; however, the analysis remains in the model.

Task 2 - Perform an advanced cross-section analysis.

An advanced cross-section analysis is a more advanced analysis that enables you to define multiple section planes by either selecting or creating them, and verify their maximum and minimum wall thicknesses.

1. In the *Inspect* tab>Analysis panel, click (Section).

2. Keep the default name of **CrossSection2**.

3. On the left side of the dialog box, click (Advanced). This enables you to conduct an advanced cross-section analysis using the advanced options shown in Figure 6–37.

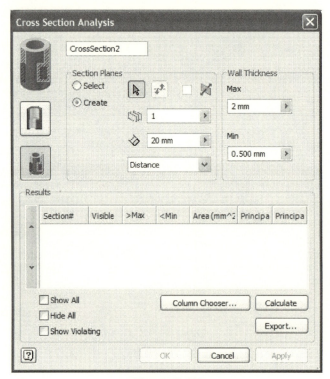

Figure 6–37

4. In this dialog box you can define whether to select an existing plane or create a new one. Keep **Create** selected and select the top plane, as shown in Figure 6–38.

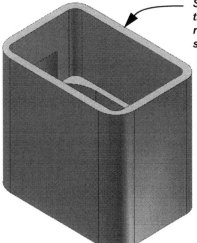

Select this top plane as the placement reference for the section plane

Figure 6–38

5. Click [icon] to flip the direction of the section planes downwards into the model.

6. Change the measurement type from *Distance* to **Spacing**, enter **10** for the number of planes, and **10 mm** for the spacing between the planes. Set the *Max Wall Thickness* to **10 mm** and the *Min Wall Thickness* to **4mm**, as shown in Figure 6–39.

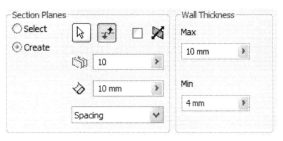

Figure 6–39

7. Click **Apply**. The model updates to display the cross-sections and the dialog box provides numerical data on the sections, as shown in Figure 6–40.

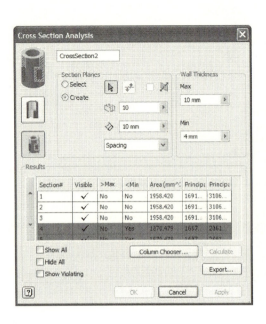

Figure 6–40

8. At the bottom of the dialog box, select **Show Violating**. This toggles off all sections that are within the min and max wall thickness restrictions. Note that seven sections remain. The blue highlighted areas on the model indicate where the wall thickness is smaller than required. The red highlighted areas indicate where the wall thickness is larger than required.

9. Review the list of sections at the bottom of the dialog box. The columns provide information on the section and whether or not it passes the wall thickness criteria that was specified.

10. Click **Cancel** to close the Cross Section Analysis dialog box. Leave the display of the Cross Section Analysis on so that as changes are made to the model, you can see the results in the analysis.

Task 3 - Edit geometry.

1. Edit **Sketch3** and change the 27.204 dimension to **24.5**.

2. Finish the sketch and note that the blue highlighted (min wall thickness) violations are gone.

3. In the Model browser, in the *Analysis* folder, double-click on **CrossSection2** to open the Cross Section Analysis dialog box. Only four sections remain that violate the wall thickness restriction.

Based on this design, there is no combination of dimensions for **Sketch3** that will satisfy both restrictions on the wall thickness. The design requires that the minimum thickness be met; however, the max thickness can be larger.

4. In the Cross Section Analysis dialog box, modify the *Max Wall Thickness* to **20 mm**. Click **Apply**.

5. At the bottom of the dialog box, select **Show Violating**. Now, there are no longer any sections in conflict.

6. Click **Cancel** to close the Cross Section Analysis dialog box.

7. Save the model and close the window.

Chapter Review Questions

1. Which of the following best describes the strips that are displayed when identifying tangent surfaces that are not curvature continuous in a Zebra analysis?

    a. Stripe edges that do not line up between surfaces indicate that the adjacent surfaces are tangent, but not curvature continuous.

    b. Stripe edges that line up between surfaces where there is a sharp angle are tangent, but not curvature continuous.

    c. Stripe edges that line up between surfaces where there is no sharp angle are tangent, but not curvature continuous.

2. Which of the following best describes the curvature comb that is displayed when identifying tangent surfaces that are also curvature continuous in a Curvature analysis?

    a. Separation of the curvature comb along the boundary indicates that adjacent faces are tangent and curvature continuous.

    b. Continuation of the curvature comb with different lengths indicates that adjacent faces are tangent and curvature continuous.

    c. Continuation of the curvature comb at the same length indicates that adjacent faces are tangent and curvature continuous.

3. Which Section analysis type enables you to analyze the min and max wall thickness for a single cross-section through the model?

    a. Simple Section Analysis

    b. Advanced Section Analysis

4. If the default comb spacing between splines is not sufficient to easily study curvature changes on a surface, which setting do you use to change it?

    a.

    b.

    c.

5. A Draft analysis was completed on a model using an acceptable range of +/- 3 degrees. If the color on one surface is outside the color gradient in the Draft Analysis dialog box, the draft on the model is within the acceptable range.

    a. True
    b. False

6. Match the Analysis Type in the left column to its icon in the right column.

Analysis Type	Icon	Answer
a. Zebra Analysis	🟦	_____
b. Draft Analysis	🟦	_____
c. Surface Analysis	🟦	_____
d. Section Analysis	🟦	_____
e. Curvature Analysis	🟦	_____

7. Which of the following statements is true regarding the Model browser shown in Figure 6–41.

    Figure 6–41

    a. Analysis2 is the currently active analysis that is being displayed on the model.
    b. There are four analysis types that are currently being displayed on the model.
    c. Analysis4 is currently the active analysis, however, its visibility is not currently displayed on the model.
    d. There is no analysis being displayed on the model.
    e. None of the above.

Command Summary

Button	Command	Location
	Curvature Analysis	• **Ribbon:** *Inspect* tab>Analysis panel
	Draft Analysis	• **Ribbon:** *Inspect* tab>Analysis panel
	Section Analysis	• **Ribbon:** *Inspect* tab>Analysis panel
	Surface Analysis	• **Ribbon:** *Inspect* tab>Analysis panel
	Zebra Analysis	• **Ribbon:** *Inspect* tab>Analysis panel

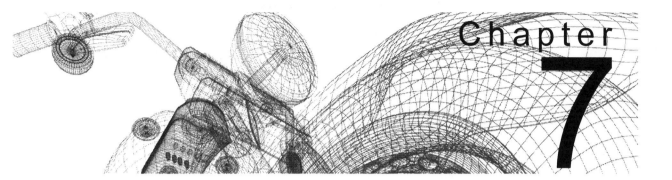

Chapter 7

Generative Shape Design

The Generative Shape Design tool available in the Autodesk® Inventor® software enables designers to set design criteria for a mass reduction target in a model. Based on assigned materials, constraints, and loads, the system returns a design suggestion that can be used to manipulate the model geometry to reduce its mass. Although this tool recommends a new shape, the manipulation is done manually using standard 3D modeling features. Once modified, stress analysis tools should be used on the model to ensure that it meets structural requirements.

Learning Objectives in this Chapter

- Create a Shape Generator study that sets a goal to meet a mass reduction target.
- Assign criteria in a Shape Generator study to accurately define a model's working environment.
- Promote a Shape Generator study to the modeling environment.

7.1 Shape Generator

The Shape Generator tool in Autodesk Inventor enables you to design light-weight models based on specified requirements. First, you must start with an Inventor model that approximates the overall volume or shape that is required. After setting the requirements and running the Shape Generator, you are presented with a 3D mesh design that you can use as a guide to redesign your initial geometry. Figure 7–1 shows the progression of a model from its initial design, through Shape Generator, to the final design.

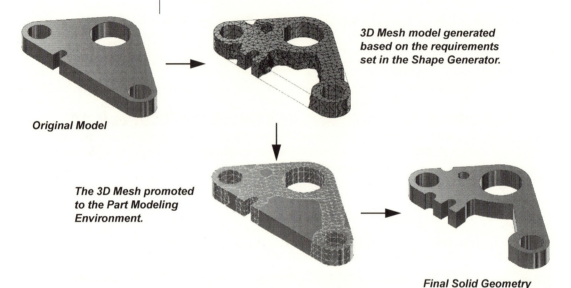

Figure 7–1

How To: Generate a Design using Shape Generator

1. Open the model in the Shape Generator environment.
2. Define the material specification.
3. Apply constraints and loads that will represent the stresses that the part will encounter.
4. Define the Shape Generator Settings.
5. (Optional) Set zones that will be preserved during the analysis.
6. (Optional) Define symmetry in the model, if required.
7. Run the Shape Generator study.
8. Modify the initial design using the Shape Generator's 3D mesh as a guide for making modifications.

Preparing a Model for Shape Generator

Prior to initiating the Shape Generator tool, ensure that the Autodesk Inventor model represents the overall volume and shape of the intended geometry. The model should contain any required contact points (such as holes) that will represent pin locations and surfaces that will sustain forces.

> **Hint: Environment Support**
>
> Shape generator is only supported for single-body part modeling. It cannot be used for multi-body part or assembly design.

Opening Shape Generator

To open the Shape Generator environment, in the *3D Model* tab>Explore panel, click   (Shape Generator). Click **OK** if prompted to review the learning tool. The *Analysis* tab opens as shown in Figure 7–2.

Figure 7–2

By default, a Shape Generator study is added to the Model browser once the *Analysis* tab is opened. The commands on this tab enable you to do the following:

- Create multiple shape generator analyzes and manage them.

- Assign material to an analysis.

- Assign constraints and loads to an analysis to define how the model is loaded in its working environment.

- Set goals and criteria for the analysis. This involves defining regions in the model that should not be changed as well as symmetry planes. Additionally, you set the criteria against which the design will be optimized. For example, reduce weight by x% to achieve a specific weight.

- Generate the optimized shape.

- Export the 3D mesh of the optimized shape to the modeling environment.

*While in the study, you can select **Modeling** at the top of the Model browser to review the features in the design while remaining in the analysis.*

To create additional Shape Generator studies, in the Manage panel, click ![icon] (Create Study), select **Shape Generator** in the Create New Study dialog box, and click **OK**.

> **Hint: Shape Generator in the Stress Analysis Environment**
>
> The Shape Generator functionality can also be accessed in the Stress Analysis environment. In the *3D Model* tab> Simulation panel, click ![icon] (Stress Analysis). Once in the *Analysis* tab, click ![icon] (Create Study), select **Shape Generator** in the Create New Study dialog box and click **OK**.

Material Assignment

In the Material panel, click ![icon] (Assign) to open the Assign Materials dialog box, shown in Figure 7–3.

Figure 7–3

- Maintain the **(As Defined)** option in the Override Material drop-down list to run the generator using the original material that was set in the modeling environment.

- Select an alternate material type in the Override Material drop-down list to study an alternative material.

- Select **Materials** to open and use the Material browser to define materials.

- Set the Safety Factor based on the **Yield Strength** or the **Ultimate Tensile Strength**.

- The material information is stored in the **Material** node for the active study. Each study that is setup in the Shape Generator environment can use a unique material setting.

Applying Constraints

You can assign constraints to the model to accurately define the translational or rotational degrees of freedom that exist in its working environment. **Fixed**, **Pin**, and **Frictionless** constraints can be assigned.

How To: Add Constraints

1. In the *Analysis* tab>Constraints panel, select the type of constraint to be assigned. Alternatively, you can right-click on the **Constraints** node in the Model browser and select the constraint type.

Constraint Type	Description
(Fixed)	Removes all degrees of freedom on a face, edge, or vertex.
(Pin)	When used with cylindrical surfaces, it prevents faces from moving or deforming in combinations of radial, axial, or tangential directions.
(Frictionless)	When used with flat or cylindrical surfaces, it prevents the surface from moving or deforming in the normal direction relative to the surface.

2. In the applicable Constraint dialog box, select (Location) and select the location to which the constraint is being assigned. Select faces, edges, or vertices, as required.

3. Click >> on the dialog box to access the additional constraint settings for each constraint type. The options in this portion of the dialog box enable you to further customize the constraint.

    - The **Display Glyph** option is used to enable/disable the visibility of the constraint glyph on the model.
    - A custom name can be assigned for the constraint, if required.
    - To apply a Fixed constraint with non-zero displacement, click **Use Vector Components** and enter X, Y, or Z values, as required.
    - For cylindrical surfaces, **Pin** constraints can be fixed radially, axially, or tangentially, as required. The default is to be fixed radially and axially.

4. Click **OK** to assign and close the dialog box. Alternatively, click **Apply** to assign the constraint and continue adding additional constraints of the same type.

Once added to the model, constraints are listed in the **Constraints** node in the Model browser. To edit them, right-click on the constraint name and select **Edit <Constraint Type>**.

Applying Loads

To accurately determine a shape using shape generator, you can assign loads that represent the applied load on the model. **Force**, **Pressure**, **Bearing**, **Moment**, **Gravity**, **Remote Force**, and **Body** loads can be assigned.

How To: Add Loads

1. In the *Analysis* tab>Loads panel, select the type of load to be assigned. Alternatively, you can right-click on the **Loads** node in the Model browser and select the load type.

Load Type	Description
(Force)	Assigns a force to a face, edge, or vertex. The force points to the inside of the part. You can assign the direction reference planar to a face or along a straight edge or axes.
(Pressure)	Assigns a pressure load to a face. Pressure is uniform and acts normal to the surface at all locations on the surface.
(Bearing)	Assigns a bearing load to a cylindrical face. By default, the load is along the axis of the cylinder and the direction of the load is radial.
(Moment)	Assigns a moment load to a face. You can assign the direction reference using a planar face, or along a straight edge or axes. The moment is applied around the direction to the selected face.
(Gravity)	Assigns the gravity load normal to the selected face or parallel with the selected edge.
(Remote Force)	Assigns a force at a specific point outside or inside the model. This option is located in the expanded Loads panel.
(Body)	Assign linear acceleration or angular velocity and acceleration for the model using a planar or cylindrical face as the input. This option is located on the expanded Loads panel.

Generative Shape Design

You can only apply one Body load per Shape Generator study.

2. In the applicable Load dialog box, select ![cursor] and select the reference to which the load is being assigned. Select faces, edges, or vertices, as required.
   - A glyph displays on the model indicating the direction in which the load is applied. To change the direction, click ![cursor] in the *Direction* area and select an alternate reference or flip the direction.
3. Define the magnitude of the load.
   - Click ![>>] for Force, Bearing, Moment, Gravity, Remote Force, and Body loads to assign the magnitude values using vector components.
4. Click ![>>] on the dialog box to access additional settings for each load type. The options in this portion of the dialog box enable you to further customize the load.
   - The **Display Glyph** option can be enabled/disabled to control the load glyph display, as required.
   - The scale and color of the glyph display can be modified.
   - A custom name can be assigned for the load, if required.
5. Click **OK** to assign and close the dialog box. Alternatively, click **Apply** to assign the load and continue adding additional loads of the same type.

Once loads are added to the model they are listed in the **Loads** node in the Model browser. To edit them, right-click on the constraint name and select **Edit <Force Load>**.

> **Hint: Multiple Loads on a Face**
>
> Consider using the **Split** command to split a single face if the face experiences multiple loading situations.

Shape Generator Settings

The Shape Generator settings enable you to define the design criteria. To open the Shape Generator Settings dialog box (shown in Figure 7–4) click ▭ (Shape Generator Settings). By default, the 3D mesh model will be generated to maximize stiffness; however, you can also define the following additional criteria:

- Reduce the mass by a specified percentage or reduce it to a specific value.

- Define a specific member size that must be maintained during 3D mesh creation. This helps ensure that the mesh does not generate a wall thicknesses that can not be manufactured or might fail structural testing.

- The *Mesh Resolution* area provides a slider and a *Value* field that can be used to set the mesh resolution. A finer setting results in a smoother, higher quality mesh; however, it requires increased run time.

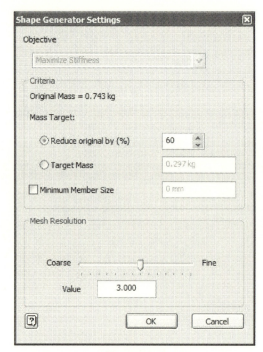

Figure 7–4

Generative Shape Design

Preserving Regions

In most models, there will be regions of the design that should not be removed when generating a suggested 3D mesh. For example, specific areas around bolt holes or other supporting features may need to be maintained to allow the model to function as required.

How To: Preserve an Area on the Model

1. In the Goals and Criteria panel, click (Preserve Region).
2. In the Preserve Region dialog box, click and select a face on the model. Based on the selection of the face, a default preserved region boundary will appear on the model.
   - If a planar face is selected, a bounding box displays around the face, as shown in Figure 7–5.

 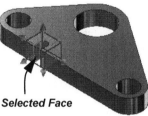

Figure 7–5

   - If a cylindrical face is selected, a bounding cylinder displays around the face, as shown in Figure 7–6.

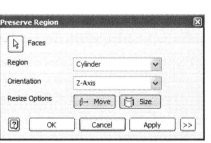 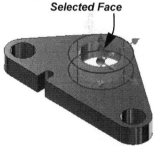

Figure 7–6

   - If the assumption of **Box** or **Cylinder** is not correct, you can switch the option in the *Region* drop-down list.

3. Refine the location and size of the bounding shape.
   - Select **Move** and drag the center point of the displayed triad to reposition the bounding shape on the model.
   - Select **Size** and activate and drag any of the handles that radiate from the bounding shape.
   - Click [>>] to enter specific values for the center point and the bounding shape dimensions.
4. (Optional) In the expanded portion of the dialog box ([>>]) you can modify the glyph color, control its visibility, or enter a custom name for the preserved region.
5. Click **OK** to create the preserved region. Alternatively, click **Apply** to create the region and continue creating additional regions.

Once preserved regions are added to the model they are listed in the **Preserved Regions** node in the Model browser. To edit them, right-click on the constraint name and select **Edit Preserved Region**.

Assigning Symmetry

Symmetry planes can be assigned in the model to force the Shape Generator to produce a 3D mesh result that is symmetric about a selected plane or up to three planes (XY, XZ, or YZ).

How To: Assign Symmetry

1. In the Goals and Criteria panel, click [icon] (Symmetry Plane).
2. By default, the symmetry planes are placed at the center of mass and are aligned with the global coordinate system. If required, use any of the following to modify the location of the default symmetry planes:
   - To align the symmetry plane with a local UCS, click [icon] (Local UCS) and select an active UCS. The symmetry plane is created in the local XY plane of the UCS.
   - To place at the center of mass, click [icon] (Center of mass). The UCS and symmetry plane are placed at the center of mass of the part.
   - To place at the center of the bounding box of the part, click [icon] (Center of bounding box). The UCS and symmetry plane are placed at the center of bounding box of the part.

Generative Shape Design

3. Toggle the active planes ( ), as required, to define the model symmetry. Active planes appear red in the model.
4. (Optional) Click >> to toggle the display of the symmetry glyph and assign a name for symmetry definition.
5. Click **OK** to close the dialog box. The symmetry Plane dialog box and a single symmetry plane are shown in Figure 7–7.

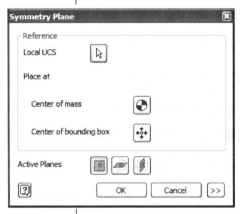

Figure 7–7

Once symmetry planes are added to the model, they are listed in the **Symmetry Planes** node in the Model browser. To edit them, right-click on the constraint name and select **Edit Symmetry Plane**.

Run the Shape Generator

Once the analysis has been setup, click (Generate Shape) to open the Generate Shape dialog box, as shown in Figure 7–8. Click **Run** to start the shape generator.

The expandable area at the bottom of the dialog box reports warnings or errors while the process is being run.

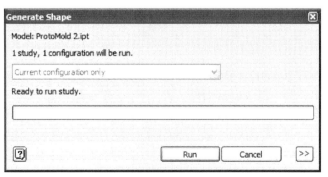

Figure 7–8

Once shape generation is complete, you are presented with a recommended 3D mesh model that can be used to guide your model design. Figure 7–9 shows the original model and a resultant mesh model after constraints, loads, and criteria were set.

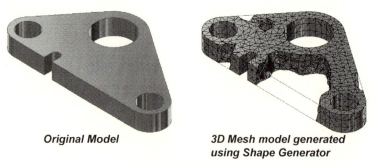

Original Model   *3D Mesh model generated using Shape Generator*

Figure 7–9

Promote the 3D Mesh Model

Once the mesh model has been generated, it can be promoted to the modeling environment to be used as a guide for making modeling changes to the geometry. In the Export panel, click

(Promote Shape) and select whether to copy the 3D mesh model directly to the part modeling environment (**Current Part File**) or to an STL file (**STL File**) that can be imported separately. Once the 3D mesh model is displayed, in the part modeling environment, you can use it as a guide to remove material from the part geometry.

Figure 7–10 shows an example of the promoted 3D mesh model in the part modeling environment and the final geometry based on suggested areas to be removed.

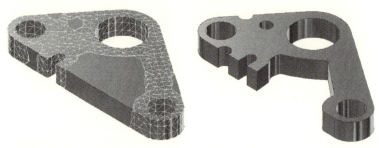

3D Model Promoted to the Part Modeling Environment   *Final Solid Geometry*

Figure 7–10

Consider the following when using a 3D mesh model to make changes to your design:

- When making geometry changes to the model, consider using lines and arcs where possible to help ensure that the final geometry is manufacturable.

- Not all geometry needs to be removed. This is a recommendation based on the criteria set.

- Consider using the Stress Analysis environment to further analyze the structural integrity of the final geometry.

The constraints and loads set in Shape Generator can be reused in the Stress Analysis environment.

> **Hint: Visual Style**
>
> Consider using the Wireframe visual style when using the 3D mesh model to make design changes. This enables you to see how the mesh model looks inside the solid geometry.

Practice 7a

Generating a Design using Shape Generator

Practice Objectives

- Create a Shape Generator study that sets a goal to meet a mass reduction target.
- Assign material, constraint, and load criteria in a Shape Generator study to accurately define a model's working environment.
- Set regions in the model that will not be removed after the Shape Generator study is complete.
- Define a symmetry plane in the model.
- Promote a Shape Generator study to the modeling environment.

In this practice, you will open a model that represents the overall shape and volume of an actuator mounting block that exists in a top-level assembly. The Shape Generator tool will be used to suggest modeling changes that helps to reduce the mass of the model to under 3 lbs. You will define the material, constraints, loads, preserved regions, and a symmetry plane prior to running the study. Figure 7–11 shows the model's progress through the practice.

 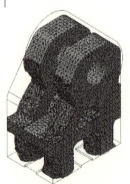  

Original Geometry   **Analyzed 3D Mesh**   **Promoted Shape Geometry**   **Modified Solid Geometry**

Figure 7–11

Task 1 - Open an existing part model in the Shape Generator environment.

1. Open **Actuator Block.ipt** from the practice files folder.

2. Change the model display to **Shaded with Hidden Edges** to better visualize the interior of the model.

Generative Shape Design

3. In the *3D Model* tab> Explore panel, click (Shape Generator).

4. Click **OK** if prompted with the Shape Generator dialog box. This provides an introduction to the tool and the option to access Help documentation. If this was previously disabled, you will not be shown this dialog box.

5. The *Analysis* tab becomes the active tab and the model and Model browser display as shown in Figure 7–12. While in the study, you can select **Modeling** at the top of the Model browser to review the features in the design while remaining in the analysis. The overall shape of the model was created using the part modeling features.

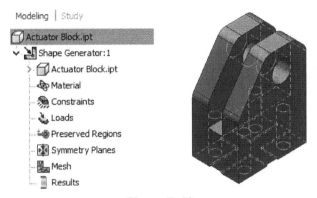

Figure 7–12

Task 2 - Define the material specification.

1. In the Material panel, click (Assign) to open the Assign Materials dialog box, as shown in Figure 7–13.

Figure 7–13

2. Maintain the **(As Defined)** option in the Override Material drop-down list. This uses the material that was defined when the model was created.

3. Click **OK**.

Pin constraints prevent faces from moving or deforming in combinations of radial, axial, or tangential directions

Task 3 - Apply constraints and loads that will represent the stresses that the part will encounter.

1. In the *Analysis* tab>Constraints panel, click (Pin).

2. Ensure that the (Location) button is active and select the cylindrical surface shown in Figure 7–14.

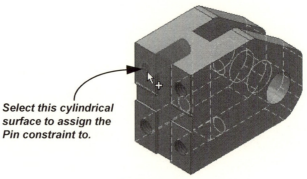

Select this cylindrical surface to assign the Pin constraint to.

Figure 7–14

3. Click **Apply** to assign the constraint and leave the dialog box open. The Pin glyph displays on the model.

4. Continue to apply three additional Pin constraints to the remaining 3 support holes on the bottom of the model. Once assigned, the model and Model browser should display as shown in Figure 7–15.

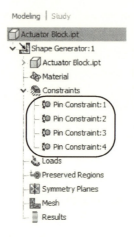

A Pin constraint glyph displays on each support holes and the Constraints node is populated in the Model browser.

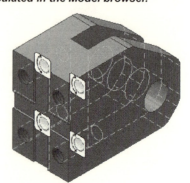

Figure 7–15

5. Click **Cancel** to close the dialog box.

Generative Shape Design

6. Change the view display to **Shaded** if you had been working in an alternate view style.

7. In the *Analysis* tab>Loads panel, click  (Bearing).

8. Ensure that the  (Faces) button is active and select the two cylindrical faces shown in Figure 7–16 as the reference faces to which the **Bearing** load is being assigned (blue faces).

9. By default, the load is along the axis of the cylinder and the direction of the load is radial. Click  in the *Direction* area and select the face shown in Figure 7–16 as the direction reference (green face). A glyph displays on the model indicating the direction in which the load is applied.

To assign the load based on the vector directions, expand the dialog box and enter the values in the additional fields that are provided.

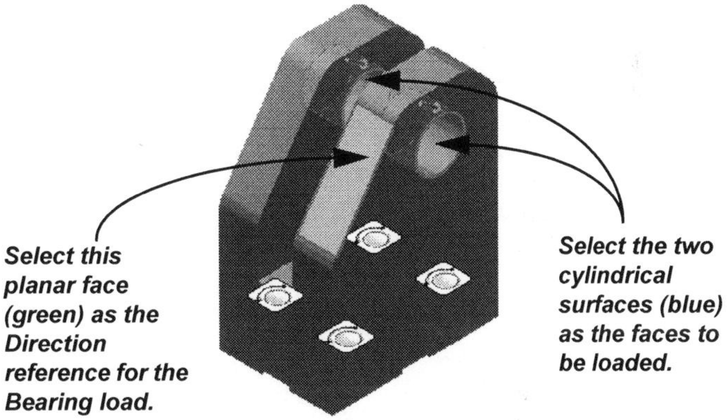

Select this planar face (green) as the Direction reference for the Bearing load.

Select the two cylindrical surfaces (blue) as the faces to be loaded.

Figure 7–16

10. Set the load *Magnitude* to **5000 N**, as shown in Figure 7–17.

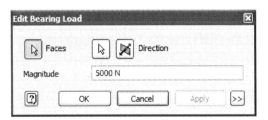

Figure 7–17

11. Click on the dialog box to access the additional settings. Enter **Bearing** as the custom name for the load.

12. Click **OK** to assign the load and close the dialog box. The **Bearing** load has been added to the **Loads** node in the Model browser.

Task 4 - Define the Shape Generator Settings.

The current mass of the model is 4.51 Lbs. The design goal in this model is to reduce the weight to under 3 lbs.

1. To open the Shape Generator Settings dialog box, click ![icon] (Shape Generator Settings).

2. Select **Target Mass** and enter **2.99lbmass**, as shown in Figure 7–18.

3. Maintain the *Mesh Resolution* slider at **3.000**, as shown in Figure 7–18.

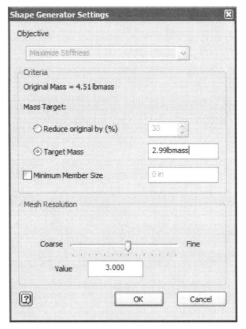

Figure 7–18

4. Click **OK**.

Task 5 - Set zones that will be preserved

1. In the Goals and Criteria panel, click ![icon] (Preserve Region).

2. In the Preserve Region dialog box, click ![icon] and select one of the cylindrical faces that was used in placing the **Bearing** load.

Generative Shape Design

3. The Preserve Region dialog box updates to create a cylindrical region. Use the arrows on the various sides of the cylindrical bounding box to drag it, as shown in Figure 7–19. Ensure that the preserved area extends the width of the part and preserves the material above and around the holes.

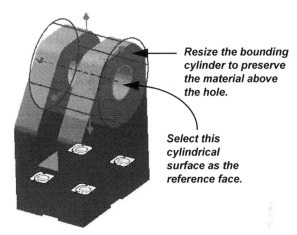

Resize the bounding cylinder to preserve the material above the hole.

Select this cylindrical surface as the reference face.

Figure 7–19

4. Click **OK**.

5. Reorient the model to the **BOTTOM** view using the ViewCube.

6. In the Model browser, expand the **Constraints** node. Right-click on **Pin Constraint1** and clear the **Visibility** option, as shown in Figure 7–20. This removes the glyph from the model display.

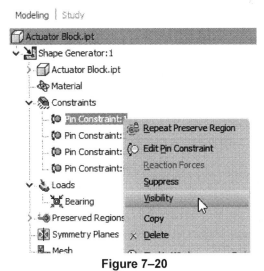

Figure 7–20

7. Clear the glyph display for the other three Pin constraints.

8. In the Goals and Criteria panel, click (Preserve Region).

9. Ensure that is active and select the edge of the circular hole, as shown in the BOTTOM view in Figure 7–21.

10. Click to expand the dialog box. In the *Region Dimensions* area, set the *Radius* value to **0.4 in** and the *Length* value to **1.1 in**. Ensure that the length is extending into the model, as shown in the FRONT view in Figure 7–21. In the *Center Point* area, set the *Y* value to **.55in**.

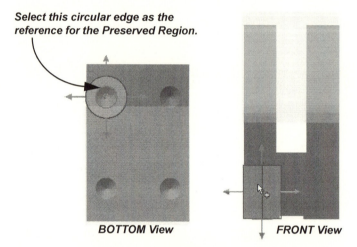

Figure 7–21

11. Create three identical preserved regions on the other support holes. The model should display as shown in Figure 7–22.

Figure 7–22

One additional preserve area is required to ensure that material is not removed that will affect the stability along the X axis.

12. Click (Preserve Region), if the dialog box is not already open.

13. Select the planar face that connects the two symmetric sides. Using the ViewCube, reorient the model to size the bounding box similar to that shown in Figure 7–23. The box should extend the width of the model and extend into the preserve areas for the support holes. Click **OK** to create the preserved area.

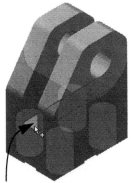 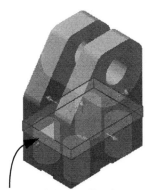

Select this planar face to place the bounding box.   *Resize the bounding box to create this preserved area.*

Figure 7–23

14. All six preserved areas are listed in the **Preserved Regions** node in the Model browser.

Task 6 - Define symmetry in the model.

The model is symmetric about the YZ plane. This should be assigned as criteria to ensure that the 3D mesh model is symmetric.

1. In the Goals and Criteria panel, click (Symmetry Plane).

2. By default, the symmetry planes are placed at the center of mass and are aligned with the global coordinate system. No change is required to reposition the planes for this model.

3. Toggle the active planes so that the YZ plane is the only plane highlighted in red, as shown in Figure 7–24.

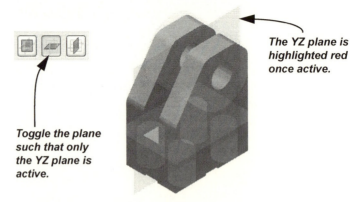

Figure 7–24

4. Click **OK** to assign the symmetry plane.

Task 7 - Run the Shape Generator and promote the study.

Now that the analysis has been setup, you can run the shape generator and promote the study to the model environment.

1. Click (Generate Shape) to open the Generate Shape dialog box.

2. Click **Run** to start the shape generator analysis.

3. Once complete, a 3D mesh should be returned, similar to that shown in Figure 7–25.

The analysis may take a few minutes to complete. The run time will vary depending on your computer.

Additionally, warnings may be presented as the geometry is optimized.

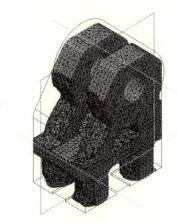

Figure 7–25

4. In the Export panel, click (Promote Shape) and select **Current Part File** to promote the optimized 3D mesh directly to the part model. Click **OK**.

5. Click **OK** in the Promote Shape dialog box that displays. This dialog box, indicates that shape promotion was successful and provides recommended steps. The 3D mesh displays embedded in the solid geometry, as shown in Figure 7–26.

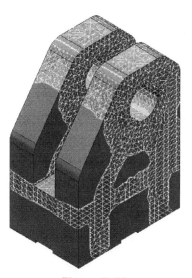

Figure 7–26

Task 8 - Modify the initial design using the Shape Generator's 3D mesh.

If time permits, try to create the sketches in your own model.

1. Open **Actuator Block_Final.ipt**. This model already has been optimized using Shape Generator and sketches that approximate the material removal have been created for you.

2. Using the **Side Cut Profiles** and **Front Cut Profile** sketches, create the geometry shown in Figure 7–27.

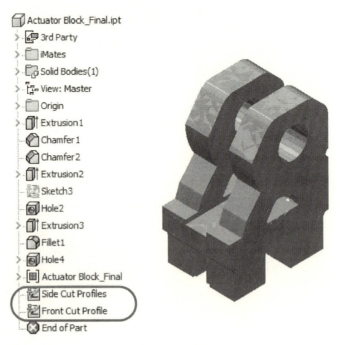

Figure 7–27

3. Open the model's iProperties dialog box and update its physical properties. Note that the mass is still slightly over 3lbs.

4. To further reduce the mass of the model, you can add fillets to the edges of the geometry, modify the sketches that were used to remove the material, and/or change to a lower weight steel. Ultimately, the changes that are made must still be analyzed for structural integrity to ensure it can withstand its loads; however, the Shape Generator has provided a satisfactory starting point.

5. Save the model and close the window.

Chapter Review Questions

1. The Shape Generator tool automatically modifies the initial geometry of the model when it is promoted to the part modeling environment.

    a. True
    b. False

2. In which Autodesk Inventor working environment can you gain access to the Shape Generator tool? (Select all that apply.)

    a. Part Modeling
    b. Assembly Modeling
    c. Drawing
    d. Presentation
    e. Stress Analysis

3. Only a single shape generation study can be setup in a model.

    a. True
    b. False

4. Which of the following constraints can be added to the model to accurately describe how it is constrained in its working environment? (Select all that apply.)

    a. **Bearing**
    b. **Fixed**
    c. **Force**
    d. **Frictionless**
    e. **Gravity**
    f. **Moment**
    g. **Pin**
    h. **Pressure**

5. Which of the following cannot be controlled using the additional options in the expandable load creation dialog boxes? (Select all that apply.)

   a. The location reference of the load.
   b. The direction reference for a load.
   c. The magnitude of the load broken down into vector components.
   d. The assignment of a custom load name.
   e. The display of the load glyph in the model.
   f. The scale of the load glyph when it is displayed in the model.

6. Which of the following are valid when setting the criteria for a Shape Generator analysis? (Select all that apply.)

   a. The volume of the model is set to reach a target value.
   b. The mass of the model is set to reach a target value.
   c. The volume of the model is reduced by a set percentage value.
   d. The mass of the model is reduced by a set percentage value.

7. A cylindrical face that is selected as the reference for a preserved region cannot use the **Box** option to define its boundary.

   a. True
   b. False

8. How many planes can be selected during a Shape Generator analysis to define symmetry in a model?

   a. 1
   b. 2
   c. 3
   d. Unlimited

Command Summary

Button	Command	Location
	Assign (material)	• **Ribbon:** *Analysis* tab>Material panel • **Context Menu:** In Model browser with Material node selected
	Bearing Load	• **Ribbon:** *Analysis* tab>Loads panel • **Context Menu:** In Model browser with Loads node selected
	Body Load	• **Ribbon:** *Analysis* tab>Loads panel • **Context Menu:** In Model browser with Loads node selected
	Create Study	• **Ribbon:** *Analysis* tab>Manage panel
	Finish Analysis	• **Ribbon:** *Analysis* tab>Exit panel
	Fixed Constraint	• **Ribbon:** *Analysis* tab>Constraints panel • **Context menu:** In Model browser with Constraints node selected • **Context menu:** In graphics window
	Force Load	• **Ribbon:** *Analysis* tab>Loads panel • **Context Menu:** In Model browser with Loads node selected • **Context menu:** In graphics window
	Frictionless Constraint	• **Ribbon:** *Analysis* tab>Constraints panel • **Context Menu:** In Model browser with Constraints node selected
	Generate Shape	• **Ribbon:** *Analysis* tab>Run panel • **Context Menu:** In Model browser with Study node selected
	Gravity Load	• **Ribbon:** *Analysis* tab>Loads panel • **Context Menu:** In Model browser with Loads node selected
	Mesh View	• **Ribbon:** *Analysis* tab>Mesh panel • **Context Menu:** In Model browser with Study node selected • **Context menu:** In graphics window
	Moment Load	• **Ribbon:** *Analysis* tab>Loads panel • **Context Menu:** In Model browser with Loads node selected
	Pin Constraint	• **Ribbon:** *Analysis* tab>Constraints panel • **Context Menu:** In Model browser with Constraints node selected
	Preserve Region	• **Ribbon:** *Analysis* tab>Goals and Criteria panel

	Pressure Load	• **Ribbon:** *Analysis* tab>Loads panel • **Context Menu:** In Model browser with Loads node selected
	Promote Shape	• **Ribbon:** *Analysis* tab>Export panel
	Remote Force Load	• **Ribbon:** *Analysis* tab>Loads panel • **Context Menu:** In Model browser with Loads node selected
	Shape Generator	• **Ribbon:** *3D Model* tab>Explore panel
	Shape Generator Settings	• **Ribbon:** *Analysis* tab>Goals and Criteria panel
	Stress Analysis	• **Ribbon:** *3D Model* tab>Simulation panel
	Symmetry Plane	• **Ribbon:** *Analysis* tab>Goals and Criteria panel

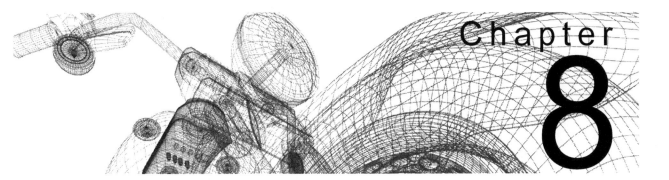

Chapter 8

Introduction to Surfacing

The Autodesk® Inventor® software enables you to combine traditional surface modeling with advanced parametric modeling technology to create seamless, hybrid surface-solid models. Features such as an extrude, revolve, loft, or sweep can also be used to create surfaces or solids.

Learning Objectives in this Chapter

- Set the Surface Output type using the Feature dialog box or the mini-toolbar, so that features are created as surfaces.
- Create a planar surface by referencing a closed sketched profile.
- Create a three-dimensional surface that is defined by a series of planar and non-planar edges.
- Create a surface that is normal, tangent, or swept from reference entities to create surface geometry.
- Combine individual surface features into one quilted surface that can be used as a single surface for modeling.
- Add or remove material to a model by referencing a surface that defines the shape of the material to be added/removed.
- Create a surface that is offset by a specified amount from the face of a solid feature or another surface.
- Create solid geometry using surface geometry.
- Control whether a surface is displayed in a drawing views.

8.1 Introduction to Surfaces

A surface is a non-solid, zero-thickness feature that can define a contoured shape. Surfaces help capture the design intent of complex shapes that are not easily defined using solids. Surfaces can also be used as references to help create other features (solid and non-solid). The term "quilt" is often used to describe surface features and can refer to a single surface feature or a group of stitched (combined) surface features. Surface features can be used to do the following:

- Create surface models that can be converted to solid models.
- Create a "skin" over an imported wireframe model.
- Create complex solid cuts and extrusions.
- Create a solid form.
- Define complex curves.

A feature created using surfaces is shown in Figure 8–1.

Figure 8–1

Surfaces display in the Model browser with symbols specific to their type, as shown in Figure 8–2. They are also listed in the **Surface Bodies** node at the top of the Model browser.

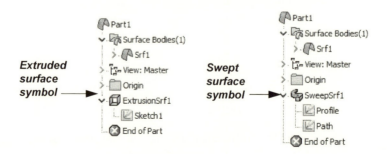

Figure 8–2

Introduction to Surfacing

8.2 Basic Surfaces

When creating most features (such as extrudes, lofts, revolves, sweeps, and coils), you must select an *Output* type. This determines if the feature is created as a solid or a surface. To set the *Output* type as a surface, click ▭ (Surface) in the feature dialog box or select **Surface output** in the mini-toolbar, as shown in Figure 8–3.

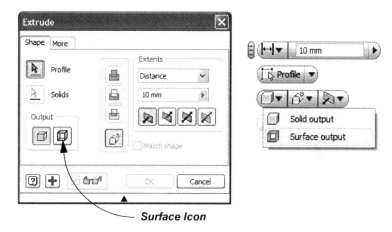

Surface Icon

Figure 8–3

- Creating a solid requires a closed profile, but a surface can be created using an open or closed profile. Defining the remaining options for a surface is the same as creating a solid feature and can be done using the dialog box or the mini-toolbar.

- All surfaces created in a part model are created as their own surface bodies, and are independently listed in the **Surface Bodies** node of the Model browser. Even if surfaces are combined, they create a new body in the list.

8.3 Patch Surfaces

Patch surfaces are surfaces created from closed 2D or 3D sketches, or existing closed boundary edges. Examples of a 2D and two 3D patch surfaces are shown in Figure 8–4.

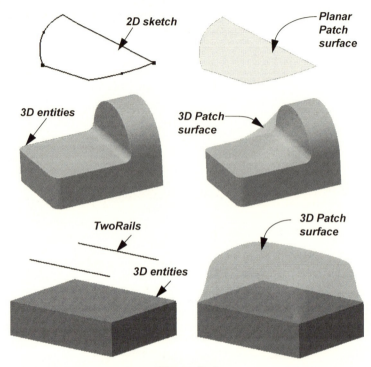

Figure 8–4

How To: Create Patch Surface

1. In the *Surface* panel, click (Patch). The Boundary Patch dialog box opens.
2. Select a closed 2D or 3D sketch, or select edges on existing objects to form a closed profile.
3. (Optional) If edges are selected, you can also assign a boundary condition (i.e., Free, Tangent, Curvature Continuous, or G2) to the edge and its adjacent surfaces in the *Condition* area.
4. To further refine the shape of the patch surface, click (Guide Rails) and select curves or points to drive the shape of the patch.
5. Click **OK** to create the surface.

- Surface patches are identified by the symbol in the Model browser.

*When selecting the edges to form a patch, consider using **Automatic Edge Chain** to select adjacent edges together instead of individually selecting them.*

8.4 Ruled Surfaces

The **Ruled Surface** option enables you to create normal, tangent, and swept surfaces. A ruled surface is a surface where a straight line lies at every point on the surface. Common uses for this type of surface includes creating parting surfaces for mold design, creating surfaces that can split a body, or adding pockets.

How To: Create a Ruled Surface

1. Click (Ruled Surface) to open the Ruled Surface dialog box, as shown in Figure 8–5.

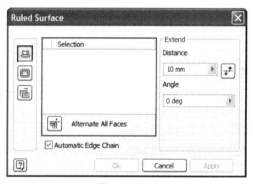

Figure 8–5

2. On the left-hand side of the dialog box, select the type of ruled surface.

   - Click (Normal) to create a ruled surface that remains normal along the edge reference.
   - Click (Tangent) to create a ruled surface that remains tangent along the edge reference.
   - Click (Sweep) to create a ruled surface that follows a direction vector along the edge reference.

3. Define references to create the ruled surface.
   - For Tangent or Normal ruled surfaces, select an edge reference to create the surface. Multiple edges can be selected. The references are listed in the *Edges Selection* area.
   - For Sweep ruled surfaces, select an edge or sketch to define the path and a vector to define the direction. The direction vector can be a face, edge, or axis. If a sketch is being used, it must already exist in the model.

The dialog box options vary depending on the type of ruled surface you select.

For Tangent and Normal ruled surfaces, select ***Automatic Edge Chain*** *so that when selecting an edge, any edge that is tangent to it is also selected. Clear this option to select individual edges.*

4. Enter a value in the *Distance* field to extend the edge(s) or sketch.

    - Select ![Flip] (Flip) to reverse the extension direction.
    - Select ![Alternate] (Alternate All Faces) to reverse the faces that are being used to define the directions.

5. (Optional) Enter an *Angle* value for the ruled surface.

6. Click **OK** to complete the ruled surface.

    Figure 8–6 shows examples of the three types of ruled surfaces.

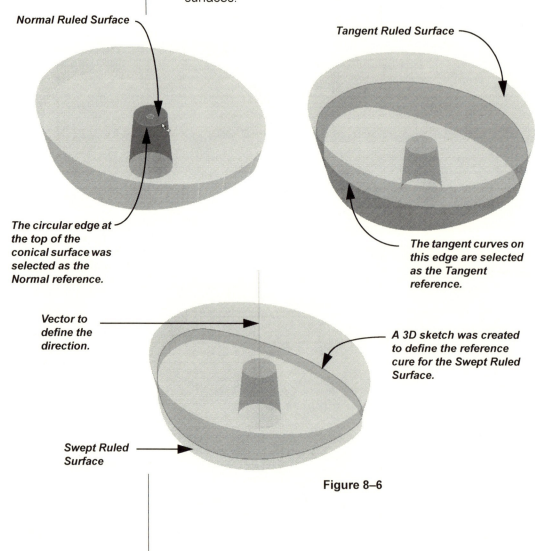

Figure 8–6

8.5 Stitch Surfaces

A Stitch surface combines individual surface features into one surface feature. This option is useful when you want to split a part or surface, solidify a group of enclosed surfaces, or replace a face with a single item. When you stitch a group of surfaces together, you form a quilt. The quilt can be converted to a solid if it forms a closed volume.

How To: Stitch Surfaces to Form a Quilt

1. In the Surface panel, click ▦ (Stitch) to create a quilt. The Stitch dialog box opens as shown in Figure 8–7.

Figure 8–7

2. Select the surfaces to create a quilt. The edges you are stitching must be the same size and adjacent to each other.
3. Click **Apply** to apply the feature. Continue stitching surfaces together or click **Done** to finish.

- Stitched quilts are listed in the Model browser, as shown in Figure 8–8 and a surface is added to the **Surface Bodies** node.

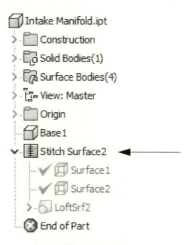

Figure 8–8

- To edit a stitched (quilt) surface, right-click it and select **Edit Feature**. When editing, you can add more surfaces to form larger quilts.

8.6 Sculpting with Surfaces

Sculpt can be used to add or remove material from a solid body using surfaces and work planes. Use Sculpt to create complex or stylized solid shapes that would be difficult to create using solid features. The selected surfaces and work planes, along with all the automatically selected solid faces of the model, are used to create a fully enclosed boundary that defines the solid volume to be added or removed.

Unlike the split and stitch options, sculpt surface references do not need to be trimmed.

How To: Add or Remove Material Using Sculpt

1. In the Surface panel, click (Sculpt). The Sculpt dialog box opens, as shown in Figure 8–9.

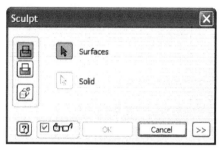

Figure 8–9

2. Click (Add) or (Remove).
3. If material is added as a result of the sculpt, you can click

    to create a new solid body from the resulting sculpted geometry.
4. Select the surfaces and work planes to form the boundary to add or remove. An example where one surface is selected and two solid faces are automatically selected is shown in Figure 8–10.

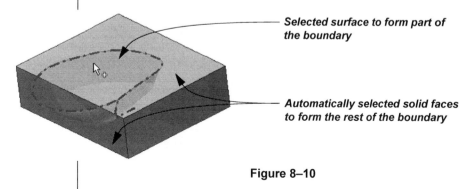

Figure 8–10

5. Define the direction, as required, by clicking >> and using the direction drop-down list for each individual surface, as shown in Figure 8–11. When adding material, the arrow highlighted in green shows what will be added. When removing material, the portion highlighted in red is what will be removed.

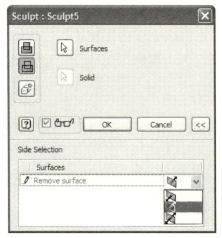

Figure 8–11

6. Click **OK** to complete the feature. An example of material removed using the sculpt feature is shown in Figure 8–12.

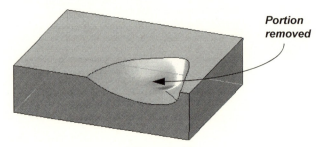

Figure 8–12

8.7 Thickening & Offsetting a Surface

Thickening and offsetting enables you to change the thickness of a part or surface or create offset surfaces from part faces or other surfaces. If you add thickness to a surface, it will become a solid. This option works only in the part environment. Surfaces in the construction environment cannot be thickened or offset. An offset surface created from a solid feature face and then thickened is shown in Figure 8–13.

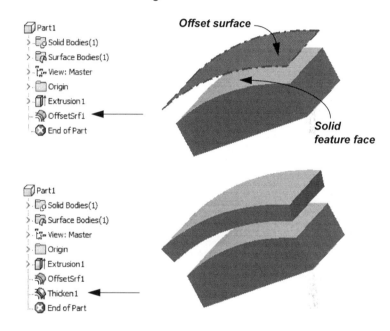

Figure 8–13

How To: Thicken/Offset a Surface Feature

1. In the Surface panel, click (Thicken/Offset) to change the thickness of a part or surface, or to create offset surfaces from part faces or other surfaces.
2. Set **Automatic Blending**, if required.
   - This option enables the blending of features when a solid face is selected. As the feature was thickened, this option blends the feature with any other interfering feature.
   - If the **Automatic Blending** option is cleared, you can select to **Join**, **Cut**, or **Intersect** the thickened face with the model.

*If a surface feature is selected to be thickened, **Automatic Blending** becomes unavailable.*

3. Define the options on the *Thicken/Offset* tab, as shown in Figure 8–14:
   - Select the reference surface (**Quilt**) or face (**Face**).
   - Enter the offset distance.
   - Define whether the new feature is a solid or a surface.
   - Define whether material is added or removed.
   - Define the direction that the new feature is created.
   - If the resulting feature is a solid, you can click [icon] to create a new solid body from the resulting thickened geometry.

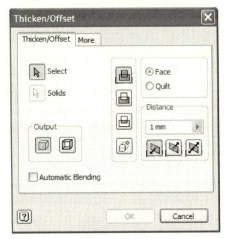

Figure 8–14

4. Select the *More* tab. The options display as shown in Figure 8–15.

Figure 8–15

Introduction to Surfacing

Option	Description
Automatic Face Chain	Automatically selects surfaces adjacent and tangent to the selected surface. This should be selected before selecting the face.
Create Vertical Surfaces	Enables you to create additional surfaces between the original and new surfaces on the edges between surfaces (not on outside edges).
Allow Approximation	Enables the system to deviate from the specified thickness when creating the surface. This can be used when a precise solution does not exist. If enabled you can select from **Mean** deviation, **Never too thin**, and **Never too thick**. Mean divides the thickness to fall both above and below the specified distance. Never too thin preserves the minimum distance. Never too thick preserves the maximum distance.
Optimized and **Specify Tolerance**	Affect the computation time when approximating a thickening. Optimized minimizes computation time by using a reasonable tolerance. Specify tolerance takes more time and uses a specified tolerance.

5. Click **OK** to complete the operation.

8.8 Surfaces in Drawing Views

When you include both solid and surface geometry in a model, the surfaces are not automatically shown in associated drawing views. In these situations, you must set the view so that it includes surfaces. To include surface bodies in views, in the Drawing View dialog box, select the *Recovery Options* tab and select **Include Surface Bodies**, as shown in Figure 8–16.

*If the **Include Surface Bodies** option was disabled when the view was created, it can be enabled by editing the drawing view.*

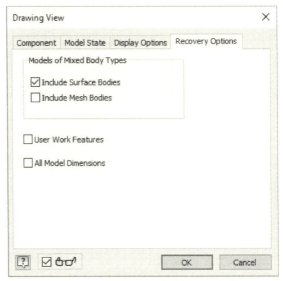

Figure 8–16

Once views with the **Include Surface Bodies** option are placed, you can individually control surface visibility for each view directly in the Model browser.

- To control the display of individual surfaces in a view, expand the view containing the surface in the Model browser and in the **Surface Bodies** node, right-click on the required surface and clear/select **Visibility**, as required, as shown in Figure 8–17.

By default, if the surface displays (is visible) in the model, it also displays in the drawing view.

Figure 8–17

- To control the visibility all surfaces that exist in a part at once, in the Model browser, expand the view node, right-click on the required part name, and clear/select **Include All Surfaces**, as required, as shown in Figure 8–18.

Alternatively, you can right-click on the Surface Bodies folder and clear/select **Visibility** *to control the visibility of all surfaces at once.*

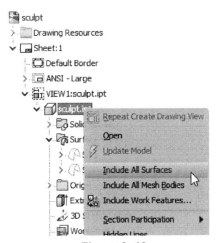

Figure 8–18

Consider the following:

- If a surface is added to the model, the drawing view only updates to reflect the display of the new surface if the **Include Surface Bodies** recovery option was originally set when the view was created.

- If a surface is deleted from the model, the drawing view updates.

- Construction surfaces cannot be included in a drawing view. If you want to include a construction surface, you must first promote it to the Part environment. Surfaces included in a **Repaired Geometry** node display in a drawing view.

Surfaces in Child Views

When a child view (such as a Projected or Auxiliary view) is created, it is generated based on the same surface display setting in the parent view. However, once the view is created, including or excluding surfaces on a parent view does not have any effect on existing child views. Both views are independent in terms of the surface display settings.

For section and breakout views, hatching is only visible on solids, not surfaces.

Annotating Surfaces in a Drawing

You can modify surface edge properties, such as line type, line weight, and color. Right-click on the surface or on the surface edge and select **Properties**. The Edge Properties dialog box opens as shown in Figure 8–19.

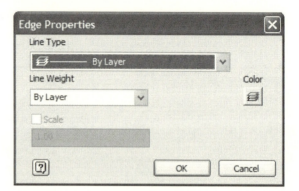

Figure 8–19

Annotations can be applied to surface edges once a surface is included in a view.

Practice 8a

Creating a Surface I

Practice Objectives

- Create an extruded surface for use as the termination plane for a solid cut.
- Mirror, fillet, and shell the geometry to achieve the required results.

In this practice, you will create a surface and use it to define an extruded cut on a bottle. You will also fillet and mirror the extruded cut and finally shell the bottle part. The resulting model is shown in Figure 8–20.

Figure 8–20

Task 1 - Create the extrusion.

In this task, you use the unconsumed sketch (**Sketch3**) to create a surface extrusion. Later in this practice, you use this surface as a termination plane for a solid cut.

1. Open **surface.ipt**.

2. The model contains **Sketch3**, an unconsumed sketch. Zoom and rotate as required to view this sketch.

3. Change the display mode to Wireframe display so that you can see the portion of the sketch inside the part, or hover over **Sketch3** in the Model browser to display it.

4. Start the **Extrude** option and click 🗔 (Surface) as the *Output* type option. The *Output* type can be specified in the Extrude dialog box or in the mini-toolbar.

5. Select **Sketch3** as the profile and set the distance to **101.6 mm**, using either the Extrude dialog box or the mini-toolbar. Extrude symmetrically on each side of the sketch plane.

6. Complete the feature. The model displays as shown in Figure 8–21.

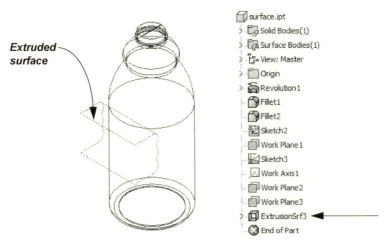

Figure 8–21

Task 2 - Sketch the cut profile and create the cut.

1. Create a sketch on Work Plane3. Sketch and dimension the geometry shown in Figure 8–22. The location of the outside vertical lines are symmetric about the Work Axis1.

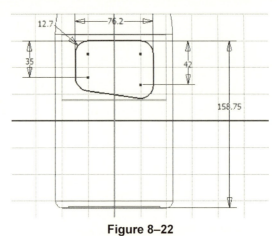

Figure 8–22

2. Start **Extrude** and click to create a solid.

Introduction to Surfacing

3. Select the new sketch as the profile. Using either the Extrude dialog box or the mini-toolbar, create the feature as a cut and set it to cut through to the surface feature.

4. In the Extrude dialog box, select the *More* tab and set the Taper angle to **-30 degrees**.

5. Complete the feature. Toggle off any visible work features and the surface. The model displays as shown in Figure 8–23.

Figure 8–23

6. Fillet the inside edge of the cutout with a radius of **3.175mm**.

7. Mirror the features (surface extrusion, cut, and fillet) about the XY plane.

8. The mirrored surface is created as its own surface body. In the Model browser, expand the **Surface Bodies** node, right-click on **Srf2**, and clear the **Visibility** option.

9. Shell the bottle with a *Thickness* of **5 mm** removing the top face of the bottle. The shaded model displays as shown in Figure 8–24.

Figure 8–24

10. Save and close the model.

Practice 8b

Creating a Surface II

Practice Objectives

- Create a lofted surface that transitions between the edges on two alternate surfaces.
- Stitch the resulting lofted surface to the existing surfaces in the model to create a single surface and form a quilt.
- Create solid geometry from the stitched geometry using the Thicken/Offset command.

In this practice, you will create the portion of the model shown in Figure 8–25 by creating a Loft surface, stitching it together with two adjacent surfaces and finally thickening this surface to create solid geometry.

Figure 8–25

Task 1 - Create a loft surface.

1. Open **Intake Manifold.ipt**. You should see two surfaces listed in the **Surface Bodies** node of the Model browser. You will create a loft between these surfaces.

2. Start the creation of a loft. The Loft dialog box opens.

3. In the Loft dialog box, in the *Output* area, click (Surface) to create a surface.

4. In the *Sections* area, click **Click to add**.

5. Select the circular surface's edge. You might need to enable **Edge Chains** in the shortcut menu.

6. In the *Sections* area, click **Click to add** again and select the edge on the other surface, as shown in Figure 8–26.

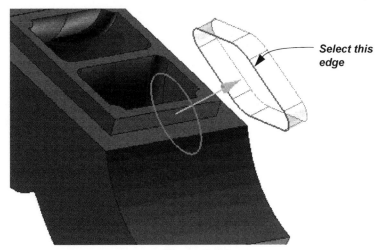

Figure 8–26

7. Select the *Conditions* tab.

8. Change both conditions from free to tangent, as shown in Figure 8–27.

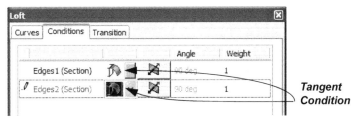

Figure 8–27

9. Click **OK** to complete the loft definition. The loft surface displays as shown in Figure 8–28.

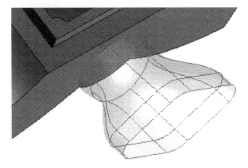

Figure 8–28

Task 2 - Stitch surfaces together.

1. In the Surface panel, click ▌ (Stitch). The Stitch dialog box opens.

2. Select the Loft surface and its two adjacent surfaces, as shown in Figure 8–29.

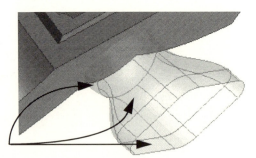

Select these three surfaces

Figure 8–29

3. Click **Apply** and **Done**. In the Model browser, in the **Surface Bodies** node, a fourth surface is added.

Task 3 - Use the Thicken/Offset option.

1. In the Modify panel, click ◈ (Thicken/Offset). The Thicken/Offset dialog box displays.

2. Select **Quilt** to easily select the stitched surface.

3. Select the stitched surface and set the *Distance* to **2 mm**.

4. Click **OK**. Toggle off visibility for the stitched surface. The model displays as shown in Figure 8–30.

Figure 8–30

5. Save the part and close the window.

Practice 8c

Sculpting a Surface

Practice Objectives

- Add material to the model by referencing a surface that defines the shape of the material to be added.
- Remove material from the model by referencing a surface that defines the shape of the material to be removed.

In this practice, you use a sculpt feature to add and remove material, as shown in Figure 8–31.

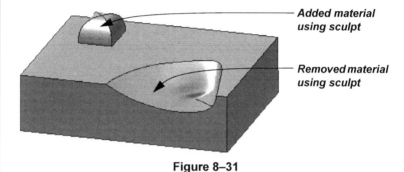

Figure 8–31

Task 1 - Add material using the sculpt option.

1. Open **sculpt.ipt**.

2. Toggle on the visibility of the surface called **Add surface**. The surface displays as shown in Figure 8–32.

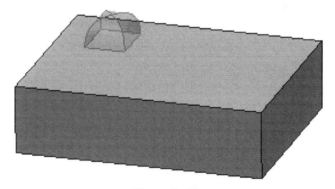

Figure 8–32

3. In the Surface panel, click (Sculpt).

4. Select the surface called **Add surface**.

5. Click **OK** to complete the feature. The model displays as shown in Figure 8–33. The material in the Add surface feature has been added to the model. Once the feature is complete, note that the Add surface feature has automatically had its visibility removed.

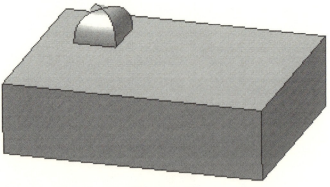

Figure 8–33

Task 2 - Remove material using the sculpt option.

1. Toggle on the visibility of the surface called Remove surface. The surface displays as shown in Figure 8–34.

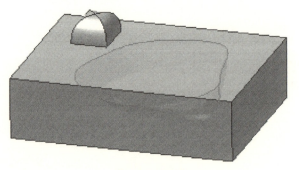

Figure 8–34

2. In the Surface panel, click (Sculpt).

3. Click (Remove).

4. Select the surface called Remove surface.

Introduction to Surfacing

5. Click >> to expand the dialog box, as shown in Figure 8–35.

Figure 8–35

6. Select the direction column to access the drop-down list that defines the side of material to be removed. The portion to be removed is highlighted in red. Verify the side containing the smaller portion of material is removed, as shown in Figure 8–36.

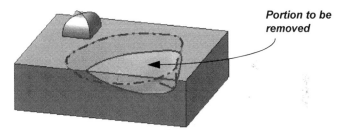

Figure 8–36

7. Click **OK**. The model displays as shown in Figure 8–37.

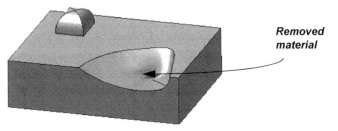

Figure 8–37

8. Save and close the model.

Practice 8d Ruled Surface Creation

Practice Objective

- Create normal, tangent, and swept ruled surfaces.

In this practice, you will learn how to use the **Ruled Surface** command to create normal, tangent, and swept ruled surfaces to complete a model. To complete the practice you will use the **Stitch** and **Thicken** commands to create solid geometry from surface geometry. The completed geometry is shown (in a top and bottom view) in Figure 8–38.

Figure 8–38

Task 1 - Create a ruled surface using the Normal type.

1. Open **Ruled_Surface.ipt** from the practice files folder.

2. In the *3D Model* tab>Surface panel, click (Ruled Surface). The Ruled Surface dialog box opens, as shown in Figure 8–39.

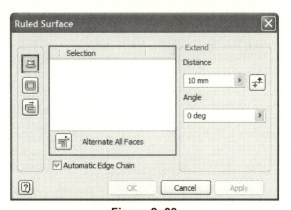

Figure 8–39

The *Shaded with Edges* Visual Style setting was assigned to improve the clarity of the images.

3. In the Ruled Surface dialog box, ensure that (Normal) is selected, if not already set.

4. Select the circular edge, as shown in Figure 8–40.

5. Set the *Distance* to **10 mm**, if not already set as the default value. The surface that is previewed should be pointing toward the center of selected circle, as shown in Figure 8–40.

   If not, flip the orientation using the button.

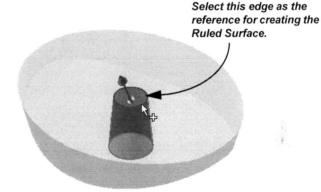

Select this edge as the reference for creating the Ruled Surface.

Figure 8–40

6. Click **Apply** to create the surface and leave the dialog box open to create additional surfaces.

7. In the Top view, zoom in on the surface. Note that the new ruled surface is perpendicular to the conical surface that is adjacent to it, not parallel to the bottom of the model. Figure 8–41 shows a sectioned view through the XY plane to visualize the ruled surface.

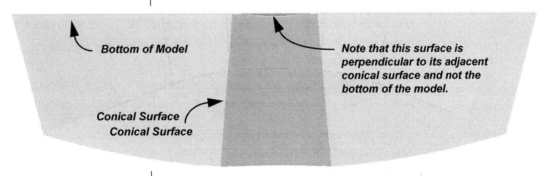

Bottom of Model

Note that this surface is perpendicular to its adjacent conical surface and not the bottom of the model.

Conical Surface
Conical Surface

Figure 8–41

Task 2 - Create a ruled surface using the Tangent type.

1. With the Ruled Surface command still active, in the Rule Surface dialog box, select ▣ (Tangent).

2. Set the *Distance* to **25 mm** and ensure that **Automatic Edge Chain** is selected.

3. Select the edge shown in Figure 8–42.

4. The preview of the tangent ruled surface displays, as shown in Figure 8–42. Click **Apply** to create the surface. Leave the dialog box open to create additional surfaces.

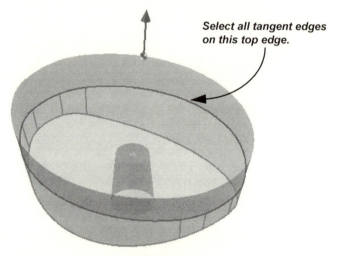

Select all tangent edges on this top edge.

Figure 8–42

Task 3 - Create a ruled surface using the Sweep type.

1. Select ▣ (Sweep) to activate the swept ruled surface option.

2. Ensure that **Automatic Edge Chain** is selected and select the lower edge of the outer surface, as shown in Figure 8–43.

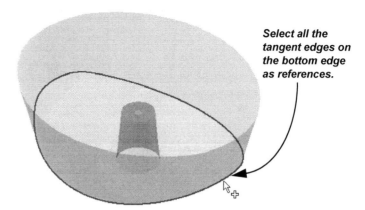

Select all the tangent edges on the bottom edge as references.

Figure 8–43

3. Select ⬚ (Vector), if not already active. Expand the origin folder and select the **Z Axis** as the sweep direction vector.

4. Set the *Distance* to **5 mm** and flip the surface creation direction, if required. A preview of the swept ruled surface displays, as shown in Figure 8–44.

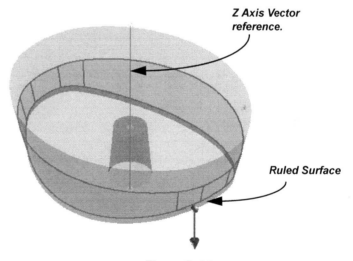

Z Axis Vector reference.

Ruled Surface

Figure 8–44

5. Click **OK** to create the surface.

Task 4 - Thicken the surfaces to create a solid part.

1. In the *3D Model* tab>Surface panel, click (Stitch).

2. Select the five surfaces shown in Figure 8–45 to add to the new quilt. Do not select the swept ruled surface, as this causes the stitch to fail.

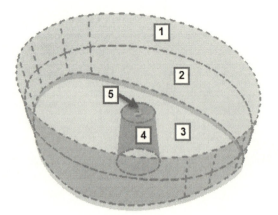

Figure 8–45

3. Click **Apply** to create the stitched surface quilt.

4. Click **Done** to complete the command. The surface updates and the edges between the tangent ruled surface and its selection have disappeared.

5. In the *3D Model* tab>Modify panel, click

     (Thicken/Offset).

6. In the Thicken/Offset dialog box select **Quilt** and select the newly created quilt.

7. Set the *Distance* to **2.5 mm**.

8. Flip the thicken direction, if required, so that the material is created to the inside of the part.

9. Click **OK** to thicken the part and create a new solid body.

10. Start the Thicken/Offset command again. Ensure that the ▣ (Join) and **Quilt** selections are active and the *Distance* value remains at **2.5 mm**.

11. Select the swept ruled surface quilt. Flip the direction to create the solid geometry to the inside of the surface, if required.

12. Click **OK** to thicken the quilt and complete the command.

13. In the *View* tab>Visibility panel, expand the **Object Visibility** drop-down list and clear the **Construction Surfaces** selection.

14. Figure 8–46 shows the completed model from the top and bottom.

Figure 8–46

15. Save and close the part.

Chapter Review Questions

1. The thickness of an extruded surface can be entered in either the mini-toolbar or in the Extrude dialog box.

    a. True
    b. False

2. Which of the following statements is true regarding surface features? (Select all that apply.)

    a. The profile of the surface must be closed.
    b. Only a single surface body can exist in a model.
    c. When creating an extruded surface, **Join** and **Cut** options are not available.
    d. When creating an extruded surface, the depth extent options are the same as those for extruding a solid.

3. Which of the following options can be used to create a planar surface from a closed 2D sketch?

    a. Extrude
    b. Loft
    c. Stitch
    d. Sculpt
    e. Thicken/Offset
    f. Patch

4. Which of the following options can be used to add or remove solid material from a model by referencing a surface body? (Select all that apply.)

    a. Extrude
    b. Loft
    c. Stitch
    d. Sculpt
    e. Thicken/Offset
    f. Patch

Introduction to Surfacing

5. The **Thicken/Offset** option enables you to add solid geometry to a model by referencing either a surface or solid face.

   a. True
   b. False

6. Which of the following options can be used to combine two or more surfaces together?

   a. Extrude
   b. Loft
   c. Stitch
   d. Sculpt
   e. Thicken/Offset
   f. Patch

7. Which of the following are valid Ruled Surface creation options? (Select all that apply.)

   a. Normal
   b. Tangent
   c. Loft
   d. Sweep

8. Which of the following best describes how excluding a surface in a drawing view affects its children views?

   a. When the visibility of a surface in a parent view is cleared, the visibility of that surface in all of its existing children views are updated to reflect the change.
   b. When the visibility of a surface in a parent view is cleared, the visibility of that surface in all of its existing children views do not change and the surface remains displayed.

Command Summary

Button	Command	Location
N/A	Include all Surfaces	• **Context menu**: In Model browser with model name selected
	Patch	• **Ribbon**: *3D Model* tab>Surface panel
N/A	Properties (edge Properties for surface in a drawing)	• **Context menu** with surface selected in the required view
	Ruled Surface	• **Ribbon**: *3D Model* tab>Surface panel
	Sculpt	• **Ribbon**: *3D Model* tab>Surface panel
	Stitch	• **Ribbon**: *3D Model* tab>Surface panel
	Thicken/ Offset	• **Ribbon**: *3D Model* tab>Modify panel

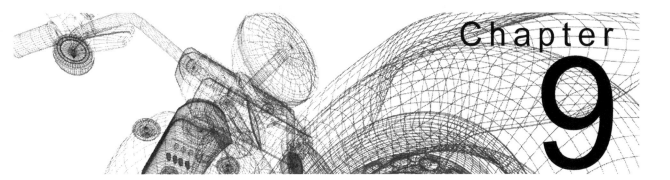

Chapter 9

Additional Surfacing Options

There are a number of tools in the Autodesk® Inventor® software that enable you to manipulate surfaces that have been created in a model. Understanding these tools and how they can be used to obtain the required surface and solid geometry enables you to create robust models.

Learning Objectives in this Chapter

- Remove portions of a surface using a reference surface or work plane.
- Increase the extent of a surface by extending it at a selected edge so that the surface maintains the curve directions of the edges adjacent to the selected edge.
- Increase the extent of a surface by stretching it at a selected edge so that the surface remains normal to the edge.
- Create a new solid face by replacing an existing solid face with surface geometry.
- Remove existing surfaces or solid faces from the model to aid in surface modeling.
- Copy surfaces to a Repaired Geometry node so that they can be opened and manipulated in the Repair environment.
- Copy surfaces from one model into another in the context of an assembly.

Trim Surface

9.1 Extend and Trim Surfaces

The **Trim Surface** option enables you to trim an existing surface feature using another surface feature or work plane.

How To: Trim a Surface

1. In the *3D Model* tab>Surface panel, click ✂ (Trim).
2. Select geometry to represent the cutting tool. In Figure 9–1, the cutting tool represents another surface.

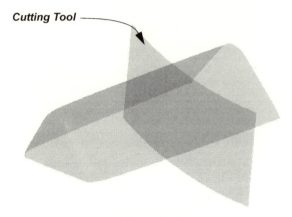

Figure 9–1

3. Select the portion of the surface you want to remove, as shown in Figure 9–2. Once the portion to be removed is selected, it is highlighted in green. You can click 🔁 in the Trim Surface dialog box to invert the selection, if required.

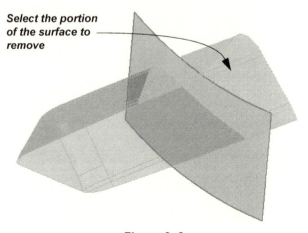

Figure 9–2

Additional Surfacing Options

4. Click **OK** to complete the feature. Figure 9–3 shows the resulting surface after trimming.

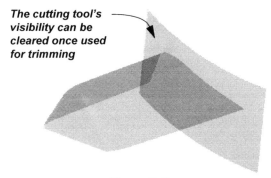

The cutting tool's visibility can be cleared once used for trimming

Figure 9–3

Extend Surface

Extend Surface enables you to increase the size of surfaces in one or more directions. You can specify a distance by which a surface is to increase or a termination face to which the surface is extended to.

How To: Extend a Surface

1. In the *3D Model* tab>Surface panel, click (Extend). The Extend Surface dialog box opens as shown in Figure 9–4.

Figure 9–4

2. Select one or more edges to extend, as shown in Figure 9–5.

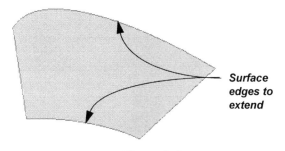

Surface edges to extend

Figure 9–5

3. Enter a distance or specify a termination reference.
4. Click >> to expand the dialog box. Select **Extend** to extend the selected edges along the same curve direction as the adjacent edges, as shown on the left side in Figure 9–6. Select **Stretch** to extend the selected edges in a straight line from the adjacent edges, as shown on the right side in Figure 9–6.

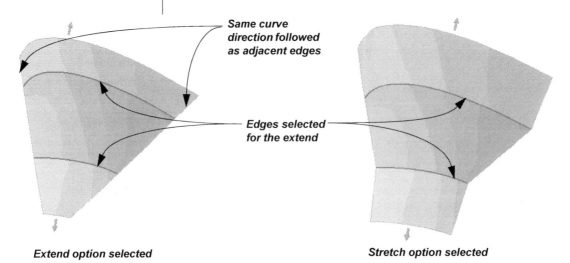

Figure 9–6

5. Click **OK** to complete the feature.

9.2 Replace Face with a Surface

The **Replace Face** option enables you to replace any face of a part with another surface. This is useful for creating parts using simple surfaces. Figure 9–7 shows a face replaced with a surface on the right side.

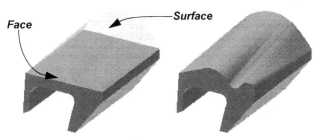

Figure 9–7

How To: Replace a Face with a Surface

1. In the *3D Model* tab>Surface panel, click (Replace Face). The Replace Face dialog box opens as shown in Figure 9–8.

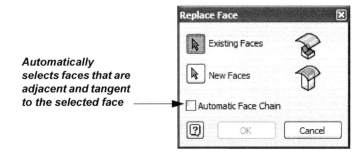

Automatically selects faces that are adjacent and tangent to the selected face

Figure 9–8

2. Select the existing part face that is to be replaced.
3. Click (New Faces) and select the replacing surface. The new face must completely intersect the part face.
4. Click **OK** to complete the feature.

When you replace a face with a face defined by a surface, you create a feature relationship between features. You can toggle off the visibility of the surface, but you cannot delete it. If you delete the surface, the new face is also deleted.

9.3 Delete Faces

The **Delete Face** option enables you to remove unwanted surfaces, solid pieces, and hollow areas from a model in the part environment. This is useful when doing hybrid solid/surface modeling. For instance, a loft operation may have created an unwanted "dent" in the object. You can clean it up by deleting the face(s), creating a new lofted surface with the required shape, then stitching everything back together to form a solid.

How To: Delete Faces

1. In the *3D Model* tab>Modify panel, click (Delete Face). The Delete dialog box opens as shown in Figure 9–9.

If a face on a solid is deleted, the solid becomes a surface.

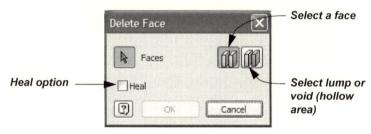

Figure 9–9

2. Select the faces to delete.

   - Use the (Select individual face) and (Select lump or void) icons to determine how faces are selected, either individually or select one face on a lump and have all faces in that lump selected.
   - A lump is a solid piece, such as a portion that remains after a Cut operation, that splits a part into multiple pieces. A void is a hollow area in a part.

*Healing can be valuable if you remove the face created by a chamfer. The **Heal** option extends the sides to restore the edge. This option is not available with Select lump or void.*

3. If required, select **Heal** when a face on a solid is deleted and you want the system to extend the adjacent faces to keep the part a solid.
4. Click **OK** to complete the feature.

Additional Surfacing Options

9.4 Copy Surfaces

The Repair environment has options to repair surface geometry for use in the Part environment.

The **Copy Object** option can be used to transfer surfaces as follows:

- Copy a surface to a Repaired Geometry node so that it can be opened and manipulated in the Repair environment.

- Copy geometry in an assembly from one part to another part. You can then use the copied geometry as reference geometry to create new geometry.

How To: Copy Objects

1. If you are using **Copy Object** to copy information between components you must first assemble the components in a temporary assembly.
2. In the assembly, activate the component into which you will be copying the surface geometry.
3. In the *3D Model* tab>expanded Modify panel, click (Copy Object) to copy surfaces to the Part environment. The Copy Object dialog box opens as shown in Figure 9–10.

Figure 9–10

4. Select the object to copy.
    - Select **Face** to select individual faces of a surface or surfaces of a solid.
    - Select **Body** to select entire surfaces or entire solids.

5. Select any additional options described below:

Create New		The **Create New Output** options depend on the selection of the face/body. Select one of the following options to copy/move surfaces or solids:
	Group (▣)	Copies/moves the selected geometry as a new group in the Construction environment.
	Repaired Geometry (▣)	Copies/moves the selected geometry as a Repaired Geometry body that can be used to access the Repair environment.
	Surface (▣)	Copies/moves the selected geometry as base surface feature(s) in the part model.
	Composite (▣)	Copies/moves the selected geometry as a single composite feature in the part model. This option is only available if two or more items are selected.
	Solid (▣)	Copies/moves the selected geometry as a base feature in the part model. This option is only available when the copied geometry can form solid geometry.
Select Existing		Enables the selection of a target composite feature or group. Associative objects are added to associative composites. Non-Associative data is added to non-associative composites.
Associative (only in Assembly, between components & not for Solid output)		When enabled, establishes a relationship source and the target geometry. The ○ symbol displays adjacent to the created feature to indicate it is associative (adaptive). To break the link, right-click on the feature in the browser and select **Break Link**.
Delete Original		Deletes the original copied/moved geometry. This option is not available for copying between parts in Assembly mode. The **Delete Original** option does not delete parametric geometry.

6. Click **Apply** to copy a surface to the part environment. Surfaces that are copied are removed from the Repair environment and are placed into the Part environment area of the Model browser.
7. Click **OK** to close the Copy Object dialog box.

Practice 9a Extending Surfaces

Practice Objectives

- Increase the extent of a surface by extending the surface at a selected edge, such that the extended surface maintains the curve directions of the edges adjacent to the selected edge.
- Increase the extent of a surface by stretching the surface at a selected edge, such that the stretched surface remains normal to the edge.

In this practice, you extend a surface using the two available extend options: **Extend** and **Stretch**, as shown in Figure 9–11.

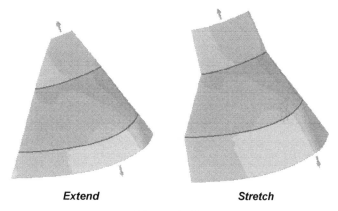

Extend *Stretch*

Figure 9–11

Task 1 - Use the Extend Surface option.

1. Open **extend surface.ipt**.

2. In the *3D Model* tab>Surface panel, click (Extend).

3. Verify that **Distance** is selected in the Extents drop-down list.

4. Reorient the model and select the edges shown in Figure 9–12.

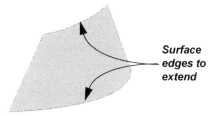

Surface edges to extend

Figure 9–12

5. Set the *Distance* to **15**.

6. Click [>>] to expand the dialog box. Verify that **Extend** is selected to extend the selected edges along the same curve direction as the adjacent edges. The preview displays as shown in Figure 9–13.

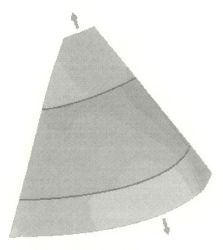

Figure 9–13

7. Select **Stretch** to extend the selected edges in a straight line from the adjacent edges, as shown in Figure 9–14.

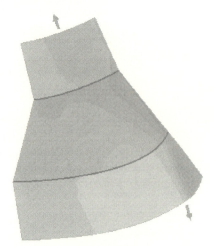

Figure 9–14

8. Click **OK** to complete the extend.

9. Save and close the model.

Practice 9b | Copying Surfaces

Practice Objectives

- Copy the geometry of one part model into another part model in the context of an assembly.
- Using copied surface geometry, replace an existing solid face with the copied surface geometry to create a new solid face.

In this practice, you copy a surface to another part in an assembly, and use the surface to replace a face on that part. The resulting component is shown in Figure 9–15.

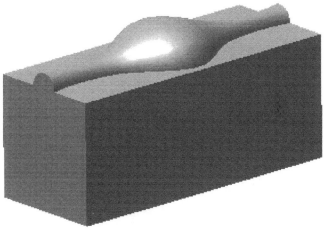

Figure 9–15

Task 1 - Create a new assembly file.

1. Create a new assembly file using the Metric template.

2. Place one instance of **blank.ipt**. Right-click and select **Place Grounded at Origin**. The first component in the assembly is grounded at the origin (0,0,0).

3. Place one instance of **shape.ipt**.

4. Show the assembly degrees of freedom (*View* tab>Visibility panel>click (Degrees of Freedom)).

5. Fully constrain **shape.ipt** as shown in Figure 9–16. The model is displayed in wireframe.

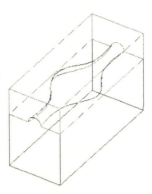

Figure 9–16

Task 2 - Copy shape.ipt.

1. Activate **blank.ipt** in the assembly.

2. In the *3D Model* tab>expanded Modify panel, click (Copy Object) to copy *shape.ipt* into **blank.ipt**.

3. Select the shape component in the graphics window.

4. Click **Apply** to copy the shape component using the default options in the Copy Object dialog box. Only the

   (Composite) option should be selected.

5. Close the dialog box. The Model browser displays as shown in Figure 9–17.

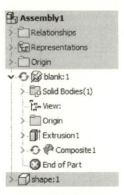

Figure 9–17

Task 3 - Replace the part face with the copied surface.

In this task, you open the blank component in a separate window and replace the blank component's top face with the copied surface.

1. Open **blank.ipt** in a separate window. The part displays as shown in Figure 9–18. Surfaces from **shape.ipt** have been added.

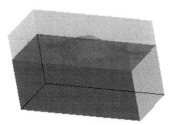

Figure 9–18

2. In the *3D Model* tab>Surface panel, click 🗔 (Replace Face) to replace a face in the part with the copied surface.

3. Select blank.ipt's top face as the existing face.

4. Click 🗔 (New Faces). Select the curved face and its two adjacent flat faces, as shown in Figure 9–19. Be sure to select all three faces.

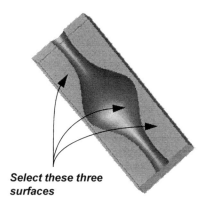

Select these three surfaces

Figure 9–19

5. Click **OK**. Toggle off the visibility of the copied surface (**Composite1**). The blank part displays as shown in Figure 9–20.

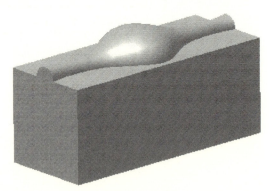

Figure 9–20

6. Save the part and assembly. If changes are made to shape.ipt, the assembly can be updated and the change will reflect in the **blank.ipt** component. If the assembly is not kept the associativity between the two components is lost and if changes are made to shape.ipt they are not reflected in **blank.ipt**.

7. Close the window.

Practice 9c

Deleting a Surface

Practice Objectives

- Combine adjacent surfaces to form a single quilted surface that can be easily selected as a reference when creating other features.
- Remove an existing surface from the model.
- Create a surface that is defined by a series of edges to create a three-dimensional surface.
- Create solid geometry from a surface using the Thicken/Offset command.

In this practice, you create a thicken feature using an imported surface. Based on the surface geometry, it cannot be created with the required thickness. To resolve the error you will delete the problem surface and create a new boundary surface. The resulting model, after a successful thicken feature is added, is shown in Figure 9–21.

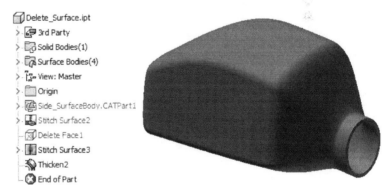

Figure 9–21

Task 1 - Open a part file.

1. Open **Delete_Surface.ipt**. Note that in the Model browser, a surface is listed in the **Surface Bodies** node. This surface has been imported from another CAD system.

Task 2 - Stitch surfaces together.

1. In the Surface panel, click (Stitch). The Stitch dialog box opens.

2. Select the surface body, as shown in Figure 9–22. All of the surfaces in the body are selected.

Figure 9–22

3. Click **Apply** and **Done**. In the Model browser, in the **Surface Bodies** node, a second surface is added.

Task 3 - Use the Thicken/Offset command.

1. In the Modify panel, click (Thicken/Offset). The Thicken/Offset dialog box displays.

2. Select **Quilt** to easily select the stitched surface.

3. Select the stitched surface and enter a distance of **4 mm**.

4. Click **OK**. The Create Thicken feature dialog box opens indicating that the feature cannot be created due to the geometry. The 4 mm value is the minimum acceptable wall thickness for this model. A smaller value will work, however, will not meet the design requirement.

5. Click **Cancel** to close the dialog box.

Task 4 - Delete a face on the model.

To resolve the failure, you will delete a surface face from the imported geometry and then recreate a new surface that will accept the required wall thickness.

1. In the *3D Model* tab>Modify panel, click (Delete Face).

2. Verify that (Select Individual Face) is enabled.
3. Select the four faces as shown in Figure 9–23.

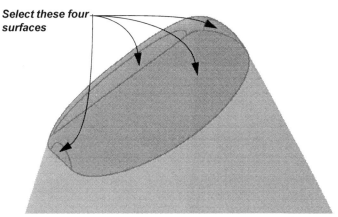

Figure 9–23

4. Click **OK**.

Task 5 - Create a boundary patch.

1. In the *3D Model* tab>Surface panel, click (Patch).
2. Select **Automatic Edge Chain** if it is not already selected. This enables you to select all the adjacent edges together instead of selecting them individually.
3. Select the circular edges bounding the face that was just deleted. A flat face immediately previews on the model, as shown in Figure 9–24.

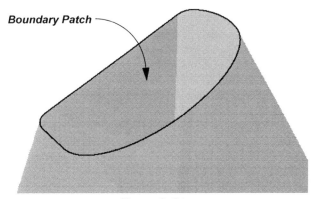

Figure 9–24

4. In the Boundary Patch dialog box, in the *Condition* area, in the selected edge drop-down list, click (Smooth G2), as shown in Figure 9–25, for the edges that defines the patch. This creates a smooth continuous condition between the patch and adjacent faces on the selected edge.

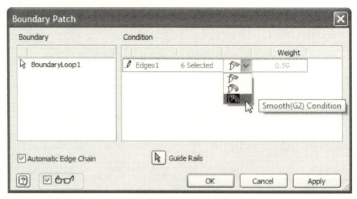

Figure 9–25

5. Maintain the default *Weight* value of **0.5**. Click **OK**. The model displays as shown in Figure 9–26.

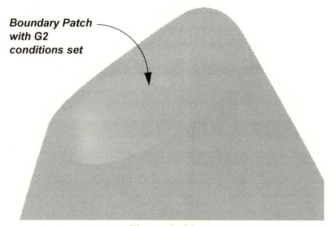

Boundary Patch with G2 conditions set

Figure 9–26

Task 6 - Stitch surfaces to create a solid.

1. In the *3D Model* tab>Surface panel, click (Stitch).

2. Select the new surface and the existing stitched surface. Click **Apply** and **Done**.

Task 7 - Use the Thicken/Offset option.

1. In the Modify panel, click (Thicken/Offset). The Thicken/Offset dialog box opens.

2. Select **Quilt** to easily select the stitched surface.

3. Select the stitched surface and set the *Distance* to **4 mm**.

4. Click **OK**. The solid geometry is created with a 4 mm thickness, as shown in Figure 9–27. By deleting the end portion of the surface geometry and simplifying it with the creation of a boundary patch that was G2 continuous with its adjacent surface, the geometry was able to be created.

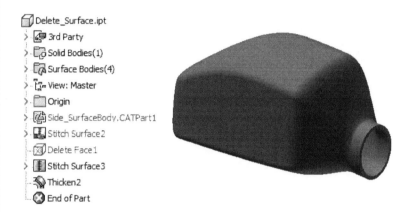

Figure 9–27

5. Save the model and close the window.

Practice 9d

Creating a Solid from Surfaces

Practice Objectives

- Trim a surface using another reference surface as the cutting tool.
- Remove an existing surface from the model.
- Create surfaces that are defined by a series of edges to create a three-dimensional surface.
- Create solid geometry by stitching surfaces together.

In this practice, you create solid geometry using imported surfaces as its foundation. Based on the surface geometry that is provided, you will trim it and create new surfaces to generate solid geometry. To complete the model you will shell it. After the solid has been created, the completed model will display as shown in Figure 9–28.

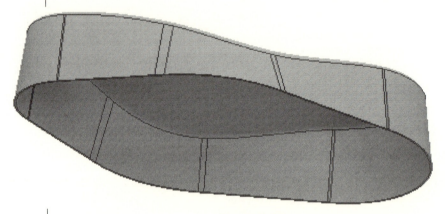

Figure 9–28

Task 1 - Trim a surface.

1. Open **Surface_to_Solid.ipt**. Note that in the Model browser, two surfaces are listed in the **Surface Bodies** node. These surfaces have been imported from another CAD system.

2. In the *3D Model* tab>Surface panel, click (Trim).

3. Select the Top surface as the cutting tool, as shown in Figure 9–29.

4. Select the portion of the surface you want to remove, as shown in Figure 9–29. Once the portion to be removed is selected, it is highlighted in green.

To invert the selection, in the Trim Surface dialog box, click , as required.

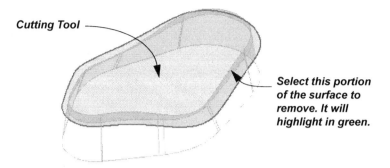

Figure 9–29

5. Click **OK** to trim the surface.

Task 2 - Delete a surface.

1. In the *3D Model* tab>Modify panel, click (Delete Face).

2. Verify that (Select Individual Face) is enabled.

3. Select the surface shown in Figure 9–30 to delete.

In the Autodesk Inventor software, *the edges of surfaces will display as yellow. The images in this practice show as black for the purposes of printing clarity.*

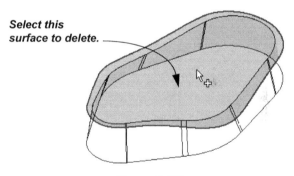

Figure 9–30

4. Click **OK** to delete the surface.

Task 3 - Create a boundary patch.

1. In the *3D Model* tab>Surface panel, click (Patch).

2. Ensure that **Automatic Edge Chain** is selected. This option enables you to select all of the adjacent edges together, instead of selecting them individually.

3. Select the chain of edges that were generated by the **Trim** option in Task 2. A flat face immediately previews on the model, as shown in Figure 9–31.

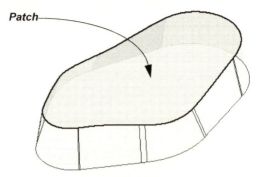

Figure 9–31

4. In the Boundary Patch dialog box, in the *Condition* area, in the Selected Edge drop-down list, click (Tangent Condition) (as shown in Figure 9–32) for the edges that define the patch. This creates a tangent condition between the patch and adjacent faces on the selected edge.

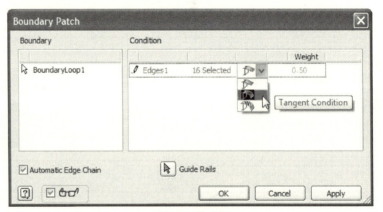

Figure 9–32

5. Set the *Weight* value to **0.2** to change the influence of tangency on the geometry. Reducing this value creates a flatter surface because tangency is maintained over a shorter distance. Click **OK**. The model appears as shown in Figure 9–33.

Additional Surfacing Options

To further refine the shape of the boundary patch, a guide rail curve or a point can also be selected to control its shape.

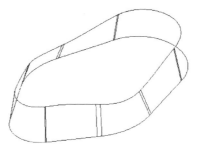

Figure 9–33

The remainder of the practice has you create a shelled solid from the imported and modified surfaces. Simply using the Thicken/Offset command does not provide for a flat lip on the bottom edge because a thickened solid remains normal to the surface, as shown in Figure 9–34. Alternatively, you will create an additional surface and then use it to create the solid geometry.

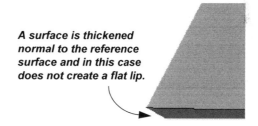

Figure 9–34

Task 4 - Create solid geometry from the surfaces.

1. In the *3D Model* tab>Surface panel, click (Patch).

2. Select the edges along the Bottom surface, as shown in Figure 9–35.

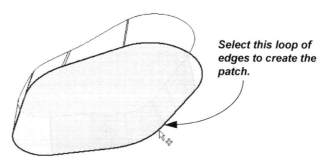

Figure 9–35

3. Click **OK**.

4. In the Surface panel, click (Stitch). The Stitch dialog box opens.

5. Select all three surfaces in the model by dragging a selection window around them. Maintain the default tolerance value and click **Apply**. The stitched surfaces form a watertight area, and therefore automatically generate a solid, as shown in Figure 9–36. Close the Stitch dialog box.

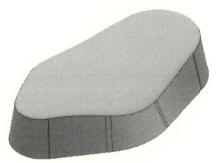

Figure 9–36

Task 5 - Add a shell to complete the solid geometry.

1. In the Modify panel, click (Shell). The Shell dialog box opens.

2. Ensure that the shell is being created on the inside of the model.

3. Select the bottom flat surface as the surface to be removed.

4. Set the shell *Thickness* to **.125 in**.

5. Click **OK**. The solid geometry is created as shown in Figure 9–37.

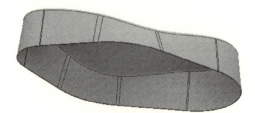

Figure 9–37

6. Save the model and close the window.

Practice 9e

Deleting a Face

Practice Objective

- Remove existing surfaces from the model so that the removed faces are automatically replaced by new surfaces.

In this practice, you will be provided a model (shown in Figure 9–38) that has been imported from another CAD system. In reviewing the model, you will note a design error and a geometry change that is required. Using the **Delete Face** option, you will fix these issues so that the geometry can be used.

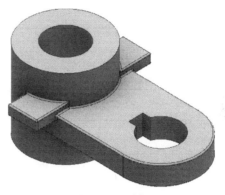

Figure 9–38

Task 1 - Delete faces on the model.

The keyway that is in the geometry is not required. The **Delete Face** option can be used to remove this.

1. Open **Delete_Face.ipt**. Note that in the Model browser, a single solid is listed in the **Solid Bodies** node and in the feature list. This solid has been imported from another CAD system.

2. In the *3D Model* tab>Modify panel, click (Delete Face).

3. Verify that (Select Individual Face) is enabled.

4. Select the three faces shown in the highlighted keyway in Figure 9–39.

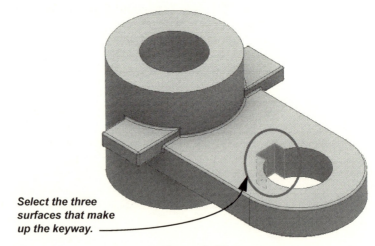

Select the three surfaces that make up the keyway.

Figure 9–39

5. Click **OK**. In the Model browser, note that the geometry is now listed in the **Surface Bodies** node. The removal of these faces has converted the solid model to surface geometry because it is no longer watertight.

To create a solid you could patch the openings with surface geometry and use **Sculpt** to create the solid. As an alternative, you will use a tool in the **Delete Face** command to heal the area where the faces were removed.

6. Double-click on the **Delete Face1** feature in the Model browser to edit the feature.

7. Select **Heal** in the Delete Face dialog box.

8. Click **OK**. Note how incorporating the use of the **Heal** option creates surfaces to replace those that are removed.

Task 2 - Delete additional faces on the inside of the model.

A modeling error was made in the original geometry and it must be corrected.

1. Rotate the model to view the hole shown in Figure 9–40. Note that there is a modeling error and that a rectangular extrusion exists in the hole.

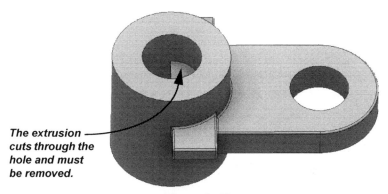

The extrusion cuts through the hole and must be removed.

Figure 9–40

2. Similar to the previous task, use the **Delete Face** command so that the three faces that must be removed are automatically healed. The final solid geometry should display as shown in Figure 9–41.

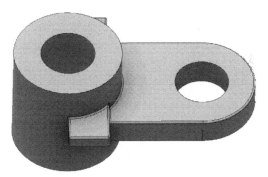

Figure 9–41

3. Save the model and close the window.

Chapter Review Questions

1. Which **Extend** surface option is used to extend the arc shown in Figure 9–42?

   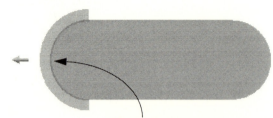

   Figure 9–42

   a. Extend
   b. Stretch

2. Which option can be used to remove surface geometry on either side of an intersecting plane or surface?

   a. Trim
   b. Stitch
   c. Sculpt
   d. Patch
   e. Delete Face
   f. Replace Face

3. Which option can be used to edit existing geometry in a model with an intersecting surface?

   a. Trim
   b. Stitch
   c. Sculpt
   d. Patch
   e. Delete Face
   f. Replace Face

4. The **Delete Face** command can only be used to remove an existing surface in the model and not a solid face.

   a. True
   b. False

5. Which of the following statements are true regarding using the **Copy Object** option to copy surfaces between components? (Select all that apply.)

    a. To copy a surface between models, right-click on the surface in the source model and select **Copy Object**. Then open the new model, right-click, and select **Paste**.

    b. To copy surfaces between models, assemble them and use the **Copy Object** command in the target model.

    c. When using the **Copy Object** command you must use the **Face** command to select individual surfaces in the source model.

    d. Once a surface is copied between components. Changes to the original surface can never be reflected in the new model.

6. Match the command in the left column to its icon in the right column.

Command	Icon	Answer
a. Trim	⬆️	_____
b. Extend	🗗	_____
c. Replace Face	⬛ₓ	_____
d. Delete Face	✂	_____
e. Copy Object	⬆️	_____

Command Summary

Button	Command	Location
	Copy Object	• **Ribbon:** *3D Model* tab>expanded Modify panel
	Delete Face	• **Ribbon:** *3D Model* tab>Modify panel
	Extend (Surface)	• **Ribbon:** *3D Model* tab>Surface panel
	Replace Face	• **Ribbon:** *3D Model* tab>Surface panel
	Trim (Surface)	• **Ribbon:** *3D Model* tab>Surface panel

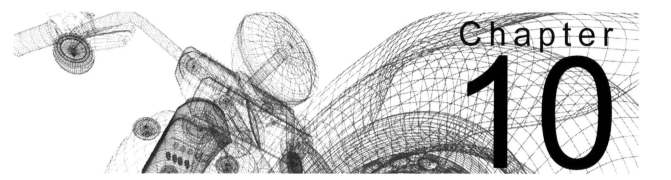

Chapter 10

Copying Between Parts (iFeatures)

The Autodesk® Inventor® software provides several methods to copy features between models. One of these methods involves the use of iFeatures. This duplication technique helps to reduce the amount of time spent duplicating a collection of features or components that are used repeatedly in an individual model, or across several models.

Learning Objectives in this Chapter

- Create an iFeature by selecting the features, parameters, and placement elements to define the iFeature.
- Place an iFeature by defining its placement plane, size values, and precise positioning to fully locate it in a model.
- Use the Copy command to duplicate features in a model or between models.
- Create a table-driven iFeature that includes variations that can be retrieved during the placement of the iFeature.
- Edit the size, position, and sketch location of an iFeature that has been placed in a model.
- Edit a source iFeature file to make changes to its initial definition.

10.1 Creating iFeatures

Several predefined iFeatures are installed with the Autodesk Inventor software and are stored in this directory.

When you create parts, you may require the same type of feature in multiple parts. By using iFeatures, you can save any sketched feature for use in other part files. iFeatures are stored in files with the extension .IDE. By default, they are stored in the *C:\Users\ Public\Public Documents\Autodesk\ Inventor 2019\Catalog* directory.

General Steps

Use the following general steps to create an iFeature:

1. Start the creation of an iFeature.
2. Select features to save as iFeatures.
3. Set the parameter size.
4. Define the iFeature position geometry.
5. Save the iFeature.

Step 1 - Start the creation of an iFeature.

Open the part that contains the sketches/features to use. In the *Manage* tab>Author panel, click (Extract iFeature). The Extract iFeature dialog box opens, as shown in Figure 10–1.

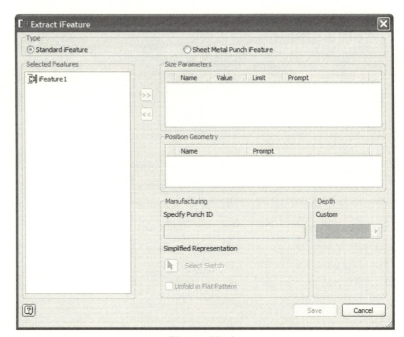

Figure 10–1

Copying Between Parts (iFeatures)

Step 2 - Select features to save as iFeatures.

Select sketches (consumed or unconsumed) and features in the Model browser or graphics window that are to become iFeatures. If the selected feature has dependent features, they are automatically selected. All elements used to create the selected feature appear below the name of the iFeature in the Selected Features area, as shown in Figure 10–2. You can use any or all of the part features in the iFeature.

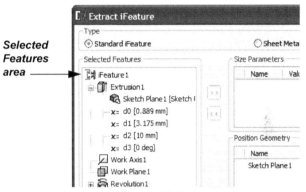

Figure 10–2

*To rename an iFeature so that its name in the Model browser is descriptive, right-click on the iFeature# at the top of the Selected Features column and select **Rename**. Enter a new name. This name identifies the iFeature whenever it is placed. Renaming the iFeature is different from naming the iFeature's .IDE filename.*

The dialog box auto populates the *Size Parameters* and *Position Geometry* areas with any renamed parameters. To add other feature parameters that are to be used in the iFeature, select them in the *Selected Features* area and use the >> icon to transfer the parameters one by one. To add all parameters associated with a feature, select the feature and select **Add All Parameters** in the shortcut menu. Figure 10–3 shows all Extrusion1 parameters transferred to the *Size Parameters* area.

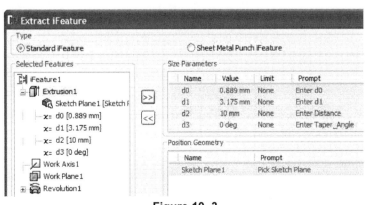

Figure 10–3

To remove a feature from a list, select the feature and select **Remove Feature** in the shortcut menu. To remove parameters, use the [<<] icon to return the parameters to the *Selected Features* area, or select **Remove All Parameters** in the shortcut menu.

Step 3 - Set the parameter size.

Once the feature parameters are transferred to the *Size Parameters* area of the dialog box you can control the size of the iFeature by applying a range or limits to the parameters. The *Size Parameters* area consists of four columns, described as follows:

Name	Lists the name of the parameter that describes a dimension of the feature. You can change the name of the parameter by selecting on it. Use a name that is descriptive to help when reusing the iFeature.
Value	Displays the default value for the parameter.
Limit	Enables you to restrict the values of parameters using the following three options:
None	Any value is acceptable.
Range	Set the allowable range for the value by entering the upper and lower values and the operator.
List	Enables you to create a group of acceptable values and set the default value of the parameter.
Prompt	Enables you to set the text that displays in a dialog box when the iFeature is inserted. You can enter information that clarifies the use of the value or describes restrictions.

Step 4 - Define the iFeature position geometry.

In the Extract iFeature dialog box, the *Position Geometry* area specifies the elements in the iFeature that are used to locate it on a part. The Sketch Plane is automatically added to this area. You can add or remove other items, such as constraints from the feature, using the [>>] and [<<] icons.

Copying Between Parts (iFeatures)

An iFeature should contain geometry that is only dependent on the geometry in the iFeature itself. Do not use Origin work features. Horizontal and vertical constraints can make it difficult to place an iFeature, because those terms are relative to the part where the feature is placed. Use parallel and perpendicular constraints instead.

The *Position Geometry* area consists of two columns, described as follows:

Name	Names the position geometry. You can change it here, but it does not change the name in the Selected Features area.
Prompt	Defines the text prompt that is provided when the iFeature is inserted. You can enter information that prompts you where to select on the existing part to place the iFeature.

You might need to customize position geometry (for example, combine two location geometries, or make one position independent of the other). Right-click on the position in the *Position Geometry* area and select **Combine Geometry**, then select another position to combine. To make positions in a combined geometry independent, right-click on the combined position and select **Make Independent**.

Step 5 - Save the iFeature.

Using iFeatures saves time and helps ensure consistency between parts.

By default, iFeatures are saved in the *Catalog* folder (*C:\Users\Public\Public Documents\Autodesk\Inventor 2019\ Catalog*) or you can create a new folder in this *Catalog* folder to further organize the files. Once the iFeature is defined and its locating position determined, in the Extract iFeature dialog box, click **Save**. The Save As dialog box opens. Enter a unique name for the iFeature and click **Save** and close the dialog box. All iFeatures are saved with the extension .IDE.

10.2 Inserting iFeatures

An iFeature can be placed in the same part in which it was created or it can be placed in any other part, as shown in Figure 10–4.

An iFeature reduces the time spent on duplicating a collection of features or components that are used repeatedly in the same or in different models.

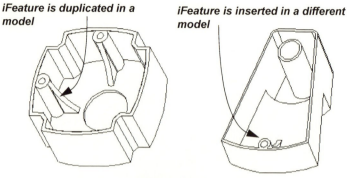

iFeature is duplicated in a model

iFeature is inserted in a different model

Figure 10–4

General Steps

Use the following general steps to place an iFeature:

1. Start the placement of the iFeature.
2. Select the position of the iFeature.
3. Determine the size of the iFeature.
4. Determine the precise position.
5. Complete the insertion.

Step 1 - Start the placement of the iFeature.

You can also drag an iFeature from Windows Explorer to the main window.

In the *Manage* tab>Insert panel, click (Insert iFeature). Click **Browse** and browse to the iFeature, select, and open the iFeature. By default, iFeatures are saved in the *Catalog* folder (*C:\Users\Public\Public Documents\Autodesk\Inventor 2019\ Catalog*).

Copying Between Parts (iFeatures)

As an alternative to initiating the **Insert iFeature** option and selecting an iFeature, you can select an iFeature directly from the ribbon. All iFeatures stored in the Catalog are listed in the drop-down list, as shown in Figure 10–5. Scroll through the list and select the iFeature.

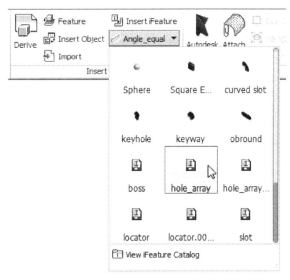

Figure 10–5

Step 2 - Select the position of the iFeature.

*Once the iFeature is open, a green symbol on the left side of the Insert **iFeature** dialog box shows you that you are in the "Position" step.*

The Position step enables you to select a planar face or work plane to locate the feature. Once you select the plane, you can select the rotation or the position symbol, shown in Figure 10–6, to rotate or move the iFeature, as required.

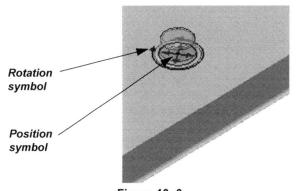

Figure 10–6

Alternatively, you can enter a rotation angle in the dialog box.

Click ✈ to flip the direction of the iFeature. A checkmark displays to the left of the name of the feature or sketch when the placement for the iFeature is fully defined, as shown in Figure 10–7.

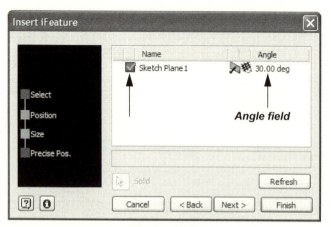

Figure 10–7

Step 3 - Determine the size of the iFeature.

Once the position is defined, click **Next** to move to the Size step. The Size step lists the names and default values of the parameters of the iFeatures. An example is shown in Figure 10–8.

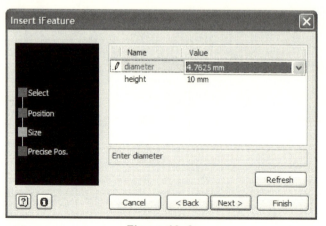

Figure 10–8

Select a value to change it. Once you change the size, click **Refresh** in the dialog box to update the display of the iFeature.

Step 4 - Determine the precise position.

Once the sizes are defined, click **Next** to move to the Precise Pos. step. The Insert iFeature dialog box displays as shown in Figure 10–9.

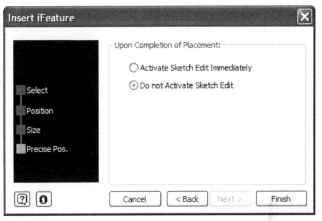

Figure 10–9

The Precise Pos. step determines what happens when the operation is complete.

- If you select **Activate Sketch Edit Immediately**, **Edit Sketch** is activated so that you can locate the sketch precisely before you continue with the part.

- If you select **Do not Activate Sketch Edit**, **iFeature** is added without accessing the sketch environment.

You can move back and forth through the steps using **Next** and **Back**, or by selecting the steps in the tree graphic.

Step 5 - Complete the insertion.

Once the location and size of the iFeature are defined, click **Finish** to complete the operation. Depending on the option that was selected in the Precise Pos. step, the sketch environment might open to refine the iFeature's placement.

No link exists between the .IDE file and the iFeature once the iFeature is placed. Therefore, changes to the .IDE file do not affect iFeatures that are already placed. Even if you insert a revised iFeature into a file that contains an older version of the feature, the original iFeature is not affected. To update a placed iFeature, delete the old iFeature and insert the new one.

10.3 iFeatures vs. Copy Feature

Some features in your models can be simply copied and pasted as a means of duplicating them within or to another model. For those features that cannot be copied, you can use iFeatures. In general, features that have sketched sections can be copied; however, features that are located on surface or reference edges (e.g., holes, fillets, shells) cannot be copied.

How To: Copy and Paste a Feature

1. Verify that the **Select Features** filter is enabled and select the feature in the model or the Model browser.
2. Once selected, right-click and select **Copy**. If the **Copy** option is not available, this action is not permitted and you should consider recreating the feature or using an iFeature.
3. Activate the model that is to be the target model, if it is not already the active model.
4. Right-click and select **Paste**. A Paste Features dialog box similar to that shown in Figure 10–10 opens, indicating the references required to place the feature.

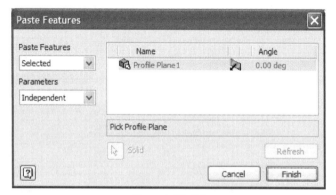

Figure 10–10

5. Select a *Parameters* option. This enables you to define whether the copied feature is dependent or independent. If the feature is copied in the same model, you can select whether or not the new feature is dependent on the source feature. If you are copying to a new model, the copied feature can only be independent.
6. Define the placement reference for the copied feature.
7. Click **Finish**. Depending on the placement references that were defined, you might need to further edit the feature to fully locate it in the model.

10.4 Table-Driven iFeatures

iFeatures are made up of parameters independent of each other, unless they are related by an equation. Table-driven iFeatures provide additional control by presetting these parameters to permitted values. For example, a threaded stud can be an iFeature. The diameter of the stud may have several preset values, and each diameter, preset lengths. Not all lengths apply to all of the diameters; therefore, you can change the iFeature to allow only certain lengths. Through the use of keys in a Table-driven iFeature you can logically group the iFeature members to enable quicker access to the required configuration.

General Steps

Use the following general steps to create a table-driven iFeature:

1. Open the iFeature file.
2. Select the configurable attributes.
3. Create the table.
4. Set up keys.
5. Complete the table.

Step 1 - Open the iFeature file.

Open an iFeature. In the iFeature panel, click (iFeature Author Table). The dialog box opens as shown in Figure 10–11.

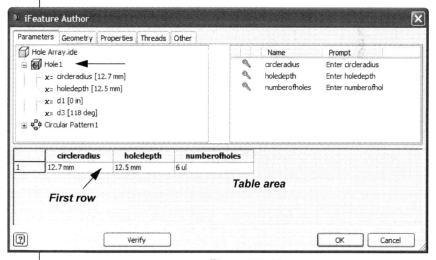

Figure 10–11

Step 2 - Select the configurable attributes.

The tabs in the iFeature Author dialog box contain the configurable attributes that can be varied to create the different iFeature configurations.

Tabs	Description
Parameters tab	Contains the parameters used in the part and they are listed under the features in which they belong. Parameters that have names other than d# are listed automatically in the Selected Parameters list.
Geometry tab	Displays the geometry used to position the iFeature. You can change the names and prompts for the geometry in this tab.
Properties tab	Lists the properties of the feature. Any custom properties in an iFeature can be made available in the Part files in which they are inserted. In the *Properties* tab, expand the **Custom** node and select the required custom parameter, then add it to the table as a property using the arrow icons. Once a property has been moved to the right side of the dialog box, you can set keys on these properties.
Threads tab	Enables you to include thread variables. Each thread variable is defined as a key. Designations such as UNC are case-sensitive.
Other tab	Enables you to create additional columns in the table. These columns do not control the size of the part, but can be used as keys in the table.

*To create a custom property in an iFeature, open the iFeature, right-click on the iFeature name in the Model browser, and select **iProperties**. Select the Custom tab and create any custom properties that are required.*

You can insert the iFeature with any of the attribute values that were set in the iFeature Author dialog box. For example, you can insert an iFeature with the hole depth parameter values shown in Figure 10–12.

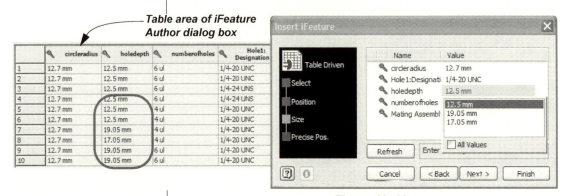

Figure 10–12

Copying Between Parts (iFeatures)

You can also enter custom values (ones not predefined) for an attribute by setting its column as custom. This enables you to enter custom values when the iFeature is inserted.

How To: Enter Custom Attribute Values

1. Right-click the attribute column in the table and select **Key> Not A Key** if a key is assigned to the parameter.
2. Right-click the attribute column in the table and select **Custom Parameter Column**. The column displays in blue.

The shortcut menu is shown in Figure 10–13.

You can also control permitted values for an attribute by defining a range and/or increment.

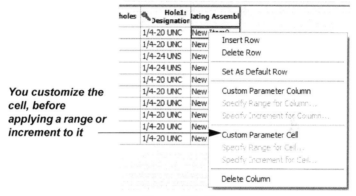

You customize the cell, before applying a range or increment to it

Figure 10–13

Step 3 - Create the table.

It is possible to edit the iFeature table in a spread sheet format using (Edit Using Spread Sheet).

Each row in the table represents a different version of the iFeature. To add more versions, right-click in the first row and select **Insert Row**. Select the table cells and enter the attribute values for each cell. Once filled in, the table area displays similar to that shown in Figure 10–14.

	circleradius	holedepth	numberofholes	Hole1: Designation	Mating Assembly
1	12.7 mm	12.5 mm	6 ul	1/4-20 UNC	New Item0
2	12.7 mm	12.5 mm	6 ul	1/4-20 UNC	New Item0
3	12.7 mm	12.5 mm	6 ul	1/4-24 UNS	New Item0
4	12.7 mm	12.5 mm	6 ul	1/4-24 UNS	New Item0
5	12.7 mm	12.5 mm	4 ul	1/4-20 UNC	New Item0
6	12.7 mm	12.5 mm	4 ul	1/4-20 UNC	New Item0
7	12.7 mm	19.05 mm	4 ul	1/4-20 UNC	New Item0
8	12.7 mm	17.05 mm	4 ul	1/4-20 UNC	New Item0
9	12.7 mm	19.05 mm	6 ul	1/4-20 UNC	New Item0
10	12.7 mm	19.05 mm	6 ul	1/4-20 UNC	New Item0

Figure 10–14

Step 4 - Set up keys.

An iFeature contains attribute values that define each iFeature member. Keys enable you to group iFeature members according to their attribute values in a hierarchical manner. This sorts the iFeature members more logically, enabling quicker access to the required configuration. A key ⚷ symbol displays in front of each attribute in the iFeature Author dialog box. Toggle the key symbols on (blue) and off (gray) to define a particular attribute as a key. For the attributes you set as keys, assign the key order (starting from 1 as the first key). The attribute set as Key 1 is the first attribute that is used for sorting or grouping the iFeature members. If Length was the first key, then all the iFeature members will be sorted according to length. To change the order of key numbers, or to assign a key number to an attribute, right-click it and select **Key** and the required number, as shown in Figure 10–15.

*You can customize the name displayed in the Model browser for an iFeature to show the Key1 parameter name and its value. Select **Use Key 1 as Browser Name column** in the Application Options dialog box (iFeature tab). This helps identify which iFeature value set is used.*

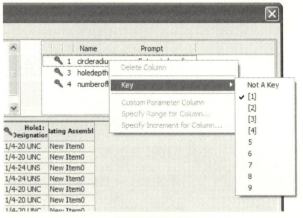

Figure 10–15

If five members had the same length of 500mm, then all five would be listed under that length (length = 500mm) in the Model browser. Next, the members are sorted according to the second key, for example width. The five members with length=500mm would be grouped according to width. If two of those members had widths of 100mm and the other three had widths of 150mm, then they would be sorted under width = 100mm and width = 150mm. The sorting continues until no more keys are defined.

Step 5 - Complete the table.

Once the table is defined, click **OK** to complete the operation.

10.5 Editing iFeatures

Edit Inserted iFeature

Once the iFeature is inserted, you can only edit its size, position, and sketch location on the sketch plane. To edit the size and position, right-click on the iFeature and select **Edit iFeature**. To edit the sketch location, right-click on the iFeature and select **Edit Sketch**. You can add dimensions and constraints; however, not change its dimensions.

Edit iFeature file

You might need to change the iFeature file (.IDE) once it has been created. To do so, open the iFeature file in a separate window. The iFeature panel displays as shown in Figure 10–16.

The (Edit iFeature) option enables you to modify sizes and position.

Figure 10–16

To view stored iFeatures, including standard predefined iFeatures, in the iFeature panel, click (View Catalog). The Catalog viewer displays in a standard Windows Explorer view, as shown in Figure 10–17.

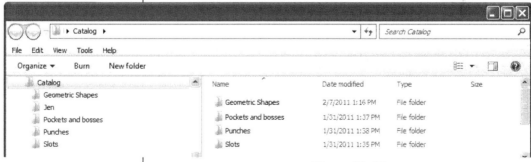

Figure 10–17

Tables are covered in more detail in table-driven iFeatures.

Click (iFeature Author Table) to create or modify iFeature tables. If an iFeature table is used, you can use (Edit Using Spread Sheet) to edit the values in a spread sheet format.

Editing the iFeature Image

When an iFeature is created, it is assigned the default icon image (🔳). This image identifies the iFeature in the Model browser of any part that you place it in, as well as in the ribbon when selecting the iFeature from the Insert panel. You may want to change the iFeature image to help identify it in the Model browser. To do this, open the iFeature file in a separate window and in the iFeature panel, click 🔲 (Change Icon). The Edit Icon dialog box opens as shown in Figure 10–18.

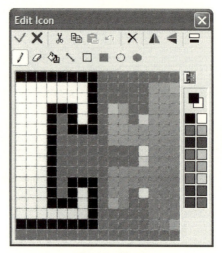

Figure 10–18

Using the colors and the tools in the dialog box, create a new image to represent the iFeature. To obtain a white background, you must use the Magenta color in all areas that are required to be displayed as white. Once the icon is complete, save the .IDE file. The new icon will display once you restart the Autodesk Inventor software.

Placement Help

You can create a separate document to help describe, to future users of the iFeature, how it is to be placed and used in a model. To attach a placement help file, open the iFeature's .IDE file and on the *Tools* tab>Insert panel, click 🔲 (Insert Object). Select **Create from File** and click **Browse** to browse to the document. Click **Open** when you have selected the required document.

The placement help file can be added as a linked or an embedded object. Embedded objects are not dependent on the external file, whereas linked files are dependent. Click **OK**. The file displays in the Model browser, as shown in Figure 10–19.

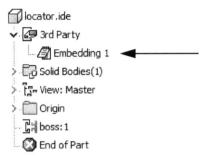

Figure 10–19

In the Model browser, right-click on the placement help file and select **Placement Help** to set this as the placement help document. Save the iFeature file.

To open the placement help file, double-click on the file in the Model browser.

Practice 10a Create and Insert an iFeature

Practice Objectives

- Assign parameter names and equations to existing dimensions in a model to prepare for iFeature creation.
- Create an iFeature from existing geometry so that a limit and range is established for selected iFeature dimensional values and an appropriate prompt is defined for the placement plane.
- Insert a placement help file to be used as a reference for locating an iFeature in a model.
- Insert an iFeature into a new part file.

In this practice, you create an iFeature. You set the limits for the iFeature's sketch diameter and set a range for one of the features' height. You then place help text in the iFeature file to help insert it. The completed model is shown in Figure 10–20.

Figure 10–20

Task 1 - Change the name of model parameters.

iFeatures are created from existing features or sketches. To make it easier to create the iFeature, use parameters that have descriptive names and apply those parameters to items in the sketches and features that will become your iFeature. Creating an iFeature with default parameters (such as d0) can be confusing to identify. In this task, you change the name of model parameters (dimensions).

1. Open **createif.ipt**. The model displays as shown in Figure 10–21.

Figure 10–21

2. In the *Manage* tab>Parameter panel, click f_x (Parameters) to open the Parameters dialog box.

3. Change the names of parameters as follows:
   - *d1* to **diameter**
   - *d2* to **height**

Plan your iFeatures so that a minimum number of parameters are required. If a dimension is always half of another dimension, use an equation rather than forcing you to enter both numbers.

4. Change the equations as follows:
   - *d0* to **diameter/3**
   - *d4* to **diameter/2**

The Parameters dialog box displays as shown in Figure 10–22.

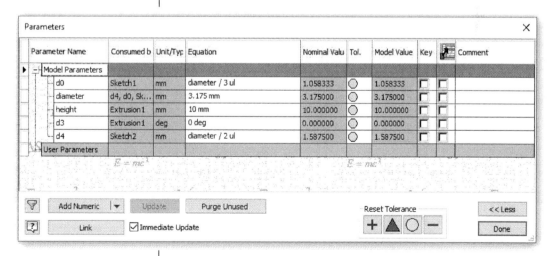

Figure 10–22

5. Click **Done** to close the dialog box.

Task 2 - Create an iFeature.

1. In the *Manage* tab>Author panel, click (Extract iFeature) to open the Extract iFeature dialog box.

2. Select **Extrusion1** in the Model browser. The *Selected Features* area displays **Extrusion1**, **Revolution1**, and the work features because the other features are children. The renamed parameters are automatically entered in the *Size Parameters* area and the **Extrusion1** sketch plane is displayed in the *Position Geometry* area. The Extract iFeature dialog box displays as shown in Figure 10–23.

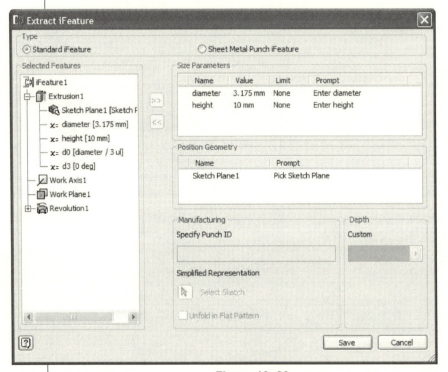

Figure 10–23

3. Note that the Limit for both parameters is set to **None**. Select **None** for the diameter parameter, and select **List** in the drop-down list. The List Values for the diameter dialog box opens.

4. Select **Click here to add value** at the bottom of the list and add the following diameters: **1.5875**, **4.7625**, **6.35**, **9.525**.

5. Set **4.7625** as the *Default*, as shown in Figure 10–24.

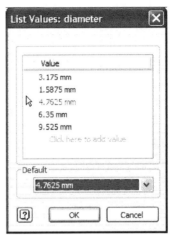

Figure 10–24

6. Click **OK** to close the dialog box.

7. Select **None** for the height parameter, and select **Range** in the drop-down list. The Specify Range for the height dialog box opens.

8. Set the *Range* to **2.5<10<25**, as shown in Figure 10–25.

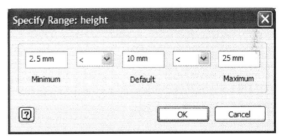

Figure 10–25

9. Click **OK** to close the dialog box.

10. Change the *Prompt* for **Sketch Plane1** to **Pick plane for base of locator**, as shown in Figure 10–26.

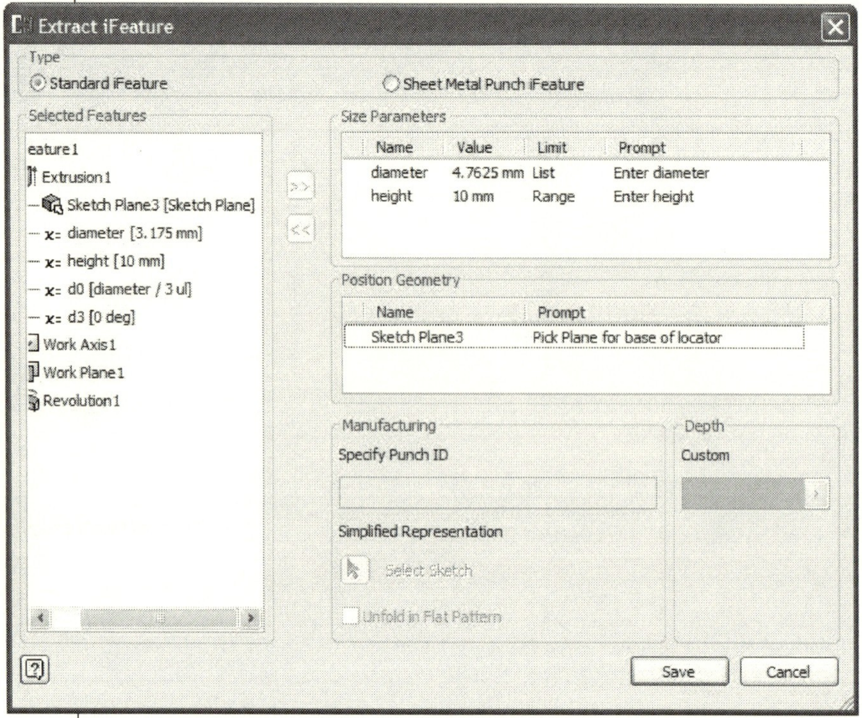

Figure 10–26

11. Right-click on **iFeature1** at the top of the *Selected Features* pane and select **Rename**. Enter **boss** as the new name. This name will be used to identify the iFeature in a Model browser whenever it is placed.

Once the iFeature is defined and its locating position is determined, it is saved in the *Catalog* folder. Alternatively, you can create a new folder in the *Catalog* folder to save your iFeatures.

Renaming the iFeature is different from naming the iFeature's .IDE filename.

12. In the Extract iFeature dialog box, click **Save**. The Save As dialog box opens.

13. In the Save As dialog box, ensure that you are in the *Catalog* folder. Right-click in the white area, and select **New>Folder**. Create a new folder in the *Catalog* folder with your own name. Store your iFeatures in this folder.

14. Double-click on the new folder, type the name **locator** for the iFeature filename, and click **Save** to save the iFeature. iFeatures are saved with the extension .IDE.

Copying Between Parts (iFeatures)

15. Close the createif.ipt file. You do not need to save the changes, since they are already saved in the catalog.

Task 3 - Insert a placement help file in iFeature.

1. Open the file **locator.ide** that you just created (*C:\Users\Public\Public Documents\Autodesk\Inventor 2019\Catalog\<yourname>* folder or the specified path that was used on your computer).

2. In the *Tools* tab>Insert panel, click (Insert Object) to open the Insert Object dialog box.

3. Select **Create from File** and click **Browse** to browse to the **locator.doc** file in your practice files folder. Click **Open**. This file is a Placement Help file that can be added as a linked or an embedded object. Embedded objects are not dependent on the external file, whereas linked files are dependent.

4. Click **OK**. Expand the **3rd Party** node and the file displays in the Model browser, as shown in Figure 10–27.

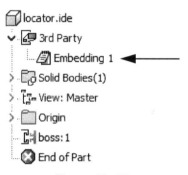

Figure 10–27

5. Right-click on **Embedding 1** in the Model browser, and select **Placement Help** to set this as the placement help document.

6. Save the iFeature file and close the window. You cannot insert an open iFeature.

Task 4 - Insert an iFeature.

In this task, you insert and place the locator.ide file into a part.

1. Open **fanbase.ipt**.

2. In the *Manage* tab>Insert panel, click (Insert iFeature).

3. Browse to and open the **locator.ide** file.

   The green symbol in the graphic on the left side of the Insert iFeature dialog box indicates that you are in the Position step. This step enables you to select a face to locate the feature. Once you select the face, you can select the rotation or the position symbol to rotate or move the part. Alternatively, you can type the rotation angle in the fields.

4. Select the face shown in Figure 10–28 as the position plane.

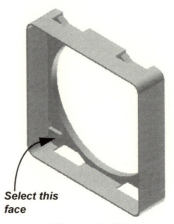

Select this face

Figure 10–28

   A checkmark displays to the left of the name of the feature or sketch when the placement for the iFeature has been fully defined.

5. Once the position is defined, click **Next** to move to the Size step. The Size step lists the names and default values of the parameters for locator.ide, as shown in Figure 10–29.

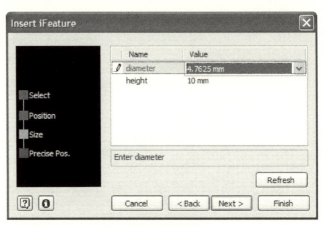

Figure 10–29

6. Note that the diameter *Value* column shows the default, **4.7625mm**.

7. Enter **8mm** in the height *Value* column. Remember the height range is between 2.5mm and 25mm.

8. Once you select the size, click **Refresh** to update the iFeature on the screen.

9. Click **Next** to move to Precise Pos. step.

The Precise Pos. step determines what happens when the command is completed.

10. Click [icon] to open **locator.doc**, as shown in Figure 10–30.

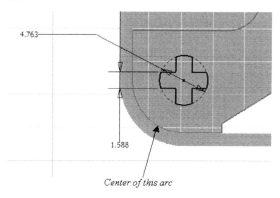

Instructions for Placement of the LOCATOR:

[Move the iFeature sketch to the center of the arc shown below and constrain the center of the sketch to the center of arc shown below. This will fully locate the iFeature]

end

Figure 10–30

11. Read the instructions on how to locate the locator.ide.

12. Close **locator.doc**.

13. Select **Activate Sketch Edit Immediately** to activate the sketch environment.

14. Click **Finish** to complete the operation.

There is no link between the .IDE file and the iFeature once the iFeature is placed. Therefore, changes to the .IDE file do not affect iFeatures that are already placed. Even if you insert a revised iFeature into a file that contains an older version of the feature, the original iFeature is not affected. To update an already placed iFeature, delete the old iFeature and insert the new one.

15. Locate the iFeature sketch according to the instructions and exit the sketch. The locator displays on the model, as shown in Figure 10–31. The placement help file displays in the **fanbase.ipt** part Model browser, where you can edit it.

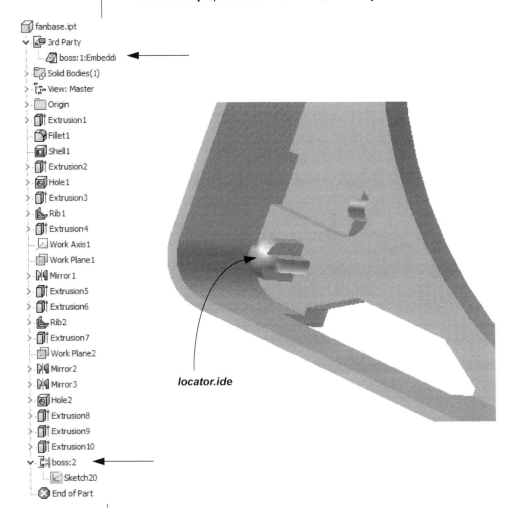

Figure 10–31

Note that although you inserted the **locator.ide** iFeature, the iFeature is identified in the Model browser as boss.

16. Insert three instances of **locator.ide** in the three corners of **fanbase.ipt**. Select the same plane as before for the position. Try to set the height of the feature to **30mm**. Since it is outside the specified range, the value is not allowed. Change the diameter; note that you can select from the values you specified in the list.

17. Save and close the model.

Practice 10b Table-Driven iFeature

Practice Objectives

- Create an iFeature that is driven by a table defining the possible variations that can be retrieved during placement.
- Insert a table driven iFeature into a new part file.
- Edit a placed iFeature to change the table instance that was inserted into a new part file.

In this practice, you create a table-driven iFeature from a hole pattern, and use the iFeature in a part. The final model displays as shown in Figure 10–32.

Figure 10–32

Task 1 - Create an iFeature.

1. Open **circle.ipt**.

2. In the *Manage* tab>Author panel, click (Extract iFeature) to open the Extract iFeature dialog box.

3. In the Model browser, select **Hole1** (**Circular Pattern2** is automatically selected with **Hole1** because it is a child of Hole1). The Extract iFeature dialog box displays as shown in Figure 10–33.

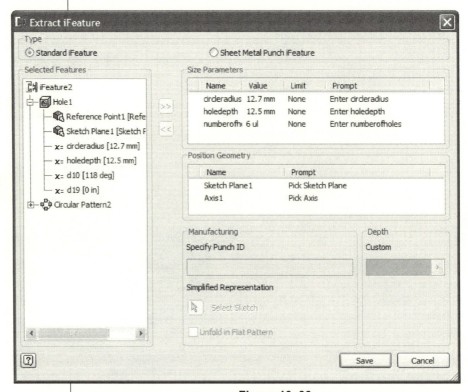

Figure 10–33

4. At the top of the *Selected Features* pane, right-click on **iFeature2** and select **Rename**. Enter **hole_array** as the new name.

5. In the Extract iFeature dialog box, click **Save**.

6. Save the file as **hole_array** in the *C:\....\Catalog\<yourname>* folder.

7. Close **circle.ipt**. You do not need to save the changes, since they are already saved in the catalog.

Task 2 - Create a table-driven iFeature.

1. Open **hole_array.ide** (*C:\Users\Public\ Public Documents\ Autodesk\Inventor 2019\Catalog \<yourname>* folder or the specified path that was used on your computer). The iFeature file only contains the selected features, as shown in Figure 10–34.

Figure 10–34

2. In the *iFeature* tab>iFeature panel, click (iFeature Author Table). The dialog box opens as shown in Figure 10–35. The named parameters and their values are already listed.

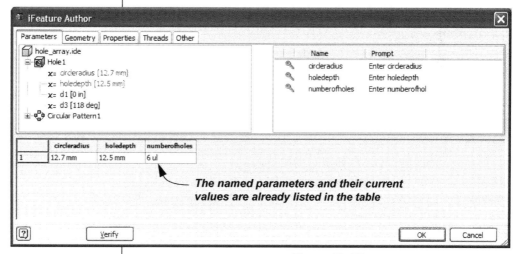

Figure 10–35

3. Select the *Threads* tab and copy **Hole1: Designation** from the left to the right side using the >> icon to add it as a column in the table.

4. Select the *Other* tab. Click **Click here to add a value** if a value doesn't already exist in the right-hand column. Enter **Mating Assembly** as the *Name* and **Mating Assembly** for the *Prompt*, as shown in Figure 10–36. It is added as a column.

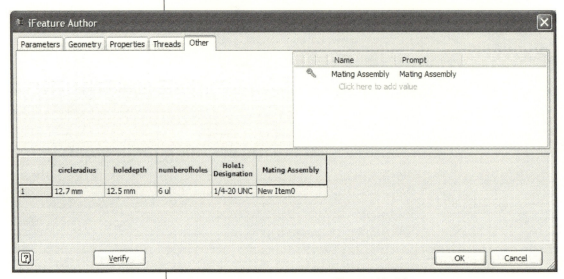

Figure 10–36

5. Select the *circleradius* column header, right-click, and select **Key>1** in the shortcut menu. Then, do the following:

   - Assign Key 2 to the *Hole1:Designation* column.
   - Assign Key 3 to the *holedepth* column.
   - Assign Key 4 to the *numberofholes* column.

6. Verify that the *Mating Assembly* column is not defined as a key by right-clicking the column header and selecting **Key> Not a Key**.

7. To enter custom values in the *Mating Assembly* column you must set it as a custom parameter. Right-click on the *Mating Assembly* column header and select **Custom Parameter Column**.

Copying Between Parts (iFeatures)

8. Select the *Properties* tab. Currently, no custom properties are listed. You must first assign a custom property to the .IDE file. Click **OK** to close the iFeature Author dialog box.

9. In the Model browser, right-click on **hole_array.ide** and select **iProperties**. Select the *Custom* tab.

10. Enter **Internal Drill Number** as the name, accept **Text** as the type, and enter **IDN7** as the value. Click **Add** and click **OK**.

11. In the iFeature panel, click (iFeature Author Table).

12. Select the *Properties* tab. Expand Custom at the bottom of the list and use >> to add *Internal Drill Number* as a property.

13. Select the first row and select **Insert Row** in the shortcut menu. Add 8 additional rows for a total of 10 rows. Edit the table values as shown in Figure 10–37. No edits are required in the *Mating Assembly* or *Internal Drill Number* columns.

	circleradius	holedepth	numberofholes	Hole1: Designation	Mating Assembly	Internal Drill Number
1	12.7 mm	12.5 mm	6 ul	1/4-20 UNC	New Item0	IDN7
2	12.7 mm	12.5 mm	6 ul	1/4-20 UNC	New Item0	IDN7
3	12.7 mm	12.5 mm	6 ul	1/4-24 UNS	New Item0	IDN7
4	12.7 mm	12.5 mm	6 ul	1/4-24 UNS	New Item0	IDN7
5	12.7 mm	12.5 mm	4 ul	1/4-20 UNC	New Item0	IDN7
6	12.7 mm	12.5 mm	4 ul	1/4-20 UNC	New Item0	IDN7
7	12.7 mm	19.05 mm	4 ul	1/4-20 UNC	New Item0	IDN7
8	12.7 mm	17.05 mm	4 ul	1/4-20 UNC	New Item0	IDN7
9	12.7 mm	19.05 mm	6 ul	1/4-20 UNC	New Item0	IDN7
10	12.7 mm	19.05 mm	6 ul	1/4-20 UNC	New Item0	IDN7

Figure 10–37

14. Click **OK** to close the iFeature Author dialog box.

15. Save and close **hole_array.ide**.

Task 3 - Insert the iFeature.

1. Open **drivenif.ipt**.

2. In the *Tools* tab>Options panel, click (Application Options). Select the *iFeature* tab and verify that **Use Key 1 as Browser Name column** is enabled. By enabling this option, you can customize the name displayed in the Model browser for an iFeature to show the Key1 parameter name and its value. Click **OK**.

3. In the *Manage* tab>Insert panel, click (Insert iFeature) or use the menu below this option to open **hole_array.ide**.

4. Select the face shown in Figure 10–38 as the position plane. Select the Axis row and select one of the cylinders as **Axis1**. A checkmark displays to the left of the name of the feature or sketch when the placement has been fully defined.

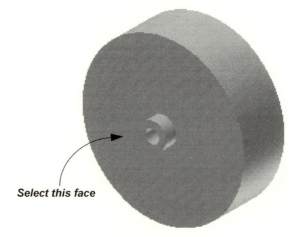

Select this face

Figure 10–38

5. Once you define the position, click **Next** to move to the Size step.

6. Accept the defaults in the *Size* area. Click **Next** to move to the Precise Pos. step.

7. Select **Do not Activate Sketch Edit**.

8. Click **Finish** to complete the operation.

   Note: As of the release of this material (April 2018), the addition of the iFeature was causing a failure. When the iFeature is initially displayed it is unexpectedly snapping to the central axis of the part. To resolve this issue the following workaround has been found. Keep in mind that the preview of the iFeature placement is not always the same as the actual geometry placement. You can always make changes to its position once it is placed.

9. Cancel the iFeature placement in the failure dialog box.

10. In the *Manage* tab>Insert panel, click **Insert iFeature** ( ) or use the menu below this option to open **hole_array.ide**.

11. Select the same face (Figure 10–38) as the position plane.

12. Select the Axis row and select one of the cylinders as **Axis1**. A checkmark displays to the left of the name of the feature or sketch when placement has been fully defined.

13. Select the Move grip that is positioned on the central axis and drag the iFeature away and place it away from the central axis, while still remaining on the geometry.

14. Once you define the position, click **Next**.

15. Accept the defaults in the *Size* area. Click **Next**.

16. Select **Do not Activate Sketch Edit**.

17. Click **Finish** to complete the operation. The model displays similar to that shown in Figure 10–39. The circle diameter is dependent on where you placed the Move grip. You can edit the feature and add dimensions to place the holes as required.

Figure 10–39

18. In the Model browser, expand the iFeature, right-click on the table, and select **Edit iFeature**. The Insert iFeature dialog box opens.

19. Enter new hole values, as shown in Figure 10–40.

20. Select the *Mating Assembly* value and enter **MCP0813** (shown in Figure 10–40) so that when the component is placed in an assembly, the mating component is identified.

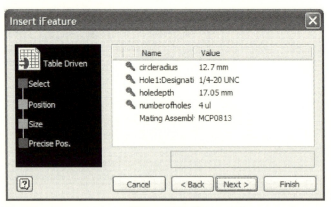

Figure 10–40

21. Click **Finish** to complete the operation. The model displays with four holes.

22. In the Model browser, right-click on **drivenif.ipt** and select **iProperties**. Select the *Custom* tab. Note that *Internal Drill Number* is listed as a custom property. Close the iProperties dialog box.

23. Save and close the model.

Practice 10c | (Optional) Slotted Hole iFeature

Practice Objectives

- Create an iFeature ensuring that all of the required geometry is included in the iFeature for accurate placement.
- Insert an iFeature into a new part file and vary the dimensional sizes to produce a required result.

In this practice, you will create an iFeature of a slotted hole. When placing the iFeature you will vary its angle and size. Minimal instructions are provided. Refer to the material for iFeatures if required. The completed model is shown in Figure 10–41.

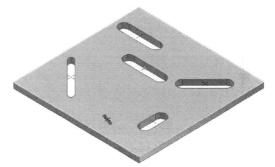

Figure 10–41

Task 1 - Create a part with a slotted hole.

1. Create a new part based on the **Standard (in).ipt** template. Create the part as a ½" thick plate measuring 12" x 12", as shown in Figure 10–42.

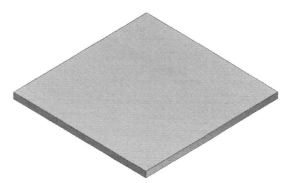

Figure 10–42

2. Start a new sketch on one of the large faces of the plate and randomly place six points using the ╬ (Point) option. It is not required to constrain or dimension these points. Finish the sketch. The model displays similar to that shown in Figure 10–43.

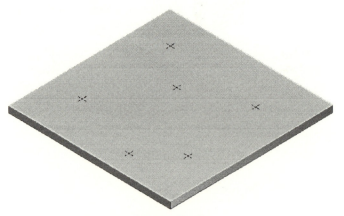

Figure 10–43

3. Start a new sketch on the same face as the sketch from Step 2. Do not just edit the previous sketch. Use the **Project Geometry** tool to project a point created in Step 2, as shown in Figure 10–44.

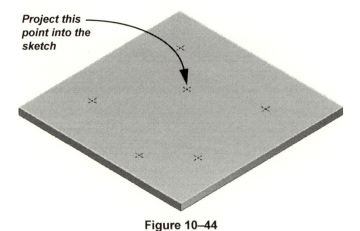

Figure 10–44

4. Sketch a slot, similar to that shown in Figure 10–45. Constrain the projected point to the midpoint of the center-to-center line. When editing the two values, enter **Slot_Length=3** and **Slot_Radius=.5** to rename the parameters, while at the same time editing the values of the parameters.

Renaming parameters while you are editing their values prevents you from having to open the Parameters dialog box to reassign names.

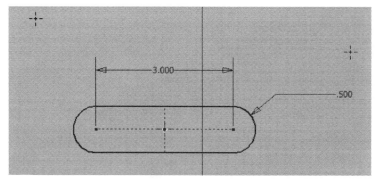

Figure 10–45

5. Finish the sketch.

6. Create the slotted cut shown in Figure 10–46 using **Extrude**. Extrude the slot through **All** of the model.

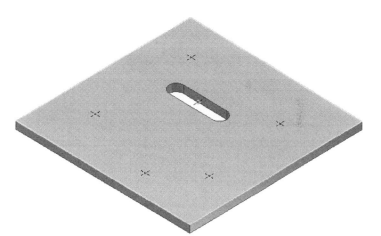

Figure 10–46

Task 2 - Create an iFeature.

1. In the *Manage* tab>Author panel, click ▣ (Extract iFeature) to open the Extract iFeature dialog box.

2. Select the extrude (slot) feature.

3. Because the point was used as a reference in the slot sketch, it is available as a reference for the slot iFeature. In the *Selected Features* area, select **Reference Point1** and transfer it to the right area to add the work point to the iFeature.

4. Reorder the *Position Geometry* by dragging **Profile Plane1** above **Reference Point1**. Edit the prompts, as shown in Figure 10–47.

5. In the *Selected Features* area, right-click on **iFeature#** and select **Rename**. Enter **slot** as the new name.

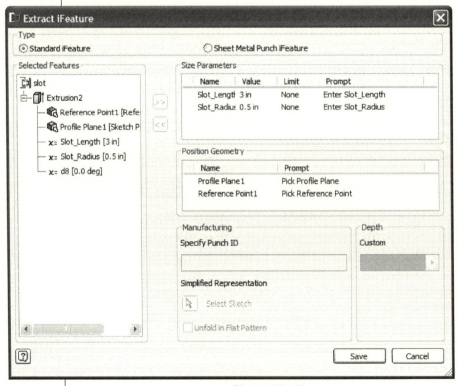

Figure 10–47

6. Save the iFeature to your *Catalog* folder as **slot.ide**.

Copying Between Parts (iFeatures)

Task 3 - Insert the iFeature.

In this task, you insert a number of instances of the slot.ide feature in the same model.

1. In the *Manage* tab>Insert panel, click (Insert iFeature) or use the menu below this option to open **slot.ide**.

2. Select the profile plane and slot center points to place the slots, as shown in Figure 10–48. You will need to add separate features for each instance. To rotate the slot on the profile plane, in the Insert iFeature dialog box, enter an *Angle*. To vary the sizes, you need to enter new values for the radius and length, as required. Keep in mind that the preview of the iFeature placement is not always the same as the actual geometry placement. You can always make changes to its position once it is placed.

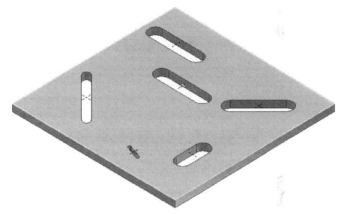

Figure 10–48

3. Save and close the model.

Chapter Review Questions

1. Renamed model parameters are automatically included as variable size parameters when creating an iFeature.

   a. True
   b. False

2. Which file extension type is used to store an iFeature?

   a. .IDW
   b. .IDE
   c. .IPN
   d. .IPT

3. Which of the following are valid menu options that can be used when defining limits on the parameter size of an iFeature? (Select all that apply.)

   a. Range
   b. List
   c. User Entry
   d. None

4. If you insert a revised iFeature into a file that contains an older version of the feature, the original iFeature is automatically updated.

   a. True
   b. False

5. Which of the following statements are true regarding the **Copy** option used to copy features. (Select all that apply.)

   a. It can only be used to copy features in the same model.
   b. It can be used to copy a chamfer from one edge and duplicate it on another edge.
   c. It can be used to create a copy of a sketched extrusion.
   d. A copied feature can always be created independent of the original; however, there are restrictions on when a dependent copy is possible.

6. Which of the following statements are true regarding the table-driven iFeatures? (Select all that apply.)

   a. The table for a table-driven iFeature is created during iFeature creation in a part model.

   b. All parameters defined during iFeature creation are automatically added as columns in the iFeature's table.

   c. The *Other* tab in the iFeature Author enables you to add iProperties to the table.

   d. Custom columns can be added in the iFeature Author and add a unique attribute value for each instance.

Command Summary

Button	Command	Location
	Change Icon	• **Ribbon:** *iFeature* tab>iFeature panel
N/A	Copy (features)	• **Context menu:** In Model browser with feature name selected
	Edit iFeature	• **Ribbon:** *iFeature* tab>iFeature panel • **Context menu** from the Model browser
	Edit Using Spread Sheet	• **Ribbon:** *iFeature* tab>iFeature panel
	Extract iFeature	• **Ribbon:** *Manage* tab>Author panel
	iFeature Author Table	• **Ribbon:** *iFeature* tab>iFeature panel • **Context menu:** In the graphics window
	Insert iFeature	• **Ribbon:** *Manage* tab>Insert panel
	Insert Object	• **Ribbon:** *Tools* tab>Insert panel
	View Catalog	• **Ribbon:** *iFeature* tab>iFeature panel

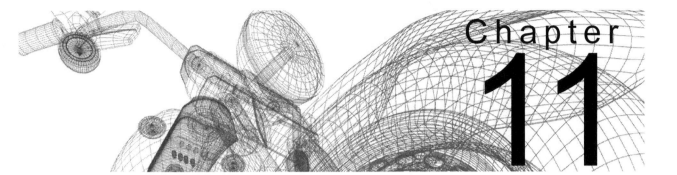

iParts

The Autodesk® Inventor® iPart option is a design option that enables you to create variations in your part designs quickly and easily. iParts can be used to create similar models, instead of recreating the same model repeatably with slight variations. Once a part has been created with iPart members, the members can also be documented in a drawing using tables.

Learning Objectives in this Chapter

- Create an iPart that can generate different configurations of a model.
- Group iPart attributes into keys to logically sort the members for quick access to the configurations.
- Insert standard or custom iParts into an assembly based on specified Keys, Tree, or Table lists for the iPart factory.
- Replace an iPart in an assembly with a new iPart instance.
- Modify an iPart factory using the Edit Table or Edit via Spreadsheet options to add or modify parameters and attributes.
- Specify whether an edit made to an iPart should reflect only in the active member or in all members.
- Use a table-driven iPart to create an iFeature.
- Use a drawing table to clearly document the members and attributes that make up an iPart.

11.1 iPart Creation

Many similar parts are used in creating assemblies. For example, one bolt may differ from another bolt only in its length. Rather than create several bolts that are identical in all ways but length, you can create one iPart to cover all lengths. Like other part files, iPart files have the extension .IPT. The iPart in Figure 11–1 shows three configurations of a cover plate.

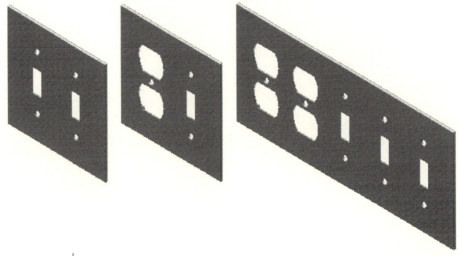

Figure 11–1

iPart files are called iPart Factories. The factory produces parts based on the part geometry and attribute values stored in a table. The new parts created by an iPart factory are unique files. By default, a part file is not created until the iPart is placed in an assembly.

General Steps

Use the following general steps to create an iPart:

1. Create or open a part with parameters.
2. Start the creation of an iPart.
3. Select the configurable attributes.
4. Add iPart members.
5. Verify the table.
6. Set up keys.
7. (Optional) Assign custom parameters.
8. Complete the operation.
9. Verify iPart instances in the Model browser.
10. (Optional) Generate iPart Members.

Step 1 - Create or open a part with parameters.

Create or open a part. To make it easier to create the iPart, use parameters that have descriptive names and apply those parameters to items in the features that will become your attributes. Consider the following:

- Plan your iPart so that a minimum number of parameters are required. If a dimension is always half of another dimension, use an equation rather than input both numbers.

- Consider what design variations are required and can be created. The parameters and dimensions that control this are used to create the iPart.

Step 2 - Start the creation of an iPart.

In the *Manage* tab>Author panel, click (Create iPart). The iPart Author dialog box opens, as shown in Figure 11–2.

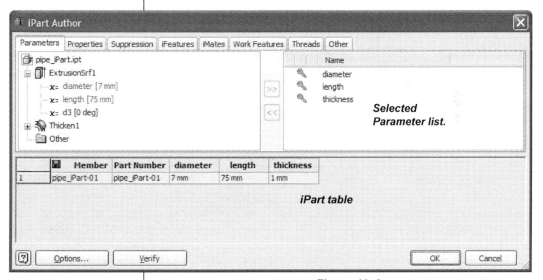

Figure 11–2

Step 3 - Select the configurable attributes.

The tabs in the iPart Author dialog box contain the configurable attributes that can be varied to create the different iPart configurations. Any parameter that has been renamed is automatically added as a configurable attribute. Use the >> and << buttons to add and remove additional parameters, as required.

The iPart Author tabs are described as follows:

Tabs	Description
Parameters tab	Contains the parameters used in the part, which are listed under the features in which they belong.
Properties tab	Enables you to add feature information, such as the part number or the name of the manufacturer.
Suppression tab	Enables you to specify individual features to compute or suppress for each instance of the part.
iFeatures tab	Enables you to specify which table-driven instance of an iFeature to include in the iPart, or set the suppression status. Add the **Table Replace** item and assign rows from the iFeature to instances in the iPart.
iMates tab	Enables you to include iMates. You can specify to do any of the following: include, suppress, set offset values, specify matching name, and specify sequence number.
Work Features tab	Enables you to specify work features to include.
Threads tab	Enables you to add thread variables to the iPart. Designations such as UNC are case-sensitive.
Other tab	Enables you to create additional columns in the table. These columns do not control the size of the part, but can be used as keys in the table.

Step 4 - Add iPart members.

Right-click on the first row, and select **Insert Row**. Continue adding rows, as required. Each additional row is an additional iPart member or configuration.

*Alternatively, you can use Excel to add new iPart members. This enables you to use some of the built-in Excel functionality, such as copy, paste, formulas, and sorting. To do so, click **OK**, right-click on Table in the Model browser, and select **Edit via Spreadsheet**.*

iParts

The columns in the table shown in Figure 11–3 list the parameter names and other attributes added from the tabs. Each row lists the values for one iPart instance. Select each table cell and enter the required attribute value.

	Member	Part Number	diameter	length	thickness
1	Pipe-7x75x1	Pipe-7x75x1	7 mm	75 mm	1 mm
2	Pipe-7x80x1	Pipe-7x80x1	7 mm	80 mm	1 mm
3	Pipe-7x85x1	Pipe-7x85x1	7 mm	85 mm	1 mm
4	Pipe-7x75x1_1	Pipe-7x75x1_1	7 mm	75 mm	1.1 mm
5	Pipe-7x80x1_1	Pipe-7x80x1_1	7 mm	80 mm	1.1 mm
6	Pipe-7x85x1_1	Pipe-7x85x1_1	7 mm	85 mm	1.1 mm
7	Pipe-8x75x1	Pipe-8x75x1	8 mm	75 mm	1 mm
8	Pipe-8x80x1	Pipe-8x80x1	8 mm	80 mm	1 mm
9	Pipe-8x85x1	Pipe-8x85x1	8 mm	85 mm	1 mm
10	Pipe-8x75x1_1	Pipe-8x75x1_1	8 mm	75 mm	1.1 mm
11	Pipe-8x80x1_1	Pipe-8x80x1_1	8 mm	80 mm	1.1 mm
12	Pipe-8x85x1_1	Pipe-8x85x1_1	8 mm	85 mm	1.1 mm

Figure 11–3

- The row highlighted in green is the default part used when placing the iPart in an assembly. To change the default row, right-click on the required row and select **Set As Default Row**.

- To suppress a feature in a part, enter one of the following in the *iPart* table cell: Suppress, S, s, Off, OFF, off, 0.

- To compute the feature, enter one of the following in the cell: Compute, C, c, U, u, ON, on, On, 1.

- When entering values that require either **Exclude** or **Include**, the first letter in each word can be entered as lowercase, but the entire word is required to be a valid entry.

Step 5 - Verify the table.

To ensure all entered values are valid, click **Verify**. Invalid values highlight in the table in yellow. Correct all invalid values before continuing.

Step 6 - Set up keys.

Keys enable you to group iPart members according to their attribute values in a hierarchical manner. This sorts the iPart members logically, enabling quicker access to the required configuration.

If you do not assign keys, it can be much more difficult to find a specific configuration. Without creating any keys, configurations are listed as follows:

In the...	The configurations are listed...
iPart table	According to the order of the columns in the iPart table, as shown in Figure 11–4.
Model browser	According to the member name, as shown in Figure 11–5.
Place Standard iPart dialog box	Separately at the top-level branch, as shown in Figure 11–6.

	Member	Part Number	diameter	length	thickness
1	Pipe-7x75x1	Pipe-7x75x1	7 mm	75 mm	1 mm
2	Pipe-7x80x1	Pipe-7x80x1	7 mm	80 mm	1 mm
3	Pipe-7x85x1	Pipe-7x85x1	7 mm	85 mm	1 mm
4	Pipe-7x75x1_1	Pipe-7x75x1_1	7 mm	75 mm	1.1 mm
5	Pipe-7x80x1_1	Pipe-7x80x1_1	7 mm	80 mm	1.1 mm
6	Pipe-7x85x1_1	Pipe-7x85x1_1	7 mm	85 mm	1.1 mm
7	Pipe-8x75x1	Pipe-8x75x1	8 mm	75 mm	1 mm
8	Pipe-8x80x1	Pipe-8x80x1	8 mm	80 mm	1 mm
9	Pipe-8x85x1	Pipe-8x85x1	8 mm	85 mm	1 mm
10	Pipe-8x75x1_1	Pipe-8x75x1_1	8 mm	75 mm	1.1 mm
11	Pipe-8x80x1_1	Pipe-8x80x1_1	8 mm	80 mm	1.1 mm
12	Pipe-8x85x1_1	Pipe-8x85x1_1	8 mm	85 mm	1.1 mm

Figure 11–4

Figure 11–5

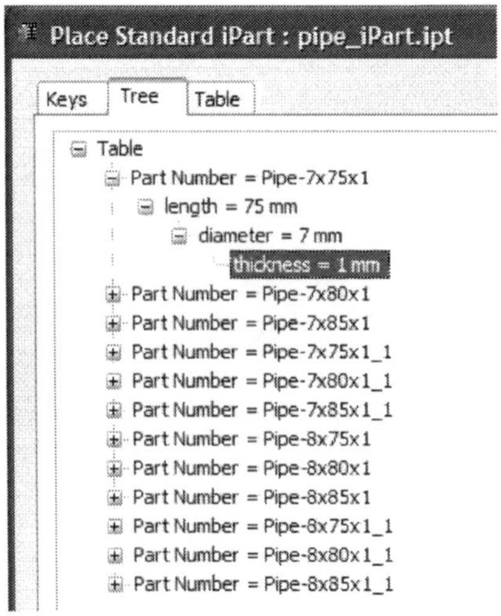

Figure 11–6

iParts

By assigning keys, you are able to organize these configurations into a logical and hierarchical structure, as shown in Figure 11–7. In the example shown, the iParts have been assigned keys for their diameter and thickness. This enables you to quickly expand the branches to find a required configuration, or easily view all of the different lengths that are available for a specific diameter and thickness.

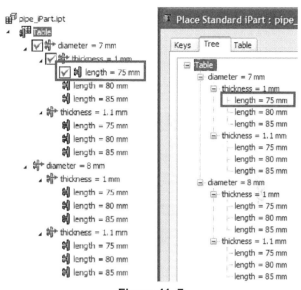

Figure 11–7

Not all attributes need keys. If assigned keys already narrow down the configurations to one, then no remaining keys are required.

To organize in this way you specify keys when you create the iPart factory. A key symbol displays in front of each parameter, as shown in Figure 11–8.

- Blue keys indicate that the attribute is set as a key.
- Gray keys indicate that the attribute is not used as a key.

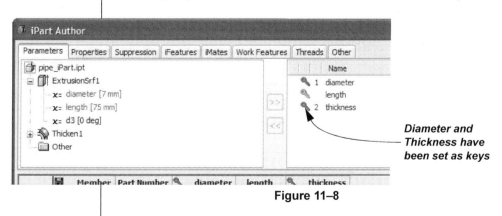

Diameter and Thickness have been set as keys

Figure 11–8

- The number next to the key indicates the hierarchy: 1 is the first key used for sorting, followed by 2, etc. Use the most descriptive or logical attribute as the first key.

- Up to nine keys can be used in a part factory. Click on a key to toggle it on or off.

- To change the order of key numbers, or to assign a key number to a parameter, in the *Name* column or table, right-click on the parameter and select **Key**. Select the required key number, as shown in Figure 11–9. You can also select a key to assign it to the next non-assigned key value.

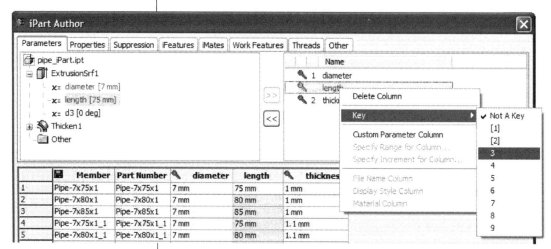

Figure 11–9

Step 7 - (Optional) Assign custom parameters.

A keyed column cannot be set as a custom column.

Parameters can be set up so that when you are placing the iPart factory member in an assembly, you are prompted to enter its value. When a custom parameter is assigned, the iPart is considered a custom iPart or custom iPart factory.

To assign a custom parameter, right-click on the parameter's heading and select **Custom Parameter Column**, as shown in Figure 11–10. Once assigned, the entire column turns blue, indicating that it is custom. It can be disabled later, if required, by clearing the **Custom Parameter Column** option.

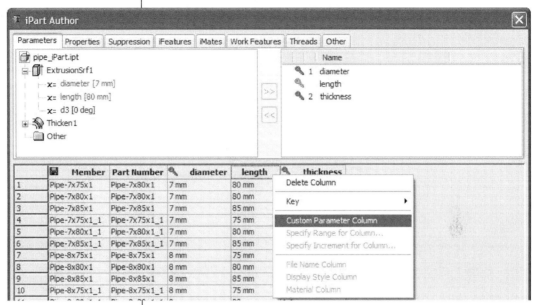

Figure 11–10

Step 8 - Complete the operation.

Once the iPart is defined, click **OK** to complete iPart creation.

Step 9 - Verify iPart instances in the Model browser.

After you have defined the iPart Factory, the table is listed in the Model browser. The members can be listed by their name or by key. Right-click on **Table** in the Model browser and select **List by Keys** or **List by Member Name** to customize the display of the members to either option.

Expand the table to see the configurations of the part defined in the table (organized according to the key attribute(s) you defined). The left side of Figure 11–11 shows the members displayed by key. The member name display is shown on the right side.

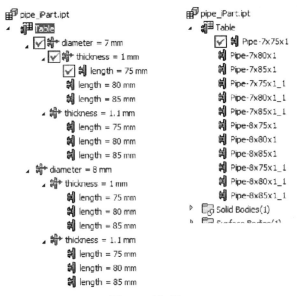

Figure 11–11

The active iPart member is marked with a checkmark. Double-click on the most-nested branches to activate that configuration (or right-click and select **Activate**). The most-nested branches are not expandable (i.e., an arrowhead symbol does not exist next to it in the Model browser).

Step 10 - (Optional) Generate iPart Members.

Once the iPart is created, you can create the member when it is used in an assembly or you can generate all the files at once.

iParts

How To: Generate All the Files at Once

1. In the Model browser, right-click on **Table** and select **List By Member Name**.
2. Hold <Shift> and select all member names.
3. Right-click and select **Generate Files**, as shown in Figure 11–12.

*If you selected **List By Keys**, you must select the most nested member names.*

Figure 11–12

The iPart members are created in a folder with the same name as the iPart file. In the above example, a folder called *hex_bolt* was created and contains four files.

If a Custom Parameter column is specified in the table, you will not be able to generate files. This is because the parameter is a required entry when the component is placed in an assembly; therefore, generating the files does not prompt you for user entry.

11.2 iPart Placement

Inserting iParts in assemblies is similar to inserting parts, except you must specify a member to use. The procedure varies depending on if they are a standard factory (does not contain any custom cells) or from a custom iPart factory (contains at least one custom cell).

When selecting iPart members for placement, the three tabs provide different ways of listing the same iPart members. This helps you quickly find the part you are looking for.

- The *Keys* tab, as shown in Figure 11–13, lists members in the order specified in the iPart Factory along with their current values. Click on a value to select a different standard value or to change a custom value. After the value for one attribute is selected, only the valid corresponding values will be listed for the other attributes.

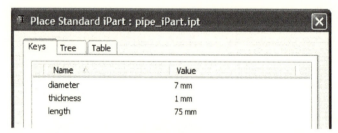

Figure 11–13

- The *Tree* tab, as shown in Figure 11–14, lists the values for each instance of the iPart. Expand the tree to see and select the instances of the part defined in the table (organized according to the key attributes).

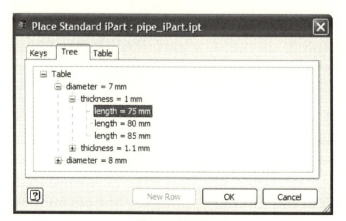

Figure 11–14

- The *Table* tab, as shown in Figure 11–15, lists the values for each instance of the iPart in the iPart Factory. Right-click on a column header to select ascending or descending sort order.

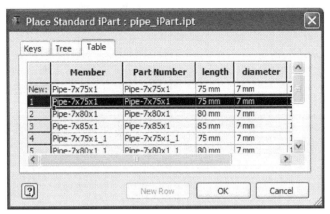

Figure 11–15

Placing a Standard iPart

How To: Place a Standard iPart

1. In the *Assemble* tab>Component panel, click (Place).
2. Select and open the iPart. The Place Standard iPart dialog box opens.
3. Select an iPart member using one of the following methods:
   - Select the current value in the *Keys* tab.
   - Select an instance from the *Tree* tab.
   - Select a row in the *Table* tab.
4. Select a point on the screen to place the component.
5. Repeat Steps 1 to 3 to place any additional iPart members.
6. Right-click and select **OK**.
7. Constrain the component in the assembly, as required.

When you place a standard iPart for the first time, the Autodesk Inventor software creates a new directory in the same directory as the iPart factory. The directory is created using the same name as the iPart factory. As you place iParts from the factory, each part is created and it is added to the folder.

Placing a custom iPart

How To: Place a Custom iPart

1. In the *Assemble* tab>Component panel, click (Place).
2. Select and open the iPart. The Place Custom iPart dialog box opens as shown in Figure 11–16. The right column contains the values you can customize.

Figure 11–16

3. Select an iPart member using one of the following methods:
   - Select the current value in the *Keys* tab.
   - Select an instance from the *Tree* tab.
   - Select a row in the *Table* tab.
4. Set the values for the custom items as required.
5. (Optional) Click **Browse** to change the *Destination Filename* for the new part. Standard iParts are named by default.
6. Select a point on the screen to place the component.
7. Right-click and select **OK**.
8. Constrain the component in the assembly, as required

Replacing an iPart

How To: Replace iPart Components

1. In the Model browser, expand the component, right-click on the **Table** node and select **Change Component**.
2. Select the new iPart instance to use.
3. Click **OK** to replace the instance.

iParts

11.3 Editing an iPart Factory

Edit Table

How To: Edit the iPart factory

1. Open the iPart factory as you would open any part file.
2. In the Model browser, right-click on the **Table** node in the Model browser and select **Edit Table** to open the iPart Author dialog box.
3. Add or change the entries in the dialog box, and click **OK**.
4. Save the changes to the file.

Changes that are made to an iPart Factory reflect in the iPart instances already placed in assemblies once their assembly has been updated.

Alternatively, in the Model browser, right-click on the **Table** node in the Model browser and select **Edit via Spreadsheet** to access the spreadsheet in Excel. You can add equations and relate the cells to each other. Equations that are entered in Excel display in red and cannot be changed in the iPart Author dialog box.

Adding Features to an iPart

When adding features to an existing iPart, considering the scope of the change is important. Consider whether the new feature should reflect in only the active factory member (**Edit Member Scope**) or reflect in all factory members (**Edit Factory Scope**). In the Author panel, the **Edit Member Scope** and **Edit Factory Scope** options, as shown in Figure 11–17, enable you to control the scope of change.

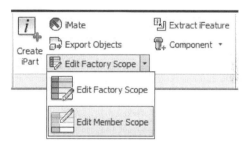

Figure 11–17

- By default, the scope is automatically set to change the entire factory (**Edit Factory Scope**), which means that if a feature is added, it is added to all members and no changes are made to the iPart table.

- If **Edit Member Scope** is specified and a feature is added, the feature and any dimensional parameters used to create it are automatically added to the table. The feature's cell for the active member will be marked to "Compute". Other members are automatically "Suppressed", but can be modified if required.

11.4 Creating iFeatures from a Table-Driven iPart

The entire table of data for the iPart is included in the new iFeature. You do not need to manually enter all instances of the iPart into the table.

Table-driven iParts, in their entirety, can be used to create a table-driven iFeature. This enables you to create an iFeature directly from a whole table-driven iPart.

How To: Create a Table-driven iFeature from a Table-driven iPart

1. Create a table-driven iPart using the standard workflow.
2. In the *Manage* tab>Author panel, click (Extract iFeature). The Extract iFeature dialog box opens.
3. In the Model browser, select the required features, or select those directly from the model geometry. To select the entire iPart, select the base feature first, and all following features will automatically be selected. Assign any of the *Size Parameters* or *Position Geometry*, as shown in Figure 11–18.

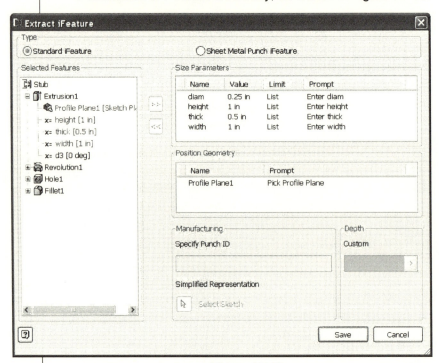

Figure 11–18

4. Save the iFeature in the catalog directory. The iFeature can be placed using the same techniques as placing any iFeature.

11.5 Tables for Factory Members

You can create tables for iParts and iAssemblies to show factory members and their attributes, as shown in Figure 11–19.

Table		
Member	Part Number	vise_screw_length
Short	Vise_Screw-01	138.75 mm
Medium	Vise_Screw-02	158.75 mm
Long	Vise_Screw-03	178.75 mm

Figure 11–19

How To: Create a Table for iPart Factory Members

1. Open or create a drawing that contains a view of an iPart member.
2. Select the *Annotate* tab>Table panel and click (General). The Table dialog box opens.
3. Select a drawing view containing the required iPart for which you want to create a table. The Table dialog box updates, as shown in Figure 11–20.

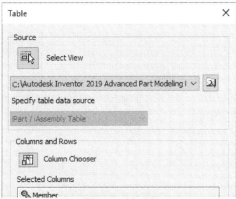

Figure 11–20

4. Click ▣ (Column Chooser). The Table Column Chooser dialog box opens, as shown in Figure 11–21.

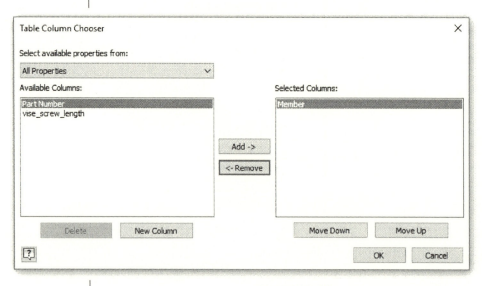

Figure 11–21

5. Customize the columns that will be displayed in the table and click **OK**.
   - Move the required column properties from the *Available Columns* list to the *Selected Columns* list to create it as a column in the table and display the attribute value for each factory member.
   - You can reorder the column properties in the *Selected Columns* list as required by clicking **Move Down** and **Move Up**.
6. Click **OK** to close the Table dialog box.
7. Move the cursor to the required location and click to place the table. The table populates with the columns and attributes of the iPart factory members.

Practice 11a Bolt iPart Factory

Practice Objectives

- Create an iPart factory using custom parameters to show different configurations of the part.
- Group iPart attributes into Keys to sort the iPart members logically, enabling quick access to the configuration.
- Add a new feature to the model and edit the member scope to define how the new feature will appear in the iPart.
- Generate the members of the iPart factory to create new part models.

In this practice, you rename part parameters so they have a descriptive name and are easily identifiable. You then establish logical relationships between these parameters so that only a small number of parameters control them all. Using these parameters you then create an iPart factory to quickly produce multiple bolt parts. The hex_bolt you will be working with is shown in Figure 11–22.

Figure 11–22

Task 1 - Change parameter names.

In this task, you change the bolt dimension (parameter) names to descriptive names. You also relate the parameters.

1. Open **hex_bolt.ipt**.
2. In the *Manage* tab>Parameters panel, click f_x (Parameters) and change the parameter names as follows:

   - d0 = stub_len
   - d6 = major_dia
   - d7 = minor_dia
   - d9 = h_width
   - d10 = h_height
   - d23 = thread_len
   - d24 = grip_len

3. Enter the following equation for the thread_len parameter:

   - thread_len = stub_len - grip_len

   This equation calculates the length of the thread when the stub length is changed.

4. Close the Parameters dialog box.

Task 2 - Create an iPart factory.

1. In the *Manage* tab>Author panel, click (Create iPart). The iPart Author dialog box opens. Note that the named parameters are already listed in the column on the right side and in the lower table.

2. Insert three more rows to the table by right-clicking on row **1** and selecting **Insert Row**. Enter the values shown in the Figure 11–23.

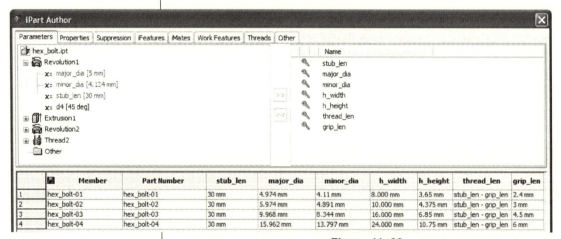

Figure 11–23

3. Select the *Threads* tab and add **Thread2:Designation** to the right column. The attribute is also added in the iPart table as a new column.

4. Enter the values shown in Figure 11–24 for the Thread Designation.

Member	Part Number	stub_len	major_dia	minor_dia	h_width	h_height	thread_len	grip_len	Thread2: Designation
hex_bolt-01	hex_bolt-01	30 mm	4.974 mm	4.11 mm	8.000 mm	3.65 mm	stub_len - grip_len	2.4 mm	M5x0.8
hex_bolt-02	hex_bolt-02	30 mm	5.974 mm	4.891 mm	10.000 mm	4.375 mm	stub_len - grip_len	3 mm	M6x1
hex_bolt-03	hex_bolt-03	30 mm	9.968 mm	8.344 mm	16.000 mm	6.85 mm	stub_len - grip_len	4.5 mm	M10x1.5
hex_bolt-04	hex_bolt-04	30 mm	15.962 mm	13.797 mm	24.000 mm	10.75 mm	stub_len - grip_len	6 mm	M16x2

Figure 11–24

iParts

If the Model browser is already displayed by keys, **List by Keys** *will not be available.*

If your iPart table is created with recognizable part numbers as the Member name you might want to consider setting the Table to **List by Member Name** *so you can easily activate a member of the iPart family.*

The Autodesk Inventor software enables you to create an iFeature from an iPart if the design intent exists.

Task 3 - Assign keys.

1. In the *Threads* tab, next to **Thread2:Designation**, click to assign it as Key 1. The key turns blue.

2. Assign Keys 2 and 3 to **stub_len** and **major_dia**, consecutively.

3. Click **OK** to close the iPart Author dialog box.

4. In Model browser, expand the Table. To configure the Model browser to display the iPart configurations listed by keys, right-click on Table and select **List by Keys**. Expand the branches for the first thread designation, as shown in Figure 11–25.

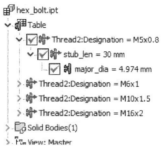

Figure 11–25

5. To activate another iPart configuration, expand it in the Model browser until it cannot expand further and double-click on the last key describing the configuration. This single iPart can be used in assemblies to add different configurations of the bolt.

6. Save the model.

Task 4 - Add a feature to the iPart.

1. Review the Author panel and note that the (Edit Factory Scope) is enabled. This is the default option, as shown in Figure 11–26.

Figure 11–26

2. Create a cut feature similar to that shown in Figure 11–27 on the active factory member.

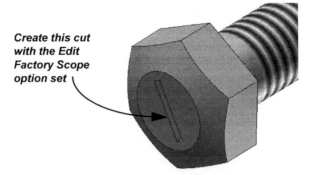

Create this cut with the Edit Factory Scope option set

Figure 11–27

3. In the Model browser, right-click on **Table** and select **List By Member Name**.

4. Double-click on the three other factory members to verify that this feature has been added to all members. If the values for the cut must be varied for each member, use the standard editing tools to add the parameters and modify them in the table.

5. Activate **hex_bolt-01**.

6. In the *Manage* tab>Author panel, click (Edit Member Scope), as shown in Figure 11–28.

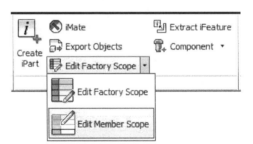

Figure 11–28

Consider setting up equations to ensure that the dimensions of both cuts are the same, or use sketching techniques to build both sketches into a single sketch but use it to create two extrusions.

7. Create a cut feature similar to that shown in Figure 11–29. For this practice, use similar dimensions to those used to create the previous cut.

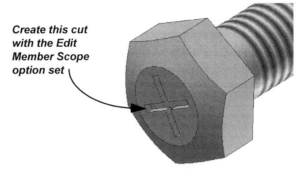

Create this cut with the Edit Member Scope option set

Figure 11–29

8. Double-click on the three other factory members to verify that this feature has not been added to the other members. It is only shown in the **hex_bolt-01** member because this was the active member when the feature was created.

9. Activate **hex_bolt-01**.

10. Right-click on Table in the Model browser and select **Edit Table** to open the iPart Author dialog box.

11. Note the new column shown in Figure 11–30. Note that Suppress is enabled for the cut in **hex_bolt-02**, **hex_bolt-03**, and **hex_bolt-04**, and the cut is computed in **hex_bolt-01**. The Suppression/Compute setting can be modified, if required. The values of the sketch dimensions can also be added to the table, if required, to control the size of the cuts in each factory instance.

eight	thread_len	grip_len	Thread2: Designation	Extrusion3
mm	stub_len - grip_len	2.4 mm	M5x0.8	Compute
5 mm	stub_len - grip_len	3 mm	M6x1	Suppress
mm	stub_len - grip_len	4.5 mm	M10x1.5	Suppress
5 mm	stub_len - grip_len	6 mm	M16x2	Suppress

Figure 11–30

12. Close the iPart Author dialog box.

Task 5 - Generate the members of the factory.

1. Verify that the Model browser is still set to **List By Member Name**.

2. Hold <Shift> and select all four member names.

3. Right-click and select **Generate Files**, as shown in Figure 11–31.

Figure 11–31

4. If you did not previously save the iPart file, you are prompted to save the file prior to file generation. Open Windows Explorer and review the four files in the new *Hex_Bolt* folder in the practice files directory.

5. Return to the Autodesk Inventor software.

Task 6 - Assign a custom parameter.

Although values have been assigned to the *grip_len* parameter for each iPart member, the values might need to vary depending on the current requirements when the hex_bolt is placed in an assembly. In this case, the column will be set as custom. The default values that were provided in the table will be used; however, designers will still have the option to enter custom values, if required.

1. In the Model browser, right-click on **Table** and select **Edit Table**. The iPart Author dialog box opens.

2. Right-click on the *grip_len* column header and select **Custom Parameter Column**, as shown in Figure 11–32. The column will turn purple, indicating that it is a custom column.

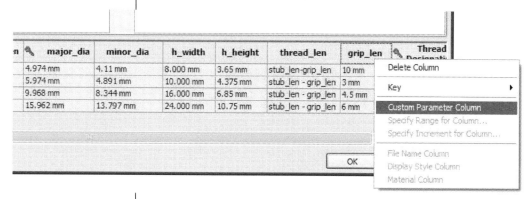

Figure 11–32

3. Click **OK** to close the iPart Author dialog box.

If a Custom Parameter Column is specified in the table, you are not able to generate files using the **Generate Files** command. You can only generate files when the part is assembled. This is because the parameter is a required entry when the component is placed in an assembly, and using the **Generate Files** command does not prompt you for user entry.

4. The iPart factory is ready to be placed. Save the file with the name **hex_bolt_iPart** and close the window.

Practice 11b | Create an iPart Factory

Practice Objectives

- Create an iPart factory using user parameters to show different configurations of the part.
- Modify and edit the iPart factory parameters and attributes in Autodesk Inventor software and Microsoft Excel.
- Place an iPart into an assembly file.
- Replace an iPart component in an assembly file with another instance from its factory.

In this practice, you create two user-defined parameters for a light-switch cover and assign them to part dimensions. To sort the instances of the part, you create an iPart factory to produce cover parts for varying combinations of switches and jacks. You edit the cover part and add a new row and column to the iPart factory via a spreadsheet. Finally, you place and constrain one instance in an assembly file. The final assembly is shown in Figure 11–33.

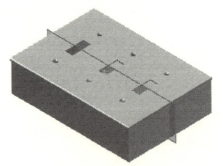

Figure 11–33

Task 1 - Create user-defined parameters.

In this task, you create two user-defined parameters and assign these parameters to part dimensions to sort various instances of the cover part.

1. Open **cover.ipt**. The model displays as shown in Figure 11–34.

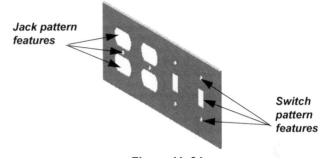

Figure 11–34

2. Use the Model browser to examine the cover part features and pattern numbers for the switch and jack pattern features.

3. In the *Manage* tab>Parameters panel, click f_x (Parameters). The Parameters dialog box opens.

4. Click **Add Numeric** and create two user-defined unitless (ul) parameters called **switches** and **jackpairs**, as shown in Figure 11–35.

d60	mm	58.42 mm	58.420000	58.420000	
User Parameters					
switches	ul	2 ul	2.000000	2.000000	
jackpairs	ul	2 ul	2.000000	2.000000	

Figure 11–35

5. Change the equation for the d0 dimension to the following to make it equal to the overall length of the part:

   • 25.4+(45.72*(switches+jackpairs))

6. Change the equation for the d18 dimension to **switches**.

7. Change the equation for the d50 dimension to **jackpairs**. The d18 and d50 dimensions are pattern numbers for the switches and jackpairs in the cover part.

8. Click **Done** to close the Parameters dialog box.

9. Update the model, if required.

10. Show the dimensions for the **Extrusion1**. Change the dimension display to **Expression.** The model displays as shown in Figure 11–36.

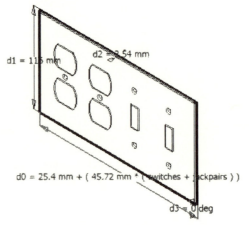

Figure 11–36

Task 2 - Create an iPart factory.

In this task, you create an iPart factory to sort the various instances of the cover part by pattern numbers for the switches and jackpairs.

1. Suppress the switch pattern and jack pattern features.

2. In the *Manage* tab>Author panel, click ![i] (Create iPart). The iPart Author dialog box opens. Note that the named parameters are already listed in the column on the right side of the table.

3. Select the key symbol next to the parameter switches in the right side panel. Key 1 is automatically assigned, the key turns blue, and a number 1 displays beside it.

4. Select the key symbol next to jackpairs to set it as Key 2. The key turns blue and a number 2 appears beside it.

5. Select the *Suppression* tab. The suppressed features are already listed in the column on the right side of the table.

6. Add **switch**, **switch holes**, **jacks**, and **jack holes** to the column on the right side. The features are also added as columns at the bottom of the table.

7. Right-click on row 1 and select **Insert Row**. Insert four more rows to the table and add the entries shown in Figure 11–37.

    - To suppress a feature in a part in the iPart table, enter one of the following entries in a cell: Suppress, S, s, Off, OFF, off, 0.
    - To compute the feature, enter one of the following entries in the cell: Compute, C, c, U, u, ON, on, On, 1.

	Member	Part Number	switches	jackpairs	switch pattern	jack pattern	switch	switch holes	jacks	jack holes
1	cover-01	cover-01	1 ul	3 ul	Suppress	Compute	Compute	Compute	Compute	Compute
2	cover-02	cover-02	2 ul	1 ul	Compute	Suppress	Compute	Compute	Compute	Compute
3	cover-03	cover-03	3 ul	0 ul	Compute	Suppress	Compute	Compute	Suppress	Suppress
4	cover-04	cover-04	1 ul	1 ul	Suppress	Suppress	Compute	Compute	Compute	Compute
5	cover-05	cover-05	0 ul	1 ul	Suppress	Suppress	Suppress	Suppress	Compute	Compute
6	cover-06	cover-06	3 ul	2 ul	Compute	Compute	Compute	Compute	Compute	Compute

Figure 11–37

8. Right-click on row 6 and select **Set As Default Row**.

9. Click **OK** to close the iPart Author dialog box. The cover part displays as shown in Figure 11–38. The features are computed according to the conditions you set in the table.

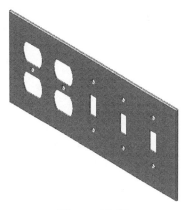

Figure 11–38

10. Save the model.

Task 3 - Edit the iPart factory.

1. Expand Table and ensure that the table display is as shown in Figure 11–39 showing all the keys not Model Names. If not, right-click on **Table** and select **List by Keys**. Expand **switches = 3**. The Model browser displays as shown in Figure 11–39.

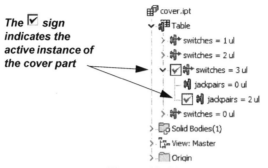

Figure 11–39

2. In the Model browser, expand **switches = 2 ul** and double-click on the **jackpairs = 1ul** node. The part displays as shown in Figure 11–40.

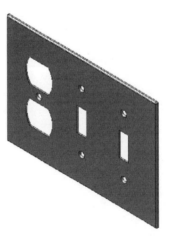

Figure 11–40

3. In the Model browser, right-click on **Table** and select **Edit Table**. The iPart Author dialog box opens.

4. Make row 3(cover-03) the default and click **OK**. The cover part displays as shown in Figure 11–41.

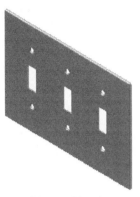

Figure 11–41

Task 4 - Edit the iPart factory via spreadsheet.

In this task, you add a row to the iPart table using a spreadsheet. You also add a column to the table to calculate the overall length of various instances.

1. In the Model browser, right-click on **Table** and select **Edit via Spreadsheet**. Click **OK** to confirm that the changes made via the Spreadsheet will take effect after the Excel process is closed.

2. Edit the iPart table in Microsoft Excel to remove the "ul" dimension from columns C and D, as shown in Figure 11–42.

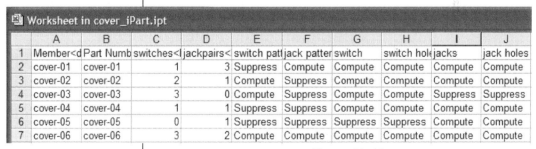

Figure 11–42

3. Add a row to the table with the values shown in Figure 11–43. The values are shown in row 8 of the table.

Worksheet in cover.ipt

	A	B	C	D	E	F	G	H	I	J
1	Member	Part Number	switches	jackpairs	switch pattern	jack pattern	switch	switch holes	jacks	jack holes
2	cover-01	cover-01	1	3	Suppress	Compute	Compute	Compute	Compute	Compute
3	cover-02	cover-02	2	1	Compute	Suppress	Compute	Compute	Compute	Compute
4	cover-03	cover-03	3	0	Compute	Suppress	Compute	Compute	Suppress	Suppress
5	cover-04	cover-04	1	1	Suppress	Suppress	Compute	Compute	Compute	Compute
6	cover-05	cover-05	0	1	Suppress	Suppress	Suppress	Suppress	Compute	Compute
7	cover-06	cover-06	3	2	Compute	Compute	Compute	Compute	Compute	Compute
8	cover-07	cover-07	4	2	Compute	Compute	Compute	Compute	Compute	Compute

Figure 11–43

4. Save the Microsoft Excel file and close excel to return to cover.ipt.

5. Activate the new row. The cover part displays as shown in Figure 11–44.

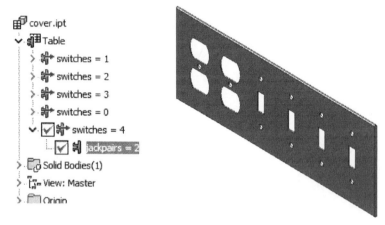

Figure 11–44

6. Open the iPart table using Microsoft Excel and add a column called **Overall Length** to the table.

7. Enter the formula below in each cell of the new column by replacing the "switches" and "jackpairs" with the corresponding C# and D#, as shown in Figure 11–45. Verify that none of the values under the switches and jackpairs columns contain "ul". The formula for the overall length is:

- 25.4+(45.72*(switches+jackpairs))

The table displays as shown in Figure 11–45.

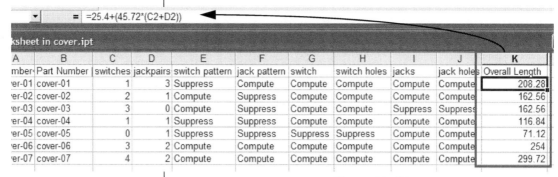

Figure 11–45

8. Save and close the Excel file and return to the part.

9. Edit the table. Note the color of the *Overall Length* column. Equations that are entered in Microsoft Excel cannot be changed in the iPart Author dialog box. Additionally, cells that contain these values display in red in the iPart Author dialog box.

10. Right-click the heading of the *Overall Length* column and select **Key>3** to assign Key 3 to the overall length column.

11. Make row 3 default. Close the dialog box.

12. In the Model browser, expand **Table** (change the Table to list by keys, if required). The overall length for each instance displays in the Model browser, as shown in Figure 11–46.

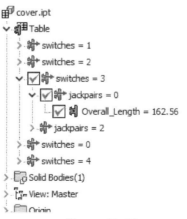

Figure 11–46

13. Save Copy As the part with the name **cover_iPart** and close the window. Do not save cover.ipt. This enables you to retain the original cover part.

Task 5 - Place the cover_iPart.

1. Create a new assembly file using the **Standard (mm).iam** template.

2. Place one instance of the **box_cover.ipt** part in the assembly. Right-click and select **Place Grounded at Origin** to place the first file in the assembly at (0, 0, 0).

3. Place one instance of the **cover_iPart.ipt** Component. The Place Standard iPart dialog box opens, as shown in Figure 11–47, showing the default key parameter values you previously set.

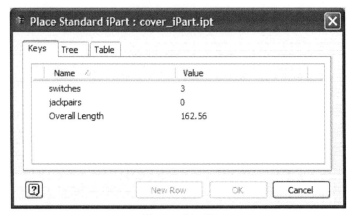

Figure 11–47

4. Select a point on the screen, right-click and select **OK**.

5. When you place a standard iPart for the first time, the Autodesk Inventor software creates a new directory in the same directory as the iPart factory. The directory is created using the same name as the iPart factory. As you place iParts from the factory, each part is created and is added to the folder. Open Windows Explorer and review the folder called *cover_iPart* in the practice files directory.

6. Fully constrain the cover_iPart. The assembly displays as shown in Figure 11–48.

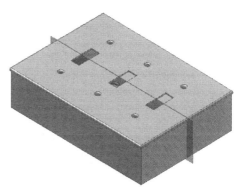

Figure 11–48

Task 6 - Change the cover-03 component in the assembly.

1. In the Model browser, expand **cover-03**, right-click on **Table** and select **Change Component**. The Place Standard iPart dialog box opens.

2. The only other component that will fit with the current size of the box_cover is **cover-02**. Select the *Table* tab, select **cover-02** (row 2) and click **OK**. The assembly displays as shown in Figure 11–49.

You can select iPart factory components to use in an assembly using any of the three tabs; Keys, Tree, and Table. In this situation it was easier to review the table for the correct length and select the required configuration.

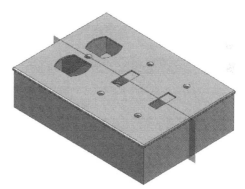

Figure 11–49

To further automate this assembly, you can design it using Adaptivity or iAssemblies so that selecting a different cover_iPart causes an update in the cover_box.

3. Save the assembly as **assembly_iPart** and close the window.

Practice 11c iParts in Assemblies

Practice Objective

- Place an iPart into an assembly by modifying a custom parameter and editing the iPart to include a new configuration.

In this practice, you modify an iPart table in the hex-bolt part to create a configuration that can be used in an assembly with the plate and switch covers. The final assembly is shown in Figure 11–50.

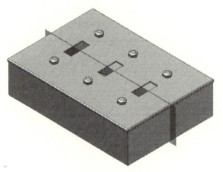

Figure 11–50

Task 1 - Open an assembly file and measure the diameter of a hole.

1. Open **outlet.iam**. The model displays as shown in Figure 11–51.

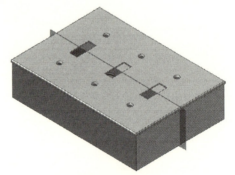

Figure 11–51

2. Measure the diameter of a hole in the cover component. This value will be used to create a new entry in the **hex_bolt_ipart_final.ipt** that fit the holes.

iParts

Task 2 - Create a new entry for the hex_bolt to fit the assembly.

1. Open **hex_bolt_ipart_final.ipt**.

2. Add an entry of **M5x0.8** to the Designation with a diameter that can be used in the assembly. Verify that the configuration can be generated and opens.

3. Place **hex_bolt_ipart_final** into the outlet assembly using the configuration that you just created. The Place Custom iPart dialog box opens, enabling you to enter a custom value for the **grip_len** parameter. This parameter was set as a custom parameter in the iPart file. Click in the *Value* cell beside **grip_len** and enter **3** as the custom value, as shown in Figure 11–52. Select the appropriate **major_dia** for the hole.

Figure 11–52

4. Assemble the remaining five bolts. The final assembly displays as shown in Figure 11–53.

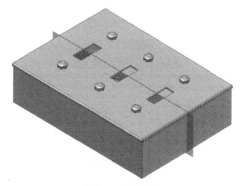

Figure 11–53

5. Save all files and close the window.

Practice 11d iPart Member Tables

Practice Objectives

- Replace the iPart factory instance that is displayed in a drawing view with another instance.
- Place an iPart member table in a drawing to display its factory members and their attributes.

In this practice, you practice switching a view of an iPart to an alternate member. In addition you will create a table of the iParts, as shown in Figure 11–54.

Table		
Member	Part Number	vise_screw_length
Short	Vise_Screw-01	138.75 mm
Medium	Vise_Screw-02	158.75 mm
Long	Vise_Screw-03	178.75 mm

VIEW2
SCALE 1 : 1

Figure 11–54

Task 1 - Switch the views to display an alternate iPart member.

1. Open **Vise_screw.dwg** from the *iPart Table* folder. The drawing displays as shown in Figure 11–55. The views reference **Short.ipt**, which is a member of Vise_Screw iPart. The three members of the iPart factory vary only in length.

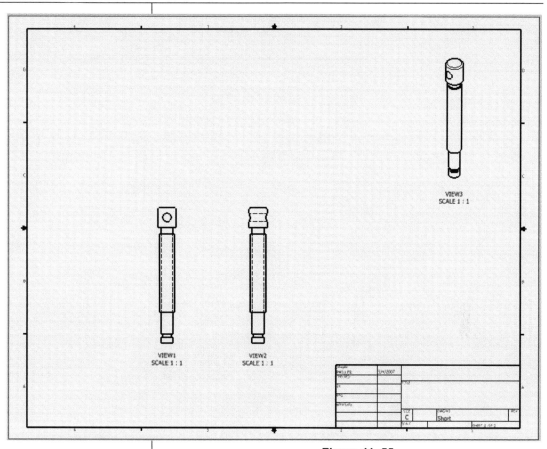

Figure 11–55

2. Right-click the isometric view (View 3, top right corner) and select **Edit View**. The Drawing View dialog box opens.

3. Select the *Model State* tab as shown in Figure 11–56. The *Member* area displays a list of the available iPart members you can display in the drawing views.

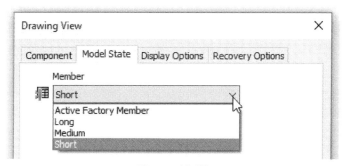

Figure 11–56

4. In the *Member* drop-down list, select **Long** and click **OK**. The views all update to display the newly selected iPart member.

5. Select the View labels and move them below their view.

Task 2 - Create a table for the iPart.

1. In the *Annotate* tab>Table panel, click (General). The Table dialog box opens.

2. Select **VIEW2**. The Table dialog box updates as shown in Figure 11–57.

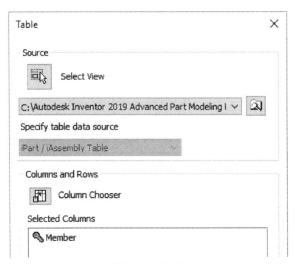

Figure 11–57

3. Click (Column Chooser). The Table Column Chooser dialog box opens.

4. With Part Number selected in the *Available Columns* area, click **Add** to move the column property to the *Selected Columns* area.

5. Add the **vise_screw_length** property to the *Selected Columns* area as well. The Table Column Chooser displays as shown in Figure 11–58.

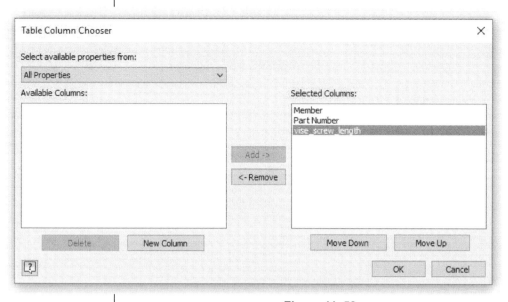

Figure 11–58

6. Click **OK** to close the Table Column Chooser dialog box.

7. Click **OK** to close the Table dialog box.

8. Move the cursor to the right of **VIEW2** and click to place it. The table populates with the columns and attributes of the iPart factory members and displays as shown in Figure 11–59.

Table		
Member	Part Number	vise_screw_length
Short	Vise_Screw-01	138.75 mm
Medium	Vise_Screw-02	158.75 mm
Long	Vise_Screw-03	178.75 mm

Figure 11–59

9. Save and close the drawing.

Chapter Review Questions

1. Which of the following best describes the difference between a standard iPart Factory and a custom iPart Factory?

    a. Custom iPart Factories include parameters that enables you to enter values when the iPart file is opened. In standard iPart Factories, all values for all parameters are preset.

    b. Custom iPart Factories include parameters that enables you to enter values when the iPart is placed in an assembly. In standard iPart Factories, all values for all parameters are preset.

    c. Both custom and standard iPart Factories include parameters that enables you to enter values when the iPart Factory file is used.

    d. None of the above.

2. Which of the following tabs in the iPart Author should be accessed to add features to the table so that they can be suppressed in iPart members?

    a. Parameters
    b. Properties
    c. Suppression
    d. iFeatures
    e. iMates
    f. Other

3. Which of the following can be entered in an iPart table to suppress a feature in a part? (Select all that apply.)

    a. Suppress
    b. Compute
    c. S
    d. C
    e. 0
    f. 1
    g. Off
    h. On

Refer to Figure 11–60 when answering Questions and below:

		Member	Part Number	stub_len	major_dia	minor_dia	grip_len	Thread2: Designation
1		hex_bolt_ipart_final-01	hex_bolt_ipart_final-01	30 mm	4.974 mm	4.11 mm	2.4 mm	M5x0.8
2		hex_bolt_ipart_final-02	hex_bolt_ipart_final-02	30 mm	5.974 mm	4.891 mm	3 mm	M6x1
3		hex_bolt_ipart_final-03	hex_bolt_ipart_final-03	30 mm	9.968 mm	8.344 mm	4.5 mm	M10x1.5
4		hex_bolt_ipart_final-04	hex_bolt_ipart_final-04	30 mm	15.962 mm	13.797 mm	6 mm	M16x2
5		hex_bolt_ipart_final-05	hex_bolt-05	30 mm	4.142 mm	3.98 mm	3 mm	M5x0.8

Figure 11–60

4. How many Keys have been set in the iPart Factory shown in Figure 11–60?

   a. 1

   b. 3

   c. 7

   d. None

5. Which parameter in the iPart Factory shown in Figure 11–60 is custom?

   a. Part Number

   b. stub_len

   c. grip_len

   d. Thread2:Designation

   e. None

6. The equations that are entered in Excel cannot be changed in the iPart Author dialog box.

   a. True

   b. False

7. Which command should be used when adding a new feature that is only required in the active factory member?

   a. **Edit Member Scope**

   b. **Edit Factory Scope**

8. Which of the following drawing **Annotation** options can you use to document the members of an iPart factory in a drawing?

   a. Parts List

   b. Revision Table

   c. General Table

   d. Hole Table

Command Summary

Button	Command	Location
N/A	Change Component	• **Context menu**: In Model browser with Table selected
(icon)	Create iPart	• **Ribbon**: *Manage* tab>Author panel
N/A	Edit Factory Scope	• **Ribbon**: *Manage* tab>Author panel
N/A	Edit Member Scope	• **Ribbon**: *Manage* tab>Author panel
N/A	Edit Table	• **Context menu**: In Model browser with Table selected
N/A	Edit via Spreadsheet	• **Context menu**: In Model browser with Table selected
(icon)	Extract iFeature	• **Ribbon**: *Manage* tab>Author panel
(icon)	General (table)	• **Ribbon**: *Annotate* tab>Table panel
(icon)	Place (Component)	• **Ribbon**: *Assemble* tab>Component panel

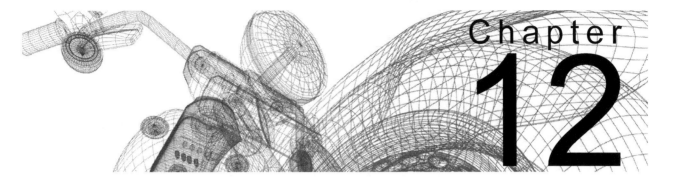

Chapter 12

Importing & Editing CAD Data

The Autodesk® Inventor® software supports the import of files from many different types of 3D CAD programs. In some cases, an associative link can be maintained between the source file and the Autodesk Inventor software. Once a CAD file has been imported, the geometry is brought into an Autodesk Inventor file where it can be further manipulated using tools available in the software. Understanding the editing tools that are available to further manipulate the imported geometry is essential to ensuring the efficient creation of the required model.

Learning Objectives in this Chapter

- Import CAD data into the Autodesk Inventor software.
- Export CAD data from the Autodesk Inventor software in an available export format.
- Use the Edit Base Solid environment to edit solids that have been imported into the Autodesk Inventor software.
- Create Direct Edit features in a model that move, resize, scale, rotate, and delete existing geometry in both imported and native Autodesk Inventor files.
- Index a supported point cloud data file, attach, and edit it for use in a file.

12.1 Importing CAD Data (AnyCAD)

You can import supported file formats using the AnyCAD import functionality. This enables you to either open the files as reference models or convert the files and break the link to the original data. The Autodesk Inventor software can open the file formats shown in Figure 12–1.

The ability to import Fusion 360 files into Inventor is currently available as a preview, for test purposes, before it is fully released. This functionality, AnyCAD for Fusion 360, enables you to import Fusion 360 files as reference models into your Inventor files. For more details on the requirements refer to the Help documentation.

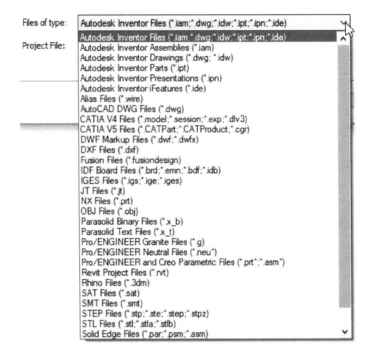

Figure 12–1

How To: Import Data

1. In the **File** menu or Quick Access Toolbar, select **Open**. The Open dialog box displays.
2. In the Files of type drop-down list, select the file format that is to be imported.
3. Select the file to import and click **Open**. The Import dialog box opens.

Importing & Editing CAD Data

> **Hint: Importing into an Existing File**
>
> You can import CAD Data into existing files using the following options:
>
> - In an open part file, in the *3D Model* tab>Create panel, click (Import). The **Import** command is also available on the *Manage* tab>Import panel.
>
> - In an assembly file, in the *Assemble* tab>expanded Place commands, click (Place Imported CAD Files).

- If a part file is imported, a new Autodesk Inventor part file is created.
- If an assembly is imported, a new Autodesk Inventor assembly is created.
- The available options in the dialog box vary depending on the file format that is being imported.

In the example shown in Figure 12–2, a CATIA part file and an .IGS file were selected, as indicated by the filenames at the top of the dialog boxes.

Figure 12–2

4. In the *Import Type* area, select how the data will be imported:
   - Select **Reference Model** to import the data so that a reference is maintained to the source file. If this option is used, when changes are made to the source file, you can update the model in Autodesk Inventor to reflect the changes.
   - Select **Convert Model** to import the geometry and break the link with the original model.
5. In the *Object Filters* area, select the data type to import (i.e., Solids, Surfaces, Meshes, Wires, Work Features, or Points).
6. In the *Inventor Length Units* area, specify the type of length unit to use for the imported geometry. The options enable you to maintain the same units as the data being imported (**From source**), or select from a list of standard units (e.g., inch, foot, millimeter, meter, etc.).
7. Depending on the *Import Type*, proceed as follows:
   - If the data is being imported using the **Reference Model** option, there are no additional options that are available. Continue to Step 11.
   - If the data is being imported using the **Convert Model** option, continue to Step 8.
8. (Optional) If you are importing a large data set on a system with limited memory, enable **Reduced Memory Mode**. This option enables you to increase memory capacity, at the cost of performance.
9. In the *Assembly Options* and *Part Options* areas, select how the assembly structure and surfaces are to be imported using the drop-down lists. The options vary depending on the file format being imported as follows:

File Format	Drop-down List	Options
Parts	• Surfaces	• **Individual:** Surfaces are brought in individually. • **Composite:** A single composite feature.
IGES or STEP files	• Surfaces	• **Individual:** Surfaces are brought in individually. • **Composite:** A single composite feature. • **Stitch:** Automatically stitches surfaces together on import.

Importing & Editing CAD Data

Assemblies	• Structure • Surfaces	• **Assembly:** The original assembly structure is maintained. • **Multi-body part:** Each component is imported as individual solid bodies in a single part. • **Composite Part:** Each part in an assembly is a composite. • The Part surface options that are available for assemblies are the same as those available for parts.

10. By default, the name of the newly created file that contains the imported geometry is the same as the imported filename. In the *File Names* area, enter a prefix or suffix to append to the default name in the *Name* field. Additionally, you can browse to a new directory or accept the default file location for the new file.
11. In the *Select* tab, click **Load Model** to add all of the model data to the dialog box and display a preview of the model in the graphics window.
12. (Optional) Click the circular node associated with each node to toggle its inclusion. By default, all nodes are included (⊕).

    When the ⊖ node is displayed, the geometry is excluded. To toggle multiple surfaces, select them and use the appropriate Status symbol at the top of the Import dialog box.

    • Whether or not you can include or exclude geometry depends on the type of part or assembly that is being imported.

13. (Optional) You can map properties from CATIA, Solidworks, NX, STEP, and Pro-ENGINEER/Creo to standard Autodesk Inventor properties using the **Property Mapping** option. Select the file type that you want to map the Autodesk Inventor properties to fill the values, as required. Click **Save**.
14. Once the options are set, click **OK** to open the imported solid in the Autodesk Inventor software.

> **Hint: Resolve Missing References**
>
> Once data is imported as a reference, the source files is required whenever the Inventor file is active. If the source file is missing, you can use the Resolve Link dialog box to search for the file. This is the same tool used to located missing part files in an assembly file.

Hint: Additional Information on Importing CAD Formats

For more details on the specific formats and versions of other CAD software products that are supported for import, search the Autodesk Inventor Help for "Importing Files".

12.2 Exporting Geometry

To export files, select **Save As>Save Copy As** in the **File** menu. The export file formats that are available for part, assembly, and drawing files are shown in Figure 12–3.

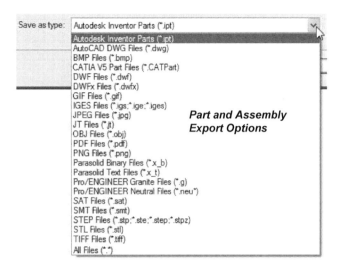

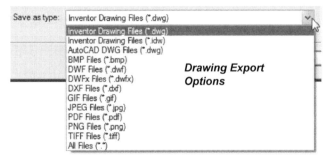

Figure 12–3

Consider the following when exporting:

- Presentation files can be exported to the following file formats: .DWF, .DWFX, .BMP, .PDF, .PNG, .GIF, .JPG and .TIFF.

- Image files can also be exported by selecting **Export>Image** in the **File** menu.

- Sketches or planar faces can be exported to .DWG or .DXF by right-clicking on a sketch and selecting **Export Sketch As**, or by selecting a planar face, right-clicking on it, and selecting **Export Face As**.

- If you save a file as a .BMP file, a snapshot of the part, assembly, presentation, or drawing file is created as the file displays on the screen.

- SAT files are generally used to translate from a program that uses an ACIS kernel to another. It can also be used to include sketches in the file.

- Sheet metal flat patterns can be exported to .SAT, .DWG, or .DXF formats by right-clicking and selecting **Save Copy As**.

- The .STL file format provides options that enable you to control the facets quality, format, and structure of the file so that an accurate prototype of a part or an assembly file can be sent to a 3D printer.

- The IGES file format enables you to export part geometry and base surfaces and assign them to different layers. Note that only the surfaces visible in the model when exported are included in the exported IGES file.

- Exporting an assembly as a Step file saves all of the files in a single file.

12.3 Editing the Base Solid

To edit a solid base feature that has been imported, right-click on the base feature in the Model browser and select **Edit Solid**. The *Edit Base Solid* tab displays, as shown in Figure 12–4, providing the editing options for imported solids.

Figure 12–4

Move Face

The (Move Face) options enable you to select faces to be moved. There are three move options in the mini-toolbar drop-down list - **Free Move**, **Direction and Distance**, and **Points and Plane**, as shown in Figure 12–5.

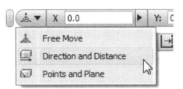

Figure 12–5

Figure 12–6 shows the mini-toolbar for the **Free Move** option. The hole face can be dragged or assigned to an X, Y, Z location.

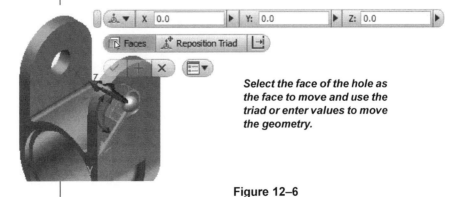

Select the face of the hole as the face to move and use the triad or enter values to move the geometry.

Figure 12–6

Figure 12–7 displays the mini-toolbar for the **Direction and Distance** option. The hole face can be moved relative to the selected distance reference.

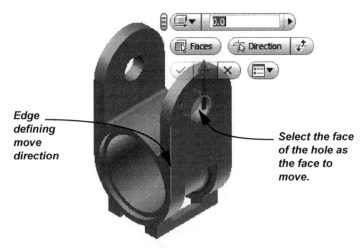

Figure 12–7

Figure 12–8 displays the mini-toolbar for the **Points and Plane** option. The hole face can be moved to a selected point.

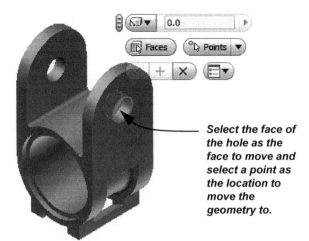

Figure 12–8

Importing & Editing CAD Data

Offset

The (Offset) option enables you to offset the existing face by a specified value or by dynamically pressing and pulling the face, as required. The face shown on the left in Figure 12–9 is selected and offset to change its diameter.

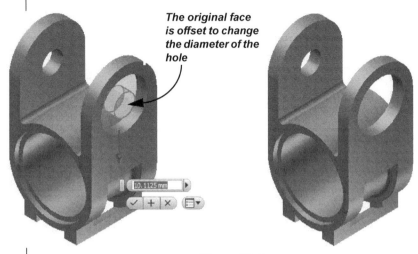

The original face is offset to change the diameter of the hole

Figure 12–9

Extend or Contract Body

The (Extend/Contract Body) option enables you to resize an imported solid in a direction perpendicular to a selected plane. In Figure 12–10, a plane was selected at the bottom of the part as the reference for an extension. The imported geometry is extended by the specified distance.

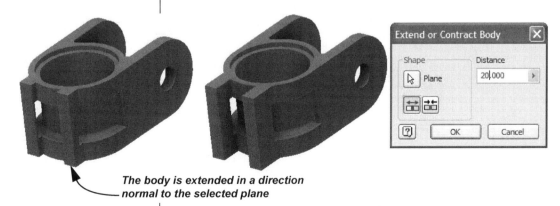

The body is extended in a direction normal to the selected plane

Figure 12–10

Delete Faces

To delete faces from the imported solid, select the faces and select **Delete** in the shortcut menu. In Figure 12–11, a face is selected and deleted from the imported solid. The geometry updates to account for the deleted face.

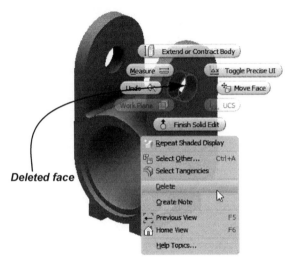

Figure 12–11

12.4 Direct Edit

Direct Edit is a method of editing both imported data and native Autodesk Inventor parametric models. These tools enable you to delete and adjust the size, scale, shape, and location of features by directly manipulating geometry in the model.

Uses of Direct Edit include:

- Incorporating quick yet precise changes to parametric data without changing the initial feature settings. The edits can still be considered parametric because they are added to the Model browser and can be edited.

- Making changes to imported Base Solid data.

To start the **Direct Edit** command, in the *3D Model* tab>Modify panel, click (Direct). Alternatively, you can right-click on imported geometry in the Model browser and select **Direct Edit**. The Direct Edit mini-toolbar opens, which provides access to all of the Direct Edit tools, as shown in Figure 12–12. These tools are activated in the top row of the mini-toolbar and the remaining tools in the mini-toolbar update to support the selected editing type.

Figure 12–12

Move

How To: Move Geometry

1. In the mini-toolbar, click **Move**. The tools in the mini-toolbar update, as shown in Figure 12–13, to permit the moving of the geometry.
2. Use the Geometry Type drop-down list to select the geometry type that is going to be selected for moving. The options include faces and solids. Select the geometry in the model that you want to move. A triad displays on the model to define the move direction, as shown in Figure 12–13.

Figure 12–13

3. Enable/disable the **Automatic Blending** option, as required.
   - Enable the **Automatic Blending** option to ensure that when a face is moved, it takes into account any adjacent tangential faces and creates new blends, if required.
   - Disable the **Automatic Blending** option to ensure that adjacent tangential faces are not taken into account when a face is moved. If a face is moved to a location that prevents any adjacent blends from being created, the move operation will fail and the ⚠ icon will displays in the mini-toolbar.
4. The triad location in the model displays based on the location where the selection was made (identified with a green dot). The commands on the third line of the mini-toolbar enable you to manipulate the triad's location:
   - Click **Locate** to select a new location on the selected face. Hover the cursor over the selected face until the required placement location is highlighted in green and select to move it.

Importing & Editing CAD Data

- Click **Locate** or **World** to reorient the direction of triad axis based on the selected object (local) or the model origin (world), respectively.
- When a local system is used, click [icon] to realign the triad to other geometry in the model.

5. Select the arrow head on the appropriate triad axis to move the selected face or solid in that direction. To define the move with more accuracy, use either of the following:

   - Click **Measure From** to specify a start point and display an *Offset* field to accurately enter an offset value. In the example shown in Figure 12–14, the midpoint on the back edge was selected as a measurement reference and a value was entered.

The midpoint of this edge was selected as a reference point from which to measure.

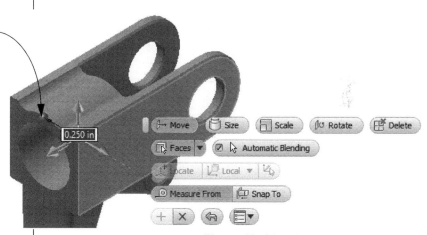

Figure 12–14

   - Click **Snap To** to select a specific reference point on the geometry to which to move.

6. Click [+] to apply the operation. [icon] displays on the model indicating a **Move** operation was added to the Direct Edit feature. The Model browser also updates to indicate that a **Move** operation was added, as shown in Figure 12–15.

Figure 12–15

7. Continue to incorporate other direct edit manipulations in the model or click [X] to close the **Direct Edit** command.

Size

How To: Resize Geometry

1. In the mini-toolbar, click **Size**. The tools in the mini-toolbar update to permit the resizing of geometry, as shown in Figure 12–16.

Figure 12–16

2. Select a face(s) in the model to resize it.
3. Drag the arrow or enter a value in the value field to define the new size. The face shown in Figure 12–17 is being resized.

Figure 12–17

4. Depending on the selected reference, the Modifier drop-down list shown in Figure 12–18 provides control over how the selected face is resized. For example, **Offset** enables you to enter a distance value, **Diameter** is used to change the size of cylindrical faces, and **Radius** changes the size of radial faces.

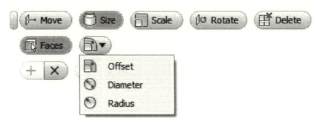

Figure 12–18

Importing & Editing CAD Data

5. Click ⊕ to apply the operation. ⬚ displays on the model indicating that resizing was done to the face and added to the Direct Edit feature. The Model browser also updates to indicate that a **Size** operation was added to the Direct Edit feature, as shown in Figure 12–19.

Figure 12–19

6. Continue to incorporate other direct edit manipulations to the model or click ✕ to close the **Direct Edit** command.

Scale

How To: Scale Geometry

1. In the mini-toolbar, click **Scale**. The tools in the mini-toolbar update to permit the scaling of geometry, as shown in Figure 12–20.

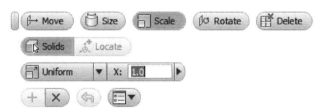

Figure 12–20

2. Select the solid that you want to scale.

3. In the drop-down list on the third line of the mini-toolbar select whether the scaling will be **Uniform** or **Non Uniform**.

4. The triad location appears at a system-defined location on the model. The commands on the second line of the mini-toolbar enable you to manipulate the triad's location:

   - Click **Locate** to select a new location on the selected face. Hover the cursor over the selected face until an acceptable placement location is highlighted in green and select to move it.

   - Click **Local** or **World** to reorient the direction of the triad axis based on the selected object (local) or the model origin (world), respectively. This option is only available if the scaling is set to **Non Uniform**.

- When a local system is used, click ⌷ to realign the triad to other geometry in the model. This option is only available if the scaling is set to **Non Uniform**.

5. Drag the arrow or enter a value in the value field(s) to define the scaling value. For a non-uniform scaling, you can enter values in all three directions. Figure 12–21 shows uniform scaling.

Figure 12–21

6. Click ⊕ to apply the operation. ⌷ displays on the model indicating that a scaling operation was added to the Direct Edit feature. The Model browser also updates to indicate that a **Scale** operation was added to the Direct Edit feature, as shown in Figure 12–22.

Figure 12–22

7. Continue to incorporate other direct edit manipulations to the model, or click ✕ to close the **Direct Edit** command.

Rotate

How To: Rotate Geometry

1. In the mini-toolbar, click **Rotate**. The tools in the mini-toolbar update to permit the rotation of geometry, as shown in Figure 12–23.

Figure 12–23

2. Use the Geometry Type drop-down list to select the geometry type that is going to be selected for rotating. The options include faces and solids. Select the geometry in the model that you want to rotate. A triad displays on the model to define the rotate direction, as shown in Figure 12–24.

Figure 12–24

3. Enable/disable the **Automatic Blending** option, as required.
   - Enable the **Automatic Blending** option to ensure that when a face is rotated, it takes into account any adjacent tangential faces and creates new blends, if required.
   - Disable the **Automatic Blending** option to ensure that adjacent tangential faces are not taken into account when a face is rotated. If a face is rotated into a new location that prevents any adjacent blends from being created, the rotate operation will fail and the ⚠ icon will appear in the mini-toolbar.

4. The triad location in the model displays based on the location on the face or solid at which you select the geometry (identified with green dot). The commands on the second line of the mini-toolbar enable you to manipulate the triad's location:
   - Click **Locate** to select a new location on the selected face. Hover the cursor over the selected face until an acceptable placement location is highlighted in green and select to move it.
   - Click **Local** or **World** to reorient the direction of the triad axis based on the selected object (local) or the model origin (world), respectively.
   - When a local system is used, click [icon] to realign the triad to other geometry in the model.
5. Select the rotation wheel on the appropriate triad axis to rotate the selected face or solid in that direction. To define the rotation with more accuracy, click **Snap Parallel** to specify another plane to which the selected face should be set parallel, as shown in Figure 12–25.

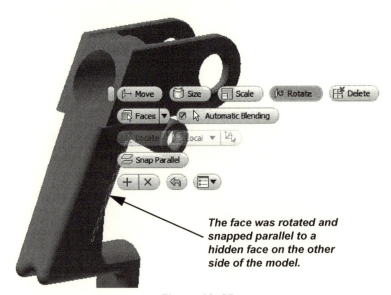

The face was rotated and snapped parallel to a hidden face on the other side of the model.

Figure 12–25

Importing & Editing CAD Data

6. Click ⊕ to apply the operation. ↻ displays on the model indicating that a **Rotation** operation was added to the Direct Edit feature. The Model browser also updates to indicate that a **Rotation** operation was added to the Direct Edit feature, as shown in Figure 12–26.

Figure 12–26

7. Continue to incorporate other direct edit manipulations to the model or click ✕ to close the **Direct Edit** command.

Delete

How To: Delete Geometry

1. In the mini-toolbar, click **Delete**. The tools in the mini-toolbar update to permit the deleting of geometry, as shown in Figure 12–27.

Figure 12–27

2. Select a face in the model to delete it.

3. Click ⊕ to apply the operation. displays on the model indicating that a deletion was made in the model. The Model browser also updates to indicate that a **Delete** operation was added to the Direct Edit feature, as shown in Figure 12–28.

Figure 12–28

4. Continue to incorporate other direct edit manipulations to the model or click ✕ to close the **Direct Edit** command.

> **Hint: Direct Edit Operation Failures**
>
> When adding a **Direct Edit** operation, ⚠ might display in the mini-toolbar after the reference has been selected. It indicates that the operation cannot be done on this reference. For example, surfaces can only be deleted if the geometry still forms a solid after deletion. The face generated from the hole geometry can be deleted, but an outside face of the model cannot. To delete an outside face, consider using the **Delete Face** command in the Modify panel. This command coverts the model to a surface model once an outside face is deleted.
>
> To undo a failed face selection, click ⟵ (Reset) to reset the operation or hold <Ctrl> and select the failing face again to remove it from the selection.

Once changes have been made with **Direct Edit** you can decide whether to edit, delete, or apply the edits to the parametric feature history (if available). This is done while the Direct Edit feature is active by right-clicking on the operation symbol that was added to the model, as shown in Figure 12–29.

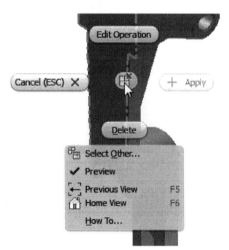

Figure 12–29

12.5 Attaching Point Cloud Data

In addition to the file formats that can be directly opened/imported into the Autodesk Inventor software, you can also attach a point cloud dataset to a new or existing Autodesk Inventor file.

A point cloud file contains a large number of individual vertices that represent the surface of an object(s). The vertices are generally defined with an X, Y, and Z coordinate. The point cloud file is created by a 3D scanning device and can consist of many different file formats. Once imported, the scanned point cloud file can be used to verify fit and function in a top-level assembly file. Figure 12–30 shows an example of a scanned pump system. This piping system could be brought into an assembly model that contains other details of the design.

Figure 12–30

To attach a point cloud file to an Autodesk Inventor file, it must be first opened in the Autodesk® ReCap software, indexed, and then saved for import into the Autodesk Inventor software.

The point cloud files that can be indexed in the Autodesk® ReCap™ software are shown in Figure 12–31.

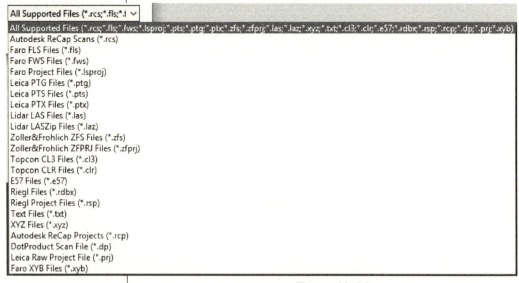

Figure 12–31

How To: Index a Point Cloud File

1. In the *Manage* tab>Point Cloud panel, click ▶ (Autodesk ReCap). In the message window that displays, confirm that the Autodesk ReCap software should be launched.
2. Close the Welcome screen.
3. In the top left corner of the interface, select **new project** to create a new project file to index the point cloud data.
4. Select **import point cloud** to create the project by importing data.
5. Enter a name for the project. A default path for the project is listed below the project name. Select the default path to open the Browse for Folder dialog box and assign a new folder path.
6. Click **proceed** once the project name and folder have been confirmed.
7. On the Import files page, select **select files to import** to open the Import Point Clouds dialog box. Browse to and select a supported point cloud file. Click **Open**.

Importing & Editing CAD Data

Refer to the Autodesk ReCap Help for more information on customizing imported Point Cloud Data.

8. Select **launch project** in the lower right-hand corner to begin indexing the data.
9. Select **launch project** in the lower right-hand corner to open the project and indexed data in the Autodesk ReCap software. Once opened, you can use additional tools to manipulate and work with the data. The project is saved in the *Project* directory and the indexed data is saved in the *Project* directory\<*project name*> folder as an .RCS file.

How To: Attach a Point Cloud File in a Model

1. In the *Manage* tab>Point Cloud panel, click (Attach).
2. In the Select Point Cloud File dialog box, select the indexed file (.RCS or .RCP) to attach. Click **Open**.
3. Select a location in the Autodesk Inventor file to place the point cloud data. The Attach Point Cloud dialog box opens enabling you to customize the attachment point and rotation values, and to adjust the density, as shown in Figure 12–32.

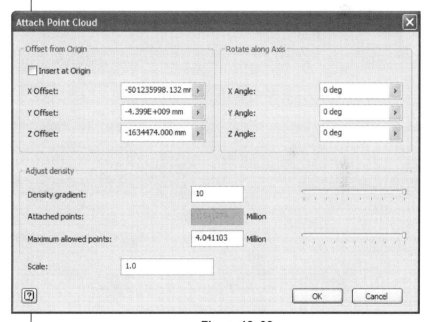

Figure 12–32

4. Click **OK** to attach the point cloud. Once imported, the Model browser updates to include a Point Clouds node that lists the imported file, as shown in Figure 12–33.

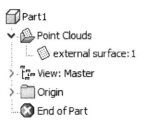

Figure 12–33

Once the point cloud data has been imported, you can use the commands in the Point Cloud panel (as shown in Figure 12–34) to work with the data.

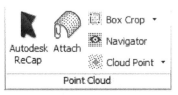

Figure 12–34

- Crop the point cloud data to remove unnecessary data from the file. To crop, click (Box Crop) in the Point Cloud panel and draw a bounding box around the area that is to be kept. Select an arrow on any of the six sides of the bounding box and drag to change the position of its wall or enter an explicit value, as shown in Figure 12–35. Continue to activate each wall and modify its position as required, to create the required bounding box. Click to crop.

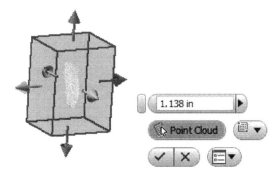

Figure 12–35

Importing & Editing CAD Data

- Use the **Uncrop** command to remove the previous crop operation and return all of the point cloud data to the file. To uncrop, expand the **Box Crop** command and click (Uncrop) in the Point Cloud panel.

- Open the Point Cloud Navigator dialog box to control the visibility status of any attached point cloud data. To open the dialog box, click (Navigator) in the Point Cloud panel and click next to the data file to toggle its visibility off. Click to toggle its visibility back on. Its visibility can also be toggled off in the Model browser.

- Add a work point to the model by using a point cloud point as a reference. To create a work point on an existing cloud point, click (Cloud Point) in the Point Cloud panel and select a point. Work points can be used to create additional geometry in the model.

- Add a Work Plane to the model by using points in the point cloud as references. To create a Work Plane, click (Cloud Plane) in the Point Cloud panel and select in the model to create the plane. The plane is inferred from a set of points in the point cloud.

Practice 12a Opening a CATIA Assembly

Practice Objectives

- Open a CATIA assembly file in Autodesk Inventor by referencing the source data.
- Incorporate changes made to the CATIA model in the Autodesk Inventor model.

In this practice, you open a CATIA assembly file using the **Reference Model** option. By importing the CAD data in this way, changes made in the source model update in the Autodesk Inventor assembly. A change in a CATIA model is made, and you will update the change in the assembly. The final model is shown in Figure 12–36.

Figure 12–36

Task 1 - Import a CATIA assembly file in Autodesk Inventor.

1. In the Quick Access Toolbar, click .

2. In the Open dialog box, navigate to the *SparkPlug* folder in the practice files folder.

3. In the Files of type drop-down list, select **CATIA V5 Files**.

4. Select **SparkPlug.CATProduct** and click **Open**. The Import dialog box opens.

5. Select **Reference Model** from the *Import Type* area. This assembly is required for use in an Autodesk Inventor assembly model. If changes are made in the source model, the changes must be updated in the Inventor version of the file.

6. In the *Object Filters* area, ensure that only **Solids** is selected. Clear any other options.

7. In the *Inventor Length Units* area, ensure that **From source** is selected. The dialog box updates as shown in Figure 12–37.

*Alternatively, the CATIA assembly could be placed in an existing assembly using **Place Imported CAD Files** on the Component panel.*

Importing & Editing CAD Data

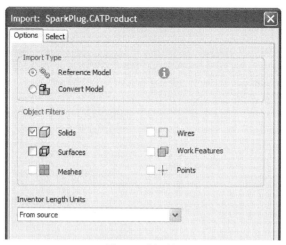

Figure 12–37

8. In the *Select* tab, click **Load Model**. A preview of the CATIA assembly displays in the graphics window and the components of the assembly are listed.

9. Click the circular ⊕ node associated with the **Wire.1** component to toggle its status to Excluded (⊖). Leave all of the other components as ⊕ Included.

10. Click **OK** to close the dialog box and import the geometry. The assembly is listed in the Model browser, as shown in Figure 12–38.

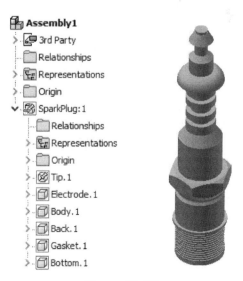

Figure 12–38

11. Save the assembly as **Sparkplug.iam** in the *SparkPlug* folder.

Task 2 - Edit the imported options.

1. In the Model browser, right-click on **SparkPlug:1** and select **Edit Import** to open the Import dialog box that was used to import the files.

2. In the *Select* tab, select ● adjacent to the **Wire.1** component to include it in the imported geometry.

3. Click **OK** to confirm the change. Note that the component is now listed in the Model browser.

Task 3 - Edit the imported model geometry.

In this portion of the practice you will simulate making a design change in the original CATIA model. To do this you will rename a file that has been provided to you so that it is used instead of the existing file. This file has had modifications made to it in CATIA. By renaming, you are simulating that the change was made locally to the CATIA file.

1. In Windows Explorer, navigate to your practice files folder and open the *SparkPlug* folder.

2. Select the **Body.CATPart** file and rename it to **Body_OLD.CATPart**.

3. Select the **Body_Updated.CATPart** file and rename it to **Body.CATPart**.

4. Return to the Autodesk Inventor software.

Importing & Editing CAD Data

5. Note in the Model browser that the ⚡ icon appears next to the **SparkPlug:1** imported geometry node (it might take a moment to update). In the Quick Access Toolbar, click ▦ (Local Update) to update the imported geometry with the change that was made in the source model. The model appears as shown in Figure 12–39.

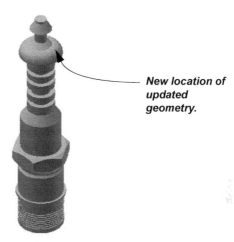

New location of updated geometry.

Figure 12–39

6. In Model browser, right-click on **SparkPlug:1** and note the **Suppress Link** and **Break Link** options. These options can be used to either temporarily break the link with the source CATIA model (**Suppress Link**) or permanently break the link (**Break Link**).

7. Save the file and close the window.

Practice 12b | Opening STEP Files

Practice Objectives

- Open a STEP file in the Autodesk Inventor software.
- Edit the imported STEP data to delete a face, move a face, and change its size.
- Add parametric Autodesk Inventor features to the imported geometry.

In this practice, you open auxpart.stp and edit the solid base model to make changes to the imported data. You also add standard Autodesk Inventor features (fillets) to the model and illustrate that the fillet is parametric although the imported geometry is not. The final model is shown in Figure 12–40.

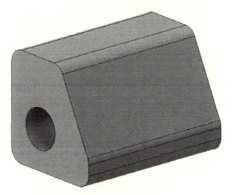

Figure 12–40

Task 1 - Open a part file.

1. In the Quick Access Toolbar, click .

2. In the Open dialog box, in the Files of type drop-down list, select **STEP Files**.

3. Select **auxpart.stp** from the top-level practice files folder. Click **Open**. The Import dialog box opens.

Step files can also be referenced, if required.

4. Select **Convert Model** from the *Import Type* area to import the file.

5. In the *Object Filters* area, ensure that **Solids** is selected. Clear any other options, if required.

Importing & Editing CAD Data

6. In the *Inventor Length Units* area, ensure that **From source** is selected.

7. In the *Part Options* area, select **Composite** from the Surfaces drop-down list.

8. Click **OK** to close the dialog box and import the geometry. The geometry is listed as **Base1** in the Model browser, as shown in Figure 12–41. The imported solid is a single feature with no associativity between it and the original file.

Figure 12–41

Task 2 - Edit the imported model geometry.

1. In the Model browser, right-click on **Base1** and select **Edit Solid**. The *Edit Base Solid* tab displays. The panels available provide editing options for imported solids.

2. Select the surface of the hole, as shown in Figure 12–42.

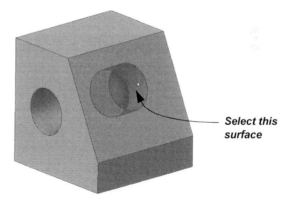

Figure 12–42

*The **Move Face** option enables you to select one or more faces on the imported solid to move them in a specified direction.*

3. Right-click and select **Delete** to remove the hole.

4. In the Modify panel, click (Move Face). The Move Face mini-toolbar opens.

5. In the mini-toolbar, expand the drop-down list and select **Direction and Distance,** as shown in Figure 12–43.

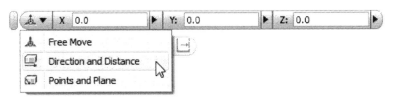

Figure 12–43

6. In the mini-toolbar, the **Faces** option is selected by default. Select the hole face as shown in Figure 12–44.

7. In the mini-toolbar, click **Direction** and select the edge indicated in Figure 12–44 to define the direction for the move.

   If required, click to flip the direction of the arrow, as shown in Figure 12–44.

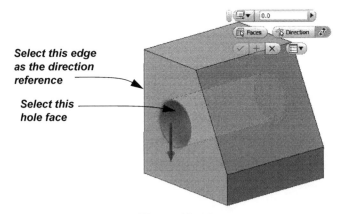

Figure 12–44

8. In the *Distance* field, enter **0.25**. Complete the move. The part displays as shown in Figure 12–45.

Importing & Editing CAD Data

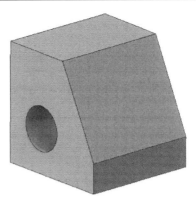

Figure 12–45

9. In the Modify panel, click (Extend/Contract Body). This option resizes an imported solid in a direction perpendicular to a selected plane. The Extend or Contract Body dialog box opens as shown in Figure 12–46.

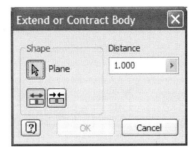

Figure 12–46

10. Select the face shown in Figure 12–47 as the reference plane for the extension.

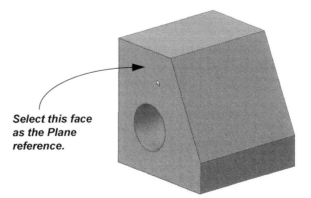

Figure 12–47

11. In the *Distance* field, enter **2** and click ⟷ (Expand) to expand the solid part.

12. Click **OK**. The part displays as shown in Figure 12–48. The imported geometry is extended in length by the specified distance.

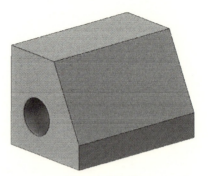

Figure 12–48

13. In the Exit panel, click ✓ (Finish Base Solid).

14. Add fillets to the horizontal edges of the model using the default radius value.

15. In the Model browser, right-click on **Fillet1** and select **Show Dimensions**.

16. Set the new *Radius* to **0.25** and press <Enter>.

17. Update the model to incorporate the dimension change. The part displays as shown in Figure 12–49. Note that the fillet is parametric although the imported geometry is not.

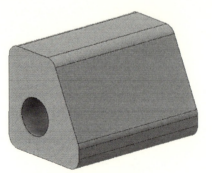

Figure 12–49

18. Save the part and close the window.

Practice 12c Direct Edit

Practice Objectives

- Open a CATIA part model and review the base solid geometry that was imported.
- Edit the base solid geometry using the Direct Edit option to move, resize, rotate, and delete faces on imported geometry.

In this practice you will learn how to use the **Direct Edit** option to edit base solid geometry that was imported into the Autodesk Inventor software. Faces will be deleted, moved, resized, and rotated to obtain the required modified geometry. To complete the practice you are also provided with a native Autodesk Inventor file to edit using the Direct Edit tools.

Task 1 - Open a CATIA model.

1. Open the **Cover.CATPart** model from the practice files folder. The Import dialog box opens.

2. In the *Import Type* area, select **Convert Model** to import the geometry and break the link with the original model.

3. In the *Object Filters* area, ensure that **Solids** is selected. Clear any other options, if required.

4. In the *Inventor Length Units* area, ensure that **From source** is selected.

5. In the *Part Options* area, select **Composite** from the Surfaces drop-down list.

6. Click **OK** to close the dialog box and import the geometry. The Model browser shows that a base feature called Casting has been imported, as shown in Figure 12–50.

Figure 12–50

Task 2 - Edit the Base Solid that was imported to move a face.

1. In the *3D Model* tab>Modify panel, click ▢ (Direct). The Direct Edit mini-toolbar opens, as shown in Figure 12–51.

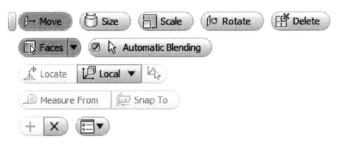

Figure 12–51

2. Ensure that **Move** is selected in the mini-toolbar. Hover the cursor over the face shown in Figure 12–52 as the face to be moved. Hold <Ctrl> to maintain this surface while locating the control point. Hover the cursor over different vertices on the face before selecting. The highlighted green dot determines where the triad will be located for moving. Ensure that you select in the area shown to place the triad and begin moving the face.

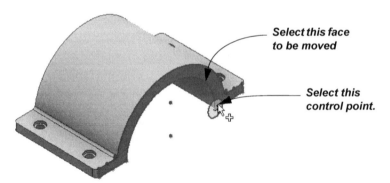

Figure 12–52

Importing & Editing CAD Data

3. By default, the x-axis (local to the model) is active. As indicated by the gold colored x-axis on the triad. Drag the face outward by dragging the arrowhead, as shown in Figure 12–53.

Figure 12–53

4. Enter **50** as the value by which the face will be moved and click ⊕ to complete the Move operation.

5. Note that ⊢ displays on the model, indicating that the move exists in the Direct Edit feature, as shown in Figure 12–54. **Move1** also displays in the Model browser in the Direct Edit feature.

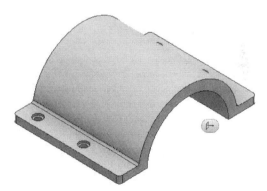

Figure 12–54

6. Right-click on ⊢ and select **Edit Operation** to edit the Move operation that was just added.

7. Instead of entering a specific value to move the face, the required depth is to be measured relative to the back surface. Click **Measure From** and select the edge shown in Figure 12–55. Enter **180** as the value.

Select this edge from which to measure

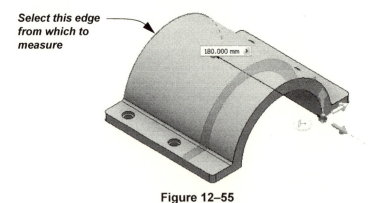

Figure 12–55

8. Click [+] to complete the changes.

9. Select the face shown in Figure 12–56 and move it **20mm**. Do the same on the opposite face. Once the two Move operations have been added the model displays as shown in Figure 12–56.

Select this face and move it 20mm

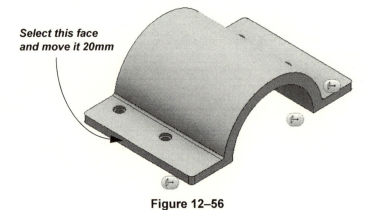

Figure 12–56

Task 3 - Edit the position and size of the holes.

1. In the mini-toolbar, select **Delete** to activate the Delete operation.

Importing & Editing CAD Data

2. Select the four faces that were created in the holes as counterbores. Two of these faces are shown in Figure 12–57, but select all four.

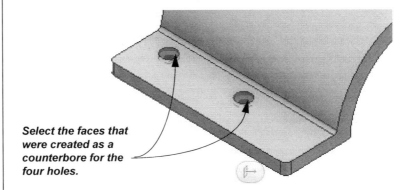

Select the faces that were created as a counterbore for the four holes.

Figure 12–57

3. Click ⊕ to complete the operation. Four operations have now been added to the Direct Edit feature.

4. Click **Size** and select the surface of the hole shown in Figure 12–58.

5. Drag the triad arrow head. Enter **-6** to enlarge the diameter by an exact value, as shown in Figure 12–58.

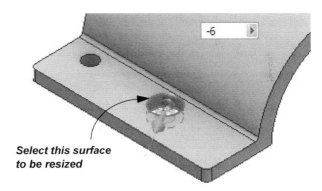

Select this surface to be resized

Figure 12–58

6. Click ⊕ to complete the operation.

7. With **Size** still active, select the inside face of the hole that you just resized.

8. Expand and select **Diameter**.

9. Select the hole faces in the three remaining holes, as shown in Figure 12–59. This sets the size of the three selected faces to that of the previously modified hole.

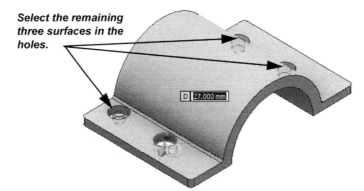

Figure 12–59

10. Click [+] to complete the operation.

11. Click **Move** and select the surface of the hole shown in Figure 12–60. Ensure that the highlighted green point is at the center of the circle to enable you to move the center of the hole.

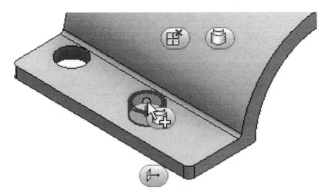

Figure 12–60

12. Ensure the x-axis arrow on the triad is selected.

13. Click **Measure From** and select the front edge (midpoint) of the model, as shown in Figure 12–61. Enter **-25mm** as the value. Do not press <Enter>.

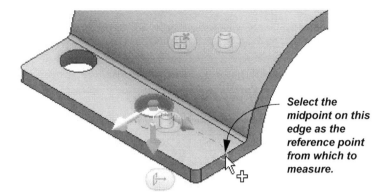

Select the midpoint on this edge as the reference point from which to measure.

Figure 12–61

14. Select the y-axis arrow on the triad.

15. Click **Measure From** and select the side edge as shown in Figure 12–62. Enter **25mm** as the value and press <Enter> to complete the operation.

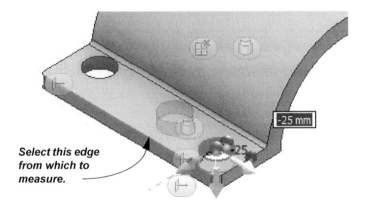

Select this edge from which to measure.

Figure 12–62

16. Adjust the positions of the other three holes in the model so that they are positioned in the same way from their nearest edges. The model should display similar to shown in Figure 12–63.

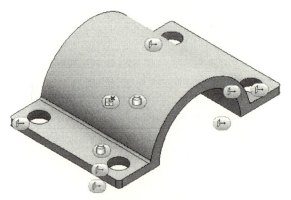

Figure 12–63

Task 4 - Rotate faces and scale the model.

1. Click **Rotate** and hover the cursor over the surface shown in Figure 12–64. Holding <Ctrl>, continue to move the mouse and ensure that the highlighted green point is at the center of the edge shown. Press the left mouse button to select it. You are now able to rotate as required from this point.

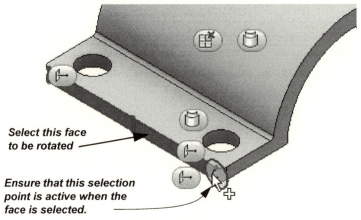

Select this face to be rotated

Ensure that this selection point is active when the face is selected.

Figure 12–64

2. Rotate the wheel as shown in Figure 12–65. Drag the triad to **20.00 deg**. Alternatively, you can enter the value. Press <Enter>.

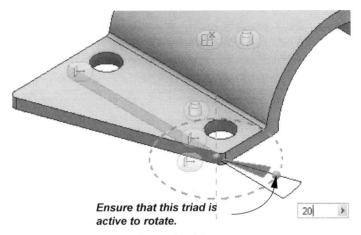

Ensure that this triad is active to rotate.

Figure 12–65

3. Rotate the opposite edge in the same way. Review the Model browser and note that all of the operations are listed in the Direct Edit feature.

4. Click ⊗ to cancel the Direct Edit feature. The model displays as shown in Figure 12–66.

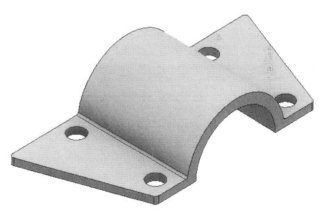

Figure 12–66

5. Note that the Model browser lists the Direct Edit feature and that the operations are no longer displayed. To edit or review the operations you must edit the feature.

6. Double-click on the **Direct Edit** feature in the Model browser.

7. Right-click on the icon in the graphics window and select **Delete** (as shown in Figure 12–67), to remove the operation from the model.

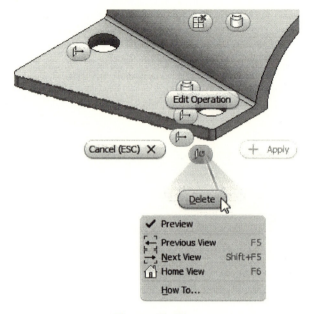

Figure 12–67

8. Remove the second **Rotate** operation.

9. Click **Scale** and select the solid body shown in Figure 12–68.

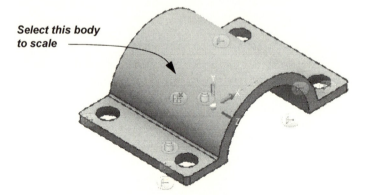

Figure 12–68

10. Ensure that the X axis manipulator is active. Enter **2** in the entry field and press <Enter> to scale the model.

11. Click ![X] to cancel the Direct Edit feature.

12. Save the model and close the window.

> **Hint: Using Direct Edit with Referenced CAD models.**
>
> It is not recommended to add Direct Edit features to a CAD model that has been imported and maintains its link to the source CAD model. This is because the Direct Edit feature may fail if the model changes in the source CAD tool.

Chapter Review Questions

1. Which of the following two Import Type opens should be used to ensure that a link to the source file is maintained and that changes that are made to the imported data can be updated.

    a. **Reference Model**

    b. **Convert Model**

2. Which of the statements are true regarding the Import dialog box when importing CAD data from another software package? (Select all that apply.)

    a. If a part file is imported, a new Autodesk Inventor part file is created.

    b. If an assembly is imported, a new Autodesk Inventor assembly is created.

    c. When importing a part into the Autodesk Inventor software, you can set the Part options to recognize each feature as a separate body.

    d. All geometry in the CAD file must be imported. Once imported, you can remove geometry as required.

3. Which of the following menu options enable you to export a .DWG file as a .BMP file? (Select all that apply.)

    a. **File** menu>**Save>Save**

    b. **File** menu>**Save As>Save As**

    c. **File** menu>**Save As>Save Copy As**

    d. **File** menu>**Save As>Save Copy as Template**

    e. **File** menu>**Export>Image**

4. Which commands can be used to edit the Base geometry shown on the left in Figure 12–69 to create the geometry shown on the right in Figure 12–69? (Select all that apply.)

Figure 12–69

   a. Move Face
   b. Offset
   c. Extend/Contract Body
   d. Delete

5. The **Extend/Contract Body** option in the Edit Base Solid ribbon enables you to resize selected features on an import solid.

   a. True
   b. False

6. How many **Delete** operations were completed on the model on the left side in Figure 12–70 to obtain the model shown on the right side in Figure 12–70?

   Figure 12–70

   a. 1
   b. 2
   c. 4
   d. None, delete would not obtain this final geometry.

7. Which of the following are Direct Edit tools that are available in the Direct Edit mini-toolbar? (Select all that apply.)

   a. **Move**
   b. **Size**
   c. **Define Envelopes**
   d. **Rotate**
   e. **Remove Details**
   f. **Delete**
   g. **Scale**

8. The green dot that is highlighted on a face that is being relocated using the **Direct Edit** command indicates where the triad is placed.

   a. True
   b. False

9. Which of the following enables you to define the measurement reference point when using **Direct Edit**?

   a. **Measure From**
   b. **Snap To**
   c. [icon]
   d. **Snap Parallel**

10. Which of the following icons displays in the Direct Edit mini-toolbar when a face in the exterior geometry on the model is selected for deletion?

    a. [icon]
    b. [icon]
    c. [icon]
    d. [icon]

11. Which software product should you use to index the point cloud data before importing it into the Autodesk Inventor software?

    a. Autodesk® Revit®
    b. Autodesk® Inventor®
    c. Autodesk® ReCap™
    d. Autodesk® Alias®

Command Summary

Button	Command	Location
(icon)	Autodesk ReCap	• **Ribbon:** *Manage* tab>Point Cloud panel
N/A	Delete Face	• **Context menu:** In graphics window
(icon)	Direct Edit	• **Ribbon:** *3D Model* tab>Modify panel • **Context menu:** In graphics window
NA	Export Face As	• **Browser:** right-click on a face
(icon)	Export Image	• **File menu:** Export
NA	Export Sketch As	• **Browser:** right-click a sketch
(icon)	Extend/ Contract Body	• **Ribbon:** *Edit Base Solid* tab>Modify panel
(icon)	Import	• **Ribbon:** *3D Model* tab>Create panel • **Ribbon:** *Manage* tab>Import panel • **Ribbon:** *Assemble* tab>expanded Place commands
(icon)	Move Face	• **Ribbon:** *Edit Base Solid* tab>Modify panel
(icon)	Offset	• **Ribbon:** *Edit Base Solid* tab>Modify panel
(icon)	Open	• **Ribbon:** *Get Started* tab>Launch panel • **Quick Access toolbar** • **File menu**
(icon)	Save Copy As	• **File menu:** Save As

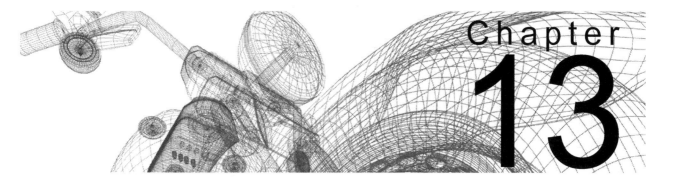

Chapter 13

Working with Imported Surfaces

The data that is imported from other CAD systems may have errors that prevents it from being created as a solid in Autodesk® Inventor®. Additionally, surfaces that are imported may need to be individually selected for modification to make a required design change. Situations like these require you to fix the problem areas or finish surface modeling. There are many options that can be used to help you identify and fix these errors.

Learning Objectives in this Chapter

- Set the import options to import surface data from other file format types.
- Transfer imported surface data into the Repair Environment to conduct a quality check for errors.
- Appropriately set the stitch tolerance value so that gaps in the imported geometry can be automatically stitched and identify the gaps that are not stitched.
- Use the Repair Environment commands to repair gaps or delete, extend, replace, trim and break surfaces to successfully create a solid from the imported geometry.

13.1 Importing Surfaces

As previously discussed, the Import dialog box can be used to import many different CAD file formats. In addition to this, it also has the flexibility to only import surface data from a file. Once the surface data is imported, you can manipulate it using the standard surfacing tools to create required geometry or edit existing surface geometry. The workflow is similar, however you should consider the following:

- Ensure that the selected **Import Type** option captures your design intent, so that the model is either referenced or converted for use in Autodesk Inventor.

- In the *Object Filter* area, select the **Surface** option to provide you with the required surfaces.

- Consider using the *Select* tab to selectively include or exclude surfaces that are to be imported, if available. For example, when importing an .IGS file, you can select the specific surfaces to import, as shown in Figure 13–1.

Figure 13–1

How To: Include or Exclude Surfaces

1. Select the *Select* tab.
2. Select **Load Model** to add all of the model data to the dialog box and display a preview of the model in the graphics window.
3. Click the circular node associated with each surface to toggle its inclusion. By default, all surfaces are included (●). When the ● node is displayed, the surface is excluded. To toggle multiple surfaces, select them and use the appropriate Status symbol at the top of the Import dialog box.

13.2 Repairing Imported Surfaces

When you import surfaces, the data might have to be repaired and stitched together into a quilt (a group of surfaces), before the surfaces can be used. Alternatively, you simply might want to make design changes to the geometry. To accomplish this, you should use the Repair environment. In the Repair environment, you can analyze, repair, and stitch the surfaces. You can then return to the Part environment to repair any remaining problem areas, such as creating missing surfaces, and finally stitching the surfaces together. If the surfaces you stitch form a closed boundary, you can obtain a solid geometry.

General Steps

Use the following general steps to repair imported surfaces:

1. Switch to the Repair environment.
2. Perform an error check.
3. Stitch surfaces together.
4. Repair imported surfaces.
5. Stitch surfaces together, as required.
6. Perform an error check.
7. Complete the repair.
8. Repair remaining problem areas, as required.
9. Stitch surfaces together, as required.

Step 1 - Switch to the Repair environment.

To access the Repair environment, right-click on the imported geometry node and select **Repair Bodies**. Alternatively, in the Surface panel, you can click (Repair Bodies) and then select the body to be repaired.

The *Repair* tab displays as shown in Figure 13–2.

Figure 13–2

Working with Imported Surfaces

Step 2 - Perform an error check.

Perform an error check to check for surface topology, geometry, and modeling uncertainty errors. In the Repair panel, click

 (Find Errors). Alternatively, you can right-click on the repair node or in the graphics window and select **Find Errors.** The Find Errors dialog box opens. Click **Select All** to select all the bodies in the imported geometry or manually select bodies. Click **OK** to run the check. The check analyzes the imported data and reports the errors, by type, in the Model browser. The error type is identified by the following symbols:

- The ✓ symbol identifies healthy geometry in the model.

- The ⓘ symbol identifies geometry that needs further investigation.

- The ⚠ symbol identifies geometry that contains errors and requires repairing.

*A glyph for each error can be displayed on the model. Right-click on the error folder and select **Error Glyph Visibility**.*

Similar errors are all grouped into folders. To locate an error in the model, in the Model browser select the error and the error symbol. Its associated entity is highlighted in the model and an error glyph is displayed. Additionally, you can use the

⇐ (Previous Error) and ⇒ (Next Error) options to progress through the list.

Heal Errors

Refer to the Help documentation for a complete list and description of the possible error types that can be found.

The **Heal Errors** command can also be used in the Repair panel when errors exist. Click (Heal Errors), select the bodies that are required to be healed, and enter a healing tolerance value.

With the required bodies selected, you can click (Analyze Selected Bodies) to analyze if the assigned tolerance will resolve the issues. Click **OK** to run the healing process. The bodies are analyzed and any problems are reported. Errors that can be healed are corrected in the model, otherwise continue to use the options in the Modify panel to correct the geometry.

Repairing using the mini-toolbar

Not all errors can be resolved using the **Heal Errors** command. As each error is selected, a Repair mini-toolbar is displayed to help resolve the error. The resolution options that are available are dependent on the error. For example, you may be provided tools to delete faces, create patches or stitch the geometry. Click ✓ once the error is healed.

Step 3 - Stitch surfaces together.

Perform a stitch to close any insignificant gaps that might have resulted from the import. It also helps to locate the significant gaps and over-extended surfaces. Stitch creates a quilt of the stitched surfaces. It is better to initially use a smaller tolerance to avoid undesirable changes in the geometry and then increase the tolerance, as required. When a gap or overlap exists that is too large to stitch without affecting the integrity of the surfaces, use the other surface repair options available.

How To: Stitch the Surfaces

1. In the Modify panel, click (Stitch) or right-click in the graphics window and select **Stitch**.
2. In the Select area of the dialog box, define whether the entities to be stitched are to be selected as faces or bodies. The faces or bodies can be selected in the Model browser or directly on the model. To select all entities in the model, select and drag a bounding box around the model. The Stitch dialog box updates showing the number of faces selected.
3. Enter a value in the *Fill gaps smaller than* field. This maximum tolerance value identifies the maximum gap and overlap between two surfaces that will be stitched together. Surface edges that contain a gap or overlap less than the maximum tolerance are stitched.

4. To preview a list of edges that will not be stitched, click
 (Find remaining gaps and free edges). Edges that could not be stitched (due to them being further apart than the defined maximum tolerance) are highlighted in the model and listed in the Stitch dialog box. An example of a model that is stitched but still contains free edges is shown in Figure 13–3.

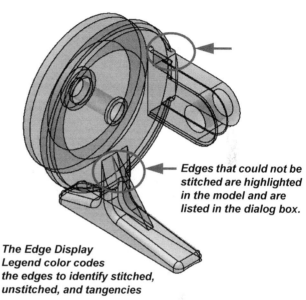

Edges that could not be stitched are highlighted in the model and are listed in the dialog box.

The Edge Display Legend color codes the edges to identify stitched, unstitched, and tangencies

Figure 13–3

5. To determine which edge in the model corresponds to which edge listed in the dialog box, select a row in the list. The corresponding edge highlights in the model. Some of the edge gaps and overlaps might be small so you might need to zoom in to see them.
6. Review the list of gaps or overlaps. If they are insignificant and can be repaired by adjusting the tolerance value without adversely affecting surrounding surfaces, change the tolerance and click **OK**. If not, maintain the original tolerance and click **OK**. Plan to use the tools on the Modify panel to fix the model.

Step 4 - Repair imported surfaces.

Use the following options in the Modify panel of the Repair environment or in the right-click on the marking or context menu to repair the imported surfaces.

Transfer Surface

The **Transfer Surface** command works in a similar way to the Stitch command. The only difference between the commands is that the Transfer Surface dialog box provides a field that enables you to select a destination body to move the selected face or body to or you can generate a new composite. To access the command, in the Modify panel, click (Transfer Surface) or right-click in the graphics window and select **Transfer Surface**.

Add Surface

The **Add Surface** command is only available in the shortcut menu directly in the model or through the Model browser. The command can be used to add a new surface to an existing face or body. To add a surface, right-click on the surface to be added and select **Add Surface**. In the Stitch: Add dialog box, select the face/body to which the new surface will be added, enter the gap tolerance value, and click **OK**.

Unstitch

There are times when you need to select particular surfaces in a quilt. Unless the required surface is unstitched from the quilt, you cannot select it. To unstitch, click (Unstitch), select the surface(s) to exclude from the quilt, and click **Apply**. You can also access the **Unstitch** command by right-clicking in the graphics window. The unstitched surface(s) can then be selected separately from the rest of the quilt.

*To select a reference to which a surface can extend up to (instead of having to specify a distance), use **Extend Surface** in the Part Features Panel.*

Extend Faces

Use Extend Faces to extend faces at an edge, as shown in Figure 13–4. To extend a face, click (Extend Faces), select the edge reference(s) for the extend, enter the extension distance, and click **Apply**. The face is extended by the specified distance.

Working with Imported Surfaces

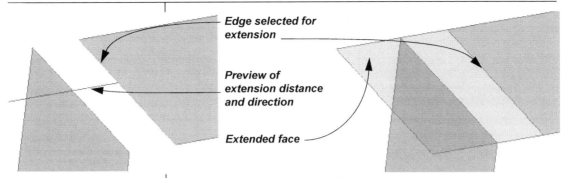

Figure 13–4

Intersect Faces

Use Intersect Faces to trim or break faces that intersect one another, as shown in Figure 13–5. To trim faces, click

 (Intersect Faces), click (Trim), and select the portions of the faces to keep when selecting the faces for the trim. The portions of the faces you did not select are removed starting at

the line of intersection. To break faces, click (Intersect

Faces), click (Break), and select the faces for the break. The faces are broken in two at the line of intersection.

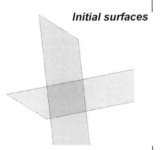
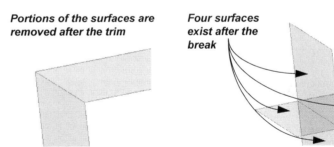

Figure 13–5

Edit Regions

Edit Regions removes unnecessary regions and loops (e.g., a surface containing a hole that needs to be removed or a self-intersecting loop needs to be removed). To edit regions, click

 (Edit Regions), select a face to repair, select regions in the face to keep, and click **Done**. The regions you selected are retained and the regions and unnecessary loops are removed.

Extract Loop and Boundary Trim

During IGES or STEP surface data translation, faces can be trimmed unexpectedly. Use **Extract Loop** to untrim surfaces and then use **Boundary Trim** to trim the surfaces using the required boundary.

To extract loop, click ▣ (Extract Loop), select one or more loops from one surface, select **Delete Wires** to delete the original loop on the surface, and click **Apply**. Click **Done** if no additional extractions are required. An example of a loop that was extracted is shown in Figure 13–6.

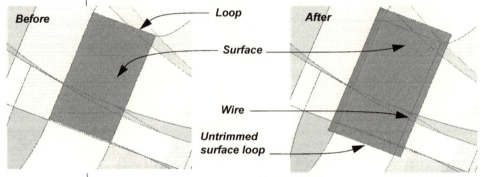

Figure 13–6

To trim a boundary, click ▣ (Boundary Trim) and select edges that form a closed loop. Once the loop is closed, select the side of the face to keep or the loop to replace. An example is shown in Figure 13–7.

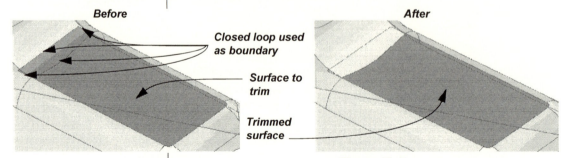

Figure 13–7

Working with Imported Surfaces

Boundary Patches can be created both in the repair and part environments.

Boundary Patch

Boundary Patch enables you to create a surface from closed boundary edges. To create a Boundary Patch, click

 (Boundary Patch), and select a closed 2D or 3D sketch, or select edges from existing objects to form a closed profile. Click **OK** to create the surface. A planar patch surface created from a closed 2D sketch is shown in Figure 13–8.

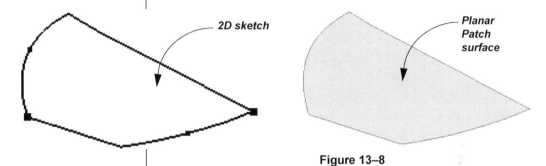

Figure 13–8

Reverse Normal

The **Reverse Normal** option enables you to toggle the direction of the surface normal for a face or a lump. Once you select a reference, the surface is highlighted in green and shows the default normal direction with an arrow. This is only available while in the Repair environment.

Step 5 - Stitch surfaces together, as required.

Stitch any additional surfaces you created together, as required. If the stitched surfaces form an enclosed boundary, it will be indicated in the Model browser as a Solid surface.

Step 6 - Perform an error check.

Perform an additional error check to verify the validity of the surfaces. If issues still remain, use any of the repair options to resolve the issues.

Step 7 - Complete the repair.

Once you have finished working in the Repair environment, you can right-click in the graphics window and select **Finish Repair** or in the Exit panel, click (Finish Repair).

Step 8 - Repair remaining problem areas, as required.

Once you have left the Repair environment you are placed in the Modeling environment. You can continue to interact with your model using the standard *3D Model* tab options (e.g., Patch, Trim, Extend) to further resolve any problem areas.

Step 9 - Stitch surfaces together, as required.

Stitch the additional surfaces that were created or modified, as required. If the stitched surfaces form a fully enclosed boundary (and assuming that no other solid bodies exist in the part) the quilt generates a solid base feature in the part.

Practice 13a | Repairing Imported Data

Practice Objectives

- Set the import options to retrieve data from an .IGS file.
- Review the Translation Report that is generated when an .IGS file is imported.
- Transfer the imported .IGS data into the Repair environment and conduct a quality check for errors in the imported geometry.
- Appropriately set the stitch tolerance value so that gaps in the imported geometry can be automatically stitched.
- Use the Repair environment commands to repair gaps, delete and replace surfaces to successfully create a solid from the imported geometry.

In this practice, you import an IGES file, analyze it, and repair the surfaces. Once you finish repairing the surfaces to obtain a fully enclosed surface, you stitch it to obtain the solid model shown in Figure 13–9.

Figure 13–9

Task 1 - Import the IGES file.

1. In the Quick Access Toolbar, click . Select **import_surf.igs**. Click **Open**. The Import dialog box opens.

2. In the *Object Filters* area, select **Solids** and **Surfaces** and leave the other options in this area cleared, as shown in Figure 13–10.

3. Maintain the default in the *Inventor Length Units* area.

4. In the *Part Options* area, select **Composite**, as shown in Figure 13–10.

5. By default, the file is created in the working directory. You can use the browse button in the *File Location* area to change directories, if required. You can also add a prefix or suffix to the filename, as shown in Figure 13–10. For this file, leave the *Name* field empty and the *File Location* as default.

Figure 13–10

6. Click **OK** to import the IGES file. The Model browser and model appear as shown in Figure 13–11.

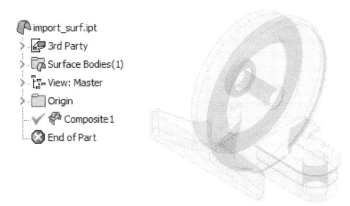

Figure 13–11

Task 2 - Examine the translation report.

Examine the translation report that is generated to review information such as the translation type, translation options used, component names, system from which the file was created, and success status.

1. In the Model browser, expand the **3rd Party** node and double-click on **import_surf.htm** to open and review the translation information.

2. Close the translation report window.

Task 3 - Examine the Model browser.

Examine the Model browser to determine what has been imported. This helps determine what is required with the model.

1. The import file contains a single composite surface. No solids have been imported (otherwise a feature named **Base1** would display in the Model browser).

Task 4 - Perform a quality check to find errors in the imported geometry.

1. In the Model browser, right-click on **Composite1** and select **Repair Bodies**. The *Repair* tab displays.

2. In the Repair panel, click ![icon] (Find Errors). The Find Errors dialog box opens. Click **Select All** to select all the Bodies in the imported geometry. Click **OK** to run the check. The bodies are analyzed and no problems are reported. If problems were reported they would be identified with symbols in the Model browser.

Task 5 - Perform a preliminary stitch.

Perform a preliminary stitch to close up any insignificant gaps that might have resulted from the import and to help locate the significant gaps and over-extended surfaces. Use a small tolerance to avoid undesirable changes in the geometry.

1. In the Modify panel, click ![icon] (Stitch). The Stitch dialog box opens.

2. Drag a bounding box around all of the geometry to select it. Ninety four (94) faces are selected.

3. Change the *Fill gaps smaller than* value to **0.05 mm**.

4. Click ![icon] (Find remaining gaps and free edges). The Stitch dialog box and model display as shown in Figure 13–12.
   - Edges that could not be stitched (due to them being further apart than the defined maximum tolerance of 0.05 mm) are highlighted in the model and are listed in the Stitch dialog box.
   - Edges that were less than 0.05 mm apart have been stitched together.
   - There are 5 remaining free edges. To determine which edge in the model corresponds to which edge listed in the dialog box, select a row in the list. The corresponding edge highlights in blue on the model. Some of the edges are small and so you need to zoom in to see them.

Working with Imported Surfaces

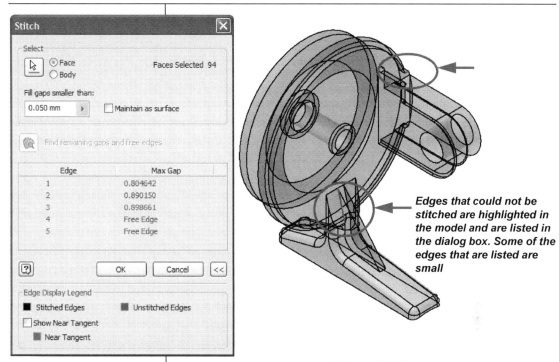

Edges that could not be stitched are highlighted in the model and are listed in the dialog box. Some of the edges that are listed are small

Figure 13–12

5. While keeping the Stitch dialog box open, rotate and zoom in on the model to get a better look at the highlighted edges that need to be resolved before the model can become solid. Some surface edges extend further than required and some adjacent surfaces contain a gap between them. There are two areas on the model (which contain the problem edges) that need to be repaired.

6. Click **OK** to close the Stitch dialog box. Note in the Model browser, the imported surface body has been changed to a single quilt, as shown in Figure 13–13, because the surfaces were stitched together. However, the gaps between surfaces still remain.

Figure 13–13

© 2018, ASCENT - Center for Technical Knowledge®

Task 6 - Use Extract Loop and then Boundary Trim.

In this task, you use **Extract Loop** to extend the edges and then **Boundary Trim** to trim back the surface to the required boundary.

1. Reorient the model and zoom as shown in Figure 13–14.

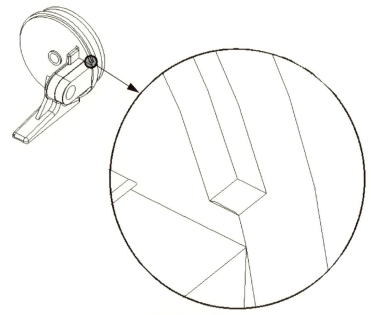

Figure 13–14

2. Position the cursor over the surface shown in Figure 13–15 in Shaded display mode to get a better idea of what needs to be repaired. Note that a gap exists.

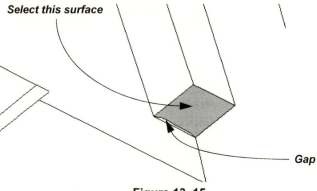

Figure 13–15

Working with Imported Surfaces

3. In the Modify panel, click ▣ (Extract Loop) to extend the surface.

4. Select the loop by selecting the surface shown in Figure 13–16.

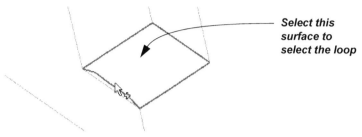

Select this surface to select the loop

Figure 13–16

5. Select **Delete Wires** to delete the original loop of the surface.

6. Click **Apply** and then click **Done**. The surface edges are extended, as shown in Figure 13–17.

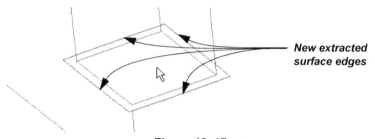

New extracted surface edges

Figure 13–17

7. In the Modify panel, click ▧ (Boundary Trim).

8. Select the edges shown in Figure 13–18 as the cutting edges.

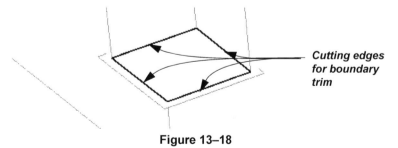

Cutting edges for boundary trim

Figure 13–18

If an incorrect surface is selected, hold <Ctrl> and select the surface to clear it.

9. Click ▶ (Face or Loop) and select the loop to keep, as shown in Figure 13–19. Verify that the required loop is selected and is displayed in green, otherwise the incorrect portion of the surface is trimmed.

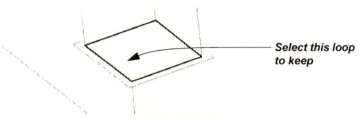

Figure 13–19

10. Click **Apply** and then click **Done**. The surface is trimmed, as shown in Figure 13–20.

Figure 13–20

Task 7 - Use Extract Loop and Boundary Trim a second time.

1. Reorient the model and zoom, as shown in Figure 13–21.

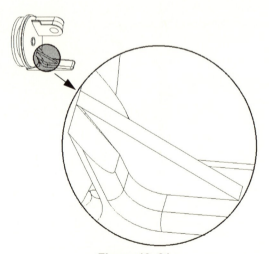

Figure 13–21

2. Position the cursor over the surfaces shown in Figure 13–22 to help visualize what needs to be repaired. Note the gap that exists between the surfaces.

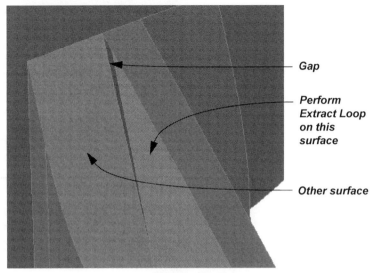

Figure 13–22

3. With **Delete Wires** selected, use **Extract Loop** to obtain the surface shown in Figure 13–23.

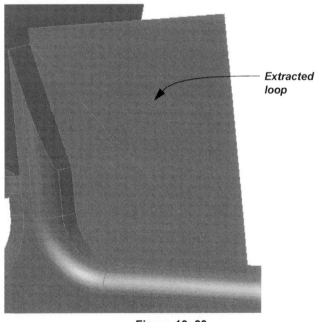

Figure 13–23

4. Perform a Boundary Trim and select the edges shown in Figure 13–24 as the cutting edges.

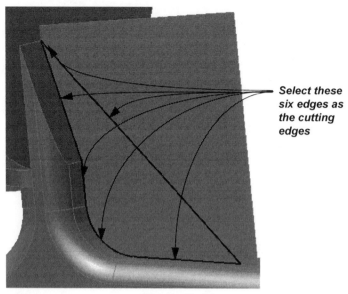

Select these six edges as the cutting edges

Figure 13–24

5. Select the Face or Loop reference, within the area to be kept, so that the model is trimmed as shown in Figure 13–25. Note that the gap no longer exists.

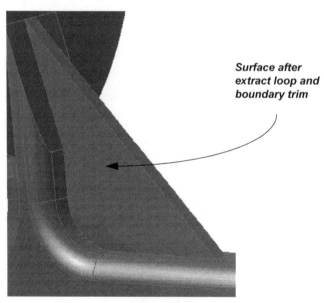

Surface after extract loop and boundary trim

Figure 13–25

Working with Imported Surfaces

Task 8 - Stitch the surfaces.

1. In the Modify panel, click (Stitch).

2. In the *Select* area, select **Body**. Select the model. Now that the model is a Quilt, the **Face** option cannot be used to select the geometry.

3. Verify that the *Fill gaps smaller than:* value is still set to **0.05 mm**.

4. Click (Find remaining gaps and free edges). No open edges remain in the model and it is automatically converted into a solid.

5. Click **OK**.

Task 9 - Delete a surface from the stitched quilt.

The design intent of the model requires that the base be longer. In this task, you delete one of the faces that has been combined to create the current solid.

1. Reorient the model so that you can see the bottom surface of the model. Right-click on the bottom face and select **Delete**, as shown in Figure 13–26.

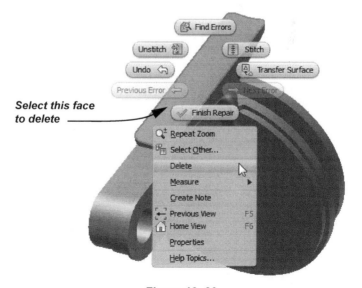

Figure 13–26

Task 10 - Stitch the surfaces.

In this task you will extend an existing surface and create a new surface to replace the one that was deleted.

1. Reorient the model so that you can see the bottom surface of the model.

2. In the Modify panel, click (Extend Faces).

3. Select the closed loop edge that represents the base of the model, as shown in Figure 13–27.

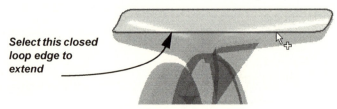

Select this closed loop edge to extend

Figure 13–27

4. Set the extend distance to **2 mm**. Click **Apply** and then click **Done**.

5. In the Modify panel, click (Boundary Patch).

6. Select the extended edge as the reference for the Boundary Patch, as shown in Figure 13–28.

Select this closed loop edge as the reference for the Boundary patch

Figure 13–28

7. Click **Apply** to create the new surface. Click **Done** to close the dialog box.

Working with Imported Surfaces

Task 11 - Add the new surface to the stitched quilt.

In this task you will add the newly created surface to the model.

*As an alternative you can also right-click on the newly created bottom surface of the model and select **Add Surface**.*

1. In the Model browser, in the repair node, right-click on **Quilt3** and select **Add Surface**. The Stitch: Add dialog box opens.

2. In the *Select* area, select **Body** and select the existing quilted surface body.

3. Change the *Fill gaps smaller than:* value to **0.05 mm**.

4. Click ![icon] (Find remaining gaps and free edges). No open edges should be reported.

5. Click **OK**.

As as alternative to modifying the bottom face in the Repair Environment, you could have also used the Direct Edit method in the 3D Model environment.

6. In the Exit panel, click ![icon] (Finish Repair) to exit the Repair environment. You are now placed in the standard part environment and can perform any regular operation on the solid model.

The model becomes a solid with the addition of the cap surface, as shown in Figure 13–29. The **Surface Bodies** node has now been changed to a **Solid Bodies** node, identifying that the model is now a solid.

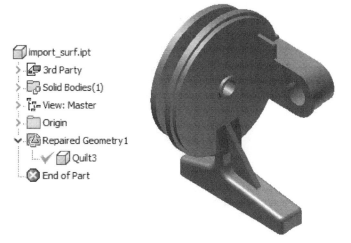

Figure 13–29

7. Save and close the model.

Practice 13b Manipulating Imported Surfaces

Practice Objectives

- Set the options to import data from a CATIA file.
- Appropriately set the stitch tolerance value so that gaps in the imported geometry can be automatically stitched to create a solid.
- Manipulate the resulting solid model using the surface Patch and Sculpt commands to add and remove solid geometry.

In this practice, you work with a file that has been imported from CATIA V5. You will import the geometry and then modify and remove features. The final part is shown in Figure 13–30.

Figure 13–30

Task 1 - Open a CATIA file.

1. In the Quick Access Toolbar, click ![icon]. Ensure that the Files of type drop-down list is set to display all files or CATIA V5 files. Select **Trim_Panel.CATPart**. Click **Open**. The Import dialog box opens.

2. In the *Import Type* area, select **Convert Model** to convert the model without keeping any associative links to the CATIA file.

3. In the *Object Filters* area, select **Solids** and **Surfaces**. Leave the other options in this area cleared.

4. Maintain the default in the *Inventor Length Units* area.

5. In the *Part Options* area, select **Composite**.

6. Maintain the defaults in the *File Names* area.

7. In the *Select* tab, click **Load Model**. The model preview displays, as shown in Figure 13–31. Individual surfaces cannot be added or removed for this model. Surface manipulation for this CATIA part can be done in the Repair Environment.

Working with Imported Surfaces

Figure 13–31

8. Click **OK** to close the dialog box and import the geometry.

Task 2 - Stitch the Trim_Panel.CATPart file.

In this task, you switch to the Repair environment and stitch together the imported surfaces.

1. In the Model browser, right-click on **Composite1** and select **Repair Bodies**. The *Repair* tab displays.

2. In the Modify panel, click (Stitch). The Stitch dialog box opens.

3. Drag a bounding box around all of the geometry to select all 29 faces.

4. In the *Fill gaps smaller than:* field, leave the default value.

5. Click (Find remaining gaps and free edges). No open edges are reported. Only free edges are located around the exterior of the model.

6. Click **OK** to close the Stitch dialog box.

7. In the Exit panel, click (Finish Repair) to exit the Repair environment. You are now placed in the standard part environment and can perform any regular operation on the model.

Task 3 - Use the Thicken/Offset command to create a solid.

1. In the Modify panel, click (Thicken/Offset). The Thicken/Offset dialog box displays.

2. Select **Quilt** to easily select the stitched surface.

3. Select the stitched surface and enter a distance of **4 mm**.

4. Click **OK**. The model displays as shown in Figure 13–32.

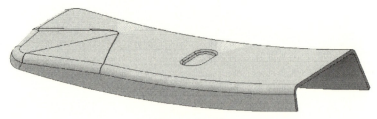

Figure 13–32

Task 4 - Modify surfaces to incorporate design intent.

In this task you will create four boundary patch surfaces that will be used to modify the model.

1. Right-click on the **Repaired Geometry1** node in the Model browser and select **Repair Bodies**. Alternatively, double-click on the node.

2. Select the nine surfaces that make up the indented area shown in Figure 13–33. Right-click and select **Delete** to remove them from the surface.

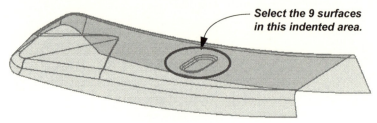

Select the 9 surfaces in this indented area.

Figure 13–33

3. In the Modify panel, click (Boundary Patch).

4. Select the loop of edges that remain once the surfaces have been deleted as the reference for the Boundary Patch.

Working with Imported Surfaces

5. Click **Apply** to create the new surface. Click **Done** to close the dialog box.

6. In the Model browser, in the repair node, right-click on **Quilt2** and select **Add Surface**. The Stitch: Add dialog box opens.

7. In the *Select* area, select **Body** and select the existing quilted surface body.

8. Change the *Fill gaps smaller than:* value to **0.05 mm**.

9. Click ▣ (Find remaining gaps and free edges). Eleven open edges should be reported. These are the outside edges of the surface.

10. Click **OK**.

11. In the Exit panel, click ✓ (Finish Repair) to exit the Repair environment.

12. The Thicken feature might fail due to the changes in the surface. If so, click **Accept**.

*Consider using the **Adjust** tool to manipulate the color of the new boundary patch so that it matches the rest of the model.*

13. Double-click on the **Thicken1** feature in the Model browser to edit it and select the reference surface again. The reference was lost when the modification was made. Click **OK**. The model displays as shown in Figure 13–34.

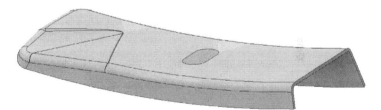

Figure 13–34

14. Save the model.

Chapter Review Questions

1. How can you bring imported data into the Repair environment, if it is not already imported into this environment?

    a. Right-click on the imported data and select **Repair Bodies**.

    b. Right-click on the imported data and select **Copy to Repair**.

    c. This cannot be done. It must be done during import.

2. In the Repair environment, which option can you use to close small gaps between surfaces?

    a. Extend Faces

    b. Intersect Faces

    c. Stitch

    d. Unstitch

    e. Boundary Trim

3. Which two commands function in the same way except that when one of the commands is executed, you specify a destination body?

    a. Stitch

    b. Transfer Surface

    c. Unstitch

    d. Boundary Patch

    e. Boundary Trim

    f. Extend Faces

4. In the Repair environment, which option can you use to create a new surface referencing a closed set of adjacent edges?

    a. Extend Faces

    b. Intersect Faces

    c. Boundary Trim

    d. Boundary Patch

    e. Extract Loop

5. Match the error types in the left column to its symbol that identifies their type in the right column.

Error Types	Icon	Answer
a. Geometry that contains errors	✓	_____
b. Geometry needing further investigation	ⓘ	_____
c. Healthy geometry	⚠	_____

Command Summary

Button	Command	Location
N/A	Add Surface	• **Context menu:** In graphics window • **Context menu:** In Model browser with surface selected
	Boundary Patch	• **Ribbon:** *Repair* tab>Modify panel
	Boundary Trim	• **Ribbon:** *Repair* tab>Modify panel
	Edit Regions	• **Ribbon:** *Repair* tab>Modify panel
	Extend Faces	• **Ribbon:** *Repair* tab>Modify panel
	Extract Loop	• **Ribbon:** *Repair* tab>Modify panel
	Find Errors	• **Ribbon:** *Repair* tab>Repair panel • **Context menu:** In graphics window
	Finish Repair	• **Ribbon:** *Repair* tab>Exit panel • **Context menu:** In graphics window
	Heal Errors	• **Ribbon:** *Repair* tab>Repair panel
	Intersect Faces	• **Ribbon:** *Repair* tab>Modify panel
	Next Error	• **Ribbon:** *Repair* tab>Repair panel • **Context menu:** In graphics window
	Previous Error	• **Ribbon:** *Repair* tab>Repair panel • **Context menu:** In graphics window
	Repair Bodies	• **Ribbon:** *3D Model* tab>Surface panel • **Context menu:** In Model browser with repair node selected
	Reverse Normal	• **Ribbon:** *Repair* tab>Modify panel
	Stitch	• **Ribbon:** *Repair* tab>Modify panel • **Context menu:** In graphics window
	Transfer Surface	• **Ribbon:** *Repair* tab>Modify panel • **Context menu:** In graphics window
	Unstitch	• **Ribbon:** *Repair* tab>Modify panel • **Context menu:** In graphics window

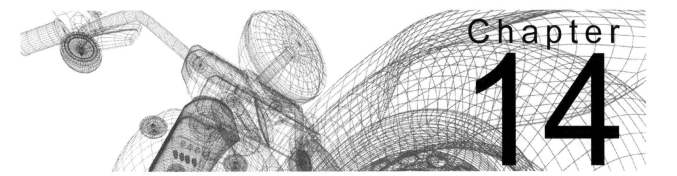

Working with AutoCAD Data

There are several ways to incorporate AutoCAD® DWG files in an Autodesk® Inventor® file. The method you use depends on your project requirements. You can open the file directly in the Autodesk Inventor software for review. You can also import and convert the AutoCAD DWG into an Inventor DWG file, where all links to the original AutoCAD DWG file are lost. Alternatively, you can import and use an AutoCAD DWG as an associative underlay in an Autodesk Inventor file. Understanding the process and results of each method helps you identify which is the best for your situation.

Learning Objectives in this Chapter

- Open an AutoCAD DWG file directly into an Autodesk Inventor part file and review the data.
- Use the DWG/DXF File Wizard and its options to import files into an Autodesk Inventor file.
- Use an AutoCAD DWG file in an Autodesk Inventor part file so that the geometry created in Inventor remains associative with the AutoCAD DWG file.

14.1 Opening AutoCAD Files

When an AutoCAD DWG file is selected for opening, you can either open the file directly or import it so that it is converted to an Autodesk Inventor DWG file. These two options represent two of the methods that can be used to view and use AutoCAD DWG files in the Autodesk Inventor software.

Opening DWG Files

By default, when a DWG file is opened using the Open dialog box, the file is opened directly in Autodesk Inventor. The file remains in a native AutoCAD DWG format, enabling you to view, plot, and measure the file contents. Objects display exactly as they do in AutoCAD. If changes to the DWG file are required, you should make the changes directly in the AutoCAD software. Figure 14–1 shows an example of the YA-Base.dwg AutoCAD file that has been opened in Autodesk Inventor. You can double-click on each of the nodes in the Model browser to activate the opened model, sheet, or layouts.

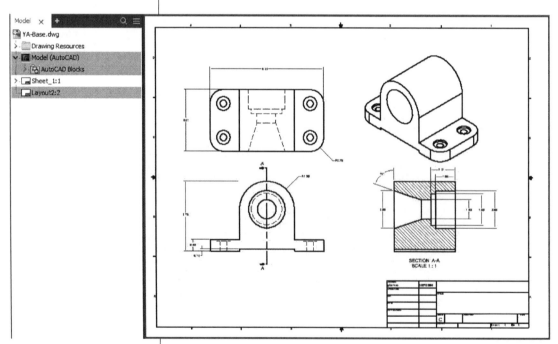

Figure 14–1

Working with AutoCAD Data

Importing DWG Files

To convert the AutoCAD DWG to a native Autodesk Inventor DWG file, the DWG/DXF File Wizard is used. The data is imported and any associative link between the source and new file are lost. When importing, you have the ability to customize many options as well as the layers that are imported.

How To: Import an Autodesk DWG File Using the DWG/DXF File Wizard

1. In the **File** menu, in the *Get Started* tab or the Quick Access Toolbar, select **Open**. The Open dialog box opens.
2. Select **DWG Files** from the Files of type drop-down list. DXF files can also be imported using the wizard
3. Select the Autodesk file to import, and click **Options**.
4. In the File Open Options dialog box (shown in Figure 14–2), select **Import** and click **OK**.

*Consider using the **Import DWG** option in the expanded **Open** command on the **File** menu to avoid using the File Open Options dialog box.*

Figure 14–2

5. Click **Open**. The DWG/DXF File Wizard dialog box opens similar to that shown in Figure 14–3.

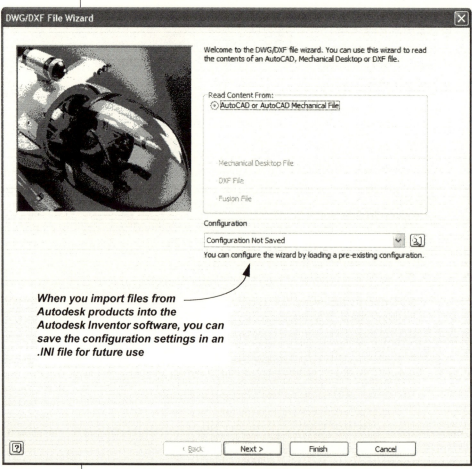

Figure 14–3

The settings you define in this wizard can be saved as a configuration file and used by during future imports.

6. In the *Read Content From* area, verify that the correct file format is selected for import. Specify a configuration file to use, as required. To use the settings defined in the selected configuration file or to accept the default file settings, click **Finish**. To continue defining import options, click **Next**.

The Layers and Objects Import Options dialog box opens. The dialog box varies depending on the file format being imported. Figure 14–4 shows the options for the import of a DXF, AutoCAD DWG, or AutoCAD Mechanical DWG file.

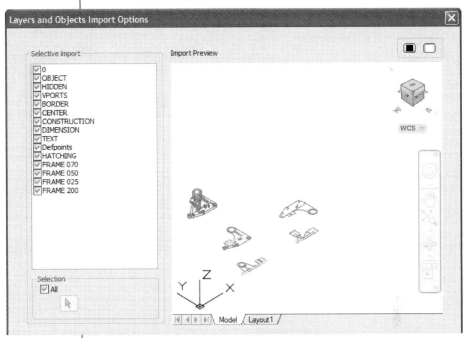

Figure 14–4

7. The Layers and Objects Import Options dialog box enables you to specify what data to translate.

   For an AutoCAD DWG file:
   - Use the *Import Preview* area to view the data. Right-click or use the Navigation toolbar to access view manipulation options or the right-click to access file options.
   - Select the data to import by selecting layers to include from the Selective import area or select specific entities to include by deactivating the **All** option in the *Selection* area and selecting entities in the Import preview area.

   For a Mechanical Desktop DWG file:
   - Use **Parts and Assemblies** to import parts and assemblies into the Autodesk Inventor software, as required.
   - Use **All Layouts as Drawings with Views** to import AutoCAD layouts into drawing views and annotations.
   - Use the **Selected Layout as Drawings with Draft Views** options to import the selected layout into an Autodesk Inventor drawing. This option is only available when a layout tab is selected and the **All Layouts as Drawings with Views** option is cleared.

8. Click **Next** when finished defining the options. The Import Destination Options dialog box opens.

9. The Import Destination Options dialog box for Mechanical Desktop DWG files also differs from the dialog box for DXF and other DWG files. Figure 14–5 shows the options that are available during the import of a DXF, AutoCAD DWG, or AutoCAD Mechanical DWG file.

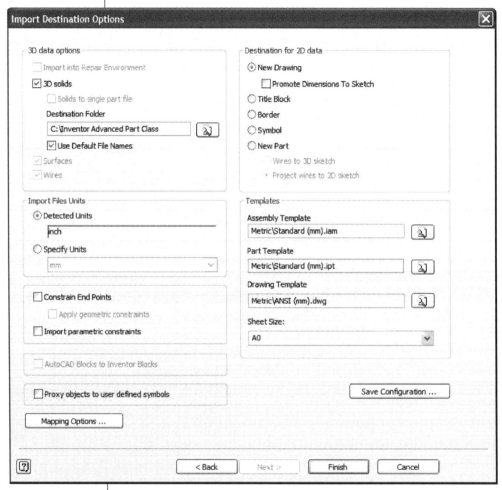

Figure 14–5

For DXF and other non-Mechanical Desktop DWG files, the available options are:

- Activate the **3D solids** option to import the 3D solids from AutoCAD, otherwise, they are not included. If **Surfaces** or **Wires** exist in the imported file, you can select these options, if required on import. Selecting a destination folder specifies the directory in which new Autodesk Inventor files are created as a result of importing 3D solids. Select **Use Default File Names** to automatically name new files based on the name of the DWG file.

*Select the **Map all layers and dimensions to a single sketch** option in the Mapping Options dialog box to avoid creating as many sketches as you have layers.*

- Specify the units to use in the *Import Files Units* area.
- Select **Constrain End Points** to automatically apply endpoint constraints. Clear this option to manually assign them. Use **Apply geometric constraints** to fully constrain the sketch.
- Select **Import parametric constraints** to translate 2D parametric constraints into a sketch.
- Select **AutoCAD Blocks to Inventor Blocks** to import AutoCAD blocks as sketch blocks when opened in an Autodesk Inventor sketch.
- Select **Proxy objects to user defined symbols** to import proxy objects from AutoCAD for use as custom symbols.
- Click **Mapping Options** to set the mapping of layers and fonts.
- Select **New Drawing** to import the 2D data on the layouts into a new drawing file. Imported 2D geometry is placed in sketches attached to a draft view. Dimensions are placed in the sketch containing the associated geometry. Unassociated dimensions, symbols, and other annotations are imported onto the drawing sheet. Blocks are imported as sketched symbols and placed in the *Drawing Resources* folder.
- Select **Promote Dimensions To Sketch** to import dimensions as sketch dimensions on a sheet in a drawing file. The promoted dimensions are associative and change if the sketch geometry is modified.
- Select **Title Block** to import 2D data from the selected layers into the title block in a new drawing file.
- Select **Border** to import 2D data from the selected layers into the border in a new drawing file.
- Select **Symbol** to import 2D data from the selected layers into a sketched symbol under the *Drawing Resources* folder in a new drawing file. An instance of the sketched symbol is also placed on the first sheet in the drawing.
- Select **New Part** to import 2D geometry from model space or paper space into a sketch in a new part. Associated dimensions are imported into the sketch, but unassociated dimensions, symbols, and other annotations are not imported.
- Select the drawing, part and assembly template files to use when new files are created during import. Also, specify the sheet size to use for new drawings.
- Click **Save Configuration** to reuse the same import settings in the future.

For Mechanical Desktop DWG files, many of the Import Destination options are the same as those available when importing DXF and other non-Mechanical Desktop DWG files. The options that are different include the following:

- Specifying **Referenced components only** or **All component definitions** for assemblies. You can also control whether to discard the .IAM file for any single part assemblies.
- Specifying whether to **Translate body only** or **As features**. For Mechanical Desktop files with unsupported features you can select the additional options.
- Importing only the selected file or external files as well for drawings with view options.
- Specifying the options for mapping mechanical symbols.
- Overwriting duplicate files that are found or using the existing file that is found.

10. Click **Finish** when you are done setting the import options and to begin the import.

Depending on the information in the AutoCAD file, the import produces different results in the form or model layouts, sheets, and imported base geometry. Consider the following:

- If you want to use 2D AutoCAD data to create features in a part, you can import the DWG file into a new part file (.IPT) or into a sketch in an active part. Alternatively, you can open the DWG and copy views to help create solid geometry. Dwg Underlays can also be used and are discussed in the next section.

- Materials applied in an AutoCAD DWG are maintained in the Autodesk Inventor software after translation. To view the materials, set the Visual Style for the part to **Realistic**.

- For AutoCAD 3D solids, they are imported as Autodesk solid bodies into an Autodesk Inventor part file (.IPT). When multiple solids are translated, a part file is created for each body and an assembly file that contains references to each part is created. AutoCAD 3D solids are not parametric, so they are brought in as non-parametric solid bodies without separately defined features (i.e., boundary representations).

14.2 DWG File Underlays

Importing an AutoCAD DWG file into an Autodesk Inventor part file enables you to import an associative underlay by referencing the AutoCAD DWG. The DWG underlay can be imported on one or more work planes or faces, enabling you to project it into sketches and use it to create associative geometry. If changes are made in the source AutoCAD DWG file, the change can be updated in the Autodesk Inventor file. Additionally, in assembly files, you can use constraints and joints to create relationships between a DWG underlay geometry and a part.

Importing a DWG File as an Underlay

How To: Import an Autodesk DWG File as an Associative Underlay

1. Start a new part file using a template and save the file.
2. In the *3D Model* tab>Create panel, click ▧ (Import). Select and open an AutoCAD DWG file.
   - If the file was not saved, a prompt displays indicating that this may cause problems in resolving links between the files.
3. Select an origin plane or planar face to import the file onto.
4. Select a origin point reference to locate the DWG file.
5. Click **OK** when prompted that inserting an AutoCAD DWG produces an associative underlay. The DWG file is listed in the Model browser as an independent node.

- To redefine the placement plane and origin point, right-click on the filename in the Model browser, and select **Redefine**, as shown in Figure 14–6. You are then prompted to select a new plane and origin point.

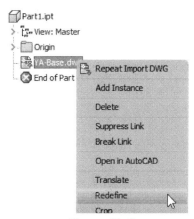

Figure 14–6

- To open the DWG file in AutoCAD, right-click on the underlay file name in the Model browser and select **Open** in AutoCAD.

Controlling Layer Visibility

Once a DWG file has been imported as an underlay, you can control its layer visibility.

How To: Control the Layer Visibility

1. Right-click on the DWG file in the Model browser and select **Layer Visibility**. The Layer Visibility dialog box opens, as shown in Figure 14–7.

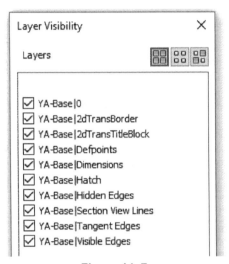

Figure 14–7

2. Toggle on/off the layer names to customize the data that will be imported.
   - Use the filter settings at the top of the dialog box to quickly clear, select all, or invert the selected layers.
   - The visibility of any of the layers can be controlled at any time using this dialog box.
3. Click **OK** to close the Layer Visibility dialog box.

Moving an Underlay

If the imported file does not appear in the correct location relative to the model's origin, it can be translated.

How To: Move a DWG Underlay

1. Right-click on the DWG file in the Model browser and select **Translate**. A translation triad is displayed on the selected origin point.
2. Using the mini-toolbar, move the AutoCAD DWG file relative to the model's origin, as required:
   - In the mini-toolbar, click **Locate** and select a new reference on the imported DWG file to reposition the triad.
   - In the mini-toolbar, click **Snap To** and select the Origin Center Point or another point to align the DWG underlay as required in the model.
3. Click ✓ to complete the translation.

Cropping an Underlay

An imported DWG underlay can be cropped to simplify the amount of detail that is displayed. Cropping can also help improve performance.

How To: Crop Entities in a DWG Underlay

1. Right-click on the DWG file in the Model browser and select **Crop**.
2. In the graphics window, drag a bounding box around the entities that you want to keep.
3. Right-click in the graphics window and select **OK (Enter)** to complete the crop. Any geometry that was not included in the selected area is automatically removed.

- Once an DWG underlay file is cropped, a **Crop** node is added to the Model browser.

- Only one crop can be made to a file, thus if a change is required, you must delete the crop element. To delete a Crop, right-click on the element in the Model browser and select **Delete**.

Using an Underlay to Create Geometry

To use the imported underlay to create solid geometry that remains associative to the AutoCAD DWG file, consider the following along with your standard sketching and feature creation techniques:

- Start the creation of a new sketch. In the *Sketch* tab>Create panel, expand the Project Geometry options and select (Project DWG Geometry). By projecting the DWG geometry you can maintain the reference between the sketch and the DWG file. Use the filter options in the mini-toolbar to project single geometry ( ), connected geometry ( ), or a DWG Block ( ). Click to close the mini-toolbar and cancel the Project DWG Geometry command.

- When projected, all of the entities are fully constrained. Consider creating Driven Dimensions to identify key dimensions in the underlay that can be used to drive solid geometry. For the example shown in Figure 14–8, the Driven Dimension can now be used to define the depth of the model.

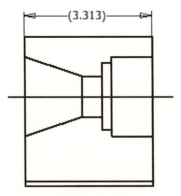

Figure 14–8

- In the Model browser, right-click on the imported DWG file to access the **Suppress Link** and **Break Link** options. These options can be used to either temporarily break the link with the source DWG file (**Suppress Link**) or permanently break the link (**Break Link**).

An imported AutoCAD DWG file can also be used as a layout reference to assemble components in an Inventor assembly file. For the example shown in Figure 14–9, the factory floor layout is an AutoCAD DWG file that can be used for assembly references in a top-level assembly.

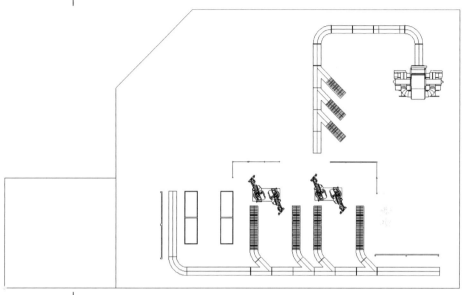

Figure 14–9

- The underlay is placed in an assembly file as a placed component. Many of the right-click menu options that are available in the part environment to edit the underlay are also available in an assembly.

The **Translate** command is not available to modify the location of an underlay placed in an assembly. To rotate it on the placement plane, you can expand the **Relationships** node in the Model browser and modify the **Angle 2** constraint, as required. As a workaround, insert the underlay into a part file, position it, and then insert the part into the assembly.

Hint: Associative DWG Underlays in Drawings

To include a DWG underlay in a drawing view, right-click on the Associative DWG file associated with the view and select **Include**, as shown in Figure 14–10. Once included, you can add text, dimensions, manage layers, or edit line types to appropriately annotate the underlay geometry.

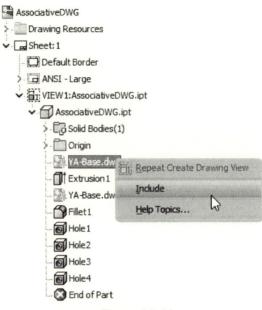

Figure 14–10

Hint: AutoCAD Mechanical files as DWG Underlays

AutoCAD Mechanical files can be imported as DWG files. If imported into an assembly file, constraints can be used to constrain the drawing. Note that cropped AutoCAD Mechanical geometry cannot be selected. Do not crop the DWG file.

Working with AutoCAD Data

Practice 14a | Import an AutoCAD DWG File into Autodesk Inventor

Practice Objective

- Use the DWG/DXF File Wizard to import an AutoCAD DWG file into an Autodesk Inventor part file and work with the data.

In this practice, you will import an AutoCAD DWG file directly into Autodesk Inventor. The AutoCAD DWG file contains a 3D AutoCAD model and a 2D layout. Once imported, you will review the file and use copy and paste techniques to copy non-associative 2D drawing data into a new Inventor model. The AutoCAD 3D model and drawing are shown in Figure 14–11.

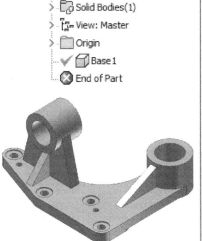
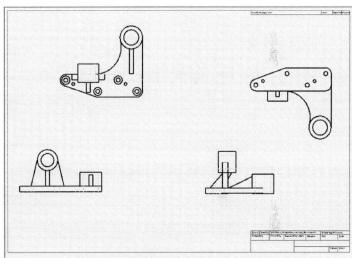

Figure 14–11

Task 1 - Import the AutoCAD DWG file.

1. In the Quick Access Toolbar, click ![icon].

2. In the File of type drop-down list, select **AutoCAD Dwg Files**.

3. Select **LEVERBRACKET.dwg** and click **Options**. The File Open Options dialog box opens. It enables you to directly open the DWG file in the Autodesk Inventor software or you can import the file. In this practice you will import the drawing.

4. Select **Import** and click **OK**.

© 2018, ASCENT - Center for Technical Knowledge®

5. Click **Open**. The DWG/DXF File Wizard displays.

6. In the *Read Content From* area, keep the **AutoCAD or AutoCAD Mechanical File** option selected. Leave the **Configuration** option set to **Configuration Not Saved** as you have not yet saved a configuration file. Click **Next**. The Layers and Objects Import Options dialog box opens. A preview of the AutoCAD 3D Solid geometry and its views are shown.

You can also zoom in and out using the scroll wheel.

7. In the dialog box, in the top right corner, click ▢ to change the background to white. You can use the Navigation bar or right-click on the background of the preview window to access the view orientation and manipulation options (e.g., pan, zoom). Manipulate the model as required.

The Layers and Objects Import Options dialog box is shown in Figure 14–12.

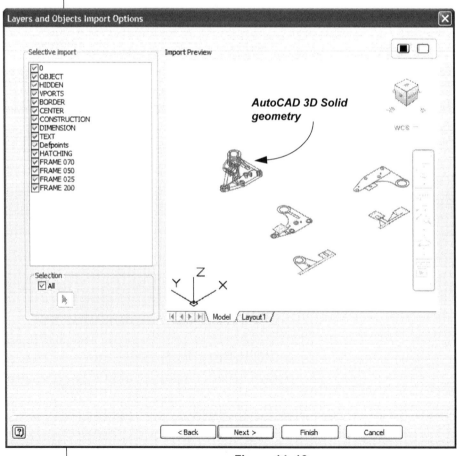

Figure 14–12

Working with AutoCAD Data

8. In the Navigation Bar, click ![icon] to fit the entire drawing in the preview area.

9. Clear **OBJECT**. Note that the model entities are removed.

10. Clear **HIDDEN** to remove the hidden lines.

11. Select **OBJECT** and **HIDDEN** again so that those entities will be imported.

12. To import specific entities from the DWG, in the *Selection* area, you can clear the **All** option and select individual entities to import. Leave the **All** option selected.

13. Select the *Layout1* tab to review the layout that will be imported.

14. Return to the *Model* tab.

15. Click **Next**. The Import Destination Options dialog box opens.

16. Activate **3D solids** to import the AutoCAD 3D solids that exist in the DWG file. Clear the **Solids to single part file** option, if selected.

17. In the *3D data options* area, verify that the *Destination Folder* field is set to the practice files directory. This is the directory where the new files will be created as a result of the import. Also verify that **Use Default File Names** is activated.

18. Select **New Drawing** to import the 2D data on the layouts into a new Autodesk Inventor drawing file. Imported 2D geometry is placed in sketches attached to a draft view. Dimensions are placed in the sketch containing the associated geometry. Unassociated dimensions, symbols, and other annotations are imported onto the drawing sheet. Blocks are imported as sketched symbols and placed in the *Drawing Resources* folder. The **Promote Dimensions To Sketch** option imports dimensions as sketch dimensions on a sheet in a drawing file. The promoted dimensions are associative and so they will change if the sketch geometry is modified. Deactivate **Promote Dimensions To Sketch**, if enabled.

19. In the *Templates* area, next to the Assembly Template, click ![icon]. In the *Metric* tab, select **Standard(mm).iam**. Click **OK**.

20. For the Part Template, in the *Metric* tab, select **Standard(mm).ipt**. Click **OK**.

21. For the Drawing Template, in the *Metric* tab, select **ANSI(mm).idw**. Click **OK**.

22. For the *Sheet Size*, select **A0**.

23. Click **Save Configuration** and enter **AutoCAD 3D Solid using metric** as the filename. Save it in the practice files directory.

24. Click **Finish** to begin the import. The DWG data is imported as a new part and drawing file.

25. Activate the LEVERBRACKET1 part file window by selecting it from the tabs along the bottom of the graphics window.

26. Return to the model's Home view using the ViewCube.

27. The color is imported from the source AutoCAD file. Change the default appearance to **Steel** using the Appearance Override drop-down list in the Quick Access toolbar, to display the model in a better color.

28. The model displays as shown in Figure 14–13. The model is a solid feature, but it is a boundary representation (rather than being made up of several features). You can now edit the solid using **Edit Solid** or **Direct Edit,** or add and remove material from the solid and use any of the edges and faces as references as you would a regular native Autodesk Inventor solid.

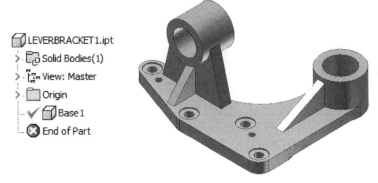

Figure 14–13

29. Save the part file using the default name.

Task 2 - Review and edit the imported drawing.

1. In the **Drawing1.dwg** drawing, expand the *Drawing Resources* folder and **Sketch Symbols** node. Right-click on ISO A2 title block and select **Insert**. Place the title block on the drawing. Click **OK** to leave the title block entries blank. Right-click and select **Cancel** to cancel placing additional title blocks.

2. The title block is small compared to sheet. To change the size, right-click on the title block, select **Edit Symbol**, enter **2** for the *Scale*, and click **OK**.

3. Use the green dot at the center of the title block to drag it to fit. Select any geometry on a view and drag it to reposition all of the views on the drawing sheet. You might have to also reposition the title block. The drawing displays as shown in Figure 14–14.

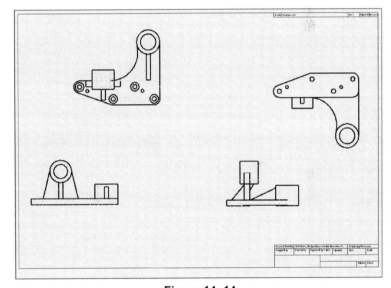

Figure 14–14

4. In the Model browser, expand the **Sheet:1** and the **ImportDraftView** branches. The 2D entities were imported into sketches, so the drawing views are actually sketched entities rather than views, unlike those in regular native Autodesk Inventor drawings.

5. Save the drawing as **Leverbracket2.idw** and save it in the practice files directory. Close the files.

Practice 14b Open AutoCAD DWG Data to Create a Solid

Practice Objective

- Open an AutoCAD DWG file directly into an Autodesk Inventor part file and work with the data.

In this practice, you will open an AutoCAD DWG file in Autodesk Inventor. You will review the contents of the DWG file and use some of its 2D data to create a sketch in new Autodesk Inventor file that can be used to create the initial geometry for an Inventor model. The geometry that will be created is shown in Figure 14–15.

Figure 14–15

Task 1 - Open an AutoCAD DWG and view the data in Autodesk Inventor.

1. In the Quick Access Toolbar, click .

2. Select **LEVERBRACKET.dwg** and click **Options**. The File Open Options dialog box opens.

3. By default, **Open** is already selected. If not, select **Open** and click **OK**.

Working with AutoCAD Data

4. Click **Open**. The **Leverbracket.dwg** file and the Browser display as shown in Figure 14–16.

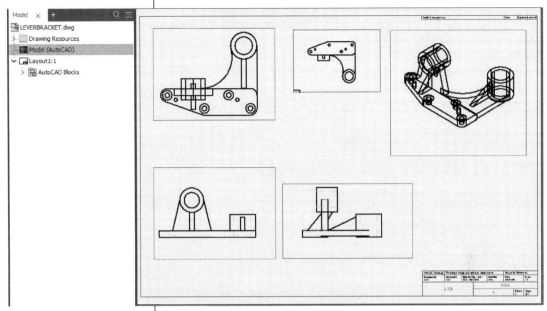

Figure 14–16

5. In the Model browser, double-click on the **Model (AutoCAD)** node.

6. To change the display color of the background, in the Model browser, right-click on **Model** and select **Background Color**. Change the color to white, if not already set as white. The model displays as shown in Figure 14–17.

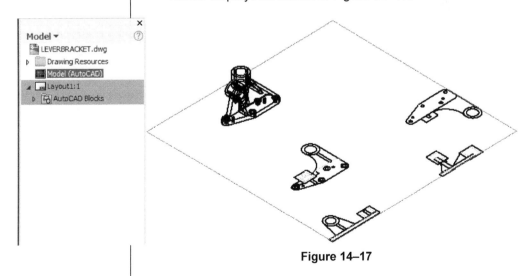

Figure 14–17

© 2018, ASCENT - Center for Technical Knowledge®   14–21

Task 2 - Use the AutoCAD DWG data to create an Autodesk Inventor part file.

1. Select and drag a selection box around the top right view, as shown in Figure 14–18.

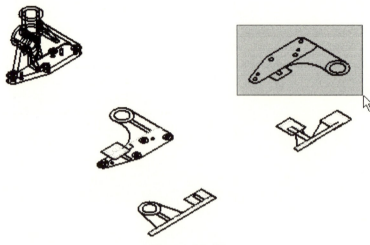

Figure 14–18

2. Right-click and select **Copy**.

3. Start a new part file using the **Standard (mm).ipt** metric template.

4. Create a sketch on the XZ plane. Once you are placed in the Sketch environment, right-click and select **Paste**. Place the entities in the sketch.

5. In the Navigation Bar, click (Zoom All) to refit the model.

6. Use the **Rotate** and **Move** tools to move the entities relative to the origin center, as shown in Figure 14–19.

   Hint: You need to create construction lines and a point at the intersection of the construction lines. Once all the reference items are created you can move the entities to the projected origin center.

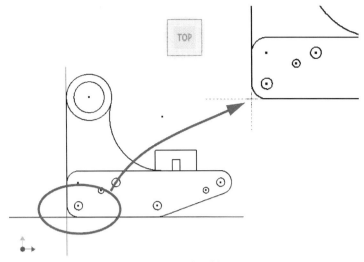

Figure 14–19

7. Project YZ and XY and locate the geometry's horizontal bottom and vertical left side entities to lie on these projected planes.

8. For simplicity, dimension the remaining entities using **Auto Dimension**. Normally, it is recommended to place dimensions based on your required design intent, but for this practice you use this tool to quickly progress to creating geometry. Finish the sketch.

9. Create an Extrude and select the three closed sections of the sketch and the six holes to obtain the solid in Figure 14–20. Extrude the feature **16mm** and flip the creation direction below the sketch plane.

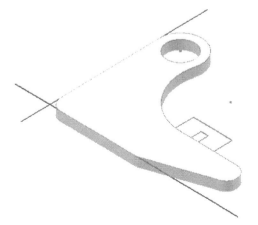

Figure 14–20

10. Expand **Extrusion1**. Right-click on **Sketch1** and select **Share Sketch**. Alternatively, you can select and drag **Sketch1** above the Extrusion to share it. By sharing the sketch it copies the sketch outside the extrusion for use with other features.

11. Toggle on the **Visibility** for the shared sketch, if it is off.

12. Extrude the two additional closed sections by **3mm**, as shown in Figure 14–21.

    Hint: When extruding the larger section you also need to select the six holes to create the solid. This enables you to then use the circular sections to create separate features later in the design process.

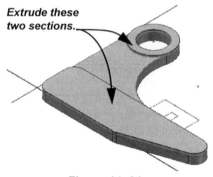

Figure 14–21

13. Create extruded cuts to represent the holes, as shown in Figure 14–22. The holes cut through the entire model. As an alternative, you could also have edited the sketch and added points to the centers of the holes. The points could then have been created with the **Hole** command to create the holes with the required diameters.

Figure 14–22

14. Save the part.

Up to this point, the method used to create the model is only one interpretation of how the model can be created. There are many other alternatives. For example, you can use the copied entities and create individual sketches for each feature, dimension and constrain them as required, and remove links to the original copied entities. Whichever method you use, consider your design intent and what information you need to communicate how the model is manufactured. Ultimately, because the data was copied from the AutoCAD file, it does not maintain any associative link.

Optional Task - Continue modeling the solid geometry.

After you have finished creating all of the practices in this chapter, continue to model the geometry for the leverbracket part that was originally created in the AutoCAD software. You can take measurements, as required, using the imported model that you created in Task 1. You need to create additional sketch planes and copy entities from the .DWG file to create the remaining geometry. In some situations you might want to consider creating features on your own instead of using copied entities.

Practice 14c

Import Associative DWG Data into a Part File

Practice Objective

- Open an AutoCAD DWG file directly into an Autodesk Inventor part file and work with the data.

In this practice, you will import an AutoCAD DWG file into an Autodesk Inventor file as an underlay. You will control the layer visibility and its location in the file so that the underlay can be used to project geometry onto sketches. The sketch geometry will then be used to create a 3D model. The geometry that will be created is shown in Figure 14–23.

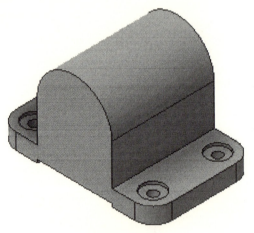

Figure 14–23

Task 1 - Create a new Autodesk Inventor model and import AutoCAD data.

1. Start a new part file using the **Standard (in).ipt** template.

2. Save the file as **AssociativeDWG.ipt**.

3. In the *3D Model* tab>Create panel, click (Import).

4. In the Import dialog box, expand the Files of type drop-down list and select **AutoCAD DWG Files (*.dwg)**.

Working with AutoCAD Data

5. Select **YA-Base.dwg** from the practice files folder and click **Open**.

6. Select the XY Origin plane as the plane to import the DWG file to.

7. Select the projected Origin Center Point as the centerpoint for the import.

8. If you had not previously saved the file as **AssociativeDWG.ipt**, you will be prompted that the file is unsaved and this may cause problems in resolving links between the files. Click **OK**.

9. Click **OK** when prompted that inserting an AutoCAD DWG produces an associative underlay.

10. If you had not previously saved the files, save it now as **AssociativeDWG.ipt**.

11. Review the three 2D views. Note that the side view is a section view.

Task 2 - Set the Layer Visibility on the AutoCAD DWG file.

1. Right-click on **YA-Base.dwg** in the Model browser and select **Layer Visibility**. The Layer Visibility dialog box opens.

2. In the filter settings at the top of the dialog box, click ▦ (Clear All) to clear all the layers from being displayed.

3. Select **YA-Base|Hidden Edges**, **YA-Base|Tangent Edges**, and **YA-Base|Visible Edges**.

4. Click **OK** to close the Layer Visibility dialog box. The visibility of any of the layers can be controlled at any time using this dialog box.

Task 3 - Crop the AutoCAD DWG file.

1. Right-click on **YA-Base.dwg** in the Model browser and select **Crop**.

2. Drag a bounding box around the two views shown in Figure 14–24. The box defines which entities in the underlay file will remain in the file.

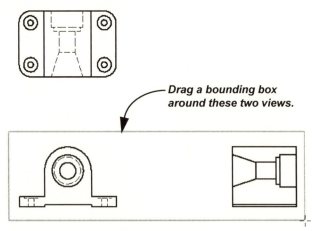

Figure 14–24

3. Right-click and select **OK (Enter)** to remove the entities outside the bounding box from view.

Task 4 - Translate the AutoCAD DWG file relative to the model's origin.

1. Expand the **Origin** node in the Model browser and toggle on the visibility of the Center Point.

2. Using the Navigation Bar, select **Zoom All** to refit the model so that both the Origin Center Point and the drawing are displayed on the screen. If you are using a white background you may have difficulty seeing the yellow origin center point. Hover the cursor over the origin planes in the Model browser to display them in the model to understand where the origin point is located.

3. Right-click on **YA-Base.dwg** in the Model browser and select **Translate**.

4. A triad displays on the Origin Center Point. Click **Locate** in the mini-toolbar. Select the center point of the internal hole, as shown in Figure 14–25.

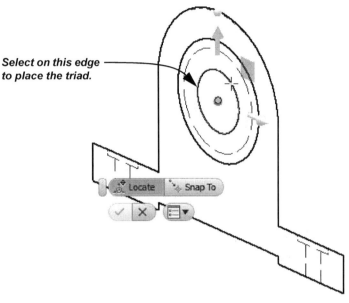

Figure 14–25

5. Click ✓ to close the mini-toolbar and complete the translation.

6. Return the model to its Home View using the ViewCube.

Task 5 - Create associative geometry from the DWG file.

1. Create a new 2D sketch on the XY plane.

2. In the *Sketch* tab>Create panel, expand the Project Geometry options and select (Project DWG Geometry).

3. In the mini-toolbar, select ![icon] (Project Connected Geometry) and select on an outside edge in the Front view, as shown on the left in Figure 14–26. All connected edges are projected. Project the outside loop of single edges on the section view, as shown on the right of Figure 14–26.

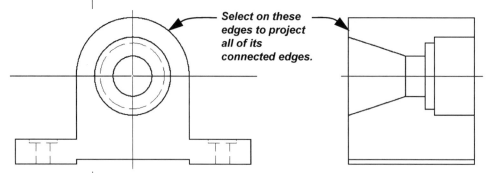

Figure 14–26

4. Click ✕ to close the mini-toolbar and cancel the Project DWG Geometry command.

5. Create a dimension in the side section view to define the depth of the model. Once placed, you will be prompted that the dimension will over-constrain the sketch. Click **Accept** to place the dimension as a Driven Dimension, as shown in Figure 14–27.

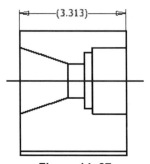

Figure 14–27

6. Finish the sketch.

7. Right-click in the graphics window and click **Dimension Display>Name** to display the name of the dimension value.

8. Create an Extrude and select the section shown in Figure 14–28. Enter **d1** (or name of your Driven Dimension) as the value for the extruded depth.

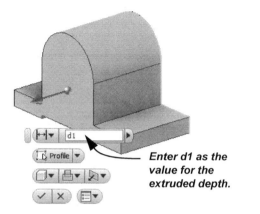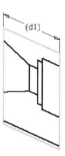

Figure 14–28

9. Complete the feature.

Task 6 - Insert the DWG on another plane and create additional geometry.

1. In the *3D Model* tab>Create panel, click (Import).

2. In the Import dialog box, select **YA-Base.dwg** from the practice files folder and click **Open**.

3. Select the plane and origin point shown in Figure 14–29 as the references to import the DWG file.

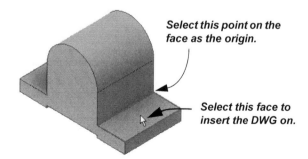

Figure 14–29

4. When prompted that inserting an AutoCAD DWG produces an associative underlay, click **OK**.

5. Right-click on the newly imported **YA-Base.dwg** in the Model browser and select **Layer Visibility**. The Layer Visibility dialog box opens. Note that the same visibility settings are set. Click **OK** to close the Layer Visibility dialog box.

6. In the Navigation Bar, select **Zoom All** to refit the model to see the solid geometry and the new underlay.

7. Right-click on newly imported **YA-Base.dwg** in the Model browser and select **Translate**.

8. A triad appears, by default, on the point that was selected on the placement face. Click **Locate** in the mini-toolbar. Select the point shown in Figure 14–30 on the newly imported underlay.

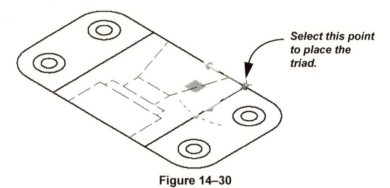

Figure 14–30

9. Click ✓ to close the mini-toolbar and complete the translation.

10. Both underlays are on different planes and are visible. Right-click on the first **YA-Base.dwg** and clear the **Visibility** option. You can toggle the display of underlays on and off as required.

11. Create a new sketch on the same face that was used to place the latest DWG underlay file.

12. In the Create panel, click (Project DWG Geometry).

13. In the mini-toolbar, ensure that (Project Single Geometry) is selected and select the four arcs on the outside corners of the view shown in Figure 14–31 to project them.

14. Project one large and one small circle, as shown in Figure 14–31. Close the mini-toolbar or cancel the command.

15. Create the three Driven Dimensions shown in Figure 14–31.

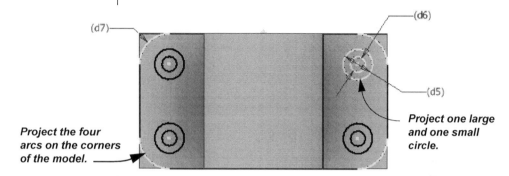

Figure 14–31

16. While in the same sketch, project the required edges and create the reference dimension shown in Figure 14–32.

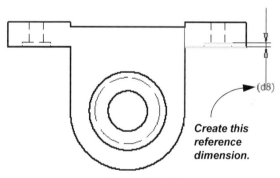

Figure 14–32

17. Finish the sketch.

18. Create a Fillet.

The dimension name may vary depending on the order that you created the Driven Dimensions in the sketch.

19. Select the four vertical edges on the outside of the model. Enter **d5** (or name of your Driven Dimension) as the value of the fillet, as shown in Figure 14–33. This ensures the size of the fillet is driven by the projected geometry.

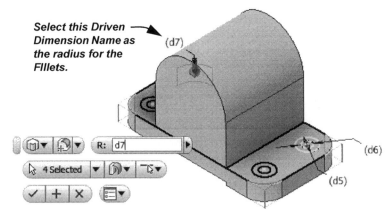

Figure 14–33

20. Complete the feature.

21. Create a concentric hole by selecting the placement plane and concentric reference shown in Figure 14–34.

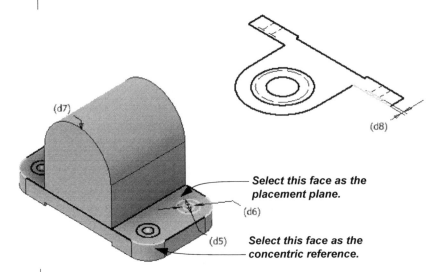

Figure 14–34

22. Enter the dimension values for the hole using the driven dimensions that were created in the sketch, as shown in Figure 14–35. Ensure that you enter the correct dimension name to match the counterbore dimensions. Create the hole as **Through All**.

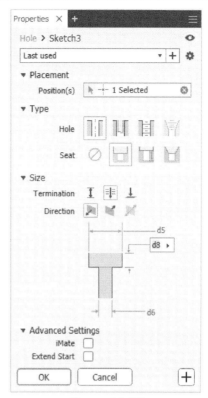

Figure 14–35

23. Complete the feature.

24. Create the additional three counterbore holes using the same settings and driven dimensions.

25. Toggle off the visibility of the second imported DWG underlay and the sketch. The model displays as shown in Figure 14–36.

Figure 14–36

26. Save the file.

Task 7 - Replace the YA-Base.dwg with a modified version.

*A copy of the original YA-Base.dwg file, called **YA-Base_ORIGINAL. dwg**, is in the Updated DWGs folder, if required.*

1. Open Windows Explorer and navigate to the *Updated DWGs* folder within the top-level practice files folder.

2. Copy **YA-Base.dwg** from the *Updated DWGs* folder into the top-level practice files folder. Confirm that you want to replace the original file with the copied version. This new file has had changes made to the file to increase the size of the holes and the depth of the model.

3. Return to Autodesk Inventor and review the **AssociativeDWG.ipt**. The Model browser indicates that **YA-Base.dwg** has been updated, as shown by the lightening bolt icons in Figure 14–37.

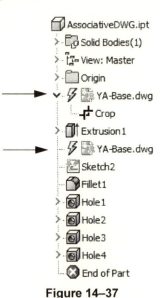

Figure 14–37

4. In the Quick Access toolbar, select ▣ (Local Update). Note that the model updates as shown in Figure 14–38.

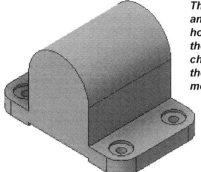

The depth of the model and the size of the holes were updated in the DWG file. The changes are reflected in the Autodesk Inventor model.

Figure 14–38

5. In the Model browser, right-click on either of the **YA-Base.dwg** files and note the **Suppress Link** and **Break Link** options. These options can be used to either temporarily break the link with the source DWG file (**Suppress Link**) or permanently break the link (**Break Link**).

6. Save the model and close the window.

Optional Task - Continue modeling the solid geometry.

After you have finished creating all of the practices in this chapter, continue to add the geometry from the DWG file into the Autodesk Inventor model. The only remaining feature is a revolved cut. To create this, consider creating a workplane and project the section that is to be revolved. Alternatively, edit one of the sketches and add more Driven Dimensions that can be used to drive additional hole features.

Practice 14d | Associative DWG Layout

Practice Objectives

- Import an AutoCAD .DWG file as an underlay in an Autodesk Inventor part file.
- Assemble the underlay part file as the base grounded component and reference it to place and create components.

In this practice, you will begin by creating a new part file that imports an AutoCAD DWG file for use as an underlay. The underlay is imported so that associativity is maintained between the files. The part file is then used in an assembly to constrain and create new components in the assembly. To complete the practice, a change is made in the original DWG file and the updates are shown to reflect in the assembly file. The geometry that will be created is shown in Figure 14–39.

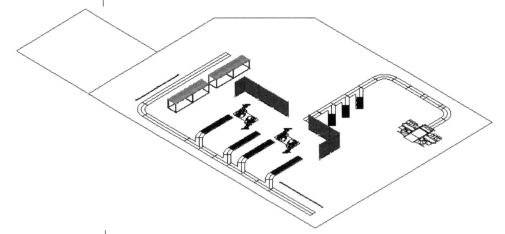

Figure 14–39

Note: With the release of the Autodesk Inventor 2018 software you were able to place a DWG underlay directly into an assembly using the **Place** option. Unfortunately, placing the underlay in this way does not provide an option to translate the underlay, as is available in the Part environment. As an alternative, if translation is required, you can insert the underlay into a Part file and place the part file into an assembly using assembly constraints to constrain the part, as required. In this practice, you must translate the placement point so that inserting it into a part and then assembling it will be the process used.

Working with AutoCAD Data

Task 1 - Create a new Autodesk Inventor model and import AutoCAD data.

1. Start a new part file using the **Standard (in).ipt** template.
2. Save the new file as **FactoryLayout.ipt**.
3. In the *3D Model* tab>Create panel, click (Import).
4. In the Import dialog box, expand the Files of type drop-down list and select **AutoCAD DWG Files (*.dwg)**.
5. Select **Layout Example.dwg** from the practice files folder and click **Open**.
6. Select the XZ Origin plane as the plane to import the DWG file.
7. Select the projected Origin Center Point as the centerpoint for the import.
8. Click **OK** when prompted that inserting an AutoCAD DWG produces an associative underlay. If you had previously not saved the file, you will be notified that saving is also required.
9. Review the factory layout. The orientation of the drawing should be rotated 180 degrees and the origin point needs to be repositioned. In the next task you will reorient the imported DWG file.

Task 2 - Translate the AutoCAD DWG file relative to the model's origin.

1. Expand the **Origin** node in the Model browser. Toggle on the visibility of the Center Point and note where it is located.
2. Right-click on **Layout Example.dwg** in the Model browser and select **Translate**.

© 2018, ASCENT - Center for Technical Knowledge®   14–39

3. A triad displays on the Origin Center Point. Select the rotation handle shown in Figure 14–40 to enable the rotation of the imported DWG file.

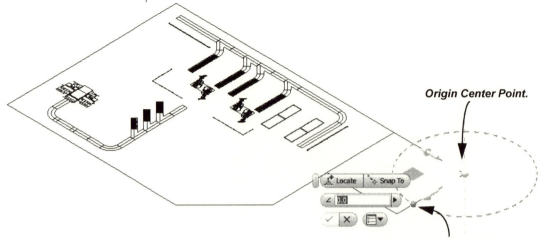

Figure 14–40

4. Enter **180** to rotate the DWG file.

5. Click **Locate** in the mini-toolbar and select the point where the two rooms join, as shown in Figure 14–41.

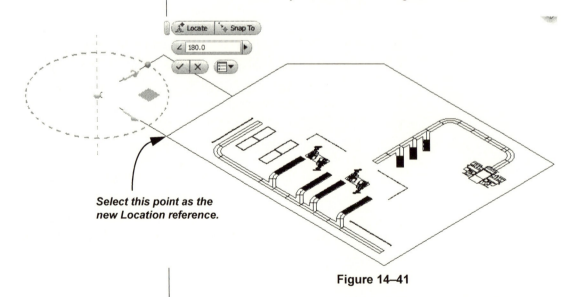

Figure 14–41

6. Click **Snap To** in the mini-toolbar and select the Origin Center Point in the Model browser to align the DWG underlay and the reference point on the drawing.

7. Click ✓ to close the mini-toolbar and complete the translation. The model should display as shown in Figure 14–42.

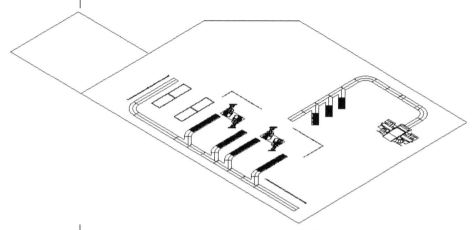

Figure 14–42

Task 3 - Set the Layer Visibility for the AutoCAD DWG file.

1. Right-click on **Layout Example.dwg** in the Model browser and select **Layer Visibility**. The Layer Visibility dialog box opens. This dialog box enables you to control the DWG layers that are displayed in the Autodesk Inventor model.

2. Select **Layout Example|Slab** in the list and note how additional entities are added to the view. As these are not required, you can leave this option cleared.

3. Select **Layout Example|Walls-Interior** to clear the option. Note how all of the entities are cleared. In this drawing all of the entities have been added to this layer. Select **Layout Example|Walls-Interior** again to enable the option.

4. Click **OK** to close the Layer Visibility dialog box. The visibility of layers can be controlled at any time using this dialog box.

5. Save the model.

Task 4 - Use the associative DWG file as a reference for assembling and creating components in an assembly.

1. Start a new assembly file using the **Standard (in).iam** template.

2. Place one instance of **FactoryLayout.ipt** into the assembly file. Right-click and select **Place Grounded at Origin** to assemble the part as the base model and ground it.

3. Press <Esc> to cancel the assembly of additional instances of the file.

4. Place a single instance of **Table.iam** into the assembly file, as shown in Figure 14–43.

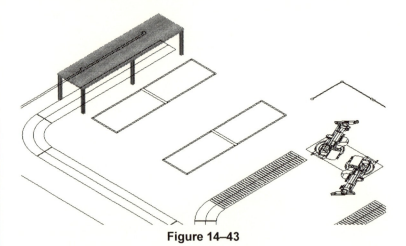

Figure 14–43

5. In the *Assembly* tab>Relationships panel, click (Constrain).

6. Using the Place Constraint dialog box, assign the following constraints to fully locate the table relative to the **FactoryLayout.ipt** file:
    - Mate the XZ plane of the table component to the XZ plane of the assembly. Use the **Flush** orientation.
    - Add two Mate constraints that align the edges of the table legs and the border of the table's layout in the X and Z directions, as shown in Figure 14–44.

Working with AutoCAD Data

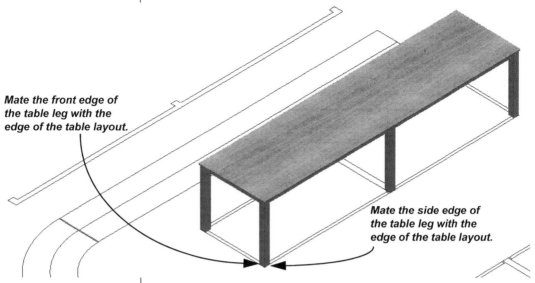

Mate the front edge of the table leg with the edge of the table layout.

Mate the side edge of the table leg with the edge of the table layout.

Figure 14–44

7. Close the Place Constraints dialog box.

8. Place a second instance of **Table.iam** and constrain it to the other table layout. The final assembly should display as shown in Figure 14–45.

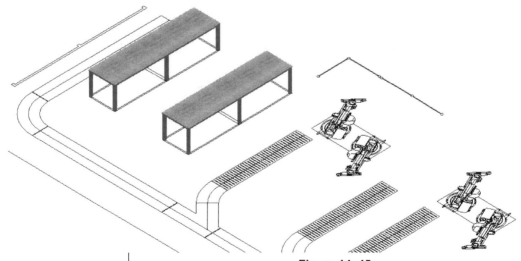

Figure 14–45

9. Save the file as **Factory.iam**.

Task 5 - Create part geometry using the AutoCAD DWG underlay as a reference.

1. In the *Assembly* tab>Component panel, click ▢ (Create) to start a new part file in the context of the assembly.

2. In the Create In-Place Component dialog box, enter **Screen.ipt** as the name of the new file and assign **Standard(in).ipt** as the part template to be used. Click **OK**.

3. Select the XZ plane of the assembly as the sketch plane reference for the new part. **Screen.ipt** becomes the active component in the assembly (if not, activate it).

4. In the *3D Model* tab>Sketch panel, click ▢ (Start 2D Sketch).

5. Select the XY plane in the Screen model as the sketching plane for the sketch.

6. In the *Sketch* tab>Create panel, expand the **Project Geometry** option, and select ▢ (Project DWG Geometry).

7. In the mini-toolbar, ensure that ▢ (Project Single Geometry) is selected. Select the 13 circular entities described in Figure 14–46. If the entire entity is not selected, it cannot be extruded in a later step.

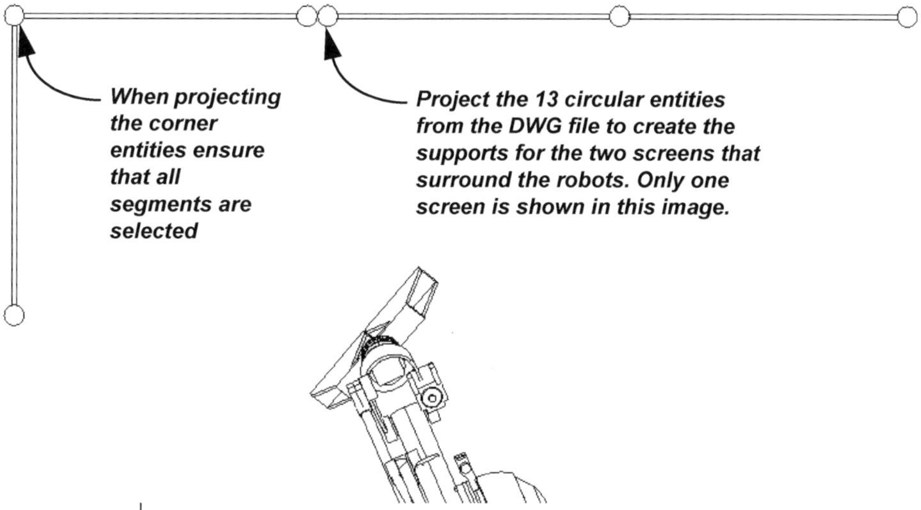

Working with AutoCAD Data

When projecting the corner entities ensure that all segments are selected

Project the 13 circular entities from the DWG file to create the supports for the two screens that surround the robots. Only one screen is shown in this image.

Figure 14–46

8. Finish the sketch and rename the sketch as **Supports**.

9. Create a second sketch on the XY plane and start the (Project DWG Geometry) option.

10. In the mini-toolbar, select (Project Connected Geometry) and project the 9 rectangles that are used to define the screen geometry between the supports, as shown in Figure 14–47.

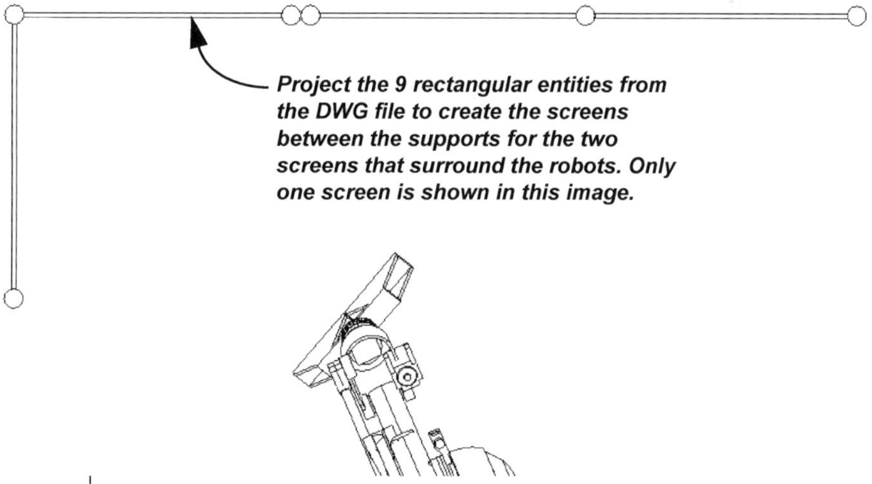

Project the 9 rectangular entities from the DWG file to create the screens between the supports for the two screens that surround the robots. Only one screen is shown in this image.

Figure 14–47

© 2018, ASCENT - Center for Technical Knowledge®   14–45

11. Finish the sketch and rename the sketch as **Screens**.

12. Use the **Extrude** command to create the screen geometry shown in Figure 14–48.

    • Extrude the 13 circular entities in the Supports sketch to a height of **72 in**.
    • Extrude the 9 rectangular entities in the Screens sketch to a height of **70 in**.

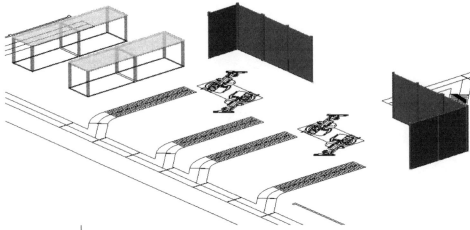

Figure 14–48

13. Reactivate the top-level assembly.

14. Save the assembly and the newly created part file.

Task 6 - Update the DWG underlay and the associated geometry.

1. Open Windows Explorer and navigate to the *Updated DWGs* folder within the top-level practice files folder.

2. Copy **Layout Example.dwg** from the *Updated DWGs* folder into the top-level practice files folder. Confirm that you want to replace the original file with the copied version. This new file has had changes made to relocate the tables and change the size of one of the screens.

*A copy of the original Layout Example.dwg file, called **Layout Example_ORIGINAL dwg**, is in the Updated DWGs folder, if required.*

Working with AutoCAD Data

3. Return to Autodesk Inventor and note that the ⊡ (Local Update) option is available in the Quick Access toolbar and that the **FactoryLayout** underlay is showing as out-of-date in the Model browser. Click ⊡ (Local Update) to update the assembly, as shown in Figure 14–49.

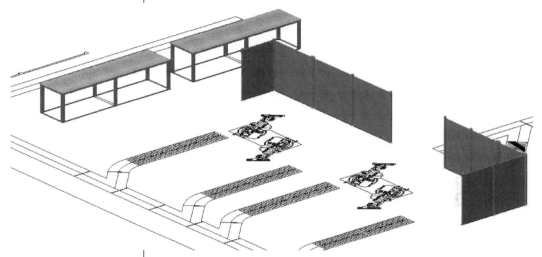

Figure 14–49

4. Save the assembly and close the files.

Chapter Review Questions

1. When using an AutoCAD .DWG file in Autodesk Inventor, which of the following Open Options should be used to view, plot, and measure the file contents?

    a. Open

    b. Import

2. Which of the following Open Options should be used to create a single solid-body base feature when an AutoCAD 3D DWG file is required for use in Autodesk Inventor?

    a. Open

    b. Import

3. Which of the following are true statements regarding importing AutoCAD DWG data as an underlay in Autodesk Inventor? (Select all that apply.)

    a. The DWG data can only be imported onto a single plane in the model.

    b. The layers in the DWG underlay can be set to display only specific layers.

    c. Use the **Project Geometry** command to project and use DWG data in a sketch.

    d. The DWG data that is imported remains unassociated with the source data.

    e. The visibility of the DWG underlays can be controlled using the **Visibility** option.

    f. An imported AutoCAD DWG file can also be used as a layout reference to assemble components.

    g. An imported AutoCAD DWG file can be displayed in a drawing view of the Inventor file.

4. Which of the following best describes how the **Translate** command can be used? (Select all that apply.)

    a. The **Translate** command enables you to relocate the DWG underlay on the same plane.

    b. The **Translate** command enables you to relocate the DWG underlay onto another plane.

    c. The **Translate** command enables you to snap the DWG underlay to the origin center point on the same plane.

5. You can crop an imported DWG underlay in multiple locations to simplify the data that displays.

   a. True
   b. False

6. Which of the following three methods for incorporating AutoCAD DWG data in Autodesk Inventor enables you to review sheets in the DWG file?

   a. Selecting **Open** in the File Open Options dialog box.
   b. Selecting **Import** in the File Open Options dialog box.
   c. Creating a new part file and selecting **Import** in the *3D Model* tab>Create panel.

Command Summary

Button	Command	Location
	Import	• **Ribbon:** *3D Model* tab>Create panel
Options...	Options (import options)	• **Ribbon:** *Get Started* tab>Launch panel>Open • **File Menu:** Open dialog box • **Quick Access toolbar:** Open dialog box
	Project DWG Geometry	• **Ribbon:** *Sketch* tab>Create panel

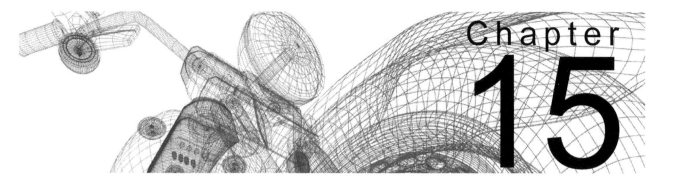

Chapter 15

Introduction to Freeform Modeling

A Freeform Modeling workflow enables you to create complex, visually appealing shapes without the complex work that is required when using a Parametric Modeling workflow.

Learning Objectives in this Chapter

- Create freeform geometry base shapes, faces, and converted geometry.
- Edit freeform base geometry by manipulating existing geometry or adding new elements to the base shape.

15.1 Creating Freeform Geometry

Using conventional modeling techniques to create organic, highly shaped, and visually appealing models is often difficult and time-consuming. Freeform modeling is an alternate modeling approach for these types of surfaces. It enables you to create shapes that can be manipulated directly, without needing to use parametric constraints. These tools can be combined with parametric tools, where required.

Creating Standard Freeform Shapes

To begin the modeling process you must create the shape that is going to form the base geometry. Select the type that provides you with the best overall shape for the required geometry. The available shapes are shown in Figure 15–1.

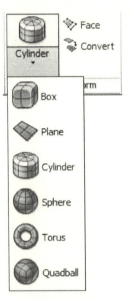

Figure 15–1

The overall procedure for creating the freeform shapes is similar and all of them use dialog boxes to define their geometry.

Introduction to Freeform Modeling

To create additional freeform shapes once in Freeform mode, select the geometry type from the Freeform tab> Create Freeform panel.

How To: Create a Base Freeform Shape

1. In the *3D Model* tab>Create Freeform panel, select the type of freeform shape to create. Figure 15–2 shows the dialog boxes that are used to create each shape type.

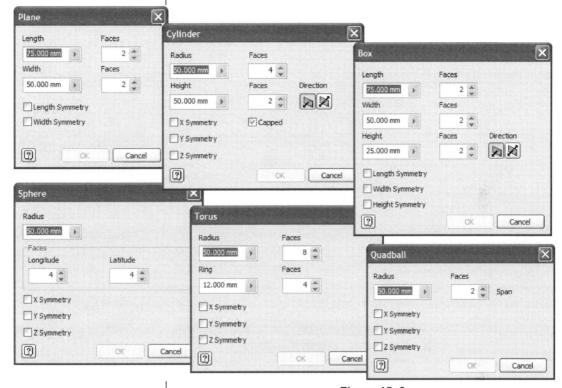

Figure 15–2

2. Select a work plane or planar face on which to place the freeform shape.
3. Select the center of the freeform shape.
   - Select the projected model origin to locate the shape at the origin center point.
   - If creating a freeform shape on an existing face, geometry points are projected from the model and can be selected as the center point reference.
   - If no reference point exists, you can also select anywhere on the plane.

4. Manipulate the size of the freeform shape using any of the following techniques:
   - Drag the arrowheads that display on the model. The active arrowhead is displayed in gold. Select any of the other arrowheads to activate them for dragging. Figure 15–3 shows the default shape and arrowheads available for a Box and Cylinder.
   - Enter values for the freeform size in its creation dialog box, as shown in Figure 15–3.

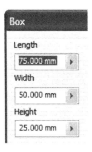   

Figure 15–3

5. Enter the number of faces that are to be added in all directions, as shown in Figure 15–4.

The freeform shape is more refined when more faces are added. Note that using too many sides can create too much control.

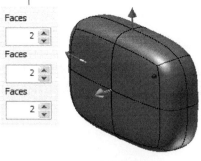 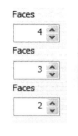 

Figure 15–4

- For a Sphere freeform, you enter the number of faces in the longitudinal and latitudinal directions. For the Quadball freeform, only a single face field is provided.

Introduction to Freeform Modeling

6. Assign symmetry by selecting the appropriate axis/directions in the creation dialog box.
   - Hover the cursor over each option to display the symmetry plane that will be used.
   - Once assigned, black edges display as a dashed yellow edge to identify the symmetry lines.

> **Hint: Defining Symmetry**
>
> If symmetry is required in the model after the base freeform shape is created, you can use ▲ (Symmetry) in the Symmetry panel to explicitly assign symmetry between selected faces.

7. For the Box and Cylinder freeform shapes, select the direction in which the freeform shape is to be created relative to the placement plane by clicking ▨ and ▨.
8. Click **OK**.

Figure 15–5 shows the available shapes. Each have been manipulated using the options in their creation dialog boxes. The Model browser shown on the left is the same regardless of the type of shape created. It indicates that a **Form** feature has been added to the model.

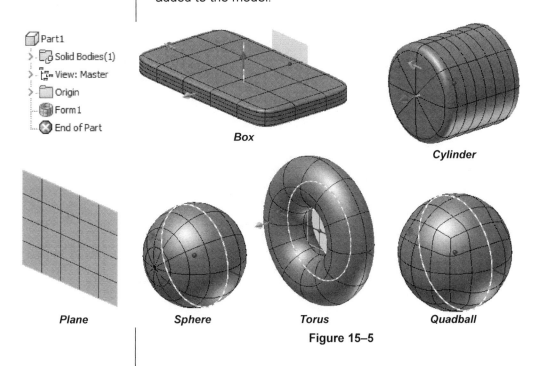

Figure 15–5

Creating a Face Freeform

To create additional faces once you are in Freeform mode, select (Face) from the Freeform tab> Create Freeform panel.

A **Face** Freeform enables you to create an irregular, planar, or non-planar face as the base freeform geometry. It can also be used to close a gap.

How To: Create a Face

1. In *3D Model* tab>Create Freeform panel, select (Face). The Face dialog box opens as shown in Figure 15–6.

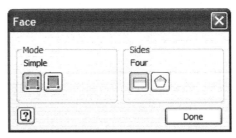

Figure 15–6

2. Set how the face is to be created using the options in the *Mode* area:

    - Select (Point) to select individual points to define the face.

    - Select (Edge) to select an edge and two points to define the face.

3. Define the number of corners in the face in the *Sides* area:

    - Select (Four) to create a face with four boundary points.

    - Select (Multiple) to create a face with any number of points. To complete the face, you must select the first selected point a second time.

4. Select points to define the face.
5. Click **Done** to complete the face.

By default, if points are selected individually without referencing existing entities, the points create a planar face.

Introduction to Freeform Modeling

Converting Geometry to a Freeform

Existing solid faces and surface 3D geometry can be converted into a freeform object using **Convert**. Once converted, it copies the shape of the original geometry and becomes freeform geometry, enabling you to use all of the editing tools to further manipulate the shape of the model.

How To: Convert to Freeform Geometry

1. In the *3D Model* tab>Create Freeform panel, click (Convert). The Convert to Freeform dialog box opens, as shown in Figure 15–7.

To convert additional faces once in Freeform mode, select (Convert) from the Freeform tab>Create Freeform panel.

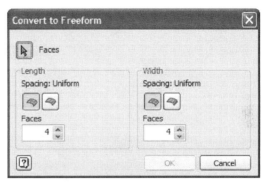

Figure 15–7

2. Select faces on a solid or surface model.
3. Define how the faces will be created in the converted freeform geometry for Length:

   - Select (Uniform) to create the converted geometry with uniform spacing and enter the number of faces to be created.

   - Select (Curvature) to create the converted geometry with curvature and enter a deviation value to define how it should be divided in the Length.

4. Set values in the *Width* area to define how the faces will be created in the converted freeform geometry. The available options are the same as in *Length*.
5. Click **OK** to complete the conversion to freeform geometry.

If the resulting shape is different from the original, increase the number of faces to more closely match it.

© 2018, ASCENT - Center for Technical Knowledge® 15–7

The solid geometry shown in Figure 15–8 was selected for conversion. Once converted, you can use the editing tools in the freeform environment to manipulate the shape, as required.

Figure 15–8

Once the freeform base solid, face, or converted freeform geometry has been created, the Freeform environment is active, as shown in Figure 15–9. All of the commands outside the *Freeform* tab are unavailable.

Figure 15–9

Hint: Toggle Smooth

Use the ![icon] (Toggle Smooth) option located in the Tools panel to toggle the freeform from a smooth to blocky mode display type, as shown in Figure 15–10. When in Blocky mode, the performance is faster. The model is still smooth once it has been toggled off or when Freeform mode is off.

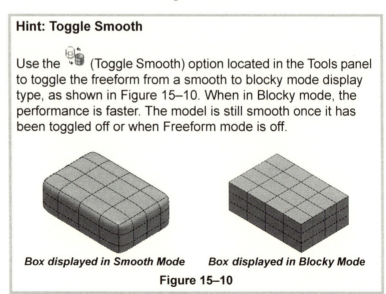

Box displayed in Smooth Mode   *Box displayed in Blocky Mode*

Figure 15–10

Introduction to Freeform Modeling

Deactivating and Activating Freeform Mode

To exit the Freeform environment, either:

- Click ✓ (Finish Freeform) in the Exit panel.

- Right-click and select **Finish Freeform** in the marking menu.

Once closed, the ribbon updates and you can access the parametric modeling tools and the Model browser adds a **Form** feature to the list of features. To reactivate the Freeform environment, right-click on the **Form** feature node and select **Edit Freeform** (shown in Figure 15–11), or double-click on the **Form** node.

Figure 15–11

15.2 Editing Freeform Geometry

The *Freeform* tab provides editing tools (shown in Figure 15–12) that enable you to further refine the freeform geometry. As changes are made to the geometry they are all incorporated into the Form feature. Feature history is not recorded to account for each of the edits. While in the same session you can undo actions, but once the model has been saved the undo history is cleared.

Figure 15–12

The mesh that overlays the geometry is used for editing. The overall mesh consists of points that are connected by edges and the enclosed edges are called *faces*. While editing you can select points, edges, faces, loops, or bodies for editing. The Box freeform shown in Figure 15–13 identifies what each of the entity types refer to in the model.

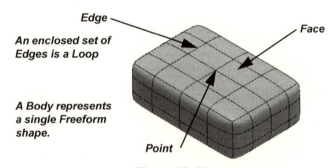

Figure 15–13

The following describes how you can use the available editing tools to manipulate the freeform shape.

Edit Form

The **Edit Form** command in the Freeform panel is the primary command that is used to manipulate geometry. It enables you to select point, edges, faces, bodies, or loops to access a manipulator triad that can be dragged to change the shape of the freeform.

How To: Edit Elements

1. In the *Freeform* tab>Edit panel, click (Edit Form). The Edit Form dialog box opens, as shown in Figure 15–14.

Figure 15–14

2. In the *Filter* area, select the element type that is to be manipulated. The options include the following:

To select multiple entities for simultaneous manipulation, hold <Shift> while selecting.

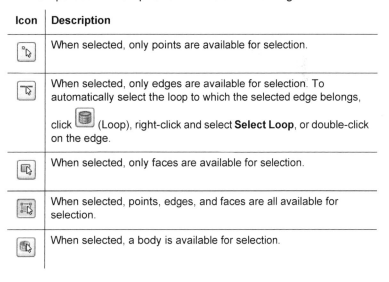

Once an element has been selected, a manipulator triad displays, as shown in Figure 15–15. The triad center is placed on the selected reference entity that is displayed in blue.

Manipulator triad on a point

Manipulator triad on an edge   **Manipulator triad on a face**

Manipulator triad on a body

Manipulator triad on a loop

Figure 15–15

3. (Optional) Filter the manipulator types that are displayed on the triad using the *Mode* settings in the *Transform* area. The available options enable you to determine whether it displays controls for (⊞) Translation, (⟳) (Rotation), (▣) (Scaling) or all of the controls at the same time (⚙), as shown in Figure 15–16. The default setting is to show all of the manipulator types.

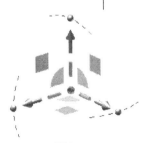  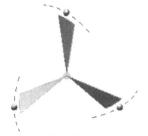

   All types   **Translation**   **Rotation**   **Scale**

Figure 15–16

Introduction to Freeform Modeling

4. Define the *Space* setting in the *Transform* area. It enables you to control the orientation of the manipulator triad.

   - Use ![] (World) to set the orientation with the model origin orientation.
   - Use ![] (View) to set the orientation relative to the current view of the model.
   - Use ![] (Local) to set the orientation relative to the selected object.

*Alternatively, you can select **Locate** in the mini-toolbar to reset the triad's location.*

5. (Optional) Click ![] (Locate) to reset the location of the manipulator triad on the geometry (not the element). Once active, select a new edge or point to locate the triad.
   - Faces cannot be selected as new references.

6. Select the remaining options as required:

   - Click ![] (Display) to toggle the model display from a smooth to blocky display style.
   - Click ![] (Extrude) in the *Transform* area to set the editing tool to entirely extrude a selected face instead of transforming it. If used, additional edges, faces, and points are created, as shown in Figure 15–17.

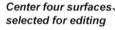
Center four surfaces selected for editing

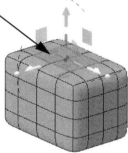

Extrude Disabled

Extrude Enabled

Figure 15–17

Soft Modification is not available if the Extrude option is being used.

   - Click **Soft Modification** to enable the edit actions to have a more gradual impact on adjacent surfaces. When enabled, you are provided additional controls to define the *Type* and *Falloff* for the modification.
   - Click ![] (Reset) to clear all of the edits.
   - Use ![] (Undo) and ![] (Redo) to clear or redo edits.

7. Reposition the geometry using either of the following:
   - Select the controls directly on the triad to reposition the geometry. Each control on the triad enables you to manipulate the geometry in a different way. Figure 15–18 shows the controls and describes their uses. You can only manipulate one triad at a time.

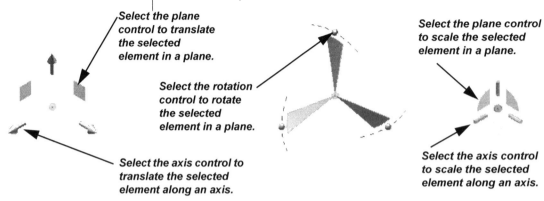

Figure 15–18

   - Enter values in the mini-toolbar entry field. The available field depends on the active triad control. For example, if the y-axis is selected for translational movement, is available in the mini-toolbar for entry. This value is not parametric and is not tied to the model.

8. Continue to select elements on the freeform model and make changes, as required.
9. Click **OK** to complete the edit.

Figure 15–19 shows the final geometry after multiple edits were made to a Box and Cylinder freeform shape.

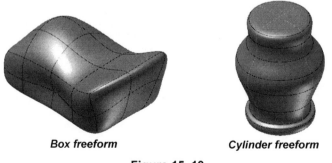

Box freeform *Cylinder freeform*

Figure 15–19

Introduction to Freeform Modeling

Working with Edges

There are a number of different editing tools on the Modify panel that can be used to modify the edges of freeform geometry. These tools include the following:

- Insert Edge
- Merge Edges
- Unweld Edges
- Crease Edges
- Uncrease Edges
- Match Edge

Insert Edge

Additional edges can be added to a freeform using the **Insert Edge** command. By adding edges you can provide additional references (edges and the points at the end of edges) that can be modified to refine the shape of the model.

How To: Insert a New Edge(s)

1. In the *Freeform* tab>Modify panel, click (Insert Edge). The Insert Edge dialog box is shown in Figure 15–20.

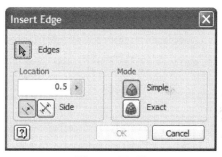

Figure 15–20

2. Click (Edges) and select an existing edge in the model as a reference.
3. Enter an offset value in the *Location* area to define where the new edge is going to be located relative to the referenced edge. If the new edge is not created on the correct side, enter a negative value to switch sides.
4. Click (Single) or (Both) to create a new single edge at the defined location or to create edges on both sides of the reference, respectively.
5. Set the mode that should be used to define the final geometry once the edge is inserted.

- Click ▣ (Simple mode) to add the new edge exactly as specified. The shape might change to add the edge.

- Click ▣ (Exact mode), which while adding the new edge as specified, also adds any additional edges that might be required to enable the model to retain its current shape.

6. Click **OK** to insert the edge.

The images shown in Figure 15–21 show how two edges are inserted and how the overall shape changes when the edges are added.

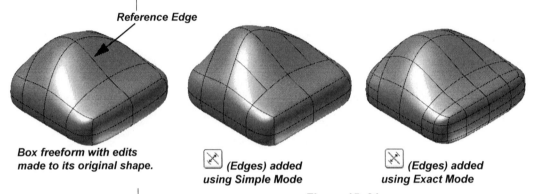

Box freeform with edits made to its original shape.

(Edges) added using Simple Mode

(Edges) added using Exact Mode

Figure 15–21

Merge Edges

Use the **Merge Edges** command to merge two open freeform edges. This can be used to blend between two freeform bodies or two edges in a single body, if the geometry permits.

How To: Merge Edges

1. In the *Freeform* tab>Modify panel, click ✏ (Merge Edges). The Merge Edge dialog box is shown in Figure 15–22.

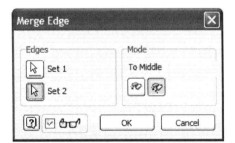

Figure 15–22

2. Click (Set 1) and select an existing edge in the model as a reference.
3. Click (Set 2), and select a second open edge to merge to. If the geometry can be created based on your selections, a preview of the geometry displays.
4. Set the **Mode** options to control the final geometry, as required.

   - Use (To Edge) to blend to the second edge selection.

   - Use (To Middle) to blend to the midpoint of the two edge selections.

5. Click **OK** to complete the merge.

Figure 15–23 shows how two edges are merged.

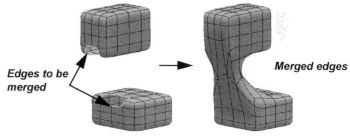

Edges to be merged

Merged edges

Figure 15–23

Unweld Edges

The (Unweld Edges) option in the Modify panel enables you to select edges to separate them from the remaining freeform body. To unweld, simply select the edge or loop of edges and click **OK**. Once unwelded, multiple bodies are created that can be moved independently, as shown in Figure 15–24.

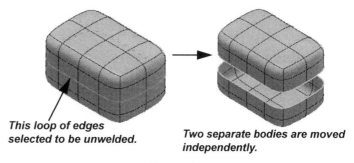

This loop of edges selected to be unwelded.

Two separate bodies are moved independently.

Figure 15–24

Crease/Uncrease Edges

The (Crease Edge) option in the Modify panel enables you to create non-curvature continuous edges on a freeform body by selecting and moving an edge. In Figure 15–25, the two edges were set to allow creasing. Once set, they display as gray. To crease an edge, simply select the edge or loop of edges and click **OK**.

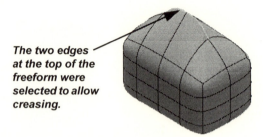

The two edges at the top of the freeform were selected to allow creasing.

Figure 15–25

To clear the crease setting, click (Uncrease Edges) and select the edges to be cleared. The crease is immediately removed and the geometry updates.

Match Edge

When designing a freeform shape, there might be a design requirement that it must match an existing solid edge or a defined sketch. To match the edge of a freeform with a geometrically constrained edge or sketch, you can use the **Match Edge** command.

Introduction to Freeform Modeling

How To: Match an Existing Freeform Edge with a Geometrically Constrained Edge

1. Click (Match Edge) in the Modify panel to open the Match Edge dialog box, shown in Figure 15–26.

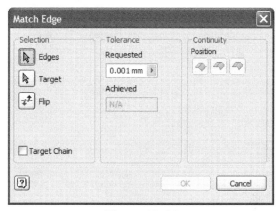

Figure 15–26

2. Click (Edges) and select the freeform edge(s) that are to be modified to match the existing constrained geometry. If you are matching a fully enclosed entity, the freeform references must also be fully enclosed.
3. Click (Target) and select the existing edge/sketch in the model to match.
4. (Optional) Click (Flip), as required, to flip the direction of the match once the references are selected.
5. In the *Tolerance* area, enter the tolerance value to attempt to meet. The freeform shape attempts to create a match with this value. If it cannot, you are prompted with an Achieved value.
6. (Optional) If the match edge is a NURB surface edge, you have access to set continuity options to further define the shape. The options enable you to maintain G0, G1, or G2 continuity with the reference.
7. Click **OK** to match the edges.

The Requested value must be less than the Achieved value for the match to be successful.

The images in Figure 15–27 represent a cylinder freeform in which three of its edges were matched to three parametric sketches.

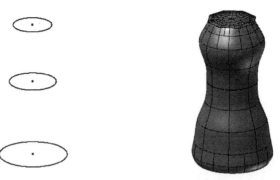

Three parametric sketches that define the top, middle, and bottom sizes of the model.

Match Edge used to match the edges at the top, middle, and bottom of the freeform with the parametric sketches.

Figure 15–27

If the referenced edge that was used for matching changes, you can rematch the edge by expanding the *Matches* folder in the Form feature, right-clicking, and selecting **Rematch**, as shown in Figure 15–28.

Rematch can be used, when required to ensure that the match is maintained. This behavior does not happen automatically.

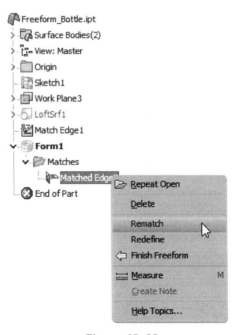

Figure 15–28

Working with Faces

The faces that make up a freeform mesh can also be manipulated to change the shape of freeform geometry. The **Subdivide** and **Bridge** commands enable you to manipulate a face.

Subdivide

The **Subdivide** command enables you to add additional faces to the model. The additional faces can help to refine the shape of the model.

How To: Subdivide an Existing Face

1. In the Modify panel, click (Subdivide) to open the Subdivide dialog box, shown in Figure 15–29.

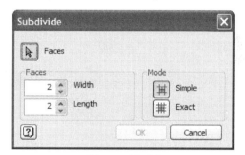

Figure 15–29

Hold <Shift> to select multiple faces for editing.

2. Click (Faces) and select an existing face in the model as a reference.
3. In the *Faces* area, enter values to define how the selected face is going to be subdivided.
4. Set the mode to be used to define the final geometry once the face is subdivided:

   - Click (Simple mode) to subdivide exactly as specified. The shape may change to add faces.

   - Click (Exact mode), which while adding the face as specified, also adds any additional faces that might be required to enable the model to retain its current shape.

5. Click **OK** to insert the face(s).

The images in Figure 15–30 show how nine faces were added (**3** in *Length* and **3** in *Width*) on a reference face using both the **Simple** and **Exact** mode options.

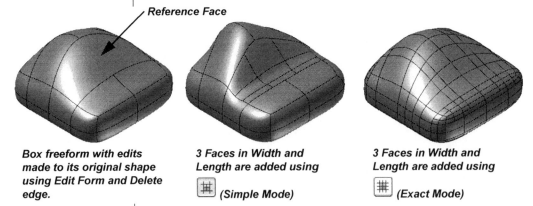

Box freeform with edits made to its original shape using Edit Form and Delete edge.

3 Faces in Width and Length are added using ⊞ *(Simple Mode)*

3 Faces in Width and Length are added using ⊞ *(Exact Mode)*

Figure 15–30

Bridge

When using multiple freeform bodies in a model, you can use the **Bridge** command to connect the space between the two shapes. Bridge can also be used to join multiple gaps in a single body.

How To: Create Bridge Geometry Between Existing Faces or Edges

1. Click (Bridge) in the Modify panel. The Bridge dialog box opens as shown in Figure 15–31.

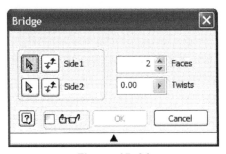

Figure 15–31

Multiple faces can be selected for both the Side1 and Side2 references.

2. Click (Side1) and select existing faces or edges on the freeform model where the bridge geometry is going to begin.

3. Click (Side2) and select existing freeform faces or edges to which the bridge geometry is going to merge.

Introduction to Freeform Modeling

4. Enter a value in the *Faces* area to define the number of faces that the new bridge geometry is going to be subdivided into.
5. (Optional) Enter a value in the *Twists* area to define how many complete rotations there are going to be on the bridge geometry.
6. Click **OK** to create the bridge geometry.

The images in Figure 15–32 show how two separate cylindrical freeform shapes are bridged by new geometry and how it can be used in a single body to create a hole.

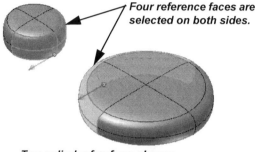

Two cylinder freeform shapes

Resulting geometry after the Bridge command was added.

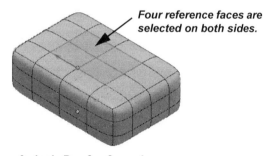

A single Box freeform shapes

Resulting geometry after the Bridge command was added.

Figure 15–32

Working with Points

The points that define the edges and faces can also be modified using tools on the Modify panel. These tools include the following:

- Insert Point
- Weld Vertices
- Flatten

Insert Point

Similar to inserting edges, points can be inserted using a similar workflow. An edge is defined when multiple points are inserted, which also defines a new face.

How To: Insert Points

1. In the Modify panel, click (Insert Point).
    - By default, the **Insert Point** command is located in the **Insert Edge** drop-down list. Subsequently, the most recent command used is displayed.
2. Select points on edges to place new points.
3. Select the *Mode* to define the shape of the new points and subsequent edges. The **Simple** and **Exact** options are the same as for when inserting edges.
4. Click **OK**.

The new point breaks the edge and creates multiple edges to fully define any adjacent faces.

Weld Vertices

Consider using this option to combine vertices once edges are merged to refine the faces that are generated.

The **Weld Vertices** option enables you to combine two selected vertices.

How To: Weld Vertices

1. In the Modify panel, click (Weld Vertices).
2. Select two points to weld.
3. Select one of the following **Weld Mode** options to customize the geometry that results from welding the vertices.

    - Select (Vertex to Vertex) to merge two selected vertices. The first vertex is moved to the position of the second vertex.

    - Select (Vertex to Midpoint) to move two selected vertices to the midpoint between the selections.

    - Select (Weld to Tolerance) to combine multiple vertices within a specified tolerance. Select the vertices and then set the *Tolerance* value.

4. Click **OK** to weld the points.

Flatten

You must select more than 3 vertices to be able to flatten.

The **Flatten** option enables you to select multiple vertices and force them to flatten to a single plane.

How To: Flatten Points

1. In the Modify panel, click (Flatten).
2. Select all the points to flatten.
3. In the *Direction* area, select an option to define how the points will flatten. The options include:

   - Use (Auto Fit) to move points to a single plane that passes through the vertices.
   - Use (Plane) to move points through a specified plane.
   - Use (Parallel Plane) to move points parallel to a selected plane.

4. Click **OK** to flatten the selected points.

Figure 15–33 shows how the **Flatten** option was used to flatten multiple vertices so that they are parallel with a selected plane.

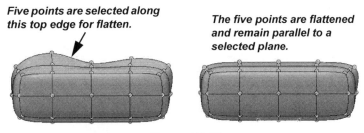

Figure 15–33

Thickening Freeform Geometry

The **Thicken** command can be used with freeform geometry to:

- Convert an open surface to a solid with soft or sharp edges.
- Create an offset surface.
- Create an interior or exterior wall if the selected freeform body is solid.

How To: Thicken a Freeform Body

1. In the Modify panel, click (Thicken)
2. In the *Type* area, select how the thickened geometry is capped. This is only available when thickening an open body. The possible options include:

    - Use (Sharp) to create a flat face to bridge the offset.
    - Use (Soft) to create a new face that is rounded to bridge the offset.
    - Use (No Edges) to leave an open gap between the thickened geometry.

3. Enter a thickness value.
4. Select the direction of the offset. The options include normal to the selected body or in a selected direction. To define a direction, you must select an axis.
5. Click **OK** to thicken the selected body.

Figure 15–34 shows some examples of geometry that has been thickened when the selected body is open.

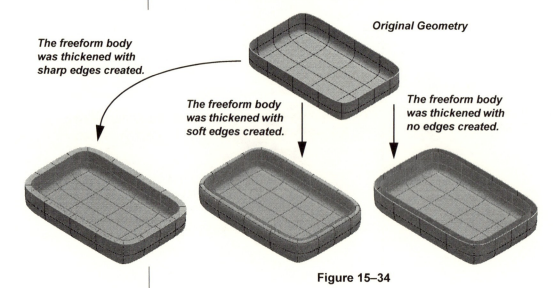

Figure 15–34

> **Hint: Reviewing Internal Geometry**
>
> When the **Thicken** command is used, geometry can be created internally. Click (Toggle Translucent) to better visualize the internal geometry.

Controlling Symmetry

When the base freeform shape was created, symmetry could have been defined for the overall geometry. The **Symmetry** option enables you to define internal symmetry between selected faces on the freeform body after the base freeform creation.

How To: Apply Symmetry Between Faces

1. In the Symmetry panel, click (Symmetry). The Symmetry dialog box is shown in Figure 15–35.

Figure 15–35

2. Click (Face1) and select the face on side 1 as the reference for symmetry. The reference displays in blue on the model.
3. Click (Face2) and select the face that is to be symmetric on the other side of the model. The reference displays in green on the model.
4. Click **OK** to assign symmetry.

If symmetry cannot be assigned based on the references that are selected you are prompted to retry making selections.

The two images shown at the top of Figure 15–36 indicate how changes are made to the base freeform to which symmetry has not been assigned. The two images shown at the bottom indicate how two faces that have been assigned to be symmetric are updated when a change is made to one of the faces.

Box freeform shape - no symmetry set

Face edited using Edit Form.

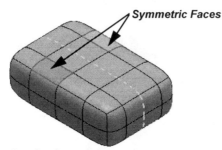

Box freeform shape - symmetry assigned to two faces

Face edited using Edit Form (both symmetric faces update)

Figure 15–36

- Symmetry that has been explicitly assigned between faces or that was assigned when the base freeform geometry was created, can be cleared by clicking (Clear Symmetry) in the expanded Symmetry drop-down list.

Mirroring Freeform Geometry

The (Mirror) command on the expanded Symmetry drop-down list enables you to mirror an entire freeform body about a selected plane.

How To: Complete the Mirror

1. In the Symmetry panel, click (Mirror).

2. Click (Body) and select the body that is to be mirrored. Only bodies can be selected for mirroring.

Introduction to Freeform Modeling

3. Click ▢ (Mirror Plane) and select a plane to mirror about.
4. If the mirrored body has an open edge and is to be merged with the original body, click **Weld** and enter a tolerance value. Based on the tolerance value, the two bodies will be merged, if possible.
5. Click **OK** to complete the mirror.

> **Hint: Repositioning a Freeform Body**
>
> When modeling or mirroring the location of the body relative to a required plane, the body's location may not be as required. To move the body, use either of the following commands:
>
> - Use the **Edit Form** command. Select the entire body and use the translation arrows to move it.
>
> - Use the **Align Form** command. With ▢ (Vertex) enabled select a vertex on the freeform body and then select a target plane to align to. If the geometry has defined symmetry, the ▢ (Symmetry Plane) option is used by default and you can align the symmetry plane to a target plane.

Deleting Entities

The mesh layout of a freeform shape may include too many points, edges, and faces. The **Delete** option enables you to delete points, edges, loops of edges, faces, and entire bodies. To open the Delete dialog box (shown in Figure 15–37), click ▢ (Delete) in the Edit panel.

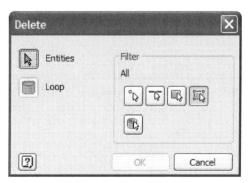

Figure 15–37

To delete entities, simply select them and click **OK**. Consider using the options in the *Filter* area to control the type of entities allowed for selection. As an alternative, you can right-click on an entity and select **Delete**. A feature history is not recorded, so keep in mind that once the freeform is finished, edits can't be undone. Figure 15–38 shows how the **Delete** command is being used to delete points, edges, and faces on a freeform shape.

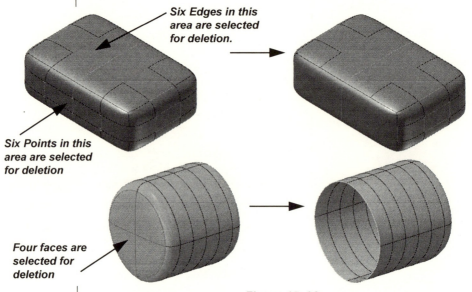

Figure 15–38

> **Hint: Selecting Faces**
>
> Toggle the (Select Through) option on the Tools panel to control how faces in a selection window are selected. When on, the selection includes hidden faces. When toggled off, the selection only includes the visible faces that fall in the selection window.

Practice 15a Box Freeform Modeling

Practice Objectives

- Create freeform base geometry using the **Box** command.
- Toggle the view display from a smooth to block visual display style.
- Edit freeform base geometry so that points, edges, and faces are translated and rotated.
- Subdivide, delete, and insert elements on freeform base geometry to permit changes to the shape of the geometry.

In this practice, you will learn how create a box-shaped freeform model and to navigate the Freeform modeling environment. Using the Edit Form and additional editing tools you will manipulate the shape of the box.

Task 1 - Create a Box freeform shape.

1. Create a new part with the default mm template.

2. In the *3D Model* tab>Create Freeform panel, click (Box). The Box dialog box opens (as shown in Figure 15–39), providing options that enable you to define the shape of the Box freeform geometry.

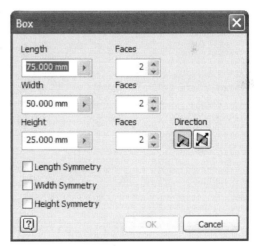

Figure 15–39

© 2018, ASCENT - Center for Technical Knowledge®

3. The Origin planes are temporarily displayed in the graphics window (as shown in Figure 15–40), so that you can select the sketch plane.

Figure 15–40

4. Hover the cursor over the origin planes in the graphics window. Note that the names display directly on the work planes in the graphics window.

5. Locate and select the XZ Plane as the sketch plane.

6. Use the ViewCube to return the model to its default orientation, if not already set.

7. By default, the Origin Center Point is projected onto the sketch plane. Select the center point as the base point for the Box.

8. You can enter values for the *Length*, *Width*, and *Height* or select manipulator arrowheads on the geometry. Select the x-direction arrowhead (*Length*) and drag it to enlarge the box. Drag it until the box is approximately **100mm**.

9. Select the y-direction arrowhead (*Width*) and drag it to a size of approximately **60mm**.

10. In the Box dialog box, set the *Height* value to **25**.

11. Ensure that exact values are entered for *Length*, *Width*, and *Height*, as shown in Figure 15–41.

12. Ensure that (Direction) is selected to create the freeform above the XZ plane.

To display the Origin 3D Indicator in the graphics window to help identify directions, open the Application Options dialog box and enable **Show Origin 3D Indicator** *on the Display tab.*

Introduction to Freeform Modeling

13. Select **Width Symmetry** to maintain symmetry on both sides of the XY plane.

14. To define the number of faces on each plane of the model, enter the *Face* values in the Box dialog box, as shown in Figure 15–41. Once all of the settings have been set, the model updates as shown on the right.

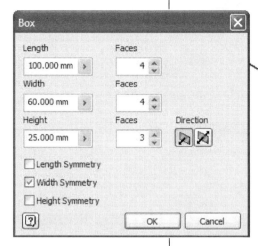
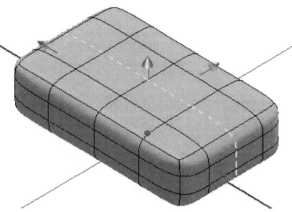

Figure 15–41

15. Click **OK** to complete the Box. The *Freeform* tab is activated.

16. In the *Freeform* tab>Tools panel, click (Toggle Smooth). The model switches from a smooth display to a block display style, as shown in Figure 15–42. This is a display type only, which can increase performance speed. The model is still smooth when it is toggled off or when Freeform mode is off.

Figure 15–42

17. Click (Toggle Smooth) again to return to the smooth display style.

© 2018, ASCENT - Center for Technical Knowledge®   15–33

Task 2 - Edit the Freeform geometry.

1. In the Edit panel, click (Edit Form). The Edit Form dialog box opens as shown in Figure 15–43.

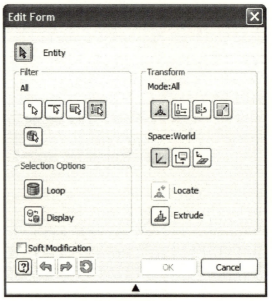

Figure 15–43

2. Note that in the *Filter* area, (All) is set as the default option. If it is not selected, do so. This enables you to select any point, edge, or face on the model. Hover the cursor over the points, edges, and faces in the model. Note that you can select any of them. Selecting the other options filters the selection to points only, edges only, or faces only, which can be useful when working with complex freeform geometry with large mesh structures.

3. Select the vertex shown in Figure 15–44 to be translated.

4. Select the y-axis manipulator arrowhead (as shown in Figure 15–44) and drag upwards similar to that shown.

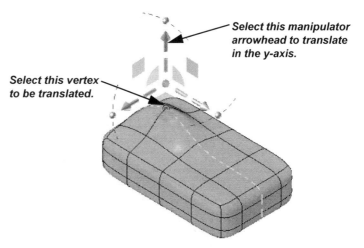

Figure 15–44

5. Select the face shown in Figure 15–45 to be translated.

6. Select the y-axis manipulator arrowhead (as shown in Figure 15–45), and drag upwards similar to that shown. Note that both sides update together. This is because the **Width Symmetry** option was used when the box was created.

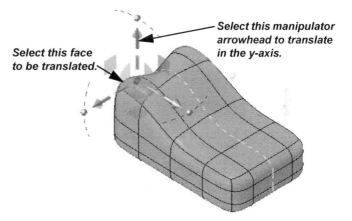

Figure 15–45

7. Select the face shown in Figure 15–46 to be translated.

8. Select the manipulator wheel shown in Figure 15–46, and drag upwards to rotate the face in the XY plane. Note that both sides update together.

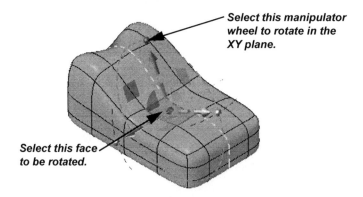

Figure 15–46

9. Select the front edge shown in Figure 15–47 to be translated.

10. Select the x-axis manipulator shown in Figure 15–47, and drag outward in the x-axis. Both sides update together.

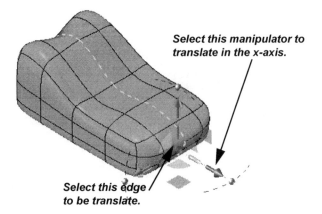

Figure 15–47

11. In the Edit Form dialog box, click [icon] to undo the last change to the model.

Introduction to Freeform Modeling

12. Select the same edge again, if not still selected and click ▨ (Loop) in the *Selection Options* area of the Edit Form dialog box. Alternatively, right-click and select **Select Loop**. The loop in which the edge exists highlights. Drag the same manipulator handle. The model displays similar to that shown in Figure 15–48. The entire loop of edges translate forward.

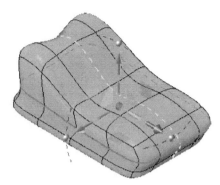

Figure 15–48

13. Click ✓ to complete the edit.

In Freeform mode all of the parametric model commands are not available.

14. Save the file as **Freeform_Box.ipt**. Note that the model cannot be saved in Freeform mode. Click **Cancel**.

15. In the *Freeform* tab>Exit panel, click ✓ (Finish Freeform). Alternatively, right-click in the graphics window and select **Finish Freeform** in the marking menu. Note that the model displays as solid geometry, as shown in Figure 15–49.

The default visual display for new models is Shaded with Edges. To clear the display of the edges, you can change to the Shaded display style.

Figure 15–49

16. Save the file as **Freeform_Box.ipt**.

Task 3 - Use Edit tools to further customize the meshed structure of the freeform.

1. In the *3D Model* tab, note that all of the parametric model commands are now available. You can continue to design the model using the familiar parametric commands. To further edit the freeform geometry, right-click on the **Form1** feature in the Model browser and select **Edit Freeform**.

2. The middle portion needs to be subdivided to include more faces. In the Modify panel, click (Subdivide) to open the Subdivide dialog box.

3. Click (Faces) if it is not already active, and select the face shown in Figure 15–50. Note that the symmetry setting that was assigned during Box creation still persists.

4. Accept the default value for the number of faces in the *Width* and *Length* fields, as shown in Figure 15–50.

5. For the *Mode* setting, maintain (Simple).

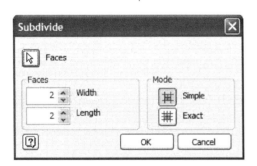
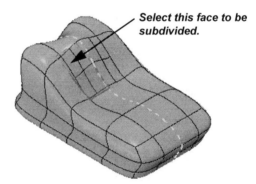

Figure 15–50

6. Click **OK** to insert the face(s). Note that the geometry changed slightly to permit the subdivision. This was acceptable. If the change is not, click (Exact) in the Subdivide dialog box when creating it. The geometry shape will stay the same but additional faces are added to maintain the shape.

7. In the Freeform panel, click (Edit Form).

Introduction to Freeform Modeling

8. Select one of the edges generated by the subdivide action, (as shown in Figure 15–51) and click ![icon] (Loop) or right-click and select **Select Loop** to automatically select all of the adjacent edges.

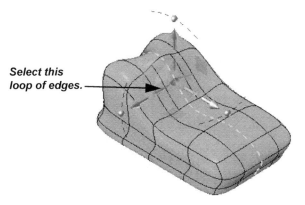

Select this loop of edges.

Figure 15–51

9. In the Edit Form dialog box, in the *Transform* area, click ![icon] (View). The triad changes to only display two axis manipulators, as shown in Figure 15–52.

Figure 15–52

10. In the ViewCube, select the **FRONT** view. Note that the triad updates to display the Manipulators in the new orientation, while retaining the x- and y-directions for the view.

11. Right-click in the graphics window and select **Previous View**. The edge remains selected. If it does not, select the loop again.

12. In the *Transform* area, click (Local) to change the triad location to the Local orientation. Drag the manipulators to create the geometry shown in Figure 15–53.

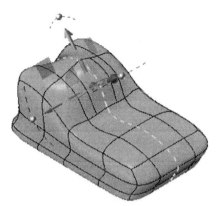

Figure 15–53

13. Click **OK** to complete the edit.

Task 4 - Delete edges from the freeform geometry.

1. Now that the reshaping is done you can delete edges in the area that was subdivided. In the Edit panel, click (Delete).

2. In the Delete dialog box, click (Edge) and select the four edges shown in Figure 15–54.

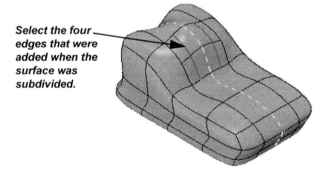

Select the four edges that were added when the surface was subdivided.

Figure 15–54

Introduction to Freeform Modeling

3. Click **OK** to delete the edges. The model updates as shown in Figure 15–55. Alternatively, because the Box was created symmetrically in the width direction, selecting two edges on one side would also have deleted the edges on the other side.

Figure 15–55

Task 5 - Insert edges on freeform geometry.

1. In the Modify panel, click (Insert Edge). The Insert Edge dialog box opens.

2. Click (Edges) if it is not already active, and select the edge shown in Figure 15–56. A preview of the new edge displays immediately.

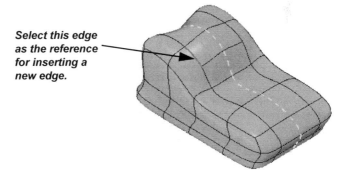

Select this edge as the reference for inserting a new edge.

Figure 15–56

3. In the *Location* area, set the offset value to **0.2**. The edge moves closer to the reference edge.

4. Return the value to **0.5** to create the new edge midway between the reference edge the next edge.

5. In the *Mode* area, click ▣ (Exact). If Simple mode had been used the geometry would change to create the edge. In this situation the exact shape must be retained so Exact mode is used.

6. Click **OK** to insert the edit. The new edge is created, but to keep both symmetry and the existing shape, more edges have been added, as shown in Figure 15–57.

Figure 15–57

7. In the *Freeform* tab>Exit panel, click ✓ (Finish Freeform). Alternatively, right-click in the graphics window and select **Finish Freeform** in the marking menu.

8. Save the file and close the window.

Practice 15b Cylinder Freeform Modeling

Practice Objectives

- Create freeform base geometry using the **Cylinder** command.
- Match edges on the freeform base geometry to that of parametric sketch geometry.
- Assign symmetry to faces on the freeform base geometry.
- Cancel assigned symmetry between faces on the freeform base geometry.
- Use the **Edit Form** command to scale elements on the freeform base geometry.

In this practice, you will learn how to create a Cylinder as the freeform base geometry. You will also assign symmetry so that when editing faces on the cylinder, the change is also mirrored on the model. Additionally, you will use the **Match Edge** command to assign an edge on the freeform model equal to that of a parametric sketch.

Task 1 - Create a sketch that will be referenced by a freeform cylinder.

1. Create a new part using the default mm template.

2. In the *3D Model* tab>Sketch panel, click (Start 2D Sketch).

3. Select the XY Plane as the sketch plane.

4. Create a circle with a diameter of **70mm** centered on the projected Origin Center Point.

5. Complete the sketch.

6. Toggle off the dimension visibility for the sketch.

Task 2 - Create a freeform cylinder.

1. In the *3D Model* tab>Create Freeform panel, click
   (Cylinder). The Cylinder dialog box (shown in Figure 15–58) opens providing options for defining the shape of the Cylinder freeform geometry.

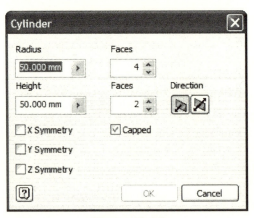

Figure 15–58

2. Locate and select the XY Plane as the sketch plane.

3. Select the projected Origin Center Point as the base point for the Cylinder.

4. In the Cylinder dialog box, click [icon] to ensure that the freeform geometry is centered on both sides of the sketch plane.

5. You can enter values for the *Radius* and *Height* or select the manipulator arrowheads on the geometry. Using either technique, create the cylinder so that its *Radius* is **40** and its *Height* is **200**.

6. Symmetry will be assigned using the **Symmetry** command in the editing tools. Ensure that symmetry is not specified in the Cylinder dialog box.

Introduction to Freeform Modeling

7. To define the number of faces on each plane of the model, enter the *Face* values shown on the left in Figure 15–59.

8. Ensure that **Capped** is selected. Once all of the settings have been set, the model updates as shown on the right in Figure 15–59.

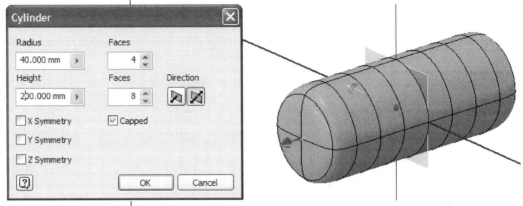

Figure 15–59

9. Click **OK** to complete the Cylinder.

Task 3 - Match an edge on the freeform geometry with the sketch.

1. In the Modify panel click (Match Edge). The Match dialog box opens as shown in Figure 15–60.

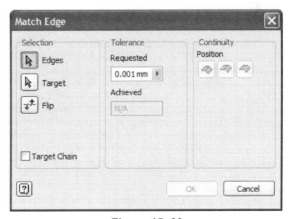

Figure 15–60

© 2018, ASCENT - Center for Technical Knowledge® 15–45

If you are matching a fully enclosed entity, the freeform references must also be a fully enclosed loop.

2. Click (Edges) if it is not already active, and select the freeform edges shown in Figure 15–61 to match the circular sketch.

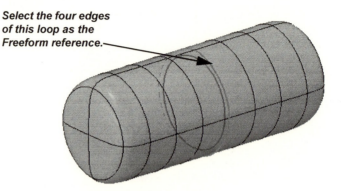

Select the four edges of this loop as the Freeform reference.

Figure 15–61

3. Click (Target) and select the existing circular sketch as the Match reference.

4. Maintain the default tolerance value.

5. Click **OK** to match the edges. The freeform geometry updates as shown in Figure 15–62.

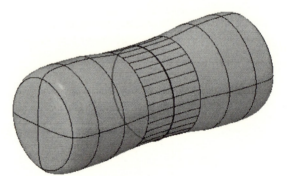

Figure 15–62

Task 4 - Assign Symmetry to the freeform geometry and edit the symmetric faces.

1. In the Edit panel, click (Edit Form). The Edit Form dialog box opens as shown in Figure 15–63.

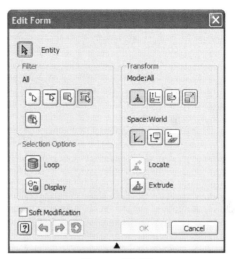

Figure 15–63

2. Reorient the model as shown in Figure 15–64.

3. In the *Filter* area, ensure that either (All) or (Face) is selected and select the face shown in Figure 15–64 to be translated.

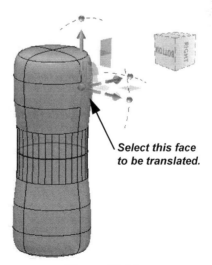

Select this face to be translated.

Figure 15–64

4. In the Edit Form dialog box, in the *Transform* area, click ⬜ (View). The triad changes to only display two axis manipulators.

5. In the ViewCube, select the edge between the Right and Bottom sides, as shown in Figure 15–65.

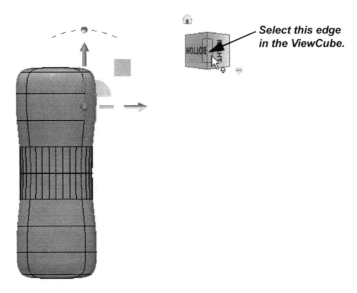

Figure 15–65

6. Select the x-axis manipulator arrowhead and drag it to the right, similar to that shown in Figure 15–66.

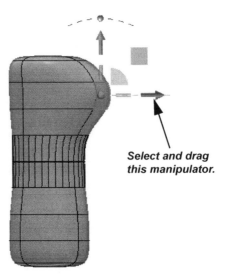

Figure 15–66

Introduction to Freeform Modeling

7. In the Edit Form dialog box, click (Reset) to reset any of the changes made in the command. Click **Yes** to confirm the reset.

8. Click **Cancel** to close the Edit Form dialog box.

9. In the Symmetry panel, click (Symmetry). The Symmetry dialog box is shown in Figure 15–67.

Figure 15–67

10. Click (Face1) if it is not already active, and select the face shown in Figure 15–68. The reference displays in blue.

11. Click (Face2) and select the face shown in Figure 15–68 as the symmetric reference on the other side of the model. The reference displays in green on the model.

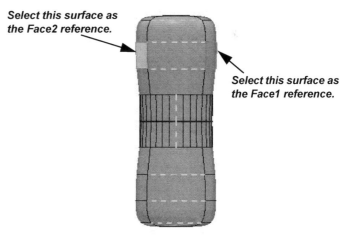

Figure 15–68

12. Click **OK** to assign the symmetry.

13. Use the **Edit Form** command again to translate the face that was just translated in the x-axis direction. Now that symmetry has been assigned with this surface, its symmetric face is also selected. Ensure that ⌨ (View Space) is set and that the ViewCube is oriented as was previously set.

14. Drag the x-axis manipulator to translate the face inward, as shown on the left in Figure 15–69. Both symmetric faces update.

15. Select the surface below it and translate it inwards, as shown on the right in Figure 15–69. Note that it also reacts as symmetric.

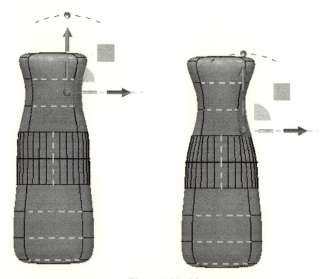

Figure 15–69

16. Complete the edit.

17. In the Symmetry panel, expand the Symmetry drop-down list, and click 🔲 (Clear Symmetry). Select the cylindrical body to clear its symmetry. Selecting this option clears all of the assigned symmetry as well as any symmetry assigned during freeform creation.

Introduction to Freeform Modeling

Task 5 - Ensure that the matched edges in the freeform remain matched.

1. Rotate the model as shown on the left in Figure 15–70. Note that the edge that was matched is no longer matched. The edits that were made have moved it. Matching does not maintain the relationship.

2. In the Model browser, expand **Form1** and the *Matches* folder. Right-click on **Matched Edge 1** and select **Rematch**. The matches edges are shown in Figure 15–70.

The degree to which the edges are mismatched is dependent on the edits that were made.

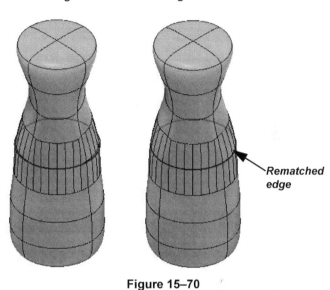

Figure 15–70

Task 6 - Scale a face in the freeform geometry.

1. Start the **Edit Form** command.

2. In the *Transform* area, click (Scale) to only display the scaling triad.

3. Select the face and scale manipulator in the z-axis as shown in Figure 15–71, and drag upward to scale the face.

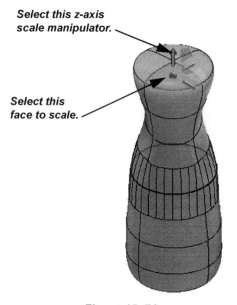

Figure 15–71

4. Complete the edit.

5. Use the ViewCube to orient the model to the **Bottom** view and note that the scaling has changed the geometry on the face that was selected.

6. Right-click in the graphics window and select **Previous View**.

7. In the *Freeform* tab>Exit panel, click (Finish Freeform). Alternatively, right-click in the graphics window and select **Finish Freeform** in the marking menu.

8. Save the file as **Freeform_Cylinder.ipt** and close the window.

Practice 15c Working with Existing Geometry

Practice Objectives

- Create freeform base geometry using the **Torus** command.
- Use the **Edit Form** command to move a freeform body.
- Delete faces that make up a freeform body.
- Convert existing surface geometry to a freeform body.
- Match edges on freeform geometry to that of parametric sketch.
- Bridge and merge edges to create freeform geometry between open edges.
- Use surface and solid modeling tools to create a solid model from the freeform geometry.

In this practice, you will begin by opening a model that provides the basic shape of a bottle in the form of surface geometry. A loft feature with parametric dimensions was used to create the base shape because the design intent for this bottle requires it to be a specific size. The design specifications require a handle. The handle for the bottle will be created using the freeform modeling workflow.

Task 1 - Open an existing model and add a base freeform shape that is to be used.

1. Open **Freeform_Bottle.ipt**. Surface geometry and a sketch (shown in Figure 15–72) have been created to use during the modeling process.

Figure 15–72

2. In the *3D Model* tab>Create Freeform panel, click (Torus).

3. Locate and select the YZ Plane as the sketch plane.

4. Select the projected Origin Center Point as the base point for the Torus.

5. Orient the model to the Right view using the ViewCube.

6. Enter values for the *Radius*, *Ring*, and *Faces*, as shown in Figure 15–73.

7. Set **Z Symmetry** and then click **OK**. The Torus should appear as shown in Figure 15–73.

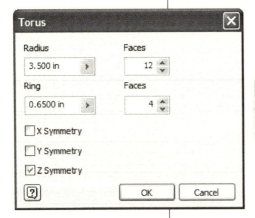
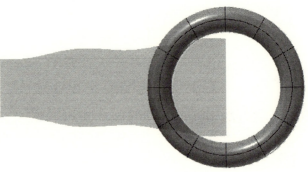

Figure 15–73

8. In the Edit panel, click  (Edit Form).

9. In the *Filter* area, select (Body) and select the Torus. Using the triad manipulators, move the body **5.5** in the *Z* axis and **1.2** in the *Y* axis. The model should appear as shown in Figure 15–74. Click **OK**.

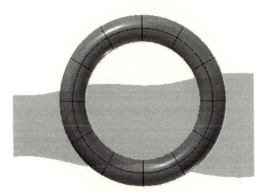

Figure 15–74

Introduction to Freeform Modeling

10. In the *Freeform* tab, in the Tools panel, ensure that ▫ (Select Through) is selected. This enables you to select both the visible and hidden side of the freeform.

11. In the Edit panel, click ▫ (Delete). Select the ▫ (Face) filter and draw the selection window shown in Figure 15–75 to select faces for deletion.

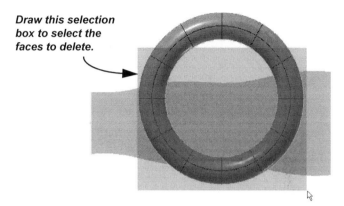

Draw this selection box to select the faces to delete.

Figure 15–75

12. Click **OK**. The freeform geometry should display as shown in Figure 15–76.

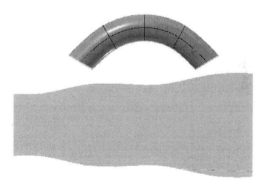

Figure 15–76

13. In the Create Freeform panel, click ▫ (Convert).

14. Select the exterior face on the existing surface model. In the Convert to Freeform dialog box, maintain the (Uniform) spacing setting in both directions and enter **12** as the number of faces for the *Length* and *Width* areas, as shown in Figure 15–77.

15. Click **OK** to complete the conversion to freeform geometry. The model should appear as shown in Figure 15–77.

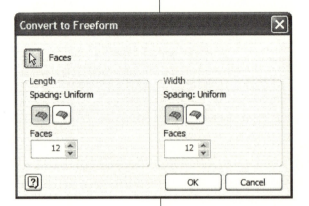
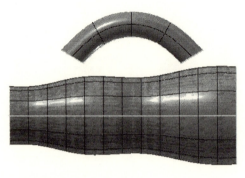

Figure 15–77

Task 2 - Match the edges of the surface geometry to the freeform.

The design intent of the bottle is that the diameter at the top of the bottle will remain unchanged. A sketch was created to define this diameter. In this task you will use the **Match** command in the Freeform environment to ensure that the edge remains matched.

1. Click (Match Edge) in the Modify panel.

2. If it is not already active, click (Edges). Double-click on the freeform edge at the top of the bottle, as shown in Figure 15–78.

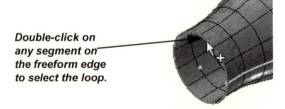

Double-click on any segment on the freeform edge to select the loop.

Figure 15–78

3. Click (Target) and select the predefined sketch at the top of the bottle as the match reference.

4. Click **OK** to match the edges.

5. In the Model browser, expand the **Form1** node and the *Matches* folder. The **Match Edge 1** operation should appear.

Task 3 - Edit the freeform geometry to merge the handle.

In this task you will merge the handle and the body of the bottle. There are many different techniques that can be used to create the geometry. The techniques shown here are some options.

1. Orient the model into the Top view using the ViewCube.

2. Preselect the 8 faces shown in Figure 15–79, right-click and select **Delete**. This is another option to delete faces instead of selecting the **Delete** command in the Edit panel. The model appears as shown on the bottom of Figure 15–79.

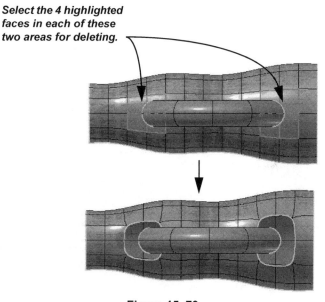

Figure 15–79

3. Orient the model to the **Right** view using the ViewCube.

In the next steps you will use two different commands to create the missing geometry. The **Bridge** command will be used on the edges at the top of the handle, and the **Merge Edges** command will be used at the edges on the bottom.

4. In the Modify panel, click ✎ (Merge Edges) and select the two sets of edges shown in Figure 15–80 at the bottom of the handle. Click 🔲 (To Edge). Click **OK** to complete the feature.

5. In the Modify panel, click ✎ (Bridge) and select the two sets of edges at the top of the handle, as shown in Figure 15–80. Enter **3** as the number of faces to be created. Click **OK** to complete the feature. The model appears as shown on the bottom of Figure 15–80.

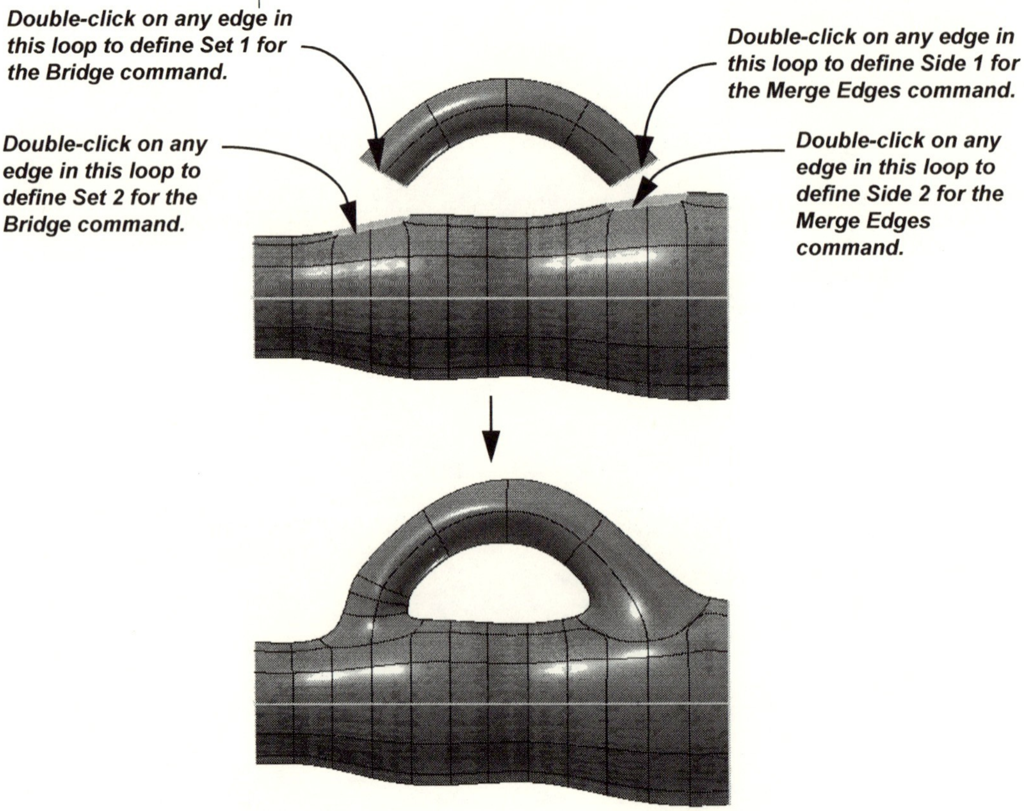

Double-click on any edge in this loop to define Set 1 for the Bridge command.

Double-click on any edge in this loop to define Set 2 for the Bridge command.

Double-click on any edge in this loop to define Side 1 for the Merge Edges command.

Double-click on any edge in this loop to define Side 2 for the Merge Edges command.

Figure 15–80

6. Spin the model and note the difference between the top and bottom of the handle in how they were created.

7. In the Check panel, click ✎ (Make Uniform). The model attempts to smooth the model.

Introduction to Freeform Modeling

*Edges that are matched in the Freeform environment may separate when subsequent edits are made. This is because this environment is not parametric and the assignment can't be automatically retained. Use **Rematch** throughout your design process to return the matched edges, as required.*

Task 4 - Rematch the matched edges.

1. In the Model browser, expand the **Form1** node and the *Matches* folder. Right-click on **Matched Edge 1** and select **Rematch**, as shown in Figure 15–81.

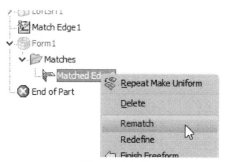

Figure 15–81

2. Finish the Freeform to exit the environment. The model displays as shown in Figure 15–82. Note that there are now two surface bodies in the model.

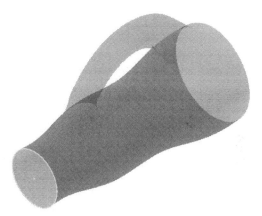

Figure 15–82

3. Save the model.

Task 5 - Use the surface geometry to create a solid model.

In this task you will use surfacing tools to finish the design so that the Form can be used to create the exterior geometry for the bottle.

1. In the Model browser, right-click on **LoftSrf1** and select **Visibility** to clear it from display. This surface was used as reference only and is not required to create the solid.

2. In the Surface panel, click (Patch) and create a new planar surface that lies at the top of the bottle, as shown in Figure 15–83. Ensure that the **Profile Edge** is selected as the reference for the patch surface. Click **OK**.

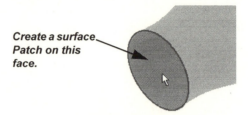

Create a surface Patch on this face.

Figure 15–83

3. Create a second patch on the bottom of the Form feature.

4. In the Surface panel, click (Stitch) to stitch the Form feature and the two new Boundary Patches together. This forms an enclosed area and creates the solid exterior of the bottle.

5. In the Modify panel, click (Shell) to remove the top face of the bottle and add a **.15** thickness to the bottle. The solid geometry should display as shown in Figure 15–84.

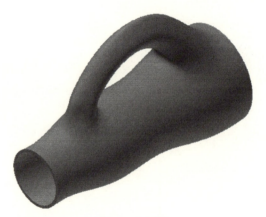

Figure 15–84

6. Save the model.

7. (Optional) If time permits, return to the Form feature and make changes to improve its shape. If changes are made, be aware that the edges that were selected for the Boundary Patches might be lost and the features might fail. If this occurs, edit them and reselect the lost edges.

Practice 15d (Optional) Bridging Freeform Geometry

Practice Objective

- Create two freeform base geometry forms and use the **Bridge** command to generate additional geometry between the forms.

In this practice, you will create two cylinder freeform base shapes in the model to help when creating the required freeform geometry. Once created you will use the **Bridge** command to create additional geometry between the two cylinders.

Task 1 - Create a freeform cylinder.

1. Create a new part using the default mm template.

2. Use the Cylinder freeform feature to create the freeform, similar to that shown in Figure 15–85. Locate the cylinder on the XY Plane and use the projected Origin Center Point as the base point for the Cylinder.

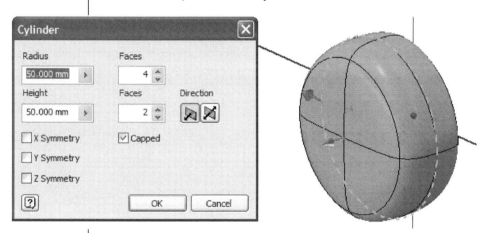

Figure 15–85

3. In the *Freeform* tab>Create Freeform panel, use the Cylinder freeform feature to create a second freeform, similar to that shown in Figure 15–86. Select the same plane, but use an origin point that is offset from the initial cylinder.

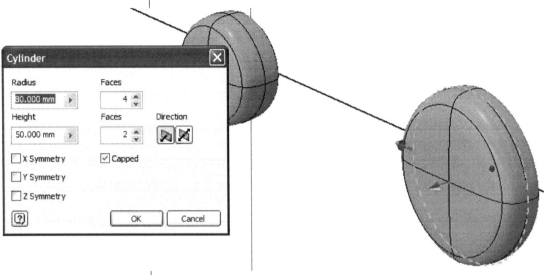

Figure 15–86

Task 2 - Create geometry between the two cylinders.

1. In the Modify panel, click (Bridge).

2. Click (Side1), if it is not already active, and select the four faces shown in Figure 15–87.

3. Click (Side2) and select the four faces shown in Figure 15–87.

Introduction to Freeform Modeling

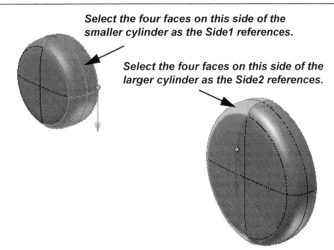

Select the four faces on this side of the smaller cylinder as the Side1 references.

Select the four faces on this side of the larger cylinder as the Side2 references.

Figure 15–87

4. Maintain the default faces for the number of faces and the twist.

5. Click **OK** to create the bridge geometry. The geometry displays as shown in Figure 15–88. Additional **Edit Form** actions can be performed on the new freeform feature, as required.

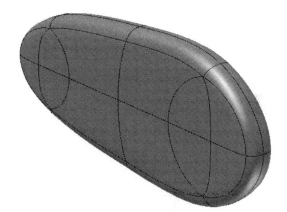

Figure 15–88

6. Exit the Freeform environment.

7. Save the file as **Freeform_Bridge.ipt** and close the window.

Chapter Review Questions

1. When modeling in the Freeform environment you can create parametric sketches for use with the **Match Edge** command.

   a. True
   b. False

2. Which of the following standard freeform shapes enables you to assign symmetry in the width, length, and height when creating the freeform base shape?

   a. Box
   b. Cylinder
   c. Sphere
   d. Torus
   e. Quadball
   f. Plane

3. The Quadball standard freeform shape enables you to assign faces along the longitude and latitude of the resulting shape.

   a. True
   b. False

4. Which of the following statements is true regarding symmetry in freeform geometry? (Select all that apply.)

   a. Symmetry can only be assigned when the base freeform shape is created.
   b. Symmetry can only be assigned using the **Symmetry** command by selecting faces on the freeform geometry.
   c. All of the symmetry assigned on the base freeform shape can be removed using the **Clear Symmetry** command.
   d. Faces adjacent to a face that was selected as a symmetry reference also update to reflect the symmetry.

Introduction to Freeform Modeling

5. When using the **Edit Form** command, which of the following describe the manipulator controls that are available when the triad displays as shown in Figure 15–89? (Select all that apply.)

Figure 15–89

   a. Translate in X, Y, or Z axis

   b. Translate in plane

   c. Rotate in plane

   d. Scale in X, Y, or Z axis

   e. Scale in plane

6. Which of the Space settings provides you with two manipulators that can be used to manipulate the freeform geometry?

   a. (World)

   b. (View)

   c. (Local)

7. Which of the following editing commands enables you to add additional elements (points, edges, or faces) to existing freeform geometry? (Select all that apply.)

   a. **Insert Edge**

   b. **Insert Point**

   c. **Subdivide**

   d. **Crease Edges**

   e. **Bridge**

   f. **Match Edge**

8. The **Flatten** command enables you to select multiple points and make them parallel to a selected plane.

   a. True

   b. False

9. When subdividing a face, ▦ (Simple mode) forces the freeform geometry to remain exactly the same once the faces have been subdivided.

   a. True
   b. False

10. Which of the following commands can be used to create the geometry between two freeform shapes? (Select all that apply.)

    a. **Insert Edge**
    b. **Subdivide**
    c. **Merge Edges**
    d. **Bridge**
    e. **Match Edge**

Command Summary

Button	Command	Location
	Align Form	• **Ribbon:** *Freeform* tab>Edit panel
	Box	• **Ribbon:** *3D Model* tab>Create Freeform panel • **Ribbon:** *Freeform* tab>Create Freeform panel
	Bridge	• **Ribbon:** *Freeform* tab>Modify panel
	Clear Symmetry	• **Ribbon:** *Freeform* tab>Symmetry panel
	Convert	• **Ribbon:** *3D Model* tab>Create Freeform panel • **Ribbon:** *Freeform* tab>Create Freeform panel
	Crease Edges	• **Ribbon:** *Freeform* tab>Modify panel
	Cylinder	• **Ribbon:** *3D Model* tab>Create Freeform panel • **Ribbon:** *Freeform* tab>Create Freeform panel
	Delete	• **Ribbon:** *Freeform* tab>Edit panel
	Edit Form	• **Ribbon:** *Freeform* tab>Edit panel
	Face	• **Ribbon:** *3D Model* tab>Create Freeform panel • **Ribbon:** *Freeform* tab>Create Freeform panel
	Finish Freeform	• **Ribbon:** *Freeform* tab>Exit panel • **Context menu:** In the graphics window
	Flatten	• **Ribbon:** *Freeform* tab>Modify panel
	Insert Edge	• **Ribbon:** *Freeform* tab>Modify panel
	Insert Point	• **Ribbon:** *Freeform* tab>Modify panel
	Match Edge	• **Ribbon:** *Freeform* tab>Modify panel
	Merge Edges	• **Ribbon:** *Freeform* tab>Modify panel
	Mirror	• **Ribbon:** *Freeform* tab>Symmetry panel

	Plane	• **Ribbon:** *3D Model* tab>Create Freeform panel
		• **Ribbon:** *Freeform* tab>Create Freeform panel
	Quadball	• **Ribbon:** *3D Model* tab>Create Freeform panel
		• **Ribbon:** *Freeform* tab>Create Freeform panel
	Select Through	• **Ribbon:** *Freeform* tab>Tools panel
	Sphere	• **Ribbon:** *3D Model* tab>Create Freeform panel
		• **Ribbon:** *Freeform* tab>Create Freeform panel
	Subdivide	• **Ribbon:** *Freeform* tab>Modify panel
	Symmetry	• **Ribbon:** *Freeform* tab>Symmetry panel
	Thicken	• **Ribbon:** *Freeform* tab>Modify panel
	Toggle Smooth/ Blocky	• **Ribbon:** *Freeform* tab>Tools panel
	Toggle Translucent	• **Ribbon:** *Freeform* tab>Tools panel
	Torus	• **Ribbon:** *3D Model* tab>Create Freeform panel
		• **Ribbon:** *Freeform* tab>Create Freeform panel
	Uncrease Edges	• **Ribbon:** *Freeform* tab>Modify panel
	Unweld Edges	• **Ribbon:** *Freeform* tab>Modify panel
	Weld Vertices	• **Ribbon:** *Freeform* tab>Modify panel

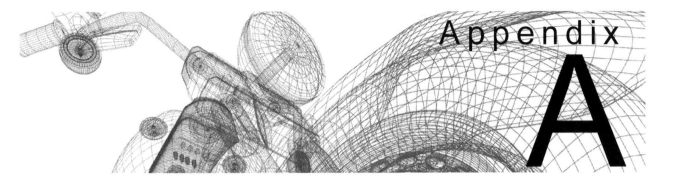

Appendix A

Creating Emboss and Decal Features

Emboss and Decal features are specialty features that can be added to model geometry to add special details to the model. Emboss features enable you to create a raised or recessed area on a part that can be used to create a flat area or add text. Labels, bar codes, brand names, art works, logos, or stamps are added to a model using the Decal features.

Learning Objectives in this Appendix

- Create a raised or recessed area on a part using the Emboss feature.
- Add an image to represent information on the surface of a model.

A.1 Emboss Features

Emboss features create a raised or recessed area on a part. They are often used to supply a flat area for a label, add text that is molded into the part (as shown in Figure A–1), or provide clearance for another part. Emboss features can add or remove material from the part.

Figure A–1

Creating the Emboss Profile

The emboss profile is a sketch of the entities that will be embossed on the model. The entities can be either standard sketched entities or you can add text.

How To: Create a Sketch that Contains Text

1. In the Model panel, click ▱ (Start 2D Sketch) and select a sketching plane.
2. Click **A** (Text) or **A** (Geometry Text) in the Create panel to add text to the sketch and select a location to place the text. Figure A–2 shows the two text options and how they differ when adding text. To place Geometry Text, select a geometry entity (e.g., arc or circle) for the text to follow.

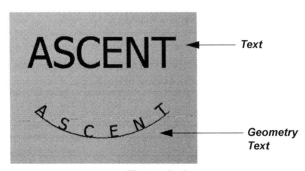

Figure A–2

Creating Emboss and Decal Features

*Text that is added to a sketch can be converted to geometry by selecting the text, right-clicking on it and selecting **Convert to Geometry**. Once converted to a selected text style, each entity acts independently and can be manipulated as required.*

3. The Format Text dialog box opens. Enter the text in the dialog box and adjust the text properties (e.g., color, font, justification, etc.) as required. Consider the use of Model and User Parameters to incorporate parametric parameter values from the model into the text.

> **Hint: Format Text Dialog box**
>
> Most settings in the Format Text dialog box (such as font, style, and justification) are similar to other Windows programs. To change the font or style of existing text, highlight the text to be changed in the dialog box and make changes as required. Changing the color, rotation, line spacing, or stretch of the text will change that property for the entire text object, and not only the selected text.

4. Click **OK** to close the dialog box.
5. Add dimensions as required to locate the text and any geometry entities on the part.
6. Finish the sketch.

Creating the Emboss Feature

Once the emboss profile has been created in a sketch it can be used to create the emboss feature.

How To: Create a Emboss Feature

1. In the *3D Model* tab>Create panel, click (Emboss). The Emboss dialog box opens as shown in Figure A–3.

Figure A–3

2. Select the Emboss profile.

3. Select the type of emboss by selecting from the three available types. The resulting geometry for each type is shown in Figure A–4.

   - Click ▭ (Emboss from Face) to create the emboss to add material, so the feature is raised.
   - Click ▭ (Engrave from Face) to create the emboss to remove material, so the feature is recessed.
   - Click ▭ (Emboss/Engrave from Plane) to create the emboss to add and remove material, so parts of the feature are above and below the sketch plane.

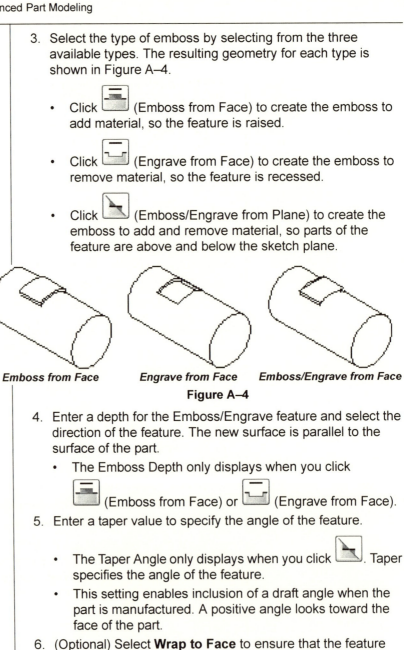

Emboss from Face   **Engrave from Face**   **Emboss/Engrave from Face**

Figure A–4

4. Enter a depth for the Emboss/Engrave feature and select the direction of the feature. The new surface is parallel to the surface of the part.
   - The Emboss Depth only displays when you click ▭ (Emboss from Face) or ▭ (Engrave from Face).
5. Enter a taper value to specify the angle of the feature.
   - The Taper Angle only displays when you click ▭. Taper specifies the angle of the feature.
   - This setting enables inclusion of a draft angle when the part is manufactured. A positive angle looks toward the face of the part.

When wrapped, text objects cannot be self-intersecting.

6. (Optional) Select **Wrap to Face** to ensure that the feature follows the surface of the part. Click ▭ (Face) to select the destination face for wrapping.
   - The **Wrap to Face** option only displays when you click ▭ (Emboss from Face) or ▭ (Engrave from Face).
7. Once the Emboss feature is defined, click **OK** in the Emboss dialog box.

A.2 Decal Features

You might want to add labels, bar codes, brand names, art work, logos, or stamps to the part when it is manufactured. When modeling, you can place these items as decals. A Decal feature can be applied directly to the part, or be created as its own part and added to an assembly. A Decal feature is created from an image. An image can be a .BMP, .XLS, or .DOC file. An example of a part with Decal features is shown in Figure A–5.

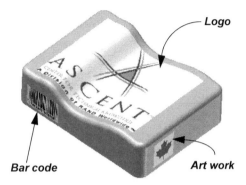

Figure A–5

Prior to creating a decal the image being used must exist in a sketch. To insert it, create a new sketch on a work plane or face and click (Image) in the Insert panel to select the image.

- Once the image is inserted, constrain the image by adding dimensions and constraints to its edges.
- When importing an image, consider using **Link** on the Open dialog box to maintain a link to the source file.
- Once the image is placed in the sketch, you can right-click on it and select **Properties** to open the Image Properties dialog box, as shown in Figure A–6. These properties enable you to set transparency masking, rotate, or mirror the image.

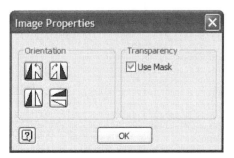

Figure A–6

Creating a Decal

*A decal cannot be applied across a seamed face. In such a case, the decal should be added to the assembly. However, the decal can be applied across tangent faces using **Chain Faces**.*

Decal features are only visible on IDW and DWG drawing views when the view is in the Shaded state. A potential workaround is to add the imagery to the drawing as a Sketched Symbol instead of as a Decal in the part file.

How To: Create a Decal Feature

1. Expand the Create panel and click (Decal). The Decal dialog box opens as shown in Figure A–7.

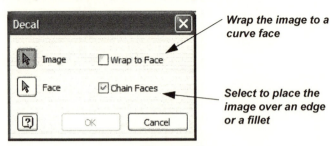

Figure A–7

2. Click (Image) and select the inserted image.
3. Click (Face) and select the face to apply the image.
4. Define how the decal will be applied to the selected face by selecting the following options, as required.
   - Select **Wrap to Face** to wrap the image to a curve face.
   - Select **Chain Faces** to place the image over an edge or a fillet.
5. Once the decal feature is defined, click **OK** in the Decal dialog box.

Practice A1

Emboss and Decals

Practice Objectives

- Create raised areas of text on surface of the model.
- Add an image on the surface of a model.

In this practice, you will create a sketch that contains text and use it to create an Emboss feature on the part shown in Figure A–8. You also place images on the part and create decals from the images.

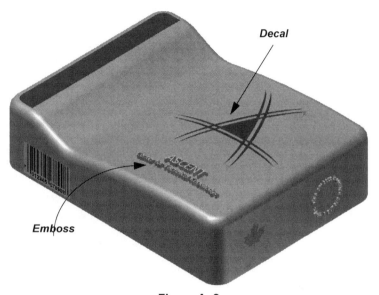

Figure A–8

Task 1 - Create the text sketch for the emboss feature.

1. Open **emboss_decal.ipt**.

2. Create a sketch using the blue face as the sketching plane. The *Sketch* tab is the active tab.

3. In the Create panel, click **A** (Text) and select a point in the lower right area of the part. The Format Text dialog box opens.

4. Enter the text shown in Figure A–9.

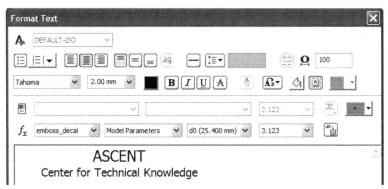

Figure A–9

5. Click **OK** to close the Format Text dialog box.

6. Dimension the text, as shown in Figure A–10.

Figure A–10

7. Finish the sketch.

Task 2 - Create the emboss feature.

1. In the *3D Model* tab>Create panel, click (Emboss) to open the Emboss dialog box.

2. Select the text as the emboss profile, and in the *Depth* field, change the emboss depth to **1.5** mm.

3. Change the color of the emboss to **Gold - Metal**. Click **OK**.

4. Accept the default (Emboss from Face).

5. Select **Wrap to Face** and select the face shown in Figure A–11.

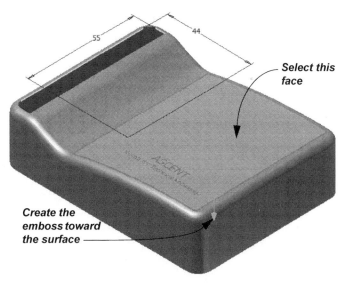

Figure A–11

6. Verify that the direction of the emboss is downward, toward the surface.

7. Click **OK** to create the feature. The emboss displays as shown in Figure A–12. If the emboss is not visible, edit the feature and verify the direction is set in the down direction.

Figure A–12

Task 3 - Insert the decal image.

1. Create a sketch using the blue face as the sketching plane. The *Sketch* tab is now the active tab.

2. In the Insert panel, click (Image). Select and open **Ascent.bmp**.

3. Place the logo image above the emboss feature, right-click and select **OK**.

4. Dimension the image, as shown in Figure A–13.

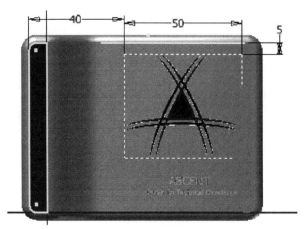

Figure A–13

5. Select the image, right-click and select **Properties**. The Image Properties dialog box opens.

6. Select **Use Mask**. This masks the background of the image to make it transparent. Click **OK**.

7. Finish the sketch and toggle off the dimension visibility.

Task 4 - Create the decal.

1. In the *3D Model* tab>Create panel, click (Decal). The Decal dialog box opens.

2. Select the logo image and select the curved face.

3. Click **OK** to create the decal. The decal displays as shown in Figure A–14.

Figure A–14

Task 5 - Add more decals and emboss features to the model.

1. Add the decals and emboss features shown in Figure A–15. Use the **Leaf.bmp** and **Barcode.bmp** images for the decals.

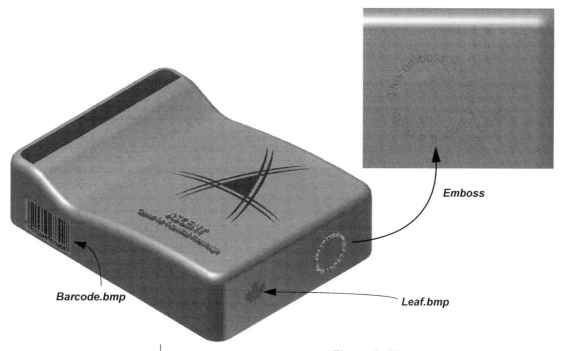

Figure A–15

2. Save the model and close the window.

Chapter Review Questions

1. Which **Emboss** option enables you to add and remove material at the same time from a model?

    a. ▭ (Emboss from Face)

    b. ▭ (Engrave from Face)

    c. ▭ (Emboss/Engrave from Plane)

2. Which **Emboss** option enables you to specify the depth to which the emboss geometry is created? (Select all that apply.)

    a. ▭ (Emboss from Face)

    b. ▭ (Engrave from Face)

    c. ▭ (Emboss/Engrave from Plane)

3. Which of the following best describes what an emboss feature can be used for in a model? (Select all that apply.)

    a. An emboss adds material to the part creating a raised area.

    b. An emboss removes material from the part creating a recessed area.

    c. An emboss is a 2D image placed on the part surface to add material to the part.

    d. An emboss is a 2D image placed on the part surface to remove material from the part.

4. Decal images can only be .BMP files.

    a. True

    b. False

5. How do you insert a decal image?

    a. During Decal creation, browse and open the image using options in the Decal dialog box.

    b. The image must be inserted into a sketch and is referenced during Decal creation.

Command Summary

Button	Command	Location
	Decal	• **Ribbon:** *3D Model* tab>Create panel
	Emboss	• **Ribbon:** *3D Model* tab>Create panel

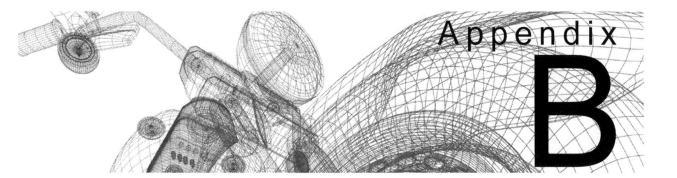

Appendix B

Custom Sketched Symbols

Creating your own custom symbols provides more flexibility than using only the standard symbols that are provided with the Autodesk® Inventor® software. To use custom sketched symbols you must learn how to create them, store them, and place them in a new drawing. Additionally, the use of AutoCAD® blocks in an Autodesk Inventor drawing file can provide additional symbols that have been created in the AutoCAD software.

Learning Objectives in this Appendix

- Create a custom Sketched Symbol using the standard sketching and text tools and save it for reuse.
- Manage the list of Sketched Symbols by creating and organizing symbols in folders.
- Edit a sketched custom symbol.
- Place a custom sketched symbol by defining its placement options and locating it relative to the defined insertion point.
- Modify the placement and definition of the sketched symbol to ensure that it communicates the required information.
- Insert an imported AutoCAD block into a new drawing.

B.1 Create Sketched Symbols

Several standard symbols (e.g., weld symbols or surface finish symbols) can be shown in drawings and allow for some customization, such as entering text in particular areas of the symbol. A custom sketched symbol enables full customization of the symbol and it consists of symbol geometry, text (if required), and its properties (e.g., placement type, instance height, attributes).

How To: Create a Sketched Symbol

1. Create or open a drawing file or drawing template for adding the sketched symbol.
2. In the *Manage* tab>Define panel, click (Symbol). The *Sketch* tab and sketching environment are activated. As an alternative, you can right-click on the **Sketch Symbols** node in the Model browser and select **Define New Symbol** to create a new symbol.
3. Use the standard sketching tools to create the symbol.
    - Text can be added to the symbol as required. The text can be static or variable. Variable text is text that is prompted for when the symbol is placed in a drawing.
    - To place text in a symbol, in the Create panel, click A (Text) and use the Format Text dialog box. If the text is to be variable, in the *Type* drop-down list, select **Prompted Entry**, as shown in Figure B–1.

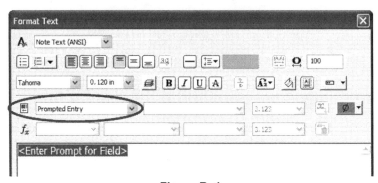

Figure B–1

Custom Sketched Symbols

4. (Optional) To define an insertion point, select a point on the sketched symbol and in the Format panel, click ⊞ (Set Insertion Point Grip), as shown in Figure B–2.

Figure B–2

If you redefine an insertion point for a sketched symbol, all of the symbols that already exist in the drawing update.

The insertion point is the location on the sketched symbol that is used during placement.

- If a leader is added to the symbol, the insertion point is where the leader connects to the symbol.
- You can also use it to snap to other drawing entities as well as move, rotate, and resize symbols after they are placed.
- Only one insertion point can be defined.

5. (Optional) To assign a connection point, select a point on the sketched symbol and in the Format panel, click (Connection Point Grip).

Connection points can be used to snap to other drawing entities or used as the attachment point for leaders.

- For example, they can be used to snap to the drawing border, views, and tables.
- In addition, they are used to move, rotate, and resize symbols after they are placed.
- Unlike insertion points, you can assign as many connection points as required.

6. Once you have finished creating the symbol, in the Exit panel, click ✓ (Finish Sketch).
7. Enter a name for the symbol and click **Save**. The sketched symbol is added to the **Drawing Resources>Sketch Symbols** node in the Model browser and can be added to the drawing.

The drawing can be saved for use as a drawing template using the **Save Copy as Template** option in the **File** menu, or it can be saved to the symbol library. Using either method enables you to quickly access custom symbols for reuse.

> **Hint: Symbol Libraries**
>
> Once saved to the drawing, you can explicitly save a custom sketched symbol to a Symbol Library. The library is a drawing file that is used to provide easy access to symbols. Multiple libraries can be created. By saving the custom sketched symbol to a library, you do not need to store the symbols in templates, or copy and paste them between drawings.
>
> ### How To: Save to the Symbol Library
>
> 1. In the Drawing Resources dialog box, in the **Sketch Symbols** node, right-click on the symbol and select **Save to Symbol Library**.
> 2. In the Save to Symbol Library dialog box, select an existing library from the list, or click ▦ (Create a new Library) to create a new library in the list.
> 3. (Optional) Click 📁 (Create a new folder) to create a new folder in the selected library to organize the symbols.
> 4. Click **Save**.
>
> The Symbol Library is stored in the Design Data directory on your system.

The list of symbols that are available in a drawing can become substantial. Consider the following tips to help you work with symbols:

Consider adding folders to your template file if you continually use the same symbol folder structure.

- Subfolders can be created in the **Sketch Symbols** node by right-clicking on it and selecting **Create New Folder**, or selecting and right-clicking on the symbol and select **Add to New Folder,** as shown in Figure B–3. Once symbols are created, you can drag and drop them into folders to organize and group.

Custom Sketched Symbols

- For sketched symbols that have multiple prompted entries, you can reorder prompts so that they are prompted for in a required order. To reorder, right-click on the **Sketched Symbols** node and select **Reorder Prompted Entries**, as shown in Figure B–3. Change the order of prompts in a dialog box.

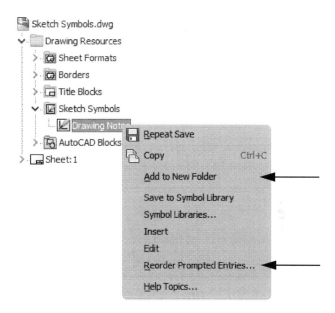

Figure B–3

Editing Sketched Symbols

Sketched symbols can be edited once they have been created. Right-click on the sketched symbol from the **Sketch Symbols** node in the *Drawing Resources* folder and select **Edit**. Make the required changes, and finish the sketch.

- If you edit a sketched symbol in a drawing, all placed instances of the symbol update in that drawing.

- If you edit a sketched symbol in a template file or library file, new drawings using that template or library file will contain the modified sketched symbol; however, any custom symbol used in a drawing based on the template or inserted from the library before the change will not reflect the change.

B.2 Place Sketched Symbols

Sketched symbols can be inserted either from the **Sketched Symbols** node in the *Drawing Resources* folder, or from a Sketched Symbols Library.

- By default, sketched symbols in the *Drawing Resources* folder contain the symbols that exist in the original drawing template. Any of these symbols can be inserted into the current drawing.

- Any symbols that have been created in the current drawing are saved to the **Drawing Resources>Sketch Symbols** node.

- Symbols can be copied between drawings. Once copied, they are placed in the **Drawing Resources>Sketch Symbols** node.

- Sketched symbols that have been explicitly saved to the Symbol Library can be inserted in the current drawing. Once inserted, they are added to the **Drawing Resources> Sketch Symbols** node.

How To: Place a Sketched Symbol

*To copy sketched symbols from one drawing to another, right-click on the sketched symbol, select **Copy**, right-click on the Drawing Resources folder in the target drawing, and select **Paste**. You can also use the Drawing Resource Transfer Wizard, which is available as a tool outside of the Autodesk Inventor software.*

1. In the *Annotate* tab>Symbols panel, click (Insert Sketch Symbol) or right-click on the symbol in the *Drawing Resources* folder and select **Insert**. The Sketch Symbols dialog box opens, as shown in Figure B–4.

    - All of the symbols available in the drawing are listed in the **Local** node and any symbols located in the library are listed in the **Symbol Libraries** node.

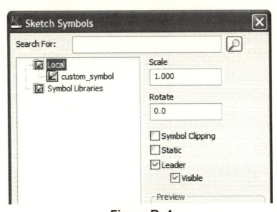

Figure B–4

Custom Sketched Symbols

Using the Insert method to add a symbol does not provide you with options for scaling, rotating, or other options that are provided in the Symbols dialog box.

To stack sketched symbols that contain geometry, press and hold <Shift> and move the cursor over the bounding box of an existing sketched symbol until the constraint icon displays.

2. Select a sketched symbol from the list of local or library symbols. Once selected a preview of the symbol appears in the Sketch Symbols dialog box.
   - Consider using the *Search For:* field to search for symbols.
3. Define the following options in the Sketch Symbols dialog box:
   - Specify a scale and rotation value.
   - Activate **Symbol Clipping** to trim dimension lines, leader lines, and extension lines behind symbols attached to drawing views.
   - Activate **Static** to prevent the symbol from being modified using the scale and rotation grip points.
   - Activate **Leader** to add a leader to the symbol. Activate or deactivate the **Visible** option to make the leader visible or invisible.
4. Click **OK** to begin placement of the sketched symbol.
5. Move the cursor to the required location and click to place it.
   - To associate the symbol with a view, select an entity on a view as the reference.
6. Continue to place symbols by clicking in the drawing. Once finished, right-click in the graphics window and select **Cancel (ESC)**. The sketched symbol is placed in the drawing and is added to the **Sketch Symbols** node for the active sheet, as shown in Figure B–5.

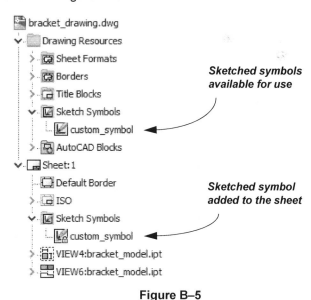

Figure B–5

To access the symbol modification options, right-click on the sketched symbol in the **Sketch Symbols** node for the active sheet, as shown in Figure B–6.

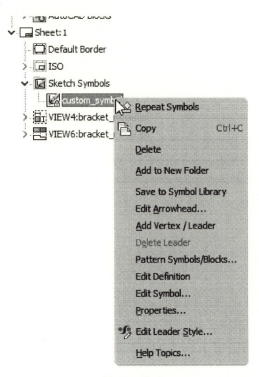

Figure B–6

The editing options include:

Option	Description
Save to Symbol Library	Enables you to save the symbol to a library for quick access and reuse without having to use a specific template or copy a symbol from another file.
Pattern Symbols/ Blocks	Enables you to pattern symbols, sketched symbols, or AutoCAD blocks. The pattern can be defined in one or two directions, similar to defining sketch or feature patterns.
Edit Arrowhead and **Delete Leader**	Enable you to manipulate existing symbol leaders. • **Add Vertex/Leader** can also be used to add leaders if placed without a leader.
Edit Definition	Returns you to the sketch environment to edit the initial definition of the symbol.
Edit Symbol	Enables you to modify the options that were selected when the symbol was placed.

B.3 AutoCAD Blocks

Consider reviewing the DWG TrueConnect Help topics for further information on using AutoCAD files in the Autodesk Inventor software.

AutoCAD templates that are converted for use in Autodesk Inventor software maintain the blocks that were created in the AutoCAD software. Although the functionality available for Autodesk Inventor symbols is reduced for AutoCAD blocks, having access is useful. Common uses for AutoCAD blocks in Autodesk Inventor drawings include simplified schematics, legacy blocks, and legacy notations. Figure B–7 shows the *Drawing Resources* folder with AutoCAD blocks available.

Figure B–7

Any AutoCAD blocks that have been converted into an Autodesk Inventor template include the original attributes. When the block is placed, the user is prompted for these values and the block can be scaled and rotated. Once inserted into a drawing, the block is a native object in the drawing. For example, you can reference the block with other entities. AutoCAD blocks cannot be edited in the Autodesk Inventor software and you cannot create them; however, you can scale and rotate them. To scale and rotate, select the block in the graphics window and use grips, as shown in Figure B–8.

*If grip handles do not display when you select an AutoCAD Block, right-click, select **Edit AutoCAD Block**, and clear the **Static** option in the AutoCAD Blocks dialog box.*

Figure B–8

- If changes must be made to the sketched content of the block, it is recommended to recreate it as a sketched symbol. If an AutoCAD block is required in an Autodesk Inventor drawing, consider opening the Autodesk Inventor .DWG file in AutoCAD and adding the block. When the .DWG is opened again, the block will be available.

- AutoCAD blocks can be imported directly from other .DWG files into an Autodesk Inventor .DWG file. To import, right-click on the **AutoCAD Block** node in the *Drawing Resources* folder and select **Import AutoCAD Block**, as shown in Figure B–9. In the Import Block dialog box, you can modify the scale and rotation values, and select the required block definition to be imported. Once imported, you can place the AutoCAD block in the drawing using the standard **Insert** command.

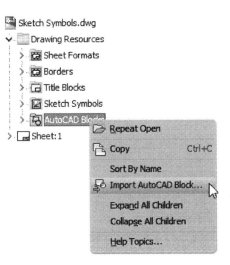

Figure B–9

The Pattern Symbols/Blocks dialog box can also be used to pattern symbols in a drawing.

- An inserted AutoCAD block can be patterned by right-clicking on the inserted block and selecting **Pattern Symbols/Block**. Using the Pattern Symbols/Blocks dialog box, as shown in Figure B–10, you can define a reference direction, number of instances, and spacing of the instances. The interface is similar to pattern sketches in the sketch environment.

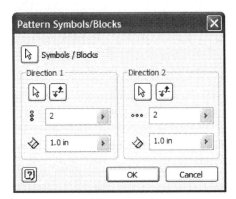

Figure B–10

Practice B1 Custom Sketched Symbols I

Practice Objectives

- Create a custom Sketched Symbol using standard sketching tools.
- Copy a custom Sketched Symbol to the Drawing Resources folder of a target drawing and display it on a sheet.
- Save a custom symbol to the Symbol Library, and place it in the drawing.

In this practice, you create a custom sketch symbol for reuse in drawings. The custom sketch symbol is shown in Figure B–11.

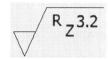

Figure B–11

Task 1 - Create a new drawing and add a custom sketch symbol.

1. Create a new drawing using the **standard.dwg** drawing template.

2. In the *Manage* tab>Define panel, click (Symbol). As an alternative, you can right-click on the **Sketch Symbols** node in the *Drawing Resources* folder and select **Define New Symbol**. The *Sketch* tab and sketching environment are now activated.

3. Sketch and add the text shown in Figure B–12. To simulate a subscript for the *Z* value, position the text lower. The sketch will consist of two separate pieces of text. Consider adding the text first to ensure the correct scale for the sketched lines.

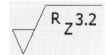

Figure B–12

4. The insertion point is defined when a symbol is created and used to locate it during placement. If a leader is used, it is where the leader connects to the symbol. Begin by selecting the bottom point of the triangular portion of the symbol. With the point selected on the symbol, in the Format panel, click

(Set Insertion Point Grip) as shown in Figure B–13. The insertion point grip is now set.

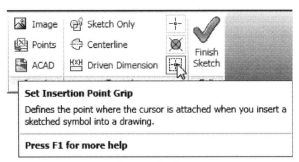

Figure B–13

5. Once finished creating the symbol, in the Exit panel, click

(Finish Sketch). The Sketched Symbol dialog box opens.

6. Enter **custom_symbol** as the name and click **Save**. The custom sketch symbol is created and added to the Model browser under the **Drawing Resources>Sketch Symbols** node, as shown in Figure B–14.

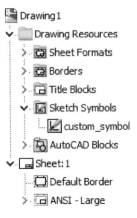

Figure B–14

7. Save the drawing as **custom_symbol_drawing**. The symbol has currently not been added to the drawing; however, it is accessible for use in the drawing.

Custom Sketched Symbols

Task 2 - Copy the custom symbol to a drawing.

Custom sketch symbols must exist in the *Drawing Resources* folder for use in a drawing. If a symbol is created in a drawing template, it will be available for use in any drawing using that template. If the symbol is created in one drawing, you need to copy the custom sketch symbol into any other drawing in which you want to use the symbol.

1. Open **bracket_drawing.dwg** from the top-level practice files folder.

2. In the Model browser, expand the *Drawing Resource* folder. Note that there are no sketched symbols.

3. Switch back to the **custom_symbol_drawing.dwg** drawing.

4. Expand the **Drawing Resources>Sketch Symbols** node, if not already expanded.

5. Right-click on **custom_symbol** and select **Copy**.

6. Switch to the **bracket_drawing.dwg** window.

7. Right-click the *Drawing Resources* folder and select **Paste**. The custom symbol is copied to the **Sketch Symbols** node. Now the custom symbol can be used in this drawing.

Task 3 - Add the custom symbol to the drawing.

*Alternatively, you can right-click on the symbol in the Drawing Resources folder and select **Insert**. Using this method does not provide you with options for scaling, rotating, or other options that are provided in the Sketch Symbols dialog box.*

1. In the *Annotate* tab>Symbols panel, click (Insert Sketch Symbol). The Sketch Symbols dialog box opens, as shown in Figure B–15. The **custom_symbol** symbol is listed in the **Local** node because it now exists as a sketched symbol in the *Drawing Resources* folder for the active (local) drawing.

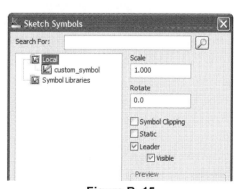

Figure B–15

*You can activate **Leader** to add a leader to the custom sketch symbol. Place it as you would for a regular surface texture symbol with a leader.*

2. Select **custom_symbol** in the **Local** node.
3. Set the *Scale* to **0.5**.
4. Verify that the **Leader** option is cleared and **Static** is selected.
5. Click **OK**. Click to place the symbol on the reference as shown in Figure B–16.

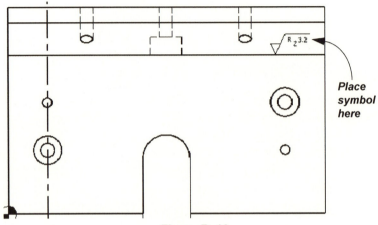

Figure B–16

*Using the **Edit Symbol** command enables you to edit the rotation and scale of symbols that are added using the **Insert** command which does not have those options available on placement.*

6. Right-click and select **Cancel (Esc)** to discontinue placing additional symbols.
7. Depending on the size of your original custom sketch, you might need to edit the scale of the symbol to correctly place the sketch in the drawing. Right-click on **custom_symbol** in the Model browser for **Sheet:1** and select **Edit Symbol**. Modify the scale, if required and close the dialog box.

The **custom_symbol_drawing.dwg** file could be saved as a template for future use by simply saving it using the **Save Copy as Template** option in the **File** menu. The next time you create a new drawing file, the new template will be available. Alternatively, you can save the symbol to a custom symbol library.

Custom Sketched Symbols

Task 4 - Create a custom symbol and save it to the library.

1. Return to the **custom_symbol_drawing.dwg** file.

2. In the *Drawing Resources* folder, right-click on **custom_symbol** in the **Sketch Symbols** node, and select **Save to Symbol Library**. The Save to Symbol Library dialog box opens, similar to that shown in Figure 2–17. It might vary if any libraries have already been created on your system.

The Save to Symbol Library dialog box always references the symbol library drawing files that have been created. This list is only empty the first time you access the command and create a library.

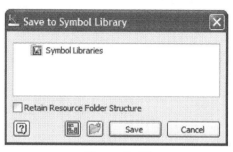

Figure 2–17

3. In the Save to Symbol Library dialog box, click (Create a new Library) to create a new library in the list. Enter **My Library** as the name of the new library. If this library already exists, select it.

4. Click **Save**. The Symbol Library (**My Library.idw**) is stored in the *Design Data* directory on your system and now contains the new symbol.

The symbol library is located in C:\Users\Public\Public Documents\Autodesk\Inventor <ver#>\Design Data\Symbol Library.

5. Close the **custom_symbol_drawing.dwg** file without saving it.

Task 5 - Add the custom symbol to the drawing.

1. Activate **bracket_drawing.dwg**.

2. Delete the previous copy of **custom_symbol** that was added to the drawing.

3. In the *Drawing Resources* folder, right-click on **custom_symbol** in the **Sketch Symbols** node and select **Delete**. This symbol is removed from the drawing. In the next task, you will add it back into the drawing from the library to simulate working with the symbol library.

4. Select the *Annotate* tab. In the Symbol panel, click **Insert Sketch Symbol**.

B–15

5. Expand the **My Library.idw** library, as shown in Figure 2–18. Note that the new symbol is listed in the library. Also, there are no symbols in the current drawing, as shown by the empty **Local** node.

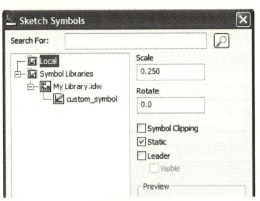

Figure 2–18

6. Select **custom_symbol.** The symbol appears in the *Preview* area in the Sketch Symbols dialog box. Maintain all of the default settings and click **OK**.

7. Place the symbol in the drawing, similar to how it was previously place. To create the symbol without a leader, right click and select **Cancel (Esc)**.

8. Save the drawing and close all the files. Now that the symbol has been saved to the library it can be reused as required, without having to have it in a template file or copying and pasting between drawings.

Practice B2 | Custom Sketched Symbols II

Practice Objectives

- Insert an imported AutoCAD Block into a new drawing.
- Create a custom Sketched Symbol that consists of text and prompted entry.
- Insert a custom Sketched Symbol that requires user entry to populate the fields in the symbol.

In this practice, you will place an AutoCAD block in a drawing and create a custom sketch symbol. The custom sketch symbol will contain user prompts and pull information from the model properties. The custom symbol that will be created is shown in Figure B–19.

Rockwell Hardness	80
Heat Treatment	Yes
Paint Application	No
Material	Cast Iron

Figure B–19

Task 1 - Create a new drawing and insert an AutoCAD Block.

1. Open **Sketch Symbols.dwg**. Three views have been added to the drawing for you.

2. Expand the **Drawing Resources>AutoCAD Blocks** node, as shown in Figure B–20.

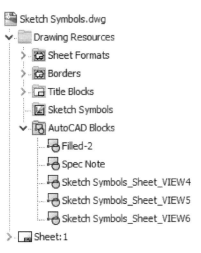

Figure B–20

*As opposed to sketched symbols, the only method you can use to add an AutoCAD block to a drawing is to right-click on the block and select **Insert**. When inserting sketched symbols, you can also use (User) in the Annotate tab.*

These AutoCAD blocks had been imported into the drawing template that was used for this drawing. Because they are in the template, they are available for use in the Autodesk Inventor drawing. As views are created in the Autodesk Inventor drawing, these are added as AutoCAD blocks upon saving. Therefore, the parametric views are visible when opened in AutoCAD.

3. Right-click on **Spec Note** and select **Insert**.
4. Place the symbol anywhere on the drawing.
5. The Edit Attributes dialog box opens, requiring you to enter a value for the *Spec Number*. Enter **5**, as shown in Figure B–21, and click **OK**.

Figure B–21

6. Right-click and select **Done** to cancel symbol placement.
7. Right-click on the symbol and note that the symbol cannot use Leaders like an Autodesk Inventor Sketched Symbol can.

Task 2 - Define a new symbol.

1. In the *Manage* tab>Define panel, click (Symbol). As an alternative, you can right-click on the **Drawing Resources> Sketch Symbols** node and select **Define New Symbol**. The *Sketch* tab is activated.

Custom Sketched Symbols

*Consider toggling on the grid display (Tools tab> Application Options> Sketch tab) and enabling grid snap (right-click and select **Snap to Grid**) to help position the text.*

2. Using the **Text** command, add the text and prompted entries shown in Figure B–22.

   - The four entries shown on the left side (Rockwell Hardness, Heat Treatment, Paint Application, and Material) are text only.
   - The top three entries on the right side (<Rockwell Hardness>, <Heat Treatment>, and <Paint Application>) use prompted entry. In the *Type* drop-down list, select **Prompted Entry** and edit the text field to display the prompts shown in Figure B–22.
   - The bottom entry on the right side (<Material>) uses a parameter from the model to populate the field. In the *Type* drop-down list, select **Properties - Model** and in the *Parameter* list, select **Material**. Ensure that you click 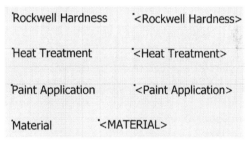 to assign the parameter.

Figure B–22

3. Constrain the text entries using the Vertical and Horizontal constraint options, located in the Constraint panel. Add dimensions, as shown in Figure B–23. These dimensions will display in the sketch environment but not be visible in the final symbol.

To set up relationships between dimensions while in a sketch, select the dimension value that is to be driven to edit it, and then select the driving dimension. The driving dimension's parameter displays in the Edit Dimension dialog box. Press <Enter> to establish the relationship.

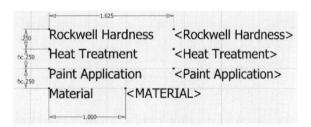

Figure B–23

4. Select the dot in the top left corner of the symbol. This dot is associated with the **Rockwell Hardness** text. In the Format panel, click (Set Insertion Point Grip). The insertion point grip is now set.

5. In the Exit panel, click ✓ (Finish).

6. Enter **Drawing Notes** as the name of the sketched symbol.

7. Expand the **Drawing Resources>Sketch Symbols** node. Right-click on the new symbol and select **Reorder Prompted Entries**. The Reorder Prompted Entries dialog box opens as shown in Figure B–24. The three prompted entries are displayed.

Figure B–24

- The **Reorder Prompted Entries** option enables you to reset the order in which entries are prompted for when the symbol is placed. In this case, with only three prompts, it is not that beneficial; however, if you are working with symbols that have a longer list of entries, it can be very helpful.

8. Click **OK** to close the dialog box without making any changes.

Task 3 - Insert the symbol.

1. In the *Annotate* tab>Symbols panel, click (Insert Sketched Symbol). As an alternative, you can right-click on the symbol in the *Drawing Resources* folder and select **Insert**.

Custom Sketched Symbols

2. Ensure that the **Drawing Notes** symbol is selected in the **Local** node in the Sketched Symbols dialog box. Clear the **Leader** option and click **OK**.

3. Click anywhere on the drawing to place the symbol.

4. The Drawing Notes Prompted Texts dialog box opens. You can enter the following values for the prompted entries, as shown in Figure B–25.

    - *Rockwell Hardness*: **80**
    - *Heat Treatment*: **Yes**
    - *Paint Application*: **No**

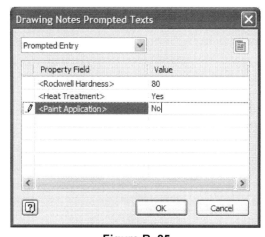

Figure B–25

*The **Drawing Notes** symbol was created in the drawing and only stored locally. This could also be stored as a library drawing template or to the symbol library so that it can be easily accessed.*

5. Click **OK**. Right-click and select **Cancel (Esc)** to finish placement. The symbols display as shown in Figure B–26. Note how the material for the model automatically populates.

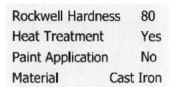

Figure B–26

6. Save the drawing and close the window.

Chapter Review Questions

1. Based on the Model browser shown in Figure B–27, how many sketched symbols have been placed in the drawing?

   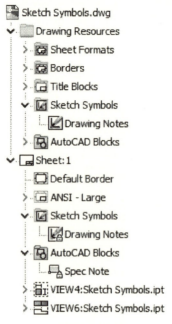

   Figure B–27

   a. 1
   b. 2
   c. 3
   d. 5

2. Which of the following is true regarding insertion points? (Select all that apply.)

   a. The insertion point is the location on the sketched symbol that is used during placement.
   b. The insertion point defines the point where the leader attaches to the symbol.
   c. A single insertion point must be assigned in the sketched symbol in order to create it.
   d. If you redefine an insertion point for a sketched symbol, all symbols that already exist in the drawing update.

3. How many connection points can be assigned to a sketched symbol?

    a. 1

    b. 2

    c. Depends on the number of vertices in the sketch.

    d. Unlimited

4. AutoCAD blocks that exist in an Autodesk Inventor file can be scaled, rotated, and the entities can be edited once placed in an Autodesk Inventor drawing file.

    a. True

    b. False

Command Summary

Button	Command	Location
 ⊠	Connection Point Grip	• **Ribbon:** *Sketch* tab>Format panel
 ↓◇	Define New Symbol	• **Ribbon:** *Annotate* tab>Symbols panel • **Context menu:** In Model browser in *Drawing Resources* folder with Sketch Symbols node selected
 ✓	Finish Sketch	• **Ribbon:** *Sketch* tab>Exit panel • **Context menu:** In the graphics window
↓◇	Insert Sketch Symbol	• **Ribbon:** *Annotate* tab>Symbols panel • **Context menu:** In Model browser in *Drawing Resources* folder with Sketch Symbols node selected
⌗	Set Insertion Point Grip	• **Ribbon:** *Sketch* tab>Format panel
A	Text	• **Ribbon:** *Sketch* tab>Create panel

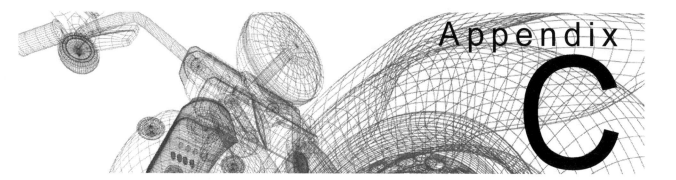

Appendix C

CAD Management

When working with drawing files, both administrators and users can benefit from knowing how to customize Title Blocks and Borders. Additionally, knowledge of the Style Library Manager enables you to create new style libraries, compare style libraries, and transfer styles between existing style libraries to ensure that company standards are met.

Learning Objectives in this Appendix

- Delete the existing title blocks that are included with a default drawing template.
- Create a title block and border using sketch and text tools.
- Add a new title block to a drawing file and save the drawing as a template that can be used to create new drawings.
- Apply a style library to an Autodesk Inventor project file to ensure that all models created in the project use this library.
- Use the Style Library Manager to create new style libraries and copy styles between existing libraries.

C.1 Title Block and Border Customization

You can add a title block and border to a drawing using one of two methods:

- Use an existing title block and border.
- Create a new title block and border.

Use Existing Title Blocks and Borders

The drawing templates included in the software contain title blocks and borders. However, you or your CAD administrator may need to customize drawing templates to show your company's specific title blocks and borders.

How To: Apply a New, but Existing, Title Block and Border

1. Create or open the drawing with the title block and border that requires changing.
2. Access the required sheet in the drawing and expand the **Sheet** node in the Model browser.
3. In the Model browser, right-click on the title block name and select **Delete**, as shown in Figure C–1.

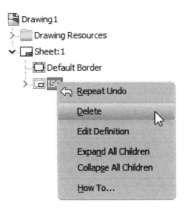

Figure C–1

4. In the Model browser, expand the *Drawing Resources* folder.

CAD Management

5. In the **Title Blocks** node, right-click on the required title block name and select **Insert**, as shown in Figure C–2.

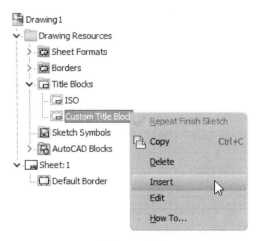

Figure C–2

6. If the title block requires entries, enter the values in the dialog box.
7. Repeat Steps 4 to 6 for the required border using Borders available in the **Borders** node.

In some cases, you might need to create a new title block.

Create a New Title Block and Border

How To: Create a New Title Block and Border

1. To create a new drawing template that includes a new title block and border, you can:
   - Open one of the existing templates from the *C:\Users\Public\Public Documents\Autodesk\Inventor 2019\Templates* directory.
   - Create a new drawing based on an existing template.

2. In the *Manage* tab>Define panel, click ▭ (Title Block) or ▭ (Border) to create a new title block or border, respectively. The current sheet becomes an active sketch.

3. Use the *Sketch* tab to draw the title block or border. Dimension the sketch, as required.

4. Add text to the title block or border by clicking **A** (Text) in the Create panel.

The Prompted Entry property type displays a prompt for you to input information when the title block is added.

- Model and drawing properties can be added so that they automatically update in the title block. Use the Type drop-down list to select the property type you want to add.

  Select the property and click [x] to add the parameter to the field. The Type and Property drop-down lists are shown in Figure C–3.

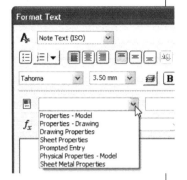

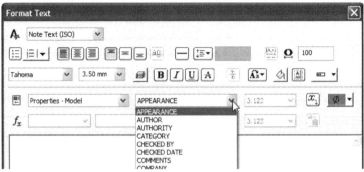

Figure C–3

5. Once you have completed the title block or border, finish the sketch or right-click and select **Save Title Block** or **Save Border**.
6. Enter a name for the title block or border and click **Save**. The new title block or border is added in the Model browser to the *Drawing Resources* folder, as shown in Figure C–4.

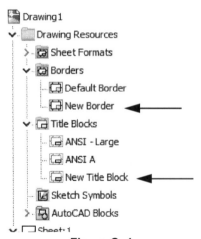

Figure C–4

To use the new title block and border as a template for future drawings, save the drawing in the *Templates* folder using **Save Copy As Template** in the **File** menu or save to a folder in the *Templates* folder.

C.2 Style Library Manager

Style

A style is a set of predefined properties, such as lighting, dimensions, and drawing standards. You can apply a style to an object, such as an annotation, edge, face, part, assembly, or drawing.

Style Library

A style library contains a set of styles, including lighting, dimensions, and drawing standards. Companies can use the style library to suit their unique needs.

To change the style library for a project, open the Projects dialog box and select the project to modify. Expand **Folder Options**, right-click on the *Design Data* folder, and select **Edit**, as shown in Figure C–5. Browse to the required style library.

*Each project uses the default style library, unless otherwise specified. The default style library is set in the Application Options (Tools tab>**Application Options**>File tab>Design Data).*

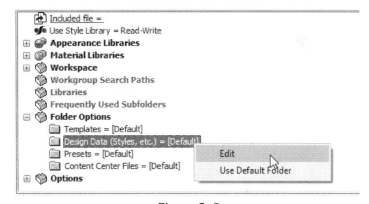

Figure C–5

Style Library Manager

The style library manager enables you to copy styles between style libraries, and rename or delete styles.

How To: Edit a Style in the Style Library

1. Access the Style Library Manager by selecting **Start>All Programs>Autodesk>Autodesk Inventor 2019>Tools> Style Library Manager 2019**. The dialog box opens as shown in Figure C–6.

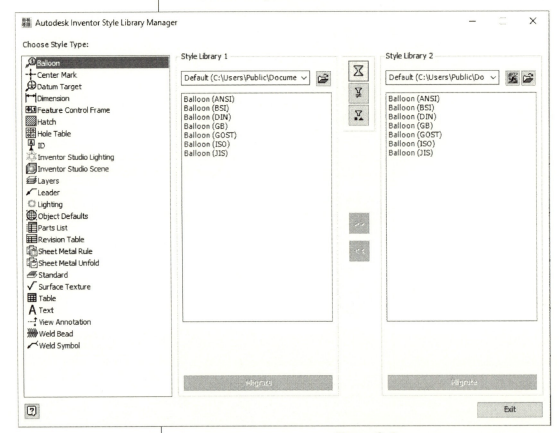

Figure C–6

2. Select the style type to edit from the list on the left side of the dialog box.
3. There are two areas on the right side: *Style Library 1* and *Style Library 2*. These two areas enable you to compare two different style libraries and transfer required styles from one style library to the other.

CAD Management

To display a different style library, in *Style Library 1* or *Style Library 2,* expand the drop-down list and select from the list of projects that use style libraries. Alternatively, use the 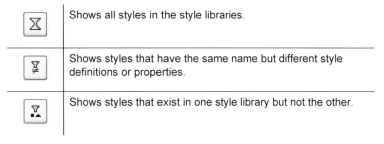 icon to browse to and open a different style library.

4. Once you have selected the required style libraries, use the filter icons to help compare the two style libraries. The filter options are described as follows:

Icon	Description
⊠	Shows all styles in the style libraries.
▽≠	Shows styles that have the same name but different style definitions or properties.
▽	Shows styles that exist in one style library but not the other.

- A style name displayed in blue, with italic and bold font indicates that the style does not exist in the other style library.

- A style name displayed in black with regular font indicates that the two styles are the same.

- A style name displayed in red, with bold and underlined font indicates that although the names are the same, their definitions are different.

An example of each is shown in Figure C–7.

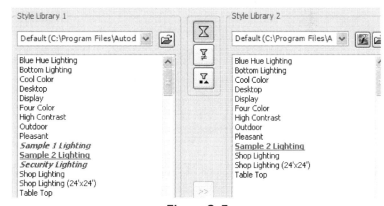

Figure C–7

Copy Styles Between Style Libraries

To copy a style from one style library to another, select the style and use the << or >> icons. Styles sometimes reference other styles, called substyles. A hole table, for example, references the text style as a substyle. When a style with a substyle is copied, the substyle is only copied if it does not already exist in the destination library. Changes made to a style library do not have any effect until the current session is closed and a new one is opened.

Rename or Delete Styles

To rename or delete a style, right-click it in the style library list and select **Rename Styles** or **Delete Styles**.

Create a New Style Library

How To: Create a New Style Library

1. Click ![icon] (Create New Style Library) to open the Create New Style Library dialog box, as shown in Figure C–8.

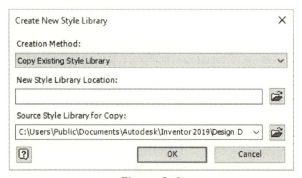

Figure C–8

2. In the *Creation Method* drop-down list, select **Copy Existing Style Library** or **Create Empty Style Library**.
3. Enter the full path directory, including the folder name, in the *New Style Library Location* field.
   - This directory specifies where the style library is stored.
   - The .XML files containing the different style types are saved into the folder specified in this field.
   - If you enter the name of a folder that does not exist, a folder with the specified name is automatically created.
4. If you selected **Copy Existing Style Library**, select the required library from the Source Style Library for Copy drop-down list or use the ![icon] icon to browse to the library.
5. Click **OK**.

Practice C1

Customizing the Title Block

Practice Objectives

- Sketch and dimension line entities that makeup the title block layout for a custom title block file.
- Add text to incorporate both static and parametric text into the title block
- Delete existing title blocks that are included with a default drawing template.
- Add a new title block to a drawing file and save the drawing as a template that can be used to create new drawings.

In this practice, you create a new title block, add it to a blank drawing, and make it available as a template.

Task 1 - Delete the existing title block from a new drawing.

1. Create a new drawing using the **ISO.idw** template in the *Metric* tab.

2. Right-click on the title block called ISO and select **Delete**, as shown in Figure C–9.

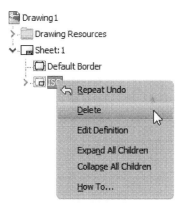

Figure C–9

Task 2 - Create the title block borders.

1. In the *Manage* tab>Define panel, click (Title Block). The sketch environment is activated.

2. Using rectangles, lines, and general dimensions, create the title block shown in Figure C–10. Align the title block as close as possible to the border.

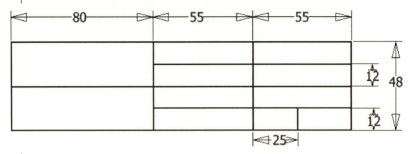

Figure C–10

Task 3 - Add regular text.

1. In the Create panel, click **A** (Text) and add the text shown in Figure C–11. Use a size of **2.00mm** for the text.

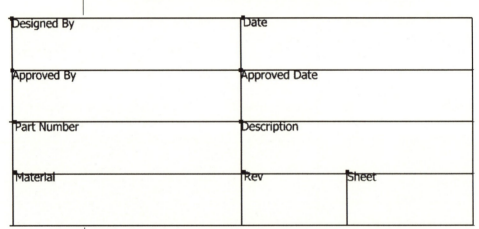

Figure C–11

Task 4 - Add model and drawing properties.

1. In the Create panel, click **A** (Text) and click in the *Designed By* cell in the title block. The Format Text dialog box opens.

2. In the Type drop-down list, select **Properties-Drawing**.

3. In the Property drop-down list, select **Designer**.

4. Click [icon]. The property is added to the text field, as shown in Figure C–12.

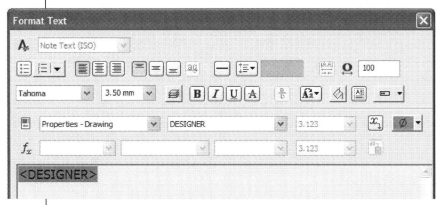

Figure C–12

5. Click **OK**. The property displays as shown in Figure C–13. Move the text, if required, by selecting the text and dragging it to the new location.

Figure C–13

6. Repeat the previous steps for the remaining properties shown in Figure C–14. **Hint**: All but the sheet properties are of the *Properties - Model* Type. Create the sheet property using a combination of the *Sheet Properties* and *Drawing Properties*.

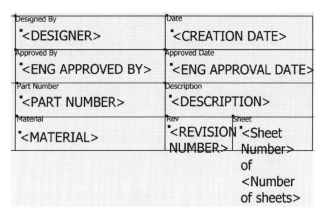

Figure C–14

Task 5 - Save the title block.

1. In the exit panel, click ✓ (Finish Sketch) to exit the sketch.

2. Enter **Custom Title Block** as the name of the new title block and click **Save**. The newly created title block is stored in **Title Blocks** node in the *Drawing Resources* folder, as shown in Figure C–15.

Figure C–15

Task 6 - Insert the newly created title block into the drawing.

1. Right-click on **Custom Title Block** and select **Insert**, as shown in Figure C–16.

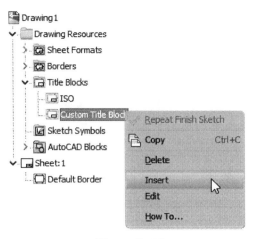

Figure C–16

CAD Management

The title block is added to the drawing and the Model browser, as shown in Figure C–17.

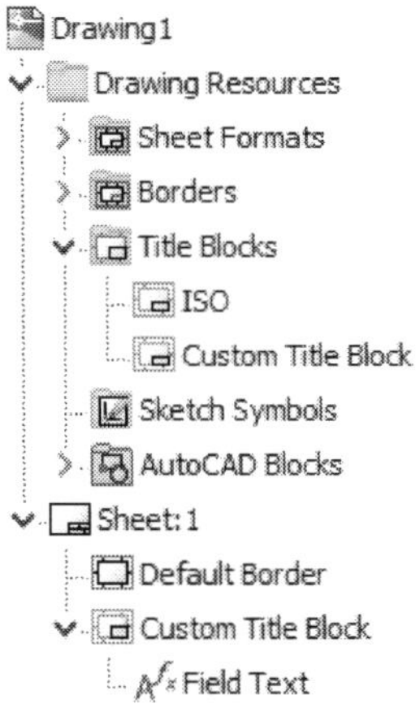

```
Drawing1
├── Drawing Resources
│   ├── Sheet Formats
│   ├── Borders
│   ├── Title Blocks
│   │   ├── ISO
│   │   └── Custom Title Block
│   ├── Sketch Symbols
│   └── AutoCAD Blocks
└── Sheet: 1
    ├── Default Border
    └── Custom Title Block
        └── Field Text
```

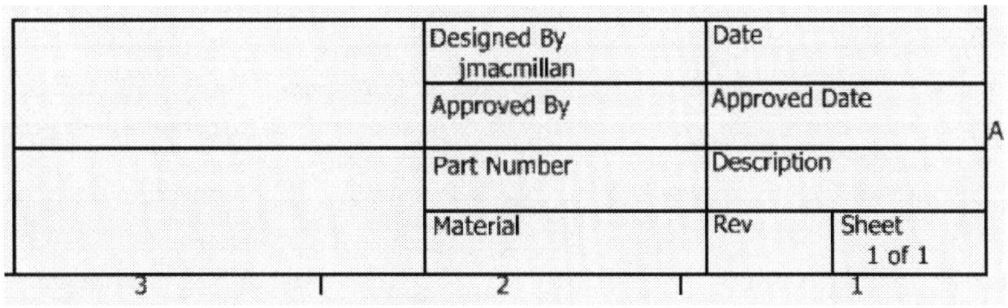

	Designed By jmacmillan	Date	
	Approved By	Approved Date	A
	Part Number	Description	
	Material	Rev	Sheet 1 of 1

Figure C–17

Note that three of the properties have been automatically filled. The information was obtained from the iproperty values and the sheet and drawing properties. The remainder of the properties were created using **Properties-Model** from the *Type* drop-down list so that their values will be populated when a model is added to the drawing.

Task 7 - Save the drawing as a template.

1. Save the drawing using **Save Copy As Template** to save the file as a template in the default *Templates* directory. The next time you access the New File dialog box, the new drawing template will be available for use.

Practice C2 Managing Styles

Practice Objectives

- Use the Style Library Manager to copy styles between libraries.
- Associate libraries to new project files.

In this practice, you use the Style Library Manager to manage styles that are associated to both style libraries and documents.

Task 1 - Open the Style Library Manager.

1. From outside of the Autodesk Inventor software, select **Start>All Programs>Autodesk>Autodesk Inventor 2019>Tools>Style Library Manager 2019**. The Style Library Manager opens as shown in Figure C–18.

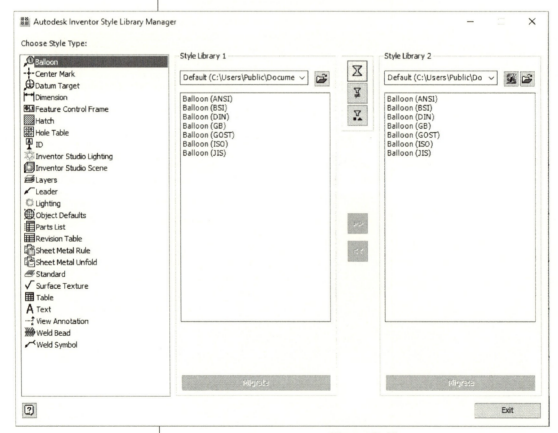

Figure C–18

Task 2 - Create two new style libraries.

In this task, you create two new style libraries. *TestStyleLibrary* and *EmptyStyleLibrary* are used to demonstrate the Style Library Manager.

1. Click ![icon] (Create New Style Library). The Create New Style Library dialog box opens as shown in Figure C–19.

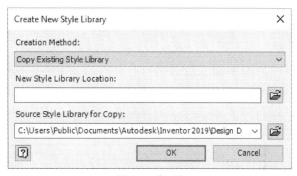

Figure C–19

2. In the *Creation Method* field, leave the default selected and next to the *New Style Library Location* field, click ![icon].

3. Browse to the practice files location for this course and create a new folder called **TestStyleLibrary**. Click **OK**.

4. In the *Source Style Library for Copy* field, leave the default selected, as shown in Figure C–20.

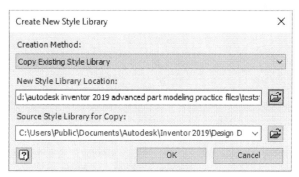

Figure C–20

5. Click **OK**.

6. Create a second style library using the **Create Empty Style Library** creation method and call it **EmptyStyleLibrary**, as shown in Figure C–21.

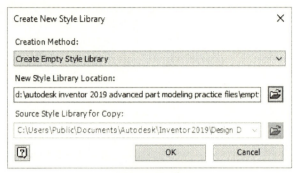

Figure C–21

Task 3 - Compare TestStyleLibrary and EmptyStyleLibrary.

In this task, you use the Style Library Manager to determine which styles are common and uncommon between TestStyleLibrary and EmptyStyleLibrary.

1. Select **User Style Library (C:\.....\teststylelibrary)** from the drop-down list for *Style Library 1*.

2. Select **User Style Library (C:\.....\emptystylelibrary)** from the drop-down list for *Style Library 2*.

3. Select a few different style types from the *Choose Style Type* column, such as Dimension, and Text. Note that the test style library (Style Library 1) contains styles shown in blue lettering, whereas the empty style library (Style Library 2) does not contain any styles.

4. Any styles that exist in the selected style library are listed. If no styles are listed, then the selected style library contains no styles for the particular style type. In the case of the empty style library, there are no styles for any style type.

    The color of the styles that are listed indicate additional information. A blue color indicates that the particular style does not exist in the other style library that is being compared.

5. Select the Lighting style type.

6. Select **Country Road - SpheronVR** from TestStyleLibrary and click [>>] to move the style to the empty style library. Note that **Country Road - SpheronVR i**s now listed in both style libraries and displays black rather than blue. The style is in black because it now exists in both the style libraries being compared.

7. Click **Exit** to close the style library manager.

Task 4 - Create a project called TestProject.

1. In the Autodesk Inventor software, in the **File** menu, select **Manage>Projects**. The Projects dialog box opens similar to that shown in Figure C–22.

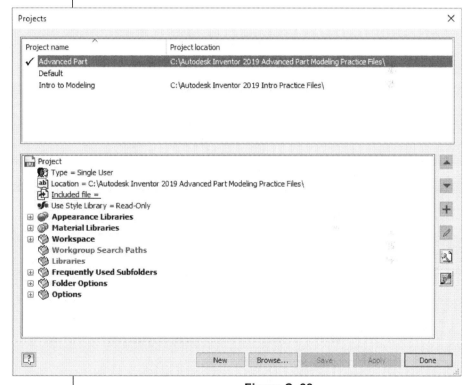

Figure C–22

2. Right-click in the upper panels where the projects are listed and select **New**. The Inventor project wizard dialog box opens.

3. Depending on whether Vault is installed, you might be prompted for what type of project you are creating. Select **New Single User Project**, if prompted. Click **Next**.

4. Define the new project, called **TestProject**, as shown in Figure C–23.

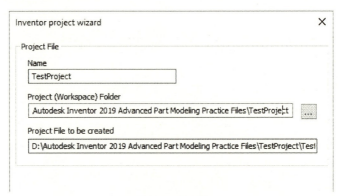

Figure C–23

5. Click **Finish** to create the project. The new project displays in the project list. If any files are open, the new project will not be set as the active project.

Task 5 - Change the project options for the project.

In this task, you set TestProject to use TestStyleLibrary for its style library. The project will also be set so that the style library can be modified.

1. In the Projects dialog box with the list of projects showing, double-click on **TestProject** to activate it, if not already active. The checkmark should now display next to **TestProject**, indicating that it is the active project.

2. In the project options area for **TestProject**, right-click on **Use Style Library** and select **Read-Write** to enable you to make changes to the style library, as shown in Figure C–24.

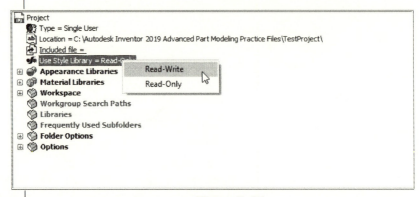

Figure C–24

3. Expand **Folder Options**, right-click on **Design Data**, and select **Edit**, as shown in Figure C–25.

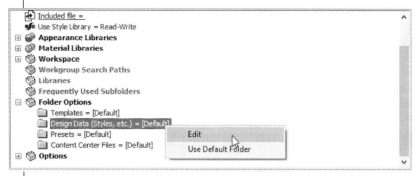

Figure C–25

4. Browse and select the *TestStyleLibrary* folder that you created earlier (*C:\.....\TestStyleLibrary*). The style library path displays, as shown in Figure C–26. Press <Enter>.

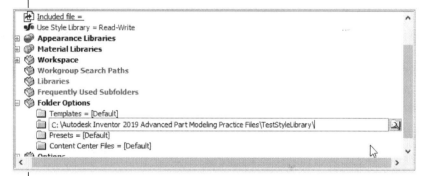

Figure C–26

5. Save the changes you made to the project by clicking **Save** in the Projects dialog box. The style library has now been assigned. Any models created in this project will use the assigned style library.

Chapter Review Questions

1. To remove an existing title block and border that is currently being displayed in a drawing, expand the *Drawing Resources* folder in the Model browser, right-click on the title block in the **Title Block** node, and select **Delete**.

    a. True
    b. False

2. Which command enables you to save an existing drawing so that it and all of its Drawing Resources can be used to create a new drawing document?

    a. **File** menu>**Manage**>**Projects**
    b. **File** menu>**Save**>**Save All**
    c. **File** menu>**Save As**>**Save Copy As**
    d. **File** menu>**Save As**>**Save Copy As Template**

3. Which tool do you use to compare the styles that exist in two style libraries?

    a. Style Library Manager
    b. Styles Editor

4. If a specific style exists in Style Library 1 and is being compared to a style with the same name but different properties in Style Library 2, how does it display?

    a. Blue, with italic and bold font
    b. Black, with regular font
    c. Red, with bold and underlined font

5. If a particular style exists in one library (Style Library 1) and does not exist in the library that it is being compared to (Style Library 2), how does it display?

    a. Blue, with italic and bold font
    b. Black, with regular font
    c. Red, with bold and underlined font

CAD Management

6. If a new library is created using the **Copy Existing Style Library** option, how would the two libraries (new and the source) display when being compared?

    a. Blue, with italic and bold font

    b. Black, with regular font

    c. Red, with bold and underlined font

Command Summary

Button	Command	Location
▭	**Border** (create)	• **Ribbon:** *Manage* tab>Define panel
N/A	**Delete** (title block)	• **Context Menu:** In Model browser with current title block selected
N/A	**Insert** (title block)	• **Context Menu:** In Model browser with title block selected
N/A	**Save Copy as Template**	• **File menu: Save As**
N/A	**Style Library Manager**	• **Start>All Programs>Autodesk>Autodesk Inventor 2019>Tools>Style Library Manager 2019**
A	**Text**	• **Ribbon:** *Sketch* tab>Create panel
▭	**Title Block** (create)	• **Ribbon:** *Manage* tab>Define panel

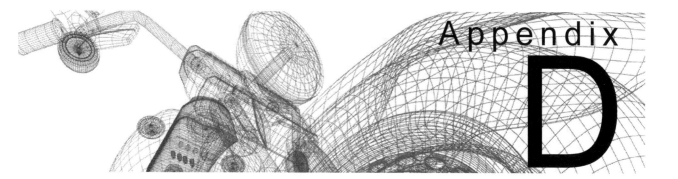

Appendix D

Engineer's Notebook

The Engineer's Notebook enables you to add non-graphical information to a model so that it can be easily communicated with other members of the design team.

Learning Objectives in this Appendix

- Create a note in a model to generate a view in the Engineer's Notebook file.
- Add notes and additional views to an Engineer's Notebook file to communicate design information.
- Use the note and view editing tools to customize the display of information in the Engineer's Notebook file to clearly communicate the design information.
- Organize notes that have been added to the Engineer's Notebook file using user-defined folders.
- Identify whether a model has notes associated with it and know how to access those notes in the Engineer's Notebook.

D.1 Engineer's Notebook

As you create your model, you might want to add non-graphical information to the file using the Engineer's Notebook that is stored with the model. This information can be about model creation, fabrication requirements, or any other information you want to retain regarding the part, as shown in Figure D–1.

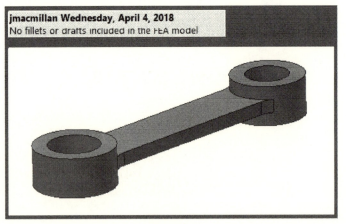

Figure D–1

Additional data is useful for communicating information between Inventor users, as shown in Figure D–2. Inventor stores this information as notes in the Engineer's Notebook.

Figure D–2

D.2 Notes

How To: Place a Note in the Engineer's Notebook

1. Notes can be attached to edges, sketches, features, components, or other elements. To create a note, right-click an object and select **Create Note**. The Engineer's Notebook opens with the first comment and view added, as shown in Figure D–3. Enter a comment, as required.

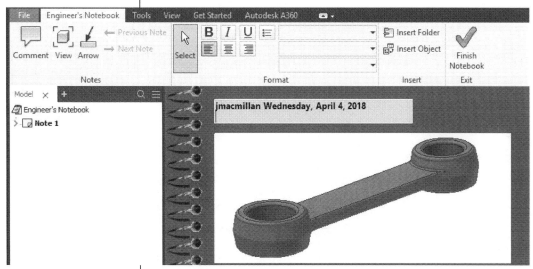

Figure D–3

*You can also access these options using the **Insert** menu or the shortcut menu.*

2. By default, a new note contains one comment and one view. You can edit these or add others in the same note. The options are described as follows:

Comment	💬	Enables you to add a comment to the notebook. With this option selected, draw a text box by selecting the two opposing corners.
View	◻	Enables you to add another view to notebook. With this option selected, draw a box by selecting the two opposing corners.
Arrow	↗	Enables you to add arrows. Start by selecting the point where the arrowhead should be located. Select additional points to add line segments to the arrow.
Previous Note	←	Enables you to activate the previous note.
Next Note	→	Enables you to activate the next note.

3. Edit a note, as required.
4. Organize notes, as required.

Notebook Comments

A Comment contains text, including the date and user name of the person who placed the note. You can edit a note as follows:

- To change the text formatting, right-click on the note and use the options available on the menu, as shown in Figure D–4.

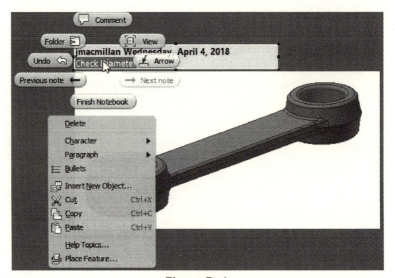

Figure D–4

- Use standard copy and paste techniques.

- Link information from spreadsheets, word processing documents, images, or even audio files, using **Insert New Object**.

- Delete a comment by right-clicking it and selecting **Delete**.

Notebook Views

A View is an illustration of the model in a certain orientation. You can edit a view using the following shortcut menu options, as shown in Figure D–5.

- Pan, rotate, or zoom.

- Change the view display.

- Delete a view.

- Use **Restore Camera** to return the view to the viewpoint that was active when it was created.

- Freeze a view so that is does not update if changes are made to the part. This is useful for documenting stages of development. When you remove the **Freeze** setting, the view automatically updates to the current state.

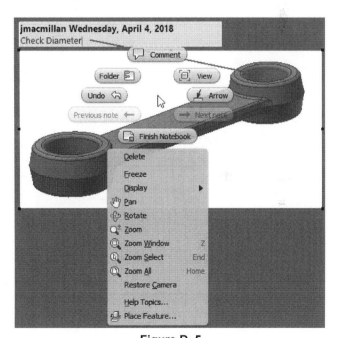

Figure D–5

Notebook Model browser

The Model browser for the Engineer's Notebook shows only notes. Organize your notes as required using the following techniques:

- In the Model browser, the shortcut menu enables you to arrange notes by name, author, date, or text, as shown in Figure D–6.

Figure D–6

- In the Model browser, the shortcut menu enables you to create folders for the notes, as shown in Figure D–7. To place a new note in a folder, right-click on the folder and select **Place New Notes Here**.

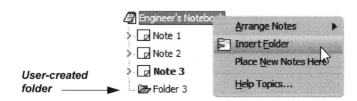

Figure D–7

- To rename a note or a folder, select it twice with two separate single clicks (do not double-click).

- Drag notes to new locations or folder in the Model browser.

It is a good idea to create a folder for each set of notes (e.g., one to place part machining notes, another to place assembly notes, etc.). Ensure that each folder name appropriately represents the notes contained in it.

Notebook Properties

By default, a note symbol (📓) displays in the graphics window when you place a note. When you move the cursor over the symbol, the text associated with that note displays, as shown in Figure D–8.

Figure D–8

Only one note symbol displays per part, so only the text for the first note displays. This helps to keep the display less cluttered. You can double-click on the symbol to open the note. Review the Engineer's Notebook Model browser to review any other notes in the model.

By default, if you delete a feature that has a note attached, the note is also deleted. You can set the properties (*Tools* tab> **Application Options**>*Notebook* tab) so that the note is retained if the feature is deleted. Retaining the note is useful when you want to keep a history of the design process. In addition to setting this property, you can also set colors and select to display the note symbol and/or text.

Practice D1 Engineer's Notebook

Practice Objectives

- Add and edit views of an existing Autodesk Inventor model to an Engineer's Notebook to communicate modeling information with other team members.
- Specify if the views in the Engineer's Notebook should be associative with the source model.
- Add and edit notes to the Engineer's Notebook to clearly identify the details that are being communicated.
- Create folders to organize the notes in an Engineer's Notebook.

In this practice, you create an Engineer's Notebook to communicate information. A page from the Engineer's Notebook created in this practice is shown in Figure D–9.

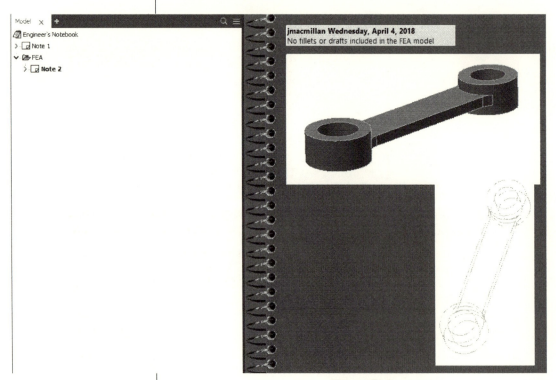

Figure D–9

Task 1 - Create a note.

The draft angle in the model does not appear to be correct. Create a note to ask someone to verify this angle.

1. Open **connecting_rod.ipt**.

2. Notes are attached to a feature or other element in the file. Multi-select all the side faces on the model, right-click and select **Create Note**, as shown in Figure D–10.

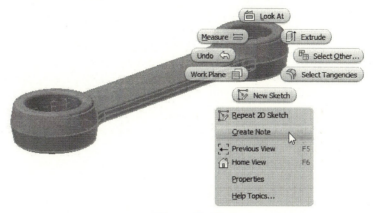

Figure D–10

3. The Engineer's Notebook opens. A comment and view are automatically created. Enter **Verify draft angle** in the comment field, as shown in Figure D–11.

4. Orient the model as shown in Figure D–11, by selecting the appropriate orientation options on the shortcut menu.

Figure D–11

5. In the Notes panel, click (Arrow).

6. Select to place the head of the arrow, drag the mouse upward towards the comment, and select again to place the tail.

7. Right-click and select **OK** to complete the arrow. The notebook displays as shown in Figure D–12.

Figure D–12

8. Select the *connecting_rod.ipt* tab at the bottom of the graphics window.

9. Hover the cursor on the note indicator icon in the graphics window. The note is displayed and the surfaces associated with the note highlight.

10. In the Model browser, expand the **Notes** item to display **Note 1**.

Task 2 - Create a folder.

Folders help to organize the notes. Create a folder to hold information for the FEA group.

1. Return to the notebook window.

2. In the Model browser, select Engineer's Notebook, right-click, and select **Insert Folder**.

3. Click on the folder twice (do not double-click) and rename it to **FEA**.

4. Right-click on the *FEA* folder and select **Place New Notes Here**.

Engineer's Notebook

Task 3 - Create another note.

Create another view of the model without any fillet or draft features. Add a comment to the view to indicate that no fillets or drafts are added to the model given to the FEA department.

1. Return to the part window.

2. Suppress the draft and fillets from the model by selecting them, right-clicking, and selecting **Suppress Features**.

3. Right-click on the part in the Model browser and select **Create Note**, as shown in Figure D–13.

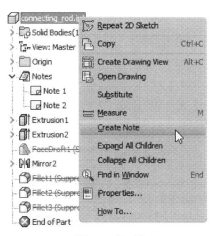

Figure D–13

4. The new view is added to the notebook. Enter **No fillets or drafts included in the FEA model** as the comment.

5. Orient the model as shown in Figure D–14.

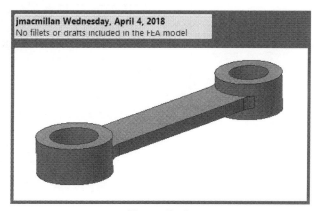

Figure D–14

© 2018, ASCENT - Center for Technical Knowledge® D–11

Task 4 - Create a second view.

1. In the Notes panel, click ▫ (View) to create another view.

2. Create a box to indicate the size of the view. Select on the page to locate the top left corner and drag the cursor down to the right side. Select again to locate the bottom right corner of the view. Orient the model as shown in Figure D–15.

3. Right-click on the model and select **Display>Wireframe** to display the model in wireframe, as shown in Figure D–15.

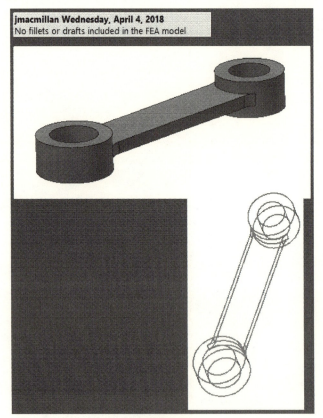

Figure D–15

Task 5 - Unsuppress features in the model.

1. Return to the part's window.

2. Unsuppress the draft feature and the fillets from the model.

3. Return to the Engineer's Notebook window. The fillets and draft are displayed in the FEA view. This is not required. What needs to be done is that the view needs to be frozen to keep the display as it was before the fillets and draft were unsuppressed.

4. Return to the part's window.

5. Suppress the draft and fillet features.

6. Return to the Engineer's Notebook window.

7. Right-click on one of the FEA views and select **Freeze** to freeze the view in its current configuration.

8. Freeze the other FEA view.

9. Return to the part's window and unsuppress the features.

10. Return to the Engineer's Notebook window to verify that the FEA views do not show the drafts and fillets.

Task 6 - Set the model material.

1. Activate the part's window.

2. In the Quick Access Toolbar, expand the Material drop-down list and select **Aluminum-6061**, as shown in Figure D–16, to assign it to the model.

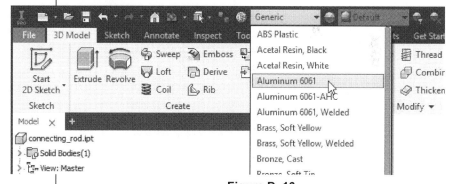

Figure D–16

3. In the Model browser, right-click on the filename or directly on the model and select **iProperties** to open the iProperties dialog box. Select the *Physical* tab to see the physical properties of the model (area, mass, etc.). Click **Update** to update the properties, if required.

4. Set the Requested Accuracy to **Very High** in the drop-down list. Note the mass and volume of the model.

5. Close the iProperties dialog box.

Task 7 - Add another comment.

Create another comment on the first note to indicate the material of the model.

1. Return to the Engineer's Notebook.

2. In the Notes panel, click ← (Previous Note).

3. In the Notes panel, click 💬 (Comment).

4. Create a box on the page to place the new comment.

5. Enter **Material = Aluminum - 6061**. The notebook displays as shown in Figure D–17.

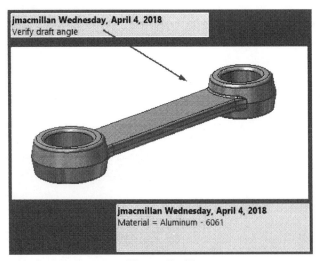

Figure D–17

6. Save the Engineer's Notebook and the model and close the windows.

Chapter Review Questions

1. How do you start the creation of an Engineer's Notebook?
   a. Create a new file using a provided Engineer Notebook template.
   b. Select an element in the model, right-click, and select **Create Note**.
   c. Select an element in the model, select the *Tools* tab and click **Engineer's Notebook**.
   d. In a drawing file, add views of the model to be documented.

2. You attach a note to which elements? (Select all that apply.)
   a. faces
   b. sketches
   c. features
   d. components

3. Which of the following are automatically added to the Engineer's Notebook when you create the first note? (Select all that apply.)
   a. Comment
   b. View
   c. Arrow

4. The orientation of a model in a part or assembly file always sets the orientation of a view in the Engineer's Notebook.
   a. True
   b. False

5. Which command enables you to prevent a model from updating in a view in the Engineer's Notebook when changes are made to the model?
   a. Right-click on a note and select **Freeze**.
   b. Right-click on a view and select **Freeze**.
   c. Right-click on the **Note** node in the Model browser and select **Freeze**.
   d. This is not possible, views update to reflect the current model display.

Command Summary

Button	Command	Location
N/A	Arrange Notes	• **Context menu:** In Model browser with Engineer's Notebook node selected
 (icon)	Arrow	• **Ribbon:** *Engineer's Notebook* tab>Notes panel • **Context menu:** In the graphics window
(icon)	Comment	• **Ribbon:** *Engineer's Notebook* tab>Notes panel • **Context menu:** In the graphics window
N/A	Create Note	• **Context Menu:** In the graphics window with geometry or entities selected • **Context Menu:** In Model browser with model name or features selected
N/A	Insert Folder	• **Ribbon:** *Engineer's Notebook* tab>Insert panel • **Context menu:** In Model browser with Engineer's Notebook node selected
N/A	Insert Object	• **Ribbon:** *Engineer's Notebook* tab>Insert panel
(icon)	Next Note	• **Ribbon:** *Engineer's Notebook* tab>Notes panel • **Context menu:** In the graphics window
N/A	Note Formatting Tools	• **Ribbon:** *Engineer's Notebook* tab>Format panel • **Context menu:** In graphics window with note selected
N/A	Place New Notes Here	• **Context menu:** In Model browser with Engineer's Notebook node selected
(icon)	Previous Note	• **Ribbon:** *Engineer's Notebook* tab>Notes panel • **Context menu:** In the graphics window
 (icon)	View	• **Ribbon:** *Engineer's Notebook* tab>Notes panel • **Context menu:** In the graphics window
N/A	View Display styles	• **Ribbon:** *View* tab>Appearance panel • **Context menu:** In the graphics window with view selected
N/A	View Orientation options	• **Ribbon:** *View* tab>Navigate panel • **Context menu:** In the graphics window with view selected

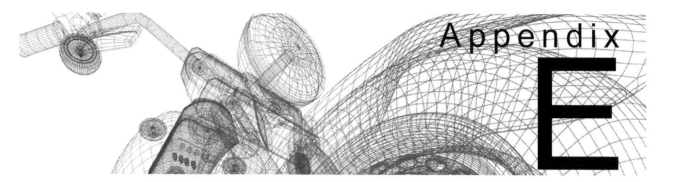

Appendix E

Autodesk Inventor Certification Exam Objectives

The following table will help you to locate the exam objectives within the chapters of the *Autodesk® Inventor® 2019: Advanced Part Modeling* learning guide to help you prepare for the Autodesk Inventor Certified Professional exam.

Exam Topic	Exam Objective	Learning Guide	Chapter & Section(s)
Advanced Modeling	Create a 3D path using the Intersection Curve and the Project to Surface commands	• Advanced Part	• 2.2
	Create a loft feature	• Advanced Part	• 5.1
		• Introduction to Solid Modeling	• 13.1, 13.2
	Create a multi-body part	• Advanced Assembly	• 4.1
		• Advanced Part	• 3.1
	Create a part using surfaces	• Advanced Part	• 8.1 to 8.7
			• 9.1 to 9.4
	Create a sweep feature	• Advanced Part	• 5.2
		• Introduction to Solid Modeling	• 12.1
	Create an iPart	• Advanced Part	• 11.1 to 11.4
	Emboss text and a profile	• Advanced Part	• A.1

© 2018, ASCENT - Center for Technical Knowledge®

E–1

Exam Topic	Exam Objective	Learning Guide	Chapter & Section(s)
Assembly Modeling	Apply and use assembly constraints	• Introduction to Solid Modeling	• 16.1, 16.2
	Apply and use assembly joints	• Introduction to Solid Modeling	• 17.1
	Create a level of detail	• Advanced Assembly	• 10.1 to 10.6
	Create a part in the context of an assembly	• Introduction to Solid Modeling	• 22.1, 22.2
	Describe and use Shrinkwrap	• Advanced Assembly	• 9.1
	Create a positional representation	• Advanced Assembly	• 8.1 to 8.3
	Create components using the Design Accelerator commands	• Advanced Assembly	• 11.1 to 11.3
	Modify a bill of materials	• Introduction to Solid Modeling	• 23.2
	Find minimum distance between parts and components	• Introduction to Solid Modeling	• 19.1
	Use the frame generator command	• Advanced Assembly	• 15.1
Drawing	Edit a section view	• Introduction to Solid Modeling	• 25.3, 25.4
	Modify a style in a drawing	• Introduction to Solid Modeling	• 26.5, 26.6
	Edit a hole table	• Introduction to Solid Modeling	• 27.6
Part Modeling	Create a pattern of features	• Introduction to Solid Modeling	• 14.1, 14.2, 14.5
	Create a shell feature	• Introduction to Solid Modeling	• 9.3
	Create extrude features	• Introduction to Solid Modeling	• 2.2, 2.3 • 3.1 to 3.4 • 5.1, 5.2
	Create hole features	• Introduction to Solid Modeling	• 6.6
	Create revolve features	• Introduction to Solid Modeling	• 2.2, 2.3 • 3.1 to 3.4 • 5.1, 5.2
	Create work features	• Introduction to Solid Modeling	• 7.1 to 7.3
	Use the Project Geometry and Project Cut Edges commands	• Introduction to Solid Modeling	• 2.2 • 5.2
	Edit existing parts using Direct Edit	• Advanced Part	• 12.4

Exam Topic	Exam Objective	Learning Guide	Chapter & Section(s)
Presentation Files	Animate a presentation file	• Introduction to Solid Modeling	• 20.1 to 20.4
Project Files	Control a project file	• Introduction to Solid Modeling	• 24.1
Sheet Metal	Create sheet metal features	• Sheet Metal	• Ch. 2 to 11 (all topics)
Sketching	Create dynamic input dimensions	• Introduction to Solid Modeling	• 2.2
	Use sketch constraints	• Introduction to Solid Modeling	• 2.2 • 3.3
	Sketch using Relax Mode	• Introduction to Solid Modeling	• 3.3
Weldments	Create a weldment	• Advanced Assembly	• 17.1 to 17.4

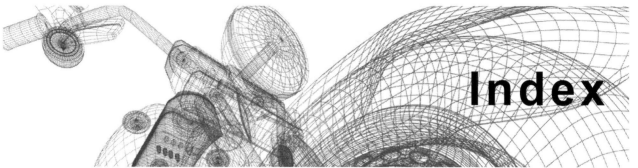

Index

#

2018.2 Enhancements
    Importing Fusion 360 **12-2**
    Resolving Missing Imported Reference Files **12-5**
2019 Enhancements
    Clear Symmetry for base forms **15-28**
    Direct Edit Automatic Blending **12-14**, **12-19**
    Helical Curve Creation Types **2-10**
    Index a Point Cloud File **12-24**
2D Sketch
    Spline **2-2**
3D Mesh **7-2**
3D Sketch
    3D Transform **2-18**
    Arc **2-12**
    Bend **2-13**
    Constraining **2-18**
    Create **2-8**
    Curve on Face **2-16**
    Dimensioning **2-18**
    Edit **2-4**, **2-9**, **2-17**
    Equation Curve **2-13**
    Helical Curve **2-10**
    Include Geometry **2-16**
    Intersection Curve **2-14**
    Line **2-9**
    Mirror **2-17**
    Point **2-13**
    Points **2-17**
    Project Curve to Surface **2-14**
    Properties **2-19**
    Silhouette Curve **2-15**
    Spline **2-2**, **2-12**
    Work Features **2-17**

A

Analysis
    Cross Section **6-5**
    Curvature **6-3**
    Draft **6-2**
    Procedure (all types) **6-7**
    Surface **6-4**
    Zebra **6-2**
AnyCAD **12-2**
Appearance
    Adding to Document **1-26**
    Assign **1-26**
    Assign Appearances **1-19**
    Browser **1-22**
    Ground Plane **1-13**
    Lighting Styles **1-15**
    New **1-23**
    Orthographic View **1-18**
    Perspective View **1-18**
    Ray Tracing **1-11**
    Reflections **1-14**
    Shadows **1-14**
    Visual Style **1-10**
AutoCAD
    AutoCAD Blocks **B-10**
    Blocks in Inventor **B-9**
    DWG files in Inventor **14-1**
Autodesk ReCap **12-23**

B

Bridge **15-22**

C

Clear Symmetry **15-28**
Coil **5-8**
Colors **1-19**
Constraints **1-4**
    Inference **1-5**
    Persistence **1-5**
    Show Constraints **1-4**
Construction Entities **1-6**
Copy Feature **10-10**
Copy Surface **9-7**
Crease Edges **15-18**
Cross Section Analysis **6-5**
Curvature Analysis **6-3**

D

Decal **A-5**
Degrees of Freedom
    Sketch **1-4**
Delete
    Delete Face **9-6**
    Face **12-21**, **15-29**
    Freeform **15-29**
Direct Edit **12-13**
    Delete **12-21**
    Move **12-14**
    Rotate **12-19**
    Scale **12-17**
    Size **12-16**
Draft Analysis **6-2**
Drawing
    Borders **C-2**
    Symbol
        Create **B-2**
        Libraries **B-4**
        Place **B-6**
    Title Block **C-2**
DWG Files **14-1**
Dynamic Dimensioning **1-7**
Dynamic Input **1-7**

E

Edit Base Solid **12-9**
Edit Form **15-10**
Edit Freeform **15-9**
Emboss **A-2**
Engineer's Notebook **D-2**
    Add Arrows **D-3**
    Add Comment **D-3**, **D-4**
    Add View **D-3**, **D-5**
    Edit Comments **D-4**
    Edit Views **D-5**
    Model Browser **D-6**
    Notebook Properties **D-7**
    Notes **D-3**
Equation Curve **2-13**
Export **12-7**
Extend Surface **9-3**
Extract iFeature **10-2**

F

Flatten **15-25**
Freeform
    Convert Geometry **15-7**
    Create Shapes **15-3**, **15-6**
    Edit **15-10**
        Bridge **15-22**
        Clear Symmetry **15-28**
        Crease Edges **15-18**
        Delete **15-29**
        Edit Form **15-10**
        Edit Freeform **15-9**
        Flatten **15-25**
        Insert Edge **15-15**
        Insert Point **15-24**
        Match Edge **15-18**
        Merge Edges **15-16**
        Mirror **15-28**
        Subdivide **15-21**
        Symmetry **15-27**
        Thicken **15-25**
        Uncrease Edges **15-18**
        Unweld Edges **15-17**
        Weld Vertices **15-24**
    Introduction **15-2**

G

Generative Shape Design **7-1**
    Constraints **7-5**
    Loads **7-6**
    Material Assignment **7-4**
    Preserving Regions **7-9**
    Promote 3D Mesh **7-12**
    Run **7-11**
    Settings **7-8**
    Symmetry **7-10**
    Workflow **7-2**
Ground Plane **1-13**
Grounded work point **4-2**

H

Helical Curve
    Constant Helical Curve **2-10**
    Variable Helical Curve **2-10**

I

iFeature
    Create **10-2**
    Create from iPart **11-16**
    Edit iFeature Image **10-16**
    Edit Inserted **10-15**
    Edit Stored File **10-15**
    Insert **10-6**
    Keys **10-14**
    Placement Help **10-16**
    Table-driven **10-11**
Import Data
    AutoCAD Data **14-2**, **14-9**
    Direct Edit
        Delete **12-21**
        Move **12-14**
        Rotate **12-19**
        Scale **12-17**
        Size **12-16**
    Editing Base Solid
        Delete Face **12-12**
        Extend or Contract **12-11**

Offset **12-11**
Import **12-2**
Surfaces **13-2**
Insert Edge **15-15**
Insert iFeature **10-6**
Insert Point **15-24**
Intersection Curve **2-14**
iPart
    Adding Features **11-15**
    Create **11-2**
    Drawing Creation **11-17**
    Edit **11-15**
    Edit Factory Scope **11-15**
    Edit Member Scope **11-15**
    Generate Members **11-10**
    Keys **11-5**
    Placement **11-12**

K
Keys **11-5**

L
Lighting Styles **1-15**
Loft
    Area Loft **5-2**

M
Match Edge **15-18**
Materials **1-19**
Merge Edges **15-16**
Mirror 3D Entities **2-17**
Mirror Freeform **15-28**
Multi-Body Part Modeling
    Assigning Features **3-4**
    Combine Bodies **3-7**
    Display **3-8**
    Move Bodies **3-5**
    New Solid **3-3**, **3-4**
    Properties **3-9**
    Split Bodies **3-6**

N
Notebook *(see Engineer's Notebook)*

O
Offset Surface **8-11**
Orthographic View **1-18**

P
Patch **8-4**, **13-11**
Perspective View **1-18**
Point Cloud Data **12-23**
Precise Input **1-7**

R
Ray Tracing **1-11**
Reflections **1-14**
Repair Environment **13-4**
Repair Environment Tools
    Add Surface **13-8**
    Boundary Patch **13-11**
    Boundary Trim **13-10**
    Edit Regions **13-9**
    Error Check **13-5**
    Extend Faces **13-8**
    Extract Loop **13-10**
    Intersect Faces **13-9**
    Reverse Normal **13-11**
    Stitch **13-6**
    Transfer Surface **13-8**
    Unstitch **13-8**
Replace Face **9-5**
Ruled Surface **8-5**

S
Save Copy As **12-7**
Scale **12-17**
Sculpt **8-9**
Shadows **1-14**
Silhouette Curve **2-15**
Sketched Symbol
    Create **B-2**
    Libraries **B-4**
    Place **B-6**
Spline **2-2**
Springs **5-8**
Stitch **8-7**, **13-6**
Styles
    Assigning to Projects **C-5**
    Copy **C-8**
    Delete **C-8**
    Lighting **1-15**
    New Library **C-8**
    Rename **C-8**
    Style Library Manger **C-6**
Subdivide **15-21**
Surface Analysis **6-4**
Surfaces
    Copy **9-7**
    Copy Object **9-7**
    Delete Face **9-6**
    Extend **9-3**
    Introduction **8-2**, **8-3**
    Patch **8-4**
    Repair **13-4**
    Repair Environment Tools
        Add Surface **13-8**
        Boundary Patch **13-11**
        Boundary Trim **13-10**
        Edit Regions **13-9**
        Error Check **13-5**
        Extend Faces **13-8**
        Extract Loop **13-10**

        Intersect Faces **13-9**
        Reverse Normal **13-11**
        Stitch **13-6**
        Transfer Surface **13-8**
        Unstitch **13-8**
    Replace Face **9-5**
    Ruled **8-5**
    Sculpt **8-9**
    Stitch **8-7**, **13-6**
    Thickening/Offset **8-11**
    Trim **9-2**
Sweeps
    Path and Guide Rail **5-5**
    Path and Guide Surface **5-7**
Symbol
    Create **B-2**
    Libraries **B-4**
    Place **B-6**
Symmetry **15-5**, **15-27**

T

Table
    Factory members (iPart) **11-17**
Textures **1-19**
Thicken **8-11**
Thicken Freeform **15-25**
Threads **5-8**
Title Block **C-2**
Trim Surface **9-2**

U

Uncrease Edges **15-18**
Unweld Edges **15-17**
User Coordinate Systems **4-4**

V

Visual Style **1-10**

W

Weld Vertices **15-24**
Work Feature
    Grounded Work Points **4-2**
    User Coordinate Systems **4-4**

Z

Zebra Analysis **6-2**